It May Not Have Been Easy…
But Was Absolutely Perfect

A mother's story of her son's passing.

Sharon Graham

ISBN 978-1-63874-856-4 (paperback)
ISBN 978-1-63874-857-1 (digital)

Copyright © 2023 by Sharon Graham

All rights reserved. No part of this publication may be reproduced, distributed, or transmitted in any form or by any means, including photocopying, recording, or other electronic or mechanical methods without the prior written permission of the publisher. For permission requests, solicit the publisher via the address below.

Christian Faith Publishing
832 Park Avenue
Meadville, PA 16335
www.christianfaithpublishing.com

Printed in the United States of America

Contents

Preface v
1) The Call 1
2) The Start of the Drive 14
3) A Few More Hours 34
4) Salt Lake Area and Airport 51
5) Saying Goodbye 63
6) Two Hours to Go 71
7) The Reality of the Hospital Visit 78
8) The Donor Process 89
9) The Wait 100
10) The Dreaded Time Arrived 120
11) It's Finally Over 130
12) What to Do Next 134
13) Where It Happened / The Truck 151
14) The Funeral Home and Making Arrangements 163
15) Messages That Altered Our Lives 174
16) Seriously: Planning for a Funeral 179
17) Surprise or Another Miracle 187
18) Our Evening Unfolds 191
19) February 11, Alyssa's Birthday 216
20) Our Amazing Sunday Day 221
21) Dinner With President Eyring and His Family 234
22) Mariah's Apartment 240
23) Aria Apartment Fireside for Dalen 246
24) Taking Care of Dalen's School Stuff 259
25) Final Preparations 271
26) Heading Into Yet Another Miracle 283
27) More Driving to Come 299

28) This is the Right Place	303
29) The Tombstone	318
30) Heading to California—Finally	325
31) Day of Love	337
32) The Arrivals Commenced	353
33) Beach Day	364
34) The Arrival of the Funeral Day	376
35) The Funeral Service	391
36) Is It Time to Eat Yet?	411
37) Sunday—Church and More Driving	419
38) Burial day—With All We Had Experienced, It Now Became Final	423
39) Driving Home	444
40) A Week—A Month	448
41) Another Desperate Call	451
42) Lesson Learned the Hard Way	463
43) Fast Forward in Time	469
44) Miracles and More Miracles	482
45) Mariah's Account of the Accident	486
46) Time Can Heal Pain-and Blessings Still Come	489
47) Anniversary Fun—February. 2019	497
48) The Awaited Meeting	505
49) One Year Mark	513

Preface

This book is not meant to diminish the passing, in any way, of a loved one from your experience.

I can promise though, that through the experience of a loved one passing on: There is peace—if only for a moment.
There is comfort—if only for a moment.
There is guidance—if only for a moment.
Once you see that *one* moment, there are others.

This book is simply a mother's story of her son's passing, that is all. There should never be comparisons to how different this story might be from yours. But with every passing of a loved one, there are also similarities. You might find comfort and see an abundance of miracles that you might not have seen before.

Let God Lead and you will be lead on an amazing journey.

Sharon Graham

The Call

February 9th, 2018, 12:53 p.m.
"Just leaving Mom," said Mariah.

"I'm so excited to see you and Dalen," I said to Mariah, our youngest. Dalen was our only boy. I walked out of the temple having spent some time there trying to fill my day with whatever I could before I got to see my kids again. I was just so excited, and we were all going to have so much fun this weekend. Mariah and Dalen were coming from Rexburg, Idaho where they were attending Brigham Young University Idaho.

"Yup, it will be fun."

"Okay, well drive carefully. You're all set, and everything is good," I stated. That meant that the tank was full of gas, they had food and clothes were packed. They just had to wait for Dalen's class to be over and then they could head out.

"Yup, see you soon Mom."

"Okay, I love you."

"Love you too." And she hung up the phone and would begin the trip down to Las Vegas for a surprise for her older sister's birthday. It had been a couple of months since the family had been together. Dalen had returned from his mission in October and got home just in time to head up to BYUI for the block semester. He was only home for one week. It was an adjustment for him, but we all felt it was good for him to be busy and in a place where others would be able to relate to him being a returned missionary. There were special arrangements made to have the whole family home for the weekend that Dalen returned. It was a great time, and the family was together for the first time after four years with other children having served their missions. It all just ended soo quickly as we only had three days with each other. Any time together, though, was a blessing for me the mom. Nothing was better than having the family around me. Of course, as with any family, there would always be personality differences, but generally they got along okay. The welcome home weekend was a good one even if it was just for three days.

Dalen's return from his mission meant that three of our four children had now served a mission for The Church of Jesus Christ of Latter-Day Saints. A mission is a dedicated period of time, that for a young man of eighteen plus years old which lasts for two years; and for a young woman of nineteen plus years old and lasts for eighteen months.

A call to serve comes directly from the prophet of the church. He prays about an individual's name and sees where in the world the church may need more missionaries. Then, this servant of the Lord, heads out and proselytes for their time period. At that time, families were only able to communicate once a week through emails and two phone calls a year: one on Christmas Day and the other on Mother's Day. Those are such sweet and priceless moments as we see the growth and dedication of our child to the service. During a mission, the missionary becomes truly converted to the Lord and their calling is then to bring others to the gospel of Jesus Christ. They dedicate their time and sacrifice all worldly issues. They strive to teach, preach, and exhort others to find the joy and peace that comes with the true gospel of our Savior, Jesus Christ. A mission is such a huge accomplishment and one that sets a precedent for the rest of their lives. They return knowing how to teach. They know how to prepare themselves, study, feel the guidance of the Holy Spirit, invite others to come unto Christ and know the importance of hard work. A mission is probably the hardest type of work both physically and especially spiritually, that someone could go through. It's an amazing experience that I would never take away from anyone, even though it's also one of the hardest things to do. A person's life is forever changed because of the service given during a mission.

1:30 p.m. "Just heading out, Mom. I'm getting really excited." Dalen was pretty good at keeping in touch with me. He would call me almost every day if I didn't call him. I would just love to hear his little "Hi Mommy" in his funny little voice. I just wanted to hug this boy.

"Me too Dalen. I just can't wait to see you. So, you aren't waiting for your new iPod, are you? That shouldn't be a reason to make Mariah wait more," I enquired.

"No Mom, we aren't waiting. But my class didn't let me out early, so we are just now starting out," Dalen commented.

"Okay, but be careful. I love you Bud."

"Love you too mom. See you soon," Dalen stated.

Dalen wasn't really excited to be at school, but he knew it was the best place for him since he didn't really have any other plans, and Mom and Dad wanted him to get some education. Even his Stake President said that school would be the best place for him, so that helped with his decision to go.

A Stake President is a religious leader of a geographic region for The Church of Jesus Christ of Latter-Day Saints. Every member of the church belongs to a ward, which is the area where you live and about 350 persons. Five to seven wards constitute a Stake under the direction of a Stake President that which might have 1200 persons that he is accountable for. The Stake President sets young people apart as a missionary; meaning they receive a special individual blessing to dedicate their next two years to the service of the Lord, with the guidance to go forth and serve where they are called. The Stake President will hold several interviews with the perspective missionary prior to them receiving their call to prove their worthiness and true desires of dedicating their time.

Dalen going away to school would mean he just wouldn't be sitting around with a lot of idle time, and his sister was already up there in Idaho, so it was supposed to be fun for the two of them to be going to school together. That part Dalen was excited about as he and Mariah were really good friends even as siblings.

Mariah just wanted some family around as she had been up to school since July with no breaks and hadn't been home except for the three days when Dalen came home from his mission. Having her big brother (and only brother) close by at school, was to help both of them move forward with life and an education; and to deepen their friendship. Mariah wouldn't be lonely knowing her brother would be there.

The kids didn't even get to come home for Christmas because of siblings that had to work, so we all decided to meet in St. George (at my mother-in-law's house) for two days so we could again celebrate a little bit of the season and be together. It was the first time Dalen met with our son-in-law Brandon. He and Alyssa had been married now for just over a year; right after her mission, but Dalen wasn't home as he was still serving in Texas. The boys were instantly brothers. It was a very good and quick few days, now a treasure of mine. I tried to get a family picture after we came home from church Christmas morning, but no one wanted to pose for it. That decision became my only regret, to have no nice family picture with Dalen and Brandon together, and I never would.

The afternoon seemed to creep by. I was trying to do anything to fill the time. I knew my kids were on the road and that their arrival time would yet be another about ten hours or so. I had to keep busy. I found myself thinking all day of the reunion we would have. I loved being with my family. It had been so long since we really had more than two days all together; and I was so grateful for all the choices that my kids had made to better their lives and to follow the Savior even if it meant that we wouldn't get together for a while. It was all so worth any sacrifice of our time. My children were happy and had made The Church of Jesus Christ of Ladder-day Saints their choice. They were righteous and obedient. I was reflecting on my blessings with a smile on my face as I found myself in the Beehive Bookstore in St. George, wondering through the aisles. Mariah had announced in December, as her Christmas present to Scott and I, that she was going to serve a mission. I was looking for a journal and missionary supplies that she might like. I took my time and enjoyed myself. I found a journal that I thought was perfect and I could get it engraved with her name on it. I thought Mariah would like it. So I finally found my way to the checkout and had finished my purchase. The clerk then took the journal to the back to print Mariah's name on it. And the phone rang.

2:32 p.m. "Mom there's been an accident. It's bad. Dalen is unconscious". Mariah was hysterical on the phone.

"What do you mean an accident? Where are you? Where is Dalen?" I sensed the urgency to know all the information at once. I knew something was wrong, really wrong. Mariah wasn't sure, so I kept asking.

"I don't know. Dalen is unconscious Mom. What do I do?"

"Is someone with you? What happened?' Panic began to run through my thoughts. I started pacing in the store thinking: '*Where the heck is this clerk with the journal?*' I walked to the back still trying to get some information from Mariah.

"Are you serious? This isn't funny Mariah. Are you okay?"

"Yes Mom. I rolled the truck. Dalen is unconscious. People are trying to help get him out of the truck."

"Is he okay?" I began to walk up to the cash register again in hopes to see where the clerk was and how I could get the book, so I could give my attention to Mariah. There were several people in line and the registers seemed so busy. I walked again to the back of the store and even began to look in some rooms opening what doors were there in hopes of finding the clerk with the journal, but no luck. The whole time my ear seemed glued to my phone.

"I don't know. I don't know," was the panicked reply of Mariah.

"Is my son alive? I need to know if my son is alive. Is he alive?" As I said this, I noticed a few people who weren't really listening, but heard the intensity in my voice and were just standing there watching me. I became very self-conscious, worried about how I was sounding and what they were understanding, but also more anxious as to the information I might be receiving from Mariah. There were no feelings present, just reactions from what was happening.

"I don't know Mom; I can't see him."

"Mariah, are you okay? How are you?"

"Yes Mom. He's not moving."

"Please Mariah; tell me if he's alive. You know how to tell if someone is breathing. I need you to go to your brother and see if he is breathing. I need to know if he is alive, Mariah. Do you think you could do that?"

"Hello, my name is Brittany. I'm with your daughter. She seems okay, but is in shock."

"Where are they?"

"We are just on the first exit at Blackfoot. The truck rolled onto the side of the road. I was right behind your daughter's truck and the first on the scene. As soon as I got out of my car and walked over to see if I could help your daughter, was out of the truck standing. Your son is still inside the truck. People are trying to get him out."

"Okay—thank you."

There was a second of processing in my mind as to who this woman was and where my daughter went. Mariah was crying pretty hard when she was on the phone, I didn't want to leave her alone. I was grateful that Brenda was there though and trying to help my daughter. I wanted to talk to Mariah and learn what was happening. It was amazing that there was help there immediately. Whatever was going on; my children were not alone and others were trying to help. That was such a huge blessing for me. [1](seeing a miracle /blessing).

"Is my son alive?" Now I walked again to the back of the store and was determined that I just needed to leave. I didn't care about the book anymore, but I just had to leave. The clerk simultaneously walked out as I thought of the need to leave, and she heard me on the phone and seemed to sense the need to hurry. She gave me the book and I began to rush out after I thanked her. I tried to explain in as few of words as possible to describe the situation and that my kids were just in an accident and that I needed to go. She understood my anxiety.

Another customer came up to me and put her hand on my shoulder which caused an anxious pause,: "I hope your son is okay."

---

[1] The car directly behind Mariah stopped as did others. They were trying to calm Mariah and get Dalen out of the truck. One that stopped was also a nurse and was huge in attending to Dalen and his needs. The first responders were called and arrived within three minutes of the accident.

"So do I. Thank you." I was trying to get to my car and continue with my phone call. "Again, is my son alive?" I asked Brenda.

"I don't know. There are people trying to help him. I will stay with your daughter and make sure she is safe." Brenda was calm and seemed to know to reassure me of the safety of my daughter.

"Thank you. Is she okay? What about my son?" I had to keep asking.

"Yes, she is okay," Brenda replied. But there was no other comment on the safety of my son.

Mariah's voice came back on the phone and said, "Mom I'm scared!"

"Mariah, it will take me a few minutes to get things organized, but I'm on my way. It's a few hours drive, but I'm on my way and will be there as soon as I can. I love you. Let me call Dad and everyone. Let me know what's happening. I don't want you to be alone. Call Rick (Mariah's boyfriend), he's closest to you. He can get there quicker than anyone else. I'm very worried too. I love you." My brain was racing with all the connections that needed to be made. It was a flood of; calling my husband Scott, keeping Mariah on the phone, finding out what happened with my son, getting in my car and driving, letting Kailee (middle daughter) know and see what's up with her, contacting Alyssa (oldest daughter) and getting them going. As a family we needed to be there, and they were all a long way away. It had to be done, so I just started doing what I felt needed to be done and that was driving.

Mariah said: "Dalen is out but I can't see him. I think they are going to transport him to the hospital by helicopter. He's not good Mom. I'm scared. I don't know if he is alive, or breathing, or what." We had learned that one of the first responders was also a nurse, and they were immediately in contact with the doctors at the hospital. Within minutes, Dalen had the best care he could have had. So amazing! The first car that stopped was Brenda. She stayed with Mariah. Three cars stopped immediately after Brenda. The third car had a nurse inside it. The police were immediately called. The first responders were arriving so very quickly. The ambulance and paramedics were dispatched immediately as well. How grateful we were to all of them. I had always admired the first responders' teams, but now their efforts were to save our son and that became so very personal.

"I'm so sorry Mariah. Are you really okay? I need to know if I can take a minute to call Dad and make some arrangements. Will you be okay for a few minutes?"

"Yes." And the phone was silent. I felt the loneliness. I jumped into my car and started to drive back to my mother-in-law's house, so I could change, pack and start to head out. First, I had to call Scott and let him know what had happened.[2]

2:35 p.m. I called Scott on the Blue-tooth. Scott was in Pomona for the Winter Nationals in California with his race car. It was always very noisy, and there have been many times when he couldn't hear his phone ring and would then call me back later when he saw that I attempted to call him. I prayed that this wasn't the case this time. He didn't respond.

2:36 p.m. I called again. Nothing! I knew that the track was noisy, but this really was an emergency. I sent a text message: "Emergency!" That was all I said. It seemed like a lifetime as the seconds and minutes went by. How could it seem to take so long for him to call me back? Scott called back within a few minutes.

2:39 p.m. "Hello."

"Scott there has been an accident. Mariah is okay, but Dalen is hurt pretty bad.

They rolled the truck just outside of Blackfoot and are taking Dalen by helicopter to the hospital. Mariah says he's not good."

"Okay so what do I need to do?" Scott asked. I don't think he thought it was as serious as it was. He also had never handled family emergencies well, but I had to make him believe me. Here

---

[2] A few days earlier I had decided to go see Kailee in St. George. Kailee was working and had plans for part of the weekend as she was visiting her boyfriend in Salt Lake City, but would drive back home Saturday night and down to Vegas on Sunday so we would be together as a family. That decision to visit her put me 7 hours closer to Mariah and she needed me.

he was an officer with the Los Angeles Sheriff Department of twenty-nine years. He could handle anything in the field and usually well. But when it came to his family; he was always squeamish and didn't always react most productively, especially if blood was involved. Scott would physically be there, but I usually handled the emotional part.

"We need to get up there. Mariah is by herself and she needs us. I don't know what's up with Dalen, but we need to go. I'm starting to drive right now."

"Okay, sounds good. I will see what I can do," Scott stated.

That was his standard reply 'sounds good'. Sometimes it meant that he would talk about it later. Sometimes it meant he would ignore the comment. How could my information be a *sounds good* comment, but that was what I got. This time, I think he knew I meant that it was serious.

We needed to get up to Mariah. I didn't even know where they were taking Dalen at that time, but we just needed to start heading up there. I hung up with Scott, and began to dial Rick, who was from Rexburg. I wanted to know if he knew about the accident and if he could get there to be with Mariah. He mentioned that he had known and that he was making arrangements to get off work and go to Mariah as soon as possible. I hated the thought that Mariah was alone and out there going through this by herself. Blackfoot was about thirty-five, forty minutes out of Rexburg. I just needed him to get there now.

2:44 p.m. I needed to call Kailee to tell her what had happened and see if she could get off work, while still driving to my mother-in-laws to get my things.

"Kailee, Dalen and Mariah were in an accident. Mariah is okay, but Dalen is not. They are taking him to the hospital by helicopter. I don't know anything else, but I'm going up. Do you think you want to come with me? It doesn't look good, so I think we need to go. When do you get off work?"

Kailee had a great boss that had always been supportive to her. I wanted Kailee to see that this was important, but we didn't even know how bad Dalen was or what we were getting into. We tried to be calm and to see that things might work out. It was just a matter of us needing to be there to help Mariah and find out the complete situation of Dalen and what that might be.

"I don't know Mom. I have to work."

"Kailee, it doesn't look good, so I think we need to go. When do you get off work?"

"Okay mom, let me talk to my boss and see what I can do."

"Okay, but you need to call me as soon as possible. I need to get going." I was almost to my mothers-in-law at this point. I knew I had to hurry, so my thoughts were of what I should take and what I would need.

I placed a call to Alyssa. She answered immediately.

2:47 p.m. "Mom I'm at work, can I call you back," Alyssa asked.

"Yes, but there has been an accident, so hurry." Within literally a few seconds Alyssa called me back.

"What happened Mom?"

"Mariah and Dalen were in a serious accident. Mariah is okay, but Dalen isn't. I'm heading up to Idaho right now."

"What should I do Mom?" Alyssa was extremely worried within a second.

"I'm not sure. I don't know if you should head up or not. I told Dad that we need to, but that is to support Mariah as well as Dalen. I don't know anything about Dalen except they are taking him to the hospital by helicopter, and he didn't look good. Dad is seeing what he can do to get up there. We don't even know how Dalen will be when we get there; or what, but right now it seems pretty serious."

"Do you want me up there?" Alyssa asked.

"Yeah, I think I do. I don't know if it's possible, but as a family we just need to be there together."

"Okay, let me call Brandon (Alyssa's husband) and see what's up. Maybe we can fly up Mom."

"That might be a good idea. I don't know how expensive that might be or the time frame, but if you need help, let me know and we will take care of it."

"Okay Mom, I'll call you right back," Alyssa responded.

"Okay." By now I literally grabbed everything I had, packed my bag and was heading towards my car when Kailee drove into the driveway. I threw my things into the back of my car. I couldn't believe how fast Kailee was able to take care of things at work and get over to her grandma's house where Kailee was living. She was there to help out her grandma and, of course, work. It wasn't far from her work to the house, but still, she got there pretty quick. There was a sense of *'get this done now'*; and also *'be calm'*. And now we could get her things gathered and be on the road.

2:49 p.m. "Mom, Brandon and I are going to come up. I'll let you know when I have more plans," Alyssa said.

'That was great news to hear.' Brandon and Alyssa had just been married for one and a half years and lived in Las Vegas. Brandon was six-foot six and was just a really good guy. You always had to look up to him. You hoped an added person fit into the family with a marriage, and that they in some way become like your own too. Brandon was that guy. We really love him, and he was so family oriented. He would do whatever he could for family and now that meant our family as well.

"Okay, that sounds good. Tell Brandon thanks for us," I stated.

"Of course, Mom. This is family!" was Alyssa's assurance to me.

"Alright. Call me back when you know more."

"K—love you Mom."

"Love you too."

2:50 p.m. Scott called me to say that he was on his way home. He got out of the usually jammed parking lot of Pomona and was on the road. He was making calls to people as well as trying to get some of his things cleared on his mind. Not knowing what to do, he just kept going.

"Okay that's good. We are just starting to leave too. Call me soon."

"Okay. I will. I love you," Scott said.

"Love you too."

What do I do about my dog? I completely forgot that I had taken him up to Utah with me, so I could surprise Mariah. Titan was her dog and she missed him so much. Mariah had asked if I could bring him up with me, and I actually said I wasn't sure things would work out; but I knew all along that I would have him there for her. I had addressed my concern with Kailee previously, and she suggested a friend that used to live in our area in California that had recently moved to St. George might help us. I had forgotten that I mentioned the dog to Kailee earlier.

"Oh my gosh, I forgot about Titan. What do I do?"

"Mom, you told me earlier, so I asked _____ if she could take him," Kailee commented.

I felt weird about that though, since I hadn't kept in much contact with this person other than yearly Christmas cards. When Kailee arrived at the house, and as she was running in to get her things, she said: "Oh yeah, _____ said she would love to watch Titan. Just leave him here and she will come over after work and get him."

"Seriously? She said it was okay?"

"Actually, she said she would love to have him and her kids would just love him to death," Kailee stated.

This lady was an angel for sure. I knew Titan wouldn't have a problem in a strange house as he was used as a therapy dog; was trained to go into all environments, and was a great cuddler. It wasn't ever a thought to have Grandma look after the dog. She just didn't have the health to take care of a dog and I didn't want to stress her out in anyway. I was in awe of _____'s kindness.

Kailee only took about five minutes to get some things together. She asked what she should take, and I told her probably enough for four or five days. She already had a weekend bag packed as she was going to Salt Lake City to visit her boyfriend, so she just added a few things. Everything was coming together quickly so we could begin this forever journey.[3]

"Okay Kailee, let's get going!"

---

[3] Our friend was willing to take Titan (our dog), and not knowing for how long. She didn't question anything at all—other than to say it was all good and she would love to have him. We hadn't even seen her for years. She simply said she would just pick him up.

The Start of the Drive

Kailee was putting things into her car. Her boss said she could go and that meant we could go together. I was relieved. Kailee still wanted to take her car because we weren't sure how much time this would take or how serious it was, but if things worked out well, she could still go and see her boyfriend that lived in the Salt Lake City, Utah, area as that was their weekend plans. We decided that we would carpool up. Kailee took only about five minutes to pack and we were ready to start heading out.[4]

We said a prayer first that we would make good time and be safe and remain calm. We also pleaded with our Heavenly Father that Dalen would be okay and that our family would get there as safely and as fast as they could. We both were loaded up and started off. I told Kailee that we would be in contact the whole time and that I wanted to make sure that she was okay. Kailee had already filled her car with gas that morning as she was planning to leave right after work. We just got to leave a few hours earlier than she had planned, so we headed up. I told her to be careful and to not speed. We didn't need to get pulled over during this trip either. I was leading the way and we headed out.

The road seemed clear. It was just before three in the afternoon, so we were ahead of people getting off work and the speed limit was raised to 80 mph. I drove 85 the whole way.

I opened Facebook while filling up my car with gas and recorded a post. I strongly felt we needed to let people know of our situation

---

[4] Kailee's boss let her off immediately upon hearing of the accident. That meant we could go together and that was comforting to me even if we were in different cars.

because I knew of the power of prayers and earnestly felt at that time that we needed them.

> **Facebook post, 2:52 p.m. "Major prayers needed!**
> **Mariah and Dalen were just in a traffic accident up in Idaho and all we know is that Dalen is being life-lined to the hospital. I will let everyone know more when I do, but we can use prayers and lots of them."**

From here on, my life was tied to my phone. It _never_ stopped ringing, or it was me dialing out. It was either me trying to contact someone, or Kailee and I getting in touch with each other; or trying to keep Mariah calm and reassured her that I was on my way: Scott letting me know what has happening, or people calling to make sure I was okay after I posted about the accident. I felt immediately the power of prayer and all the thoughts of our family and friends. Within minutes, our whole family had pages of thoughts expressing their prayers on our behalf. It really was amazing.[5]

In the past, I would go on Facebook and view the posts from my very small family and friends. I used my Facebook to keep up with family and nieces and nephews and their families. I would hear from past mission companions or persons that were co-workers of mine. I would hear occasionally from people that I sent yearly Christmas cards to. I never really knew who even read my posts, though, because so few would reply or comment back. I would get comments, but usually maybe not more than twenty or so. I didn't think that this tool of technology would really reach so many people and in such a short time and yet it did.

Very quickly, I found myself in awe again. Facebook became my lifeline, as it did for my family too. My usual twenty or thirty com-

---

[5] Posted on Facebook. Within minutes we had literally about 100 thoughts of prayers and good wishes. The quickness that the messages got out and where the messages were sent from left us all awe struck.

ments now became one hundred. I was hearing from everyone. There were messages from co-workers of the past, or even those that worked with my children. I was hearing from friends that I hadn't heard from in years. It was like an explosion and then, add the power of all their prayers with their comments. I realized that between our family members, my message (now re-posted by our children and Scott) were reaching over five hundred plus persons within minutes, mostly because of Scott's contacts between the Sheriff's Department, and his racing group. It didn't seem real, but it was, and it was amazing and very overwhelming. There was also such a huge sense of peace and comfort when I listened through Bluetooth to all the messages and their concerns for our family and our current situation.

(Samples of love and support about five minutes after post)

2:53 p.m.   "Mrs. Graham."

I don't know why Rick always called me Mrs. Graham. It seemed so weird to me because usually members of our church are referred to us as Brother So-and-So, and Sister So-and-So, which meant I would normally have been called Sister Graham. I've never had a youth of our church call me Mrs. Graham, so it just seemed unique. Rick did though and it was okay.

"I just wanted you to know that I'm on my way and will be there soon," Rick responded.

"Thanks Rick. Please hurry. I don't want Mariah to be there alone." I can't say that his comment relieved me, but it really kept the anxiousness down to where I could continue my drive and take care of whatever else I needed to.

2:54 p.m. "What's going on Mariah?"

"Mom, they are taking Dalen to the hospital in Pocatello by ambulance."

"Okay—I'm on my way. I'm about eight/nine hours away. I don't want you to be by yourself. Are you okay?

"Dalen's bleeding pretty badly. They won't let me see him. The paramedics are working on him," Mariah informed me. I thought they were taking him in a helicopter. So, I was a bit confused when Mariah mentioned they would be traveling in the ambulance.

"They won't let me see him Mom. What do I do?"

"They are trying to help him Mariah. They will make sure you are okay too. Trust them. Did you see him?"

"There's a lot of blood Mom. I don't know if he's alive. His head was covered in blood, and I couldn't see anything else.

"But he's alive?" hoping with every fiber of my being that I would hear something positive. To think of what my child was seeing and experiencing kind of mortified me. Mariah asked to see if her brother was alive. How horrific for her. Yet as a mom, I so needed to know and couldn't expect her to do any more, but I needed to know where my son was.

"Yes, but they had to shock him. He's not good Mom. He's not good."

Hearing that your son had to be shocked sent a visual of every episode in a TV hospital show where they shocked someone and watching their body jerking up and down when they tried to revive a heart. Then there was the hearing of the flat line on the heart monitor with its clear sound that was now attached to my son's chest, which showed that the pulse had stopped. The visual of the compressions to the heart to restart it and the amount of strength of each person involved to try and save a life became very real. Except this time, it was for the life of my son. To know that my son had received this procedure (later we learned that it was not just once, but three times in the field), and that really scared me a lot. What kind of damage could pumping on someone's chest do to a body? Would my son be able to come out of this and survive in a normal way? It wasn't horror or panic that struck me but a very vivid picture in my mind as to what my son had to experience. My heart hurt for him. My prayer was of gratitude that he had the proper help he needed to keep him alive and that they were there so quickly.

"On my way, Mariah. I'm hurrying as fast as I can. Just packed and filled up with gas. Kailee is driving her car up, she got off work and we are carpooling. I'm on my way Mariah. Sorry it will take a while, but we are praying hard that we all make good time. I'll be there as soon as I can."

"Mom, I'm okay, I know you're coming and I know they are helping Dalen. I just feel helpless. I can't do anything."

"Mariah, I need you to take pictures. I know that might be hard, but you need to take pictures for insurance and for our family. Please take pictures of everything. Where is Rick? Have you heard from him? Mariah, I need pictures."

In asking Mariah to take pictures, I knew that was a very difficult request for her. It was seriously for a couple of reasons: 1) to help our insurance company understand the accident, and 2) I wanted to see the condition that my children had to experience. I knew that it would be a tool for me to have the pictures. I felt so bad asking Mariah, but it was important and there really wasn't anyone else there to do it. I hoped that she could do the pictures and then concentrate on Rick coming.

"Yes, I called him (**2:50 p.m.**) and he is on his way. He should be here soon. Love you Mom."

"Oh how I love you. Please know that Mariah, we love you dearly. This is an accident. It's not your fault. I love you."

There was an immediate plea to my Heavenly Father as I ran through my thoughts of who might be close enough to help my daughter. As far as I knew, Dalen was being cared for by a multitude of people—the first people that were driving behind Mariah and stopped to help, the first responders, the paramedics and a nurse that happened to be there; but Mariah was there on the side with Brenda by themselves. That picture was harder for me to handle than wanting to envision what was happening to Dalen. I contacted Rick and asked him if he had talked to Mariah. He said that he had and that he was on his way. I asked if he could hurry, and then I also asked if he could send me the number for the hospital so I could call them. Rick said he would send it to me. It only took a few seconds, which I was very grateful for.

2:55 p.m. Calling Alyssa to let her know what I knew. "Dalen isn't good. They are taking him to Pocatello." Not knowing what other communication had gone on between the rest of the family; I didn't know if Scott was talking to his daughters or not; or if they were calling him or each other. So I assumed they didn't have any information of what was happening, so I repeated whatever I knew. "Dalen is being taken to the hospital. He is bleeding badly, and we don't know how he is. Mariah doesn't think he's doing very well. I think we need to get up there as soon as possible."

"Yeah, Brandon is on his way home, so we will try and get a flight. It will depend on the money and everything."

"Yup I know. Just let me know what you find out. I love you. Please be safe."

"Of course Mom. Okay, I love you. I'm gonna look on the internet for a flight."

"Okay, I'll call in a few minutes."

3:00 p.m. "Mrs. Graham, I'm on my way. I just found the number of the hospital, so I'll send it to you." Rick was so thoughtful to keep me informed as to what he was doing.

"Thanks, Rick. I just don't want Mariah to be by herself. Please hurry."

"I am. My family is coming as well, and I think Aubree is too," Rick said. Aubree was a mutual friend of Mariah and Rick's. Mariah had spent most of her free time from school at Rick's house. His family was so good to Mariah, and they loved that she was Rick's girlfriend. I was comforted to know that another mom would be there and could hug my daughter. Their support would be a very big deal to all of us, but especially to Mariah.

"That would be great. Can you let me know if you hear of anything? I'm sure Mariah is talking with you." I didn't know how to plead any stronger to find out any kind of information concerning my son. What was going on with my son? How would I really know because I wasn't there and couldn't see, and hear the outcome? Everything I learned was through the phone. How grateful I was for that tool—now my lifeline, but it also just didn't seem like it was enough.

"Of course," was his reply.

3:01 p.m. "Portneuf Medical Center."

"May I have the emergency room please?" It only takes seconds for a call to be transferred. I'm sure it was only seconds, but again, it seemed like a long time especially when I knew what needed to be said, I just needed the person to hear my plea.

"ER."

"I know my son is being brought in. He was in an accident in Blackfoot and is being transported there by ambulance."

"Yes, we are waiting for his arrival," the nurse stated.

"I want you to keep my son on life support till we get there. His name is Dalen Graham. He is with his sister Mariah Graham. She will be in the ambulance with him. His family is trying to come from California, Vegas, and St. George. I'm about eight/nine hours out. We are all doing what we can to get there, but I want my son put on life support please till we get there, in case we need to say goodbye. I didn't get to say goodbye to my mother in person when she passed, and I want to be able to say goodbye to my son. Please take care of my son. Please!!!'

"We are waiting for your son to arrive. We are aware of his condition and will make sure your wishes will be made known to the staff. We will take care of it for you."

"Thank you. Thank you so very much," I pleaded.

"We will do everything we can. Your son is in good hands." This was the voice of all understanding. I was so far away, and the person on the receiver end of the phone knew her position, and I sensed that she was proficient as well. She would do her job just like the paramedics, and ambulance drivers, and all who had assisted with Dalen's care up to this point. I trusted her completely. There was no reason not to.

"Thank you. Thank you," was pretty much all I could say to the nurse. I didn't know what they knew. I didn't know how serious the condition of my son was, but from what little description I had, it wasn't good. I knew it would be hours before we all got there, and I just hoped and prayed that we would make it in time to say goodbye to my son if needed. It was still so unclear and uncertain of what we would be facing.

3:03 p.m. Mariah was trying to figure out some things. I couldn't understand everything that was going on, but I was able to talk to her whenever I could and when she needed me.

"Hey Mom—they won't listen to me! I keep telling everyone Dalen's name and age and whatever, and they keep ignoring me. They keep calling him by another name."

"Who won't listen to you?"

"The paramedics!"

"Mariah, they are just trying to help Dalen and do what they need to for him."

"No Mom. They keep calling him a different name. It's stupid and I don't get it!" Mariah was pretty intense. She just kept yelling that the people couldn't get Dalen's name right. It was so frustrating for her.

"Are you going to the hospital?"

"Yes, but we are waiting for the ambulance first. They keep asking me the same things."

"Why aren't they flying him in?" For a moment, I had the thought that even though it was bad, maybe it wasn't as bad as we thought he was, or else he was doing a bit better, so the ambulance was a good sign. I would learn later the reason for the ambulance. It wasn't all that good. Once they revived Dalen, they couldn't fly him because there wouldn't be any room in the helicopter to revive him again if needed, and because his pulse and blood pressure were so low, they felt it was safer for him to be transported in the ambulance. I also had learned that they had to revive Dalen five times—three from the field and two from the ER. Not such a good piece of information for sure.

"I don't know, but I'm so frustrated. They need to help my brother and they won't listen to me!"

"They are helping him Mariah. I'm sure they are doing all they can for him. How long have they been working on him?"

"They were here pretty quick after the accident. So, they have been working with him for a bit. The ambulance is here. Gotta go."

As in any emergency, the time frame always seems so obscured in someone's mind. A minute that gets replayed in your mind can feel like an hour to the person involved. The paramedics got there within minutes literally. There was a phone call within seconds of the accident from one of the first bystanders, and supposedly, there was a nurse and attendees at the scene as soon as it occurred. The police were there within three minutes from the initial call, while the paramedics arrived under seven minutes from the accident being reported. This time frame, along with Mariah's frustration, was very real. *Why were they calling Dalen by another name?* I never understood that question. I would learn again, the reason why. When someone was in a traumatic situation, they use a pseudo name because they needed to get the medical process started. So when they started working on Dalen, Mariah was held off to the side, so they weren't told his proper name. They gave an alias name so that they could start the medications and reporting of the events to the hospital. That explanation I could handle, but I still didn't understand why they didn't correct that information once they had it. I guess it was that they wanted to give Dalen all the attention and that the report would be corrected later.

The second answer given wasn't comforting in anyway. The other reason explained to us was that when a person dies in the field, they give a pseudo name so as not to offend any family members that might be listening to all the procedures that were being performed. It is a protection for the family and workers. Knowing that they had to revive Dalen didn't make that explanation very comforting. To revive—not just that a pulse was weak; but that there was no pulse. Dalen literally had died and was brought back to life not just once, but five times. I was in awe. However, with Mariah yelling at them to use Dalen's correct name; I think they should have used his proper name, if nothing else than to comfort her. I would have been yelling at them too. I didn't agree with that procedure, but once I understood more about it—I really was grateful that they were directing their time to Dalen's condition and not worrying about what to call him. I was just visualizing Mariah constantly yelling to them Dalen's correct name and sensing her anguish.

"Okay Mariah. Call me when you get there."

"Okay."

"Love you, Mariah."

"Thanks Mom, I love you too." There was a brief sigh of relief as I knew that Mariah would soon receive some attention and that Dalen was being worked on. I hoped that Mariah would also get some kind of counseling, or at least able to express what happened in the accident and to unload some of her feelings. It had been under a half hour since the accident and Dalen was still being worked on. We also found out later that it took all that were working with Dalen about twenty minutes just to get him out of the truck. He was stuck upside down and they couldn't get the door opened. They actually pulled him out from Mariah's side of the vehicle. So, all this time and Mariah was standing there watching while thinking they were taking forever, and now calling her brother by a different name. I couldn't imagine what she would be going through—being the driver, and not knowing the condition of Dalen, but thinking in her mind, she caused it all. There were just so many overwhelming thoughts for her, and me.

How could I console my daughter? I wish we knew the outcome of Dalen, or that at least he was okay. Just keep driving. Just keep driving. It almost seemed like such a normal process. I was very aware of everything and handling the situation like I thought I should. I wasn't freakin' out or hysterical, or unaware of my surroundings. I wasn't crying or even emotional. On the contrary, I was very much in control of it all. The phone calls and messages just kept coming. They were very calming. I felt the great power of prayer, and I was comforted and of sound mind. So; just keep driving. And I did.

3:07 p.m. Scott said that Stefanie (his former lieutenant) had called him because she had seen my Facebook post and was worried. Scott was pretty upset with me. "Why would you do that? I don't think everyone needs to know our business."

"Well, I did it because I knew that we could use the help and prayers of our family and friends. Look Scott. Look at all the support we have already." I guided his attention to my Facebook post and had him read the messages. He did feel of the support and prayers. Either way, Scott would have to accept my actions because they were already there and done. Furthermore, we were being so blessed and immediately. It really was so awesome.

Prayer is an amazing thing. As members of our church, prayer is a constant. We believe that God loves us and that we are His spiritual children. For that reason, He wants to hear from us and we do that through prayer. We believe in the communication that we offer our prayers; they are heard, and then answered by our loving Heavenly Father. We pray for ourselves and by ourselves. We pray for our families and with our families. We pray for our friends. We pray for strength, comfort, help, and guidance. We pray for situations in our country and problems with other countries. We pray for our veterans and those first responders. We pray for our homes, our food, our animals, and crops. We pray for leaders both in and out of the church such as our church Prophet and Apostles, and our presidents, and our country's leader. There really isn't much we can't pray for. And with the faith that is required with praying, answers come. Peace comes. Comfort comes. Guidance and direction to our lives comes. We aren't alone, and we don't feel alone. We pray first thing in the morning to start our day. We pray on our food each time we eat, and we give our thanks for what we have. We pray at the end of our day. We say prayers together as a family, and we have a prayer in our heart constantly. When there is a specific issue, our prayers seem more intense. When someone is really searching for an answer, our prayers are more sincere. We try not to take for granite the opportunity we have in praying and are asked always by others to pray for them. I believe in prayer because I have experienced the power of prayer. I have tested it and been proven of its reality. This day was a testimony again of that divine power.

Stefanie had asked Scott what she could do. "I told her I wasn't sure, but that I needed to get up to Idaho quickly," Scott said.

She told Scott that she would check into it and that she would call back. That was unbelievable. It was just amazing that she was there and taking care of things to help Scott out.

Scott and I both hoped there wasn't much traffic so Scott could get home and begin his journey of getting up to Idaho. He just wanted to be on his way and make good time. Scott was asking what he should bring and how many days of clothes to gather. Again, not really knowing anything of Dalen's condition, but in case—I said to pack for at least a week.

3:12 p.m. Scott, while driving home from Pomona, was in touch with whoever he could reach out to for help. He received a phone call from our Bishop (our religious leader), who also saw my Facebook post, and called to see if he could help with anything. Another call was coming in from Stefanie, so Scott asked the Bishop if he could call him right back. Stefanie told Scott that she had a flight for him out of Burbank at 4:32 and landing in Salt Lake City at 7:35 p.m. He would have a thirty-five-minute layover and then arrive in Idaho Falls about 9:30 p.m. That was still going to put him up there faster than I could get there, and we were so grateful. Stefanie had arranged for everything and also wouldn't let Scott pay for any of it. She just kept telling him not to worry and that he just needed to focus on getting up to Idaho to be with his family. He was very overwhelmed by her generosity.[6]

Scott immediately called our Bishop back and explained that he needed a ride to the Burbank airport. The Bishop asked when Scott would be home and that he would be waiting for him. Scott figured out that he should be home by three as there was no traffic and he was moving well. The Bishop said he would be there. Things just don't fall into place that precisely. It just didn't seem natural. Scott literally drove into the driveway and the Bishop was waiting for him. He ran into the house and packed. It was forty-five minutes to Burbank, and they left the house at 3:12 p.m. Scott's flight was at 4:32 p.m. That meant it would be close, but before they left the driveway, the Bishop offered a prayer and asked that they would make it to the airport in time so Scott could be with his son and—definitely a huge blessing for our family for sure.[7]

Stefanie had always been a very big part in the development of Scott's career. Wherever she went, she found a way to get Scott over to work with her. She had guided and molded Scott and people

---

[6] To say that what Stefanie did was anything but amazing still wouldn't give enough credit to her. Scott didn't have to do anything but drive home. He knew it would all be taken care of. Stefanie had this handled within five minutes, five minutes! He trusted Stefanie with his life, and she knew that. But then to also, not have to pay for the flight, or rental car, was such a surprising blessing.

[7] Our bishop wasn't just checking on Scott, but was immediately available for the help Scott needed to get to the airport. The bishop's son passed away five years ago so he was willing to talk to Scott and have him express his concerns. He really was there when we needed him.

seemed to like Scott in the sense that; if Stefanie wanted him to work with her, others would agree, and it always seemed to be good for Scott too. Scott appreciated all her attention on his behalf. Now, it wasn't even being a leader, but saving Scott and me from stress and anxiety and being the friend, he needed. It was amazing and way above anything we could have asked for.

3:14 p.m. Mariah: "They have Dalen in the ambulance. They checked me out quickly too. I'm going with Dalen."

"So that means he's alive!"

"He doesn't look good Mom. He really doesn't."

"That's hard to hear but keep me informed and know how much we love you. Let me know when you get there. I know this is hard, but I need to know as much as you can tell me. I'm coming," reassuring Mariah again.

"Okay Mom, I really don't know what's going on. But they are still working on Dalen. Just get here Mom! Please hurry!" Mariah pleaded.

3:16 p.m. "Hello."

"Hello Mrs. Graham. I'm almost there." Rick was now getting close to the hospital, about another twenty miles away. Rick was so worried for Mariah. He thought enough to keep me informed as well.

"I'm so grateful you will be there to help Mariah," I stated.

"Of course. If there is anything I can do for you, just let me know."

"Well, you going to be with Mariah is huge. I just can't handle the thought of her being alone!"

3:28 p.m. "How are you?" It was like I couldn't talk enough to Mariah. I wanted to be there every minute for her and wish I could. The drive was moving along, but my daughter was so heavily on my mind. There was nothing I could do but keep driving. Just keep driving. So, I did.

"Where are you Mom?" Mariah had a hint of terror in her voice.

"We are just coming into Cedar. What's going on?"

"We're at the hospital. They have Dalen. I don't know where he is," Mariah said.

"Are you alone? Is Rick coming?"

"Yeah, he's almost here."

"I don't want you by yourself. I'm really worried about you."

"I'm okay Mom. The security lady is with me. I'm not by myself. She said she wouldn't leave me. I just want you here." There was such pain of hearing Mariah's plea, and I couldn't do anything for her.

Your heart breaks when you know you can't help your child. No matter how they hurt, you want to take away their pain. We want our children to be normal, healthy, and always safe. As parents that seems like an impossible emotion; 'Let me take away their pain' is always our constant plea for our children when we see them suffering. Life doesn't usually work out that way though. All too often, our children also have to suffer with pain and experience that part of life for themselves. Mariah was alone and had been now for way too long in my opinion. I just couldn't do anything else but keep driving. I was moving along quickly. We were making really good time, but it wasn't enough. I just wanted to be there.

"I'm coming. Let me make some calls to see who is close and can get there to be with you."

"Okay."

"Are you okay?" again I asked.

"Yeah, I am. Please just hurry." Mariah is a very strong-willed young lady who doesn't like to show any emotion and usually appears as strong minded and determined. She wasn't going to let anyone think anything else but that she was okay. That was why I kept asking—to really know her state of mind, and I believed that she was as okay as she wanted and needed to be at that time.

3:30 p.m. "Portneuf Medical Center."

"May I have the emergency room please?" I asked the operator.

"Hello ER."

"Hello, this is Mrs. Graham. I had called a few minutes ago about my son coming in and being put on life support. His name is Dalen Graham. I think he might be there by now, but I'm not sure. I forgot to tell you that he is a donor."

"That is good to know. He is just arriving. Thank you for telling us. I will let everyone know," the nurse would confirm her new knowledge to the ER staff.

"You're welcome. Please just take good care of my son and thank you."

It had now been just about an hour since Mariah called me on Dalen's phone and how our lives had changed. Now that I began to process the situation, I realized that Mariah had been calling from Dalen's phone the whole time. I came to find out that once she got out of the truck, she immediately looked for a phone to call for help and Dalen's was the first thing she found. She didn't even have shoes on her feet as she was just chilling in the truck for the trip, probably not the best idea since she was driving. The phone became all of our lifelines. Her phone would be found within a few minutes, but Mariah kept Dalen's phone in her hand; I think it brought her some kind of comfort.

It had been about half an hour since my Facebook post. So in between calling those who I felt needed to know what was going on, I was listening to all these amazing messages posted on Facebook and texts-all expressing their concern for our family and mentioning that they were adding their prayers. What an overwhelming feeling to know that our situation mattered to so many. I was in awe that literally within two seconds—I had the first response, and they just kept coming. Within one minute, I had messages of our names being put on several temple prayer lists.

In The Church of Jesus Christ of Latter-Day Saints, temples are sacred buildings where members make covenants and perform ordinances. There are opportunities to have names added to a prayer roll, because of health concerns, or spiritual needs or even physical desires. Prayers are then offered on behalf of those with needs.

Prayers can have very profound affects. I felt so grateful for the outreach from others in knowing that again, all these prayers were being offered on behalf of our son. What a great power for sure.

—Oh my goodness, I am so sorry. If there's anything we can do, please don't hesitate to call.

—Wow, so sorry. That is so scary.

—Just saw about Dalen and Mariah. We immediately said a prayer for you all.

—Just put Dalen and Mariah on the prayer roll. Praying for you.

—I love you and I'm here for you if you need me.

—Our son is in SLC and said he could be there in two hours if you need him. We will pray for Dalen.

—Keeping you all in our prayers.

—An update on the kids? Praying for them!!!

—What can we do, anything? We are praying.

—We are just a phone call away for anything, we can also head to Idaho at any time if needed.

—We are praying for Dalen and all of you.

—Your family's names are all in the Odgen Temple prayer roll.

—You have my prayers of course!

—Praying.

—Prayers sent.

—Sending prayers your way for your family.
—Is Mariah doing well? Prayers for all.
—I'm so sorry! Dalen was my sons first companion in Texas. You and your family are in my prayers.
—I know you are strong! My prayers are with you and your family.
—Praying for you guys.
—Praying for your family.
—Oh wow…so very sorry. Putting names in temple. You're all in my prayers!!!
—Praying for him and your family.
—So sorry to hear this. Prayers and hugs.
—My heart goes out to your family.
—So sorry for your family. You and your family are in my heart and prayers at this time.
—You guys are in my prayers. We understand this is a very hard time but all we want to do is help if we can.
—We are only 2 hours away and I can be there in no time if you need anything.
—Sending lots of prayers to your family.

These samples of text messages arrived within about fifteen minutes and kept going throughout the afternoon. I heard from relatives and friends from all over. I heard from one of Dalen's missionary companion's parents, having never met them before. We got messages from Utah, Canada, Australia, Wyoming, California, Florida, and others. My cousin Kelli called me. She knew all too well of the phone call that came out of a panic, as her twin sister had passed away just a year ago and how hard it had been on her. I told her that I was good, and I really was good, and would let her know more when I did. Of course, I thanked her and everyone else too, for everything they were doing for us—mostly their prayers, thoughts, and concerns.

3:31 p.m. While Scott was driving to Burbank, he had also placed a call to his fireman friend that lived in Rexburg. His name was Kevin. He thought he might be able to find out some information about Dalen from his paramedics' friends, since he knew everyone in that department. What he heard wasn't the best, but also wasn't the worst.

3:33 p.m. "I just talked to Kevin, and he said that Dalen's lung collapsed. He also had lots of bleeding on the brain. They would have to do emergency surgery to release the pressure on his brain. That's their big issue now. They were able to inflate his lung, and it sounded like things were looking up. They got his oxygen level back up too, so I'm feeling better." Scott related all the news he knew of to me.

"That still sounds scary." I hadn't heard anything about the lung or the bleeding on the brain. I just knew there was bleeding, but I didn't know where it was from.

"They had to transport him in the ambulance because of his lung, and they lost his blood pressure. But Kevin said it sounded like they were getting him to respond. So, I'm breathing better."

"Yeah, that is great news." Still didn't feel like it was enough, but it was something.

"We are just about to take off, so I won't be able to call till I land in Salt Lake City." Scott stated.

"Well, I will just keep driving. Call me the second you can. It's going to be a long drive I think. But I'm making good progress and Kailee is doing good too."

"Gotta go. Be safe."

"Talk to you soon. Love you Scott." I then reported to Kailee immediately after hearing from Scott all the information. We were relieved that his lung was back to normal and took that as a very positive improvement from what we were speculating. Another call to Alyssa of course, and our prayers would continue, but there was at least for a moment, an opportunity to breathe-even for just a minute.

Kailee's Facebook post 3:35 p.m. "Major prayers needed! Mariah Graham and Dalen

Graham were just in a traffic accident up in Idaho and all we know is that Dalen is being life-lined to the hospital; lung failed and has brain damage.

I will let everyone know more when I do but we can use prayers and lots of them. Me and my parents are all on the road driving individually up."

Mariah's Facebook post 3:48 p.m. "Quick update: I am fine with a few cuts and bruises. Dalen is not so good. Pretty scary. Thank you all for your thoughts and prayers."

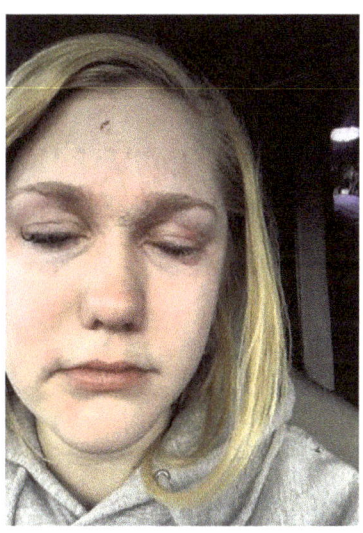

A Few More Hours

3:49 p.m. "How are you doing Kailee?" I asked.
"I'm good. It's amazing how clear the road is."
"Well, our prayers were heard. Let's just keep going. Let me know if you need to stop or can't handle the drive."
"No, I'm good. Just keep going Mom. Let's keep going."
"Sounds good. Talk to you in a minute."
"Okay, Love you."
"Love you too."

> **Facebook post @ 3:51 from Kelli Christensen (my cousin). "Love and prayers needed for this amazing woman, fellow twin cousin of mine, as her son and daughter were in a terrible accident. Love you Scott and Sharon Graham."**

3:54 p.m. I needed to find my brother Gordon. His wife Maria was usually the better way to get to him. She was always the sweetest person. I called her and she said to call Gordon as he was at home. Gordon lived in Syracuse, Utah which was about forty-five minutes north of Salt Lake City. He really was the closest family member that I could think of to get someone up to be with Mariah in Pocatello.

"There's been a serious accident. Dalen isn't doing well. Mariah was driving and rolled the truck. They are taking Dalen to Pocatello Hospital."

"So, what do you want me to do?" In his voice wasn't the sound of support or comfort, instead, he sounded irritated of what I was asking of him. He didn't really want to go. I knew that, but I needed him. Gordon was a very quiet man. Seldom did you see any type of reaction from him. He usually meant things when he said something and it was pertinent to the issue, but you still never quite knew where you stood with him or what he was feeling.

"Could you go up? You're the closest family member and I just don't want Mariah to be alone."

"Oh, it will be alright. Everything will be okay. I don't think I need to go."

"Gord, the reports aren't good. I just don't want Mariah alone in that hospital by herself, in case Dalen passes away. I just want you to go. Come on brother. This is serious, and I need your help. What are you not understanding?" My thoughts now were racing to why my brother was hesitating, and I was becoming irritated. I didn't want that to come across though, because I needed my brother and I just needed him to believe me. I needed his help and I needed it now.

"He's not going to die. It's not that bad, don't worry."

"I'm driving up from St. George but have about eight more hours ahead of me. Please could you go till I get there?"

"I can look into it if that's what you want."

"Yes, that is what I want, please? It isn't good Gord. Please just go and be with Mariah. Dalen's lung was punctured and there is bleeding on the brain, so it's not good." Again, I couldn't get mad at my brother. He was trying to be positive and not let me worry. I wasn't worried, but I was just so very concerned for Mariah and the situation she was in. "I know you're still the closest one to Mariah. Please can you go?"

"Yes—I'll go," he said hesitantly.

"Okay. Thank you so much. Could you let me know when you get there?"

"Yup. I will."

"Thanks Gord. I love you. This means so much to me."

"Love you too. It will be okay. Don't worry." That was easy for him to say because he didn't know of all the calls and information we had received. I wanted to believe him, but I truly felt that the situation merited other and more serious concerns.

"I'm hurrying." I replied.

3:56 p.m.   "Where are you at Mom?"
"Just passing Cedar. How are you? What's going on?"
"I'm okay. I don't know what's going on with Dalen. They haven't said anything to me. I don't know what to do or think."
"I wish I could help you Mariah. This is tough, so tough. I'm so sorry for what you have to experience. I love you sweetie. Oh how I love you." I knew Mariah didn't know about the emergency surgery needed on Dalen's brain, and I wasn't going to tell her.

3:57 p.m.   The thought of how amazing things were happening, kept coming to my mind. As bad as this was becoming—things were coming together with Scott getting on his flight, Kailee and I progressing, and Alyssa and Brandon getting on the road. Of course, it wasn't fast enough. The road just seemed too long in front of me. But we just kept moving. 'I wish the road was shorter. I wish I could be with Mariah. I wish Gord would be there. I wish this wasn't happening.' Off course I had several thoughts along those lines.
"Are you holding up Kailee?" I inquired.
"Yup, I'm good." Kailee was a person that would always tell you exactly what was happening. She was very literal and that was all the time. That came from her autism. Kailee as a child didn't talk till she was almost four. She went to special education classes for two years. We never knew if she would be able to go to a normal class. We worked really hard all the time on helping her progress and learn about autism. Kailee surpassed all of our expectations as she graduated from high school, served a mission for our church. and has been able to provide for herself holding down two jobs. She bought a car by herself and pays for her rent, insurance and living on her own. But when you ask Kailee a question, she would always tell you what she thought even if it didn't quite fit with the conversation. But when Kailee said she was good, it meant she was good. You believed what Kailee would say. She would tell you exactly how things were and she was usually right even if it wasn't what you wanted to hear. That's the part where

others would think that Kailee was just different enough to not quite fit in. Still, we were so proud of all of her accomplishments.

"Okay, let's keep going then."

"Any more word about Dalen?" Kailee asked.

"Nope, it's hard not to know what's going on."

"Ya, so I'll just keep following. Chris (Kailee's boyfriend) just gave me this heads up too. Northbound I-15 is closed due to two accidents," Kailee informed me.

"Okay. Let's check that out when we get closer."

"Yeah, of course."

3:58 p.m. "Mom, I don't know what's goin' on. I'm here, but I don't know where Dalen is. Rick got here a few minutes ago, so I feel a little better," Mariah said.

"Oh that is good news. I'm glad he's there for you. Now you won't be alone anymore." What a horrific feeling—to be alone in a waiting room of a hospital knowing that a family member is hurt and badly, and that you can't find out anything. Then you start to notice that even though you are okay—there are issues.

"They are going to check me out again, so I'll call you back."

"Okay that's good. Make sure you tell them everything and really have them check you over. Don't think everything is okay—let them check you out," I insisted.

"Okay Mom."

"Love you honey."

"Love you too Mom, bye."

4:15 p.m. Scott had found out about Dalen and Mariah from his friend Kevin. Mariah had a swollen eye and shoulder. She might have some other bruises, but nothing was visible at that moment. Dalen's lung collapsed. They stabilized him, but he was in critical condition and about to undergo surgery on his head to relieve pressure from bleeding on the brain. There was internal bleeding as well. It was a very serious situation, and Kevin thought we should know. They have him intubated and were able to fix the hole in his lung. He would be going in for surgery immediately. Scott felt that since he was attended to, and that his lung was now fixed, that things should be better. He thought that the surgery was needed, but that it would also resolve the issues that were threatening to Dalen.

4:18 p.m. "Mom."
"Hi Alyssa. What have you found out?"
"We are going to drive. It was too hard to get a flight. They were way to expensive and had huge layovers, so we are just getting in the car to come up. With all the layovers, it is actually going to be faster if we drive. We couldn't get a flight till after 6:30 p.m. and we had like six-hour layovers. So, we just decided to drive up."

Brandon got off work and was able to drive home and all within half an hour. He was an EMT in Vegas and wasn't supposed to get off work for another two hours. Alyssa also had a dog to worry about too. She had found a friend that would come and play and feed her dog. That was another issue that we realized: when any of us had a problem come up, the obstacle was solved almost immediately. Things were just taken care of. We might have had to make a phone call, but then everything was handled, so amazing again.[8]

4:24 p.m. Alyssa was also just heading out. She had to wait for Brandon to come home. "We are about to head out Mom."
"Okay—it's a long way. I'm only about one and a half hours ahead of you. Make sure you drive carefully. Mariah is getting checked out right now and she doesn't know anything about Dalen."
"Yeah I know, she told me."
"Okay then, just be super careful and keep in touch."
"Okay Mom, love you," Alyssa said.
"Love you too, bye."

4:25 p.m. "So, this is your brother." Gord said.
"Hi Gord. Have you left yet?"

---

[8] Brandon got off work. He said there was a family emergency and he needed to go. Alyssa was able to get someone to watch their dog, and they were on the road within an hour.

"Yeah, I'm on the road. Do you know anything else?"

"They are checking Mariah out right now. She doesn't know where Dalen is though. We know his lung collapsed and there is bleeding on the brain, but we don't know what they are doing with him now. There was surgery to release the pressure on his brain. Could you hurry? She's having a hard time. Since I can't be there, please hug her for me."

"Sure thing. I don't think you should be driving though. You need to let Maria come with you so she can drive."

"Well, I'm doing fine. Let me know when you get there, please."

"Okay—I will, but I think you need to let Maria drive for you. I don't think you should be by yourself."

"Well, I'm not really, as Kailee and I are carpooling together. I'm really doing fine and actually, I want to drive. It keeps my thoughts where they need to be."

4:28 p.m. Scott called me as he was getting off the freeway and heading into moving really quickly. In fact, when Scott arrived, he actually had ten minutes before they started boarding and at Burbank, there wasn't ever much of a wait to get through security, so he was there and had minutes to spare. Miracle for sure. We were in awe how quickly things came together. I know that Scott told me more information about his flight, but I really only remembered that he would have a layover in Salt Lake City. I couldn't remember the time frame other than he had a flight and that he made it on time. What another amazing blessing.

"My flight leaves in about ten minutes. I just made it. No traffic at all. I have about half an hour layover in Salt Lake City when I get there. That's not bad and I don't even have to get off the plane, so I should be in Idaho Falls about 9:30 p.m. and will get a rental car from there. Stefanie took care of everything."[9]

"Wow-that is amazing. She is so good to you."

---

[9] Scott had to make it to Burbank in 40 minutes. Get through security and make a flight. Not only did he get there in time, he had minutes to spare. The traffic usually just doesn't work that way in LA County especially on a Friday.

"Yeah, I should be in Pocatello by 10:30 p.m. It's all working out. What more do you know?" Scott enquired.

"Nothing really. It's kind of hard to get any information. Rick just got there so Mariah isn't alone anymore, but I'm still worried about her."

"Me too."

"We'll talk to you in a few hours. Love you."

"Love you too," said Scott.

"Are you okay?"

"Yeah, I think so. It's just the unknown."

"Yeah, that is the hardest part of this. Call me when you get to Salt Lake City. Love you babe." I said.

"I will. Love you too."

As Scott was boarding the plane, he received a call from the hospital. Kevin had talked to his paramedic friends that had just brought Dalen in and had asked them to talk to Scott with the details. He was told of the exact condition, that both of Dalen's lungs had collapsed. They were able to inflate them, but that they were taking him into surgery immediately to release pressure on his brain where there was internal bleeding.

Even though we had heard similar to this before, to actually speak with the personal that attended Dalen made it so much more real. They just said he wasn't good. As bad as that was, they made it sound hopeful or at least to Scott.

"It sounded positive to me, that Dalen had pulled through a tough few moments, but that he was good," Scott informed me again. "The hospital also said that he was very critical, but there was some improvement. They suggested that we get there quickly." Still, Scott seemed reassured.

Scott had called me with the hospital results, which wasn't as calming to me. I felt that it was still pretty darn scary and that our son was in a critical state. Scott deflected the mood as he reminded me to get someone for the animals back home because he would be gone. I had already done that. Our dear sweet neighbor Tina had always been so kind to help. She had dogs and horses too, and we rode together as often as our schedules allowed. But to help on the spur of the moment—not knowing our time frame either; just so awesome. Of course, she was very worried about Dalen and asked that I keep her informed. Thank you *'again'* Tina. What an angel.[10]

The Sister Missionaries had been taking care of the animals already as Scott never liked feeding them, so I made sure he didn't have to while I was gone. They also had a key to the house just in case they would need it. So, between the missionaries and Tina, things were taken care of at home regarding the animals and I was very grateful.

"Be safe, be still, be strong." My cousin Kelli just kept reassuring me, she was there for me and would help however she could. She called several times to check on me.

"He's in ICU right now. He did puncture both lungs. They fixed that. They're waiting for his CAT scan results and an emergency surgery to relieve some pressure on his brain from all the bleeding. I'm coming up to Nephi, so I'm making progress." Now I had information I could relay to people and Kelli was able to hear it first.

My sister-in-law called to see what she really could do. I had hoped that my brother was on his way even two hours out—still the closest. She reassured me that he was, and very thorough with my actions and thoughts. I was doing what needed to be done, and slowly the miles were passing. I was driving as if this was a normal trip, so Kailee and I just kept driving.

4:30 p.m. "Where are you Mom? I don't know what to do." Mariah was beside herself. I just couldn't imagine how the time was her enemy, and even though we were hurrying, it wasn't fast enough.

"We're just coming into Beaver. A few hours closer sweetie. Uncle Gord will be there within the hour. Anyone else there?" I asked.

"Rick is here with Aubree," Mariah stated.

"That is good to hear. So, you're not alone. Are you okay?"

"Yeah, I really am okay Mom. I wish everyone would quit asking me."

---

[10] Our neighbor Tina was not only available on the spur of the moment, and not knowing for how long we would need her to take care of our animals; but she asked if she could do anything else for us over and over again.

"Mariah, I have to know how you are. I will ask because I can't do anything else."

"Yeah, I'm good. Gotta go, the doctor is now going to check me out."

"Okay—Let me know what's up."

"Okay Mom."

4:33 p.m. "Hey Mom, I need to get gas." Kailee and I were on the same wavelength.

"Yeah, me too. I need a bathroom too."

"Okay—I'll follow you." So, nothing out of the ordinary as far as traveling went. We would stop and get gas, something to munch on and a bathroom break. Then head back out on the road. We were coming into Beaver. I thought we were making good time. Again, the road just kept going. There was still good daylight as the sun was starting to set, so I was grateful again for the blessing of getting as far as we did with the light of the day. This one little gas station was the standard stop. It just seemed to be a good space from St. George and a great place to stretch. We had stopped there regularly and actually had seen people we knew from our Stake back in California. (A Stake is a geographical region where our church exists.) Just the popular place to stop, I guess. This time, I just ran into the bathroom, so I didn't take the time to look around to see if I knew anyone. I asked Kailee if she needed anything, munchies or a drink. We were good, gave her a hug and we were on the road again.

> **Facebook post-4:34 p.m.** 'Scott wondered why I would put a traumatic event on Facebook. But the overwhelming support of love and prayers is huge. Dalen is in ICU currently.
>
> He did puncture both lungs, there is trauma on the brain and they are waiting for a CAT scan result. Scott was able to get a flight into Idaho, thanks to Stefanie Fredericks. Dalen's name is on the temple prayer roles in several temples. Thank you.

Brandon, also a paramedic, was able to get some more information about the transport. Brandon told me that we needed to get there sooner than later. "I don't think he will make it Mom," he responded.

"What do you mean? We thought he was doing better."

We had hope and a positive outlook. This news changed the reality of the situation. Kevin had also called me and said that Dalen wasn't doing well. They had to resuscitate him twice while in the field and once in the ambulance. I knew it was three times, I didn't know one was in the ambulance. That I didn't know. Just hearing this though from a different person, made it so much more real. Hence, there was no helicopter because they couldn't resuscitate in the helicopter. The truck had rolled five times. I didn't know that- the truck rolled five times, three sideways and two head over heels. Horrifying—the picture was very vivid in my mind. His pulse was really weak, but there was one. That part I was thankful for. Without a pulse there would have been no attempt to revive him as much as they did. Without a pulse, he wouldn't have been able to be a donor. Not an easy feeling to process. My son was dying or had died.

Is this real? What a phrase to have crossed your thoughts. My son had died. I was still so very far away and couldn't do anything about it. My faith was strong though, and I knew that I would be able to just keep driving and be safe and sane while doing so. There was nothing but peace abiding with me. Sure my mind was racing all over the place; between children, Scott, travel and where Dalen was at and what would happen. With all that was going on though, I was at peace. I was calm and I was facing the situation as I needed to do. Again, it was *'just keep driving and get there quickly'*. Scott wouldn't be able to know any of this as his flight had taken off. I couldn't do anything but drive. My full heart and thoughts were just; *'Please keep my son alive till we get there. Just keep him alive please!'* Gratitude became my blanket as my petitions became outwardly expressed to my Heavenly Father for the life of my son.

"My son wasn't going to make it. He wasn't going to make it. Just let us get there first, please Heavenly Father, PLEASE!"

Sheila called me. She too, had read my post on Facebook. Being a twin meant we shared some special feelings when thinking of the other. She had always been more insightful to me and my needs throughout our lives. She was so worried about all of us. This new information about Dalen helped. They had to inflate his lungs and he was going into surgery to release pressure on his brain." Some ways, it was a relief to finally have something to say. "So, we know that both of his lungs had collapsed. They had to resuscitate him three times before they even put him into the ambulance. But they now are working on relieving the pressure on his brain and have him stabilized.

"Oh my gosh, I'm so sorry! What can I do?" Sheila asked.

"Just keep praying with the rest of us. There really isn't anything else we can do. It's so hard when I'm not there and don't really know what's happening. I'm making good progress though, but I'm still about six hours out. I called Gord and practically had to beg him to go and be with Mariah."

"Yeah, I heard that," Sheila commented.

"He didn't think it was a big deal, but I begged him to go."

"That's good. I'm glad he went."

"I know. Cody (my cousin that lives in Wyoming) offered to go, knowing that he was only seven hours away and would be there for Mariah, but Gord hesitated, and he was only two hours away. I thought that was way cool of Cody. Not knowing how serious everything was I kind of understood Gord's point, but I still wanted him there. I was just really struggling with the thoughts of Mariah being alone." I knew Sheila would read my thoughts. That was hard and yet it was what had to be done.

"How is she?" Sheila inquired.

"The doctor is checking her out right now. She says she's fine of course. Can you keep the family informed for me?"

"Of course," she replied.

"Okay—Thanks Sheila. I'll call you later. Love you."

"Love you too. Just let me know what I can do," she insisted.

"Ok, I will."

4:59 p.m.   "Portneuf Memorial Hospital."
"Can I have the ER please?"
"One moment and I'll connect you," the operator said.
"ER."
"Hi. My name is Sharon Graham, and my children were in an accident and taken there. You have my daughter Mariah and my son Dalen. Can you update me on the condition of my son?"
"We just called your husband and informed him of the procedures we did. Both lungs had collapsed, and they had to resuscitate him five times," the nurse relayed her information to me.
"I heard it was only three times."
"Yes, but we had to shock him twice when he arrived at the ER."
"Is my son okay now?"
"He is in surgery to take the pressure off his brain as he is bleeding internally. But he is stable and that is good and the best we could expect." Again the nurse was just trying to give a mom all the answers she could.
"You know we asked to have him on life support? Right?"
"Yes we know of your wishes," she replied.
"I also wanted to let you know he is a donor in case you hadn't heard."
"That is very important to know. Thank you again for telling us. I will make sure the team knows that. Do you know what he wanted to donate?" she asked.
"I'm not really sure. I know the organs and his eyes were mentioned before. But other than that—I'm really not sure. I just wanted you to know that."
"Thank you. We will do whatever we can for your son," she said with conviction.
"Thank you. I'm hurrying but still about six hours out."
"We will take care of him. Be safe in your travels," the nurse stated.
"Thank you. Goodbye."

5:12 p.m.   Maria Romano. "Hi Sharon, I was in Wendy's room (a lady I visited with) when you were on the phone and I found out

about the accident. I don't know what to say but that we will be praying for Dalen and you guys and let me know if I can do anything for you while your away; feed your dogs, or horses just send me what to do, I can do it."

Maria was a good friend. I had been assigned to be her visiting teacher. All the women in the church, are assigned to take care of specific sisters. We call them visiting teachers. It basically meant we checked in on them and helped if we can with any needs, whether physically, emotionally, or spiritually. Maria and I had worked hard together over the last couple of years, to get her family back into activity in the church. We had worked hard together over the last couple of years to get Maria's family back into activity in the church. We had worked to get her family to the temple where they were sealed together for time and all eternity.

We had walked together for over a year and had been over to each other's for dinner or movie and popcorn several times. We were friends and good friends. I knew that if I needed anything, Maria would be there for me as would Wendy, and I would be there for them. Maria worked at the school and Wendy was a teacher there. A small community and close friends.

5:16 p.m. "So, what did the doctor. say Mariah? How are you? What did they do?"

"I'm good. My shoulder hurts and I'll probably have a black eye. They ran some tests and did some x-rays and I think I'm good."[11] Mariah recalled.

"That's great. Have you heard anything about Dalen?"

"Yeah, I think they are taking him up to ICU when they're done with all the testing. He doesn't look good Mom. I don't think he'll

---

[11] Mariah was totally fine. There were no broken bones, or scratches, very little bruising. How could this be possible? My daughter's car rolled 5 times. How could my daughter survive with only a bruise on her shoulder and a discolored eye? This was so amazing and more than a miracle.

make it. I think Dalen is going to die." Mariah was so blunt and straight to the point, but it was true.

"We don't know that Mariah. We don't know that."

"From what people are saying—Yeah, I think I know. Kevin spoke with the paramedics and he said he isn't going to make it and should have died in the field."

"Mom, what do I do?" Mariah pleaded again for an answer.

"Hang on till we get there. I'm just passing Fillmore. I'm making good time. Dad is flying up to Idaho Falls and then he will get a rental car and drive the rest of the way down. Alyssa and Brandon are about two hours behind Kailee and me. We are all coming. Just hang on Mariah." I reflected on what I was asking my daughter to hang on to. What did I want her to hang on to? It was like being in a raft in a storm and hanging on to the sides for dear life, that you would make it alive. Was I asking to hang on in that way? I believe I was asking to hang on to hope for Dalen and a truth of our coming. To hold on to that truth, we were coming and would arrive soon.

"Okay, but hurry Mom."

"I'm trying. So glad you're okay. Love you Mariah."

"Love you too, Mom."

Calls kept coming. I heard from Alyssa who updated us on her travels. Heard from Maria (sister-in-law) trying to get me to pick her up, so she could drive me to the hospital. I heard from Kailee as we continued to check on each other throughout the drive. Wendy Barnes called, who was my visiting teacher and friend. We had a monthly topic that we would discuss with each other, and it was always nice to know that someone cared about me. Wendy was that person for sure. She was beside herself with worry and wondered how she could help. She just couldn't imagine a mother having to accept that her son wasn't going to make it. Gord announced that he was arriving, which was the biggest relief. Kelli, my cousin, was checking in on me and making sure I was able to drive and mentally be okay. All the calls were again such a blessing. They kept me on track and focused. I felt very blessed.

—I just heard! Are you okay and do you need anything? Praying for your family.

—Sharon please drive safe. Put his name in the temple.

—Sharon, please know how much we love you and your family.

—Please let me know if there is anything I can do (Stake President Knowles).

—I just heard about Dalen and Mariah. Is there anything we can do to help the family?

—I know your phone is blowing up. Praying and love you.

—I am here if you need anything at all. I can be in Idaho in 3 hours if you need me! Love you.

—My friend, I'm not going to call you right now as I know you are driving, and I want you to be safe.

—Please know I am praying for Dalen and ALL of you. I'm in NM but will keep me updated. I love you my friend.

—Just talked to Scott. I don't want to overwhelm you with too many calls but I'm here to talk to help you guys in any way.

—Our hearts are with you all.

—You are the best mom I know. I'm so sorry, Sharon.

All my messages came through Bluetooth, so I just kept pushing that 'play message' button. I then could hear what each person was saying and not be looking at my phone. I needed to be safe too.

6:30 p.m. Passing through Payson, Utah. I received a call from Gina Lindstrom. Gina was a friend. We never really did a lot together, but our sons were the same age and on many sport teams together. Gina was one of those persons that if she needed help, she knew she could call on me and I would be there for her. She was a neighbor and a friend. We always laughed when we were together.

For some reason, she liked my advice. She was in shock with our news of Dalen. She couldn't handle this situation and really needed to talk.

"Okay, I don't do this at all, but I need you to pray with me and to pray right now."

"Gina, I'm driving. I can't pray right now. Why can't you pray?"

"I don't know how to pray out loud," she insisted.

"Well, what do you want me to do? I'm driving."

"I need you to pray with me right now!" She was demanding. She wanted this right now and felt it was absolutely necessary. She literally needed me to pray with her, which I thought was a very odd request. But I complied because I probably needed the prayer myself.

"Okay, I'm not sure if I can. I can't pull over because I'm on a freeway."

"I don't care. I need you to pray with me right now." Again she insisted.

"Okay Gina. Okay, I will."

"Okay what do I do?"

"Bow your head and close your eyes and I'll say the prayer." This was such a unique experience. Gina knew of our faith and new of our belief in the power of prayer. "Heavenly Father. This is a very serious situation that we are in as we know so little of Dalen's accident and what has happened to him. We bow our heads before thee as we humbly wish to ask for thy protection. Dear Heavenly Father, we are grateful for our understanding of thy Plan of Salvation, and we are grateful for the power of prayers that have been offered on our behalf. Please bless Gina to gain an understanding of that plan. I'm thankful for her friendship and her concerns for me currently. Please bless her with thy peace as well. At this time Heavenly Father, we wish to ask thee for one very big blessing. We don't know what is happening with Dalen, and we plea with thee at this time, for him to be comforted. That his body will be able to endure what is being asked of him. We pray for the doctors and nurses to have the knowledge of what to do for Dalen, and that they might be able to keep him alive until we are able to reach him. We asked for our journeys to be quick and in safety and for all our family to be able to be united quickly. Please Heavenly Father, our desire is to be with our son before he passes this life. If this is thy will, we will accept it. If this is thy will, we will understand. We love thee Heavenly Father, and again give thanks for all thy blessings that we have experienced thus far in this journey. Please comfort us and guide us. Please give Gina this gift as well. Let her feel of thy peace. We say these things in the name of Jesus Christ, Amen."

Gina was silent on the other end.

"I don't know if that is what you were expecting Gina?" I asked.

"I'm not sure what I was expecting, but that was amazing, and I needed that. How do you do that, pray like that?" Gina replied.

"I don't know. I just pray to my Father in Heaven knowing that He loves me and my son, and I will do His will and we will accept His. I didn't know what to say, but I trust in His plan and believe that He would take care of us."

I really didn't remember much of what I said about the prayer after that, but that my friend had needed me to pray and that I did it while driving. I know my prayer was for me too, but mostly for my friend to understand the comfort that comes with the spirit and the knowledge we had of life after death. It now was very real to me. I now had to completely believe what I had been taught my whole life; that the afterlife exists and that God's plan is real. I had believed this my whole life, and now I had to show that I believed it. I was calm and again doing all that I needed to do. Peace was my companion through this whole thing. I felt inspired and uplifted. Again-my plea was to just keep driving and to do all that I could do to get to see my boy. The rest of this was put into God's hands. He was leading us along and we were willing to follow.

Salt Lake Area and Airport

Kailee had already heard of major accidents in the Salt Lake City area. We knew that we would have to take a different route with the side streets because of the information that Chris had given Kailee. Kailee had lived in that area the previous year after her mission and had worked and drove daily the back roads to get to her job, so I was very excited when she announced that she knew the way.

"Then go ahead of me and I will follow you."

"Chris told me there was another accident. That's three on the I-15. So, it's a really good thing we aren't going that way," Kailee stated.

"I wouldn't be able to handle sitting on the freeway and not moving. This is awesome."

"Yup, so follow me and we will come around the I-15 on the other side of Salt Lake. I'll drive as far down as I can before we have to cross back over to the I-15. It's not that much farther Mom."

"If we are moving, I'm good. Lead the way Kailee."

We were coming into the Salt Lake Valley area. There was always traffic and knowing that there were multiply accidents added some stress. However, I was very excited to know that we were heading parallel to the freeway, but the traffic was cruzin' along. I was surprised that others hadn't gotten off the I-15 and were driving the same way we were, but I also wasn't complaining. Our drive was clear. I remembered my prayer, and I knew it was being answered. We were making amazing time. I was getting excited to think that we were coming through the valley with no obstacles.[12]

---

[12] It was about 6:30 p.m. on a Friday evening in the Salt Lake area and there was no traffic on the detour route we were taking. That doesn't happen unless God wants it to.

6:42 p.m. "Mom, are you almost here?" Mariah asked.

"I'm coming into the Salt Lake Valley right now. Kailee is driving us the back roads because there are some big accidents on the I-15. We are making good time sweetie. I promise that I'm hurrying."

"Okay, I'm good. I'm just anxious to see you Mom. Gord is here and Rick's family is here too. So, I'm not alone, but I just want to see you. Dalen is in the ICU unit now. It's hard to look at him Mom; his head is all full of blood and it's swollen, but I won't leave him. I won't leave him Mom."

"I want to be with you too, sweetie. I'm glad you are okay. Hang in there. We are on our way and getting closer. I'll check with you in a bit."

Alyssa had called too, and she was about two hours behind me. She was making good time but was also nervous. She kept letting her thoughts get the best of her, and she was thinking of the worst. She tried to be calm, but it was really hard on her not knowing a whole lot. She was glad that she didn't have to drive because she couldn't focus and was anxious about the unknown. We again, were just grateful that our family was making progress, and all was going well. We just kept driving. Just keep driving.

> **Facebook @ 7:03 p.m. Gina Lindstrom**-"I am requesting your prayers, love, light and positive vibes for my sweet friend Sharon Graham, and her family whom I love very dearly. Her son Dalen Graham, has been in a car accident. Dalen has been around my house as well as my parent's home throughout the years since kindergarten. He is loved like another son and grandson by us. Please lift them up in your thoughts and prayers as the Graham family reunites to be by Dalen's side."

7:05 p.m. Kevin Davis "Hey Sharon, I don't know what you have heard, but you need to know that your son isn't going to make it. The paramedics called me again after they had spoken with the surgeons and said that they worked really hard on your son, but that there was just too much internal bleeding and that there wasn't really anything more they could do. You should have been here an hour ago. But for now, your son isn't going to make it. I'm really sorry, Sharon. I'm sorry. We will stay here till you get here."

"We are just passing through the valley. I should be there in about three hours or less. We are hurrying as fast as we can. So, there isn't anything they can do for my son?"

"I really don't think so. His injuries were too severe. He had too much blood on his brain. They did put a drain in though, but the damage was extensive." Kevin had announced the death of someone several times before as he was a fireman in Rexburg and was pretty close with all the paramedics. This was different as it was his understanding of what the personnel had experienced with Dalen, and we were his friends. Not what he wanted to tell us, but I was also grateful that we heard from our friend. The hospital was waiting for us to arrive before they gave us all the detailed information.

"Okay. Thank you for telling me. I really appreciate your friendship and that you can be there for Mariah. That means a lot to us. Thank you."

Kevin hung up the phone, and it was like I expected the words. Again, I wasn't in shock. I heard what he said and knew I needed to call the family and let them know. The worst was now true. I don't know if I felt it already to be true or that it was almost expected because of the trauma that Dalen had sustained, but the words that my son wasn't going to make it meant I still needed to get there and in a hurry too.

7:08 p.m. "Kailee, Dalen isn't going to make it."

"Really? He's not going to make it."

"No. Kevin just called and said that he pretty much was only on life support because I had asked them to put him on it. He has too many internal injuries. Are you okay?"

"Yeah, I guess." There was a slight pause for processing what she had just been told. She sounded like she was in shock just a bit, but also that she could handle the news.

"Do you need to pull over for a minute? Are you okay?"

"Yeah, I'm okay Mom. I'm sad, but I also want to just keep driving."

"Me too. So, let's keep going. You have to be honest and let me know if this is too much for you. You are doing great and we are making awesome time. I really appreciate you leading me through this traffic thing."

"Okay Mom. I'm way sad, but I'm okay. I can drive. I have my music. I'm good."

Then I had to call Alyssa. She was already upset because she was so far behind everyone else. I knew that no matter what, the words weren't going to be easy to say, but had to be said.

7:10 p.m. "Alyssa, Dalen isn't going to make it. Kevin Davis just called me and said that he had too many internal injuries. I think Brandon kind of had an idea too, that he wouldn't make it." I heard the tears in her voice. I knew it was the worst thing she could have listened to. I knew that she was very upset. Again, I couldn't do anything to help her either. I was too far from Mariah, and now knowing what she knew. I was behind Kailee and knew that the news was a shock to her. I was ahead of Alyssa and couldn't console her because of the distance too. Scott was on an airplane, and I didn't really know when he would land in Salt Lake City or his time frame, and I couldn't tell him. So, I couldn't help anyone. I couldn't help any of my family, and I was just told that my son wasn't going to live. I felt so limited in my abilities to help my family, but I felt secure in my faith and knowledge and knew we would all be able to handle this situation and be comforted through it all.

"Seriously Mom, I don't want to hear that."

"I know Alyssa. It's not what any of us want to hear, but it is reality. He is on life support because I had asked them to keep him on life support."

"I don't want to hear this mom. We are driving as fast as we can. I want to be there Mom. I need to be there." She was crying hard. I couldn't console my daughter and reality of this whole thing, was that my son was going to die. My son wasn't going to make it. My son wasn't going to make it.

"I know sweetheart. I need to be there too. Keep driving and be safe. We will deal with the issues when we get there. Just keep driving and be safe. I love you sweetie."

"I love you too Mom." The tears didn't stop just because we hung up. I felt so bad for Alyssa. I just couldn't do anything to make this situation any better. We were still so far away.

Scott's friend Bob called. He was on our racing team and was just a really good guy. He had always supported Scott's racing program. He had gone to the races with us. He picked up parts for Scott. He took vacation time to go with Scott racing and really part of our family which led him to being very concerned for all of our family. I explained to Bob what I had just heard. He was devastated. He expressed his condolences and asked if he could do anything. I told him there really wasn't anything he could do. I just needed to talk to Scott and make sure he was okay and then get to Idaho. Wendy, Maria, and a few others called. All were stunned with the information I relayed to them. They didn't know what to say or do and I didn't know what to do except again, keep driving.

7:29 p.m. "Kailee I'm making sure you are okay."

"Yeah, I'm good. I'm sad but I'm okay."

"Dad's calling me. I'll call you right back."

I had sent a text to Scott not knowing actually when he would arrive in Salt Lake City or how long his layover would be. "Call ASAP!" Kailee and I were coming into the airport area. I had a thought; maybe we could reach Scott and pick him up in time. Then we could drive the rest of the way together. Maria had pretty much talked me into picking her up, even though I didn't want to get off the highway because that would mean another forty minutes off the road to drive up to her house in Syracuse and that meant that much more time before I could get to Mariah. Gord and Maria both kept asking me to pick Maria up so I wouldn't be driving alone. So, I had decided to do that and leave Kailee's car at Gord's house too, especially now that we knew how serious this had become. That way we would be able to drive together since we knew that Dalen wasn't going to make it. We would be in Idaho for at least a few days and would have to take care of whatever was needed of us. So, it was decided. Now I just needed to get a hold of Scott and hope that we wouldn't miss each other.

7:31 p.m. "Get off the plane. I'm right here, and we can pick you up. Get off the plane Scott!"

"Wow, okay. I just saw your text. I wasn't even going to turn on my phone, but I did. I will get off."

"We are literally one exit away. I need to get a hold of Kailee to get her to turn off and go to the airport. Bye."

7:32 p.m. I was flashing my lights; I was honking my horn; and I was trying to call Kailee on the phone. 'Answer Kailee. Answer—hurry and answer.' I literally had three hundred feet before she would miss the exit to the airport.

"Get off Kailee, Get off this exit NOW! Go to the airport. We are going to pick up Dad. Get off!" as I saw her signaling to turn off the highway, she was about forty feet from missing it. Holy cow!! That couldn't have been any closer. I literally had seconds to get Kailee to turn off. Seconds and we made it. It was so perfect. That actually gave us a big boost. We were excited that we made it, Scott was getting off the plane, and we made the connections. I had no idea that his plane was landing just as we were coming to the airport exit. I had no idea that all of this was so close to missing and yet so close that we made it. As we drove into the airport, I wasn't even sure where I would find Scott, and there he was, walking directly toward us. It wasn't even three minutes for him to get off the plane and walk outside. He was exactly there. How the heck did he get off the plane and not have any obstacles to go through but get off the plane? He was right there. Right there in front of us. It was so amazing. He waved for us, and we pulled right in to pick him up just as I was calling him and asking him where he was and telling him where we were. Kailee's car was first and then mine. He got into my car. We didn't even hardly stop. I didn't get out of the car or anything. We just drove in, picked him up, gave each other a kiss, and drove around to get back onto the highway. We had made it. It was so astounding that within seconds, a thought to get Scott came to my mind, and I acted upon that thought. For Scott to have turned on his phone and seen my text when he had no thought to turn it on, but he did and we made it, and it was perfect.[13]

7:36 p.m. "Dalen isn't going to make it Scott. Kevin just called me a few minutes ago. He's not going to make it."

"What, what do you mean? Everything was good when I last heard from Kevin." It took about one second for Scott to react. He started to cry and he was crying hard. He thought that our son was on the mend. That was the last he heard; that Dalen was in trouble but was doing better. It was devastating news for Scott. He couldn't handle it. I was so grateful I was driving. I was grateful he could have this time to process. I held his hand and said nothing. I just let him cry.

7:37 p.m. "Kailee we are going to drop your car off at Gord's. Maria wants us to pick her up. She doesn't think we should drive knowing that Dalen won't make it. I think I'm good; but if we leave your car there, we can be together."

"Okay Mom. I don't want to stop though."

"Me neither, Kailee. I just got tired of Gord telling me that I shouldn't be driving. So let's stop. Maria said she will be ready, so we won't have to stop for very long. One last bathroom break, I guess. You will have to change your weekend plans too Kailee."

"Dad is having a hard time. I think it would be good if we were together, okay?"

"Okay. I'll head up to Maria's house. I already told Chris I couldn't make it."

"We still have a bit to go so if you need to stop or if you need anything, let me know. I'll call you in a few minutes."

Gord's house was about another forty-five minutes from the airport. I gave the phone to Scott to talk to Kailee for just a minute.

---

[13] The airport thought; exit; and pickup could not have been executed any closer to the exact time frame without intervention. It was so miraculous. Nothing short of a major miracle for sure.

He needed to know that his other children were okay. He heard her voice and her confidence, and it seemed to help him. He was still crying though. He expressed his love to Kailee and she to him. I then explained the situation to him once he hung up with Kailee. I told him where Alyssa was and how long Gord had been up there with Mariah. I explained that there were accidents on the I-15 and that Kailee took the back way which brought us by the airport and that we didn't know when he was landing but that I took a guess. I let him try to see some of the messages we were getting, but he really couldn't stop crying. He felt so helpless. He didn't know what to feel.

"I wasn't prepared for this. How am I supposed to feel?" Scott asked.

"I don't know honey. No, this isn't what a parent is supposed to prepare for."

"I don't know what to do."

"We will keep going. We will keep driving and we will take care of what we need to when we need to."

"My son isn't supposed to die. I'm not prepared for this. I don't know how to feel!" Scott was struggling and just didn't know how he should react.

I held his hand tight. I kept driving, and he kept crying. He then called Alyssa and heard her voice. She was crying too. They expressed their love for each other. He told her to drive safely and hurry. He then tried to catch up with all the phone messages he had received since his phone had been on airplane mode while he was flying. Then he saw everything. He saw the support that had come in from messages, texts and Facebook. He saw calls from Kevin and those who knew Mariah or Dalen. He saw the support that had come in from messages about Dalen's condition. He heard the calls from so many that wanted to help. All the messages were put onto the phone's speaker, so I heard most of them too. Scott wasn't able to read them because he was crying so hard. He started calling some of the people back and explained now that Dalen wasn't going to make it. He called his dad. He and his wife Trish were hysterical on the other end. Of course Trish was on the second line of the phone while Scott was trying to talk to his dad. The two of them were always on the phone together. They told us they loved us and that they would keep praying for us. Scott mostly was on speaker phone for his calls. He felt it was easier for him to explain what happened to Dalen and that way I could also help with information when he felt overwhelmed.

7:42 p.m. Maria Romano "Sharon, I don't know what to say. I'm so sorry. Is there anything I can do for you?"

"Thanks Maria. I don't think so. Everything is taken care of. Thanks for offering though."

"Sure, no worries."

Looking outside the car window, I was actually seeing signs of winter. There wasn't a lot of snow, but way less than I was expecting, and it laid on the side of the road in patches. Again, I thought about how exciting and blessed we were to have clear roads.[14]

We made it to Gord's house and Maria was waiting. She was adamant that I not drive, but I was fine. We took our last bathroom break and got on the road again. Our stop was only about five minutes, but again, it was about another ten minutes off the road to their house. We headed back to the highway and now we were only about two hours away. Two more hours. We were getting so close. Two more hours. It better not be any longer than that. I was going by what Gord had said, and I trusted him. Google even agreed with us, as of course Kailee checked it out on her phone as soon as we mentioned it. That was almost comforting to know that we were getting so close and that we only had two more hours to go. It was almost 8:00 p.m. now, and it was very dark. We were so blessed though, because there was no snow. The roads were clear and the traffic was light. It had been dark for a while now and we were coming out of the populated area of the Salt Lake Valley. Maria would ask us questions as to how we were doing. I was fine. Scott still didn't know how to react. Kailee was fine, but glad that we were together.

---

[14] The weather had predicted a storm coming in, but for now there was nothing on the roads. The snow had cleared and almost was completely melted. The roads were perfectly cleared until about 20 miles out of Pocatello and then there was snow on the shoulder of the road. Amazing!

7:55 p.m. **Bobby Harris** "You are the best mom I know. I'm so sorry, Sharon." Bobby and Gina were amazing. They kept calling me. They called and called and called, which was a blessing for us to know of their concerns.

Bobby was a sheriff on the department that Scott had always looked up to. Scott said he was always honorable and was just a great street cop. Scott had aspirations to be like him throughout his career. There was a conversation that occurred once between the two men about two years prior to Dalen's accident.

Scott said to Bobby: "You know I'm a Mormon, don't you sir?"

Bobby replied: "Well that explains a lot."

Bobby had had many encounters with members of our church. There were a few members that lived on his street and were very good neighbors and friends. Bobby and Gina had learned about the missionaries and wanted to help take care of them. When he would first meet a missionary, Bobby would ask, "Let me see your shoes." If the shoes looked worn out or well used, Bobby and Gina would immediately take the missionary to the shoe store and purchased new ones; the missionary might not have really needed new shoes; but they always were very grateful. Bobby and Gina were invited by their church friends to every activity their ward would have, and they would participate with them and loved every bit of it. They even attended several church meetings with their friends. They studied the scriptures faithfully, but just never felt the need to convert. Still, some of the biggest hearted people I had ever met. They have been to our house twice as we celebrated Canadian Thanksgiving (October) with us. They sent packages to the missionaries that were serving from their home ward into various parts of the world. They sent packages to my kids too, Dalen on the mission and even Mariah up at school. They came to our ward when Alyssa gave her homecoming mission report and talked about her experiences. That was the first time I'd actually met them, but I felt I already knew them very well. They surprised us a few times by coming to our ward when one of us were giving a talk, for a testimony meeting, or just to say hi. I knew their concerns for us and Dalen were so very real. I was grateful. On the last contact I would have with Bobby, I told them that we would probably be staying in Pocatello because it would be so late, and we didn't know what to expect once we got there. He took that information and looked online for a Bishop serving in the Pocatello area.

"I'm not a member of your church but a good friend of mine is, and he is coming to the hospital because his son was in a traffic accident this afternoon and isn't going to make it. I need you to help him out, maybe have a place for them to stay at so they won't have to worry about anything. I don't want them to worry. Do you think you can take care of that for me?"

Not only did this amazing Bishop get us a room at the hotel right next to the hospital, but they had sandwiches in the fridge and some sodas to drink waiting for us. We were in awe as we witnessed this outpour of love from Bobby to a Bishop that didn't know us, and from this Bishop to our family. It was just so amazing, and we were so thankful for both of them.

Bobby and Gina regularly checked on us as they were concerned about the possibility of us driving in snow, but we constantly reassured them the roads were clear. They were very grateful to know that I now had Scott and Kailee with me, and they were assured that things would now be okay.

8:05 p.m. I called my dad. "Dad don't know if you had heard, but Mariah and Dalen were in an accident this afternoon. Dalen isn't going to make it. We are driving up to Idaho now. Could you let the rest of the family know? I will call them all later and let them know more when I knew more."

"Are you okay?—That's horrible. Guess there really isn't anything I can do," my dad commented.

"Nope—not really. Just call everyone for me please and let them know."

"Of course."

"Love you Dad."

"Love you too." Dad wasn't used to being the one to communicate. Since Mom passed away last July, he had learned to do a bit more. I could have called everyone, but I thought it really was something my dad could do to help me, and I wanted to focus my time on driving.

"Okay, we're getting closer." I just kept saying to myself. We were passing Tremonton, which was just on the north side of the Utah boarder approaching Idaho. There was always tons of snow there and usually some of the worst weather when passing from Utah to Idaho. Today it was clear. We just kept driving. About another hour and a half to go. I could see that Scott was drained. He wanted this to be over. Maria was also concerned about me driving in my mental condition. Again she asked if I would like a rest because she would be happy to drive. I was okay. I was making good time and I was emotionally stable, so why not keep going?

Saying Goodbye

8:12 p.m. At one point, it almost seemed to Mariah that we would never get there, and she was coming to accept that. Such a horrible thought for me; my daughter still without her family and in the hospital watching her brother knowing that he wouldn't make it and starting the sixth hour from the accident.

"I know you're trying to get here Mom, but this is really hard. I just sit by Dalen and hold his hand and cry."

"Mariah, they told us again that he wasn't going to make it. Is that what they told you too? Do you think you would be able to hold the phone to his ear, so he could hear me talk and say goodbye to him?"

"Yeah Mom, they said he was going to die so many times that I'm just frustrated. I don't know if he is going to die or not Mom. He is just lying there, and the machines are moving and there is nothing else. I just don't know what to believe."

"It is hard to believe especially when you have sat and looked at him this whole time. It is true though; he won't make it."

"I do think I know that, but I just don't want to believe it," she said.

"Me neither, Mariah. I really don't want to believe it either. But since it is real, do you think you could let me say goodbye to my son?"

"That would be pretty hard to do!" she exclaimed.

"I know Mariah, but if we aren't going to make it before he passes, I would at least like him to hear my voice and let me express how much I love him."

I couldn't imagine Mariah's thoughts as I was asking my daughter to listen to her family say goodbye to her brother, my son, and to know these would be our last words we would get to express to him. This was just a horrible experience, and yet, I also knew of this procedure as this was the way I said goodbye to my mother just before she passed away. It was going to be hard, but also fair to those of us that were trying so hard to be there for Dalen and Mariah and weren't sure that we could make it in time. We needed this closure for ourselves.

"Okay Mom. I just won't know when you are finished because I won't be able to hear what you're saying, so I'll just ask after a few minutes." Mariah wanted us to have our moment with Dalen alone.

I took the phone off Bluetooth as I felt this needed to be a private moment for each of us saying goodbye to Dalen.

"I'm ready Mom," Mariah instructed us.

Mariah was putting the phone up to Dalen's ear. I didn't know if my son had any consciousness or not; and I didn't know if he was already gone or not; but I thought this would be my last time to talk to my son.

"Hey Bud, Mom here. I just want you to know how much I love you. I wish I could be there to say goodbye. I understand if you need to go. Oh how I love you Buddy Boy." I felt my voice start to quiver just a bit as I felt tears rolling down my cheek. "I love you so very much. Love you Bud." A few more tears began to flow. "Bye Buddy Boy, goodbye."

What can you say at a moment like that? Did I comfort my son at all, or was it mostly for me to know that I attempted to say goodbye to my son? Did I need to say more or ask questions or talk about dreams I knew he had? I didn't really know what to say. I just said what came to my mind. He needed to know again, how much I loved him. He was my Buddy Boy; my only son; my example of how to use the priesthood and be grateful for it; how to include God in everything and repent quickly so we could stay close to Heavenly Father. My boy. My boy! I wasn't really crying, but there was a weird release within my thoughts—*'I'm doing it again, saying goodbye to a loved one over the phone.'*

When my mom was passing, I was so mad at my dad. For a few days, I asked if I needed to come home. My family lived in Alberta,

Canada, which is a long way away from California. Getting there wasn't an easy process as it was about a twenty-six-hour drive. It meant getting a flight, figuring out time periods of calculating the distance from the airport, figuring out if I should rent a car or have someone pick me up. For three days, I kept asking Dad if he thought I should come home. He kept saying a definite 'no' and said that she was fine. If I came home, that would give a message to my mom that she was really sick. But she was, so I was very frustrated with the situation. I was running out of options when on July 5th, 2017, it came to: "She's unconscious. You could talk to her, but I don't know if she will hear you." Sheila was the one to keep me informed about Mom. Sheila was the one that thought about how I might be feeling not being able to be there. I had asked her if she thought it would be possible for her to hold the phone up to Mom so I could say goodbye. We made an arrangement the night before. She would go to the hospital the next morning about 9:00a.m., her time (an hour later than my time), and I would say my goodbye to Mom. Sheila called me at 7:35 a.m. and said Mom wasn't going to make it and that she was on her way into Raymond, which was about ten minutes away. Raymond was a little community hospital. I thought Mom deserved better care and should have been taken into Lethbridge. Lethbridge was the city where the main hospital was for all the surrounding areas. Either way, I believed my mom would hear me while I was on the phone. I knew her spirit would accept my thoughts and I hoped she could feel of my love for her. Things were occurring quickly with my mom. Sheila said they got an emergency call into the hospital that morning very early, because Mom wasn't going to make it. I only had minutes before she passed. Sheila called me and said I needed to hurry and say goodbye. Then she held the phone up to Mom's ear so I could talk to her. I told Mom how much I loved her and needed her; and appreciated all that she had done for me throughout my life. I told her that I was grateful that she was my mom. I said I was sorry I couldn't be there, but that I just needed her to know how much I love her. She was an angel that I hoped to be like.

"I love you Mom. I love you so much." That was it. That was all I got. And Mom was gone.

Now the same thing was happening with Dalen, and again, I couldn't be there. This was all I could do for my son. I could express my love and really nothing else. I couldn't do anything else. I just wanted to see my boy. Now I wanted the same opportunity with my son and Mariah had given me this gift. I was so incredibly grateful for her during this process. There was a moment of silence.

"Are you done Mom?"

"Yes, I am. Thank you so much." It was strange because, as I expressed my love and wiped away some tears that were rolling down my cheek, my voice never sounded uncontrollable. This seemed so surreal and yet, I had just said goodbye to my son that I would never see again in this life. I was saying goodbye to his body. I was saying goodbye to his spirit. I wouldn't ever get to talk to him again. I wasn't able to kiss him goodbye. I wouldn't be able to hug him, look at him, smile at him, and hear his voice. All this was gone. I would never again be able to express my feelings to my son. I could only hope that what I had expressed was enough. Did I choose the right words? Did he know how much I really loved him? Was he able to hear me? Did my son have any consciousness at all, to know I was there? Was my son ever there or had he already moved on? He was still on life support. To me, that meant he was still there. How could someone die if they were on life support? Although we don't know when the spirit actually leaves a body; we believe that it comes after the last breath of life is taken or upon the second of death. That is what I believed. Wouldn't they have to wait to die until the life support had been stopped? We had just been told over the last few hours that it was bad and that our son wasn't going to make it; that we needed to be there twenty minutes ago. With that information, I guess someone could pass away while on life support. Their body might just give up.

Dalen had been fighting now for over six hours. He was still alive if only through the tubes and medication that he was on to keep him alive. And until we got there, as long as he wasn't in pain, I persisted with the knowledge that he was still there. I believed that he was still there. I had to believe that my boy was still there. And I kept driving believing that he was still there. Oh, how my heart pleaded with my God that he was going to be alive when we arrived.

I was still calm and at peace, but I hit the realization that I couldn't change what was happening. If it were to happen, that Dalen would pass, I felt so comforted and truly at peace and had the thought that when my son passed, that it would be very quick. Still, I so wanted to be there. I so wanted to see him one more time before he passed away. I thought of our Bishop's family where the mom didn't make it to the hospital before her son passed. The Bishop was there with their son at a scout camp, but the drive for the mom was too far away. At that moment, I knew how she felt. I just wanted to see my son. I just needed to see my son. I still prayed that Dalen would wait for us. I was still praying that we would make it in time. I really believed that we would make it on time. Again, I was consumed with the peace that all would be in God's hands, and we would be comforted through it all. Just keep driving.

8:15 p.m. "I think Dad and Kailee need to say their goodbyes too." I said to Mariah.

"Okay, let me know when they are ready." You could hear the hesitation in Mariah's voice. She would have to do this again. She was doing the best she could.

"Here is Kailee." I handed her my phone so she could say goodbye to Dalen and have a private moment with him.

"Hi Dalen. I just want you to know that I love you. I'm grateful that you're my brother. I'm grateful that you always showed me you loved me. I wish I could be there to say goodbye to you, but I guess this is how we have to do it. I love you Dalen. Okay—bye." Kailee had said what she felt she needed to and that was it. She usually wouldn't give more detail than was needed; just what was needed, and Kailee was done.

Scott kept fighting to gain his composure and just couldn't seem to get it together. I had never seen him so emotional. I don't know why, but I tried to analyze his reactions. Was he just so devastated because of his relationship with Dalen? Was he so upset because parents aren't supposed to plan on the passing of their children? Was he in shock? Dalen and Scott weren't as close as they might have been. They did love each other, but Dalen just had made several choices that were so disappointing to Scott and in so many various areas of his life. He wouldn't get a job. He didn't show much ambition with school. In fact, Dalen didn't like school. There were always financial issues with Dalen. He needed money for this or that. I would make sure he could at least live, at least get food and Scott would scold me for giving him money. He wanted Dalen to struggle a bit more, so he would understand better the need to get a job, which I also agreed with. *Every* phone conversation between Scott and Dalen was about getting a job. Everyone. Dalen knew he disappointed his dad, and it bothered him but then he also came to the conclusion and would say: "I know—I just keep disappointing dad. It's what I do. He will never be satisfied with who I am, but I love him, and I know he loves me." Dalen had struggled for years on how to please his dad, but then he didn't really ever put forth the effort needed to make any changes. And to Dalen, it would all be okay.

Even with this constant difference between Scott and Dalen; Dalen still was happy with who he was. He knew his dad wasn't happy with his choices, but he liked who he was and he really was happy most of the time. So, I thought that Scott might have been feeling some remorse for how he did talk with Dalen and that that might be the reason for his display of emotions. I then thought that maybe part of it also, was just that there wasn't any training on how we are supposed to act when as a parent, we are told a child isn't going to live. How are we supposed to feel? How should we act? Is there a protocol? Should we know to act a certain way? Scott loved Dalen, and I heard him express that almost every time they talked on the phone. They had their differences for sure, but they loved each other. There were sincere hugs after every family prayer we would have. Dalen loved his dad too, and they did share that expression with each other. Scott really was at a loss and just didn't know how to feel or act. I believe it was a pretty normal reaction for what he was going through. If there could be a normal in this situation was this it? But however hard this was, I knew that we would be okay. We really were, and however hard this was, we would be okay.

"Scott, do you think you can do this?"

"I don't know. No one prepares you for this. What do I say? How do I tell my son goodbye?" Again, his tears came.

"You say what you feel. You tell your son you love him, and you express your gratitude that he is your son. Say what's in your heart."

"Okay."

"Mariah, Dad is ready."

"Okay, I'll put the phone to Dalen's ear again. Go ahead Dad."

There was a brief hesitation.

"Hey Bud. It's Dad here," he spoke through a broken voice. "I love you Buddy. I love you so much."

That was all the wording he could get out as he pushed the phone back into my hand and just sobbed. How could I console my husband? I had to drive. I was trying to hug him in some way. I rubbed his back with my right hand and just looked into his face. I wanted to help, but I also realized that he needed this time to let out his feelings. How could all this be happening? Poor Mariah. She had to be the one listening to us all express our love to Dalen and say goodbye. This couldn't have been easy on her at all. In fact, later Mariah expressed that having the family say goodbye, was the hardest part of Dalen's passing for her. Listening to all of us say goodbye just made everything so real, and again, Mariah felt it was because of her. What an awful trial for her. My heart was just broken knowing that she was there, waiting for us, saying goodbye to Dalen who was going to pass, and not knowing what she should do.

"Mariah, I think we are all done. You need to call Alyssa and let her say goodbye too. Please can you give her that opportunity?"

"Yeah Mom, I will. This is REALLY hard Mom. This is really, really hard though."

"I can't imagine, and I'm so sorry. This had to be one of the hardest things to do. I'm so sorry Mariah. I wish I could take all of this away from you. I just don't know how to. So sorry Mariah. Just know that we are getting close and will be there as soon as possible. Will you call me back, though, when Alyssa's done?"

"Okay Mom. I will."

Again, what we were asking Mariah to do was hard; she had so much strength. She was amazing through all of this. To sit on the end of a phone and hear your family express their final goodbyes had to be so hard, almost impossible to do. Her sitting there in the hospital for hours, alone with her brother, waiting for us to get there, again just almost impossible to think of what she had to endure. For her to be alone with all her thoughts and worries was almost more than I could comprehend. My daughter was so calm though, strong, and able to control all of her emotions. She kept telling me that she really was okay. She just really wanted us to be there. Everyone was so concerned for her, but she just kept telling them that she was okay. She wanted us to believe her; she really was okay. I even heard that in her voice. Every time I spoke with her on the phone, I asked her how she was. She didn't hesitate in saying that she was doing okay. She felt comfort and was seeing blessings start to come to her. She had come to her own understanding of Dalen and what was happening. She knew she was alive for a reason. That was the hardest part for her, why wasn't she hurt? Why did she walk away and why was Dalen struggling to live? Even with those questions, Mariah was calm and okay. She was okay and we would take that because it could have been so much worse.

Scott too, was okay for a few minutes and then his phone would ring, and he would tell Dalen's story again—that he wasn't going to make it and that we were still driving but getting closer to the hospital. Everyone wanted to know what they could do for us and there really wasn't anything. We couldn't do anything. We just wanted to get there and to then see what we would have to face. Your mind imagines so many things. *'How does my son look? How does Mariah look? What will happen when we walk into the hospital? What would be the first things we would have to do? What is the process for a donor? Will Gord still be with Mariah? It looks so cold outside, is Mariah cold? Is Dalen cold? Will we really get there soon?'*

"Please Heavenly Father; just let us get there quickly and safely. Please let my son make it till we arrive." My prayer never altered.

Two Hours to Go

8:25 p.m. **Alyssa texted the family**—"I'm grateful that we know families can be together forever."

Mariah—"Me too."

Kailee—"Dalen gets to keep Grandma Hudson company now. It's a blessing and a relief to me knowing what we know of eternal families."

Alyssa—"And he gets to hang with Sam (our Bishop's son). I know he's happy and in a much better place."

Mariah—"He's not dead yet!!!!!!!"

Alyssa—"I know, Mariah. I'm just trying to think of things that will make me feel better about this whole thing."

9:04 p.m. "We are just coming into the valley and looking at the temple Mom. It is so beautiful," Alyssa stated as she was passing the Bountiful Temple. Temples at nighttime are a beacon. They are lit up purposely to have the strength of the lights seen for miles around. They are an amazing site. Alyssa was updating us and we were grateful, but also anxious as we were getting closer ourselves.

"So, we are making good time, but still out a ways," Alyssa responded. They were just coming into Ogden which was just past the Salt Lake City County line. Alyssa still had about two hours to go to get to Pocatello.

9:11 p.m. Rory called to see if we knew anything else. I guess Dad had relayed the message to him that Dalen wasn't going to make it. It was quite late in Ontario, Canada. They were two hours ahead of Utah time, so it was after 11:00 p.m. there. Rory is the third oldest in my family—the youngest brother. There are six kids in my family:

three boys and then three girls. Sheila and I are the youngest, but I am the last of the last. There are only seven years between us all. I often wondered how my mother did it, how she handled six kids in such a short time span.

Rory had chosen a different path from our family. He wasn't active in The Church of Jesus Christ of Latter-Day Saints and hadn't been since he was about fourteen years old. He was asked by a leader of our church one day, to cut his hair before he played church ball and my brother refused. That was his turning point. He chose to leave the church standards, which were always a huge heartache for the rest of us, but especially for my mom. He got to where he didn't even believe in God. So, without God, this ordeal could only be traumatic and devastating, an end to it all with no hope. I personally couldn't imagine life without God, especially in this experience. To go through life without the knowledge of the next life, the plan of salvation, and faith in answers to prayers would be a horrible end to why we exist. We all still prayed for Rory that his heart would soften one day, so he would once again, have a desire to live the gospel of Jesus Christ with the rest of his family and be united with us. We were all taught the same teachings growing up, but Rory just felt he would be better with another way. Rory was the kindest soul though. He had a huge heart. When our family was together, Rory was the jokester. He always made everyone laugh.

"I don't know what to say sis. I'm so sorry for your heartache! I just don't know what to say or how you are handling this."

At this point in Rory's life, he was going through treatment for stomach cancer. He was trying to get the strength to go through radiation and I knew that he wouldn't be able to come no matter what, but that he would want to be there. I understood that. His taking care of himself was way more important for him than to be sick while trying to travel to California to say goodbye to my son. Dalen would know his intentions for sure.

"It's okay Rory. We don't quite know what to expect when we get there other than he won't make it. Gord had called me, because I had asked him to go up and be with Mariah because geographically, he was the closest family member. He basically just told us that we needed to hurry and that the nurses were saying that Dalen was going to pass any moment. So we are hurrying."

"Wow, how are you doing this?" asked Rory.

"Well Rory, all I'm doing is driving. There really isn't anything else I can do. I'm driving and we are praying."

"I'm so beside myself." I could hear him crying. His raw feelings and his loss for words were very apparent. "Love you sis. Just know that I love you and this is just so dreadful. I just can't imagine what you are going through. I just can't imagine it."

"Thanks Rory. I love you too. Thanks for the call, I really appreciate it. Rory, we know that God is guiding us and we are at peace. It is real—this peace thing, it is real."

There was a moon out, but it was behind the passing clouds. When it came out, I was beginning to see a glisten on the ground beside the roadside. There was more snow on the road. It was quiet and calm. There was nothing that had altered our driving view. There was a road sign: 'Pocatello-64 miles away'. I felt my heart jump a beat.

We were getting so close. I just couldn't wait till we got there.

"Come on road. Let me get there." Someone finally asked if anyone was hungry. I said that I was okay and that I wasn't going to stop, so if they were hungry, they would have to wait. My mission was in sight, and nothing was going to stop me. They agreed with me.

9:13 p.m. President Taylor called—Dalen's mission president had finished his mission a few months ago and was residing in Salt Lake City area as a church leader.

"Sister Graham, President Taylor here."

"Hello President. I'm sure you have heard about Dalen."

"Yes I have. That is why I'm calling. What can I do for you? We are praying for your family."

"Dalen isn't going to make it President. We are almost to the hospital and will know more then. I promise that I will let you know what happens."

"Oh, that is just horrible. We love our Elder Graham so much. I'm so sorry. We love your son."

"I know you do. I want to thank you for all that you did for Dalen. He loved you so much. He was so grateful for your guidance, and he knew you loved him. Thank you for everything."

"Thank you Sister Graham. I know you will have the strength to handle this, but we will continue to pray for your family."

"Thank you President, and goodbye."

9:25 p.m. **Alyssa**-"We are just about one hundred miles out and we should be there around 11:00p.m."

The sign on the side of the road stated that Pocatello was forty-eight miles away. Was it possible that we were finally seeing our destination? I was almost getting excited. "Okay guys, here we go. We are getting so close."

The road was straight and clear, and we couldn't have asked for it to be better. The atmosphere wasn't morbid or depressing in the car. We were all very sad and tears were evident, but it didn't feel empty. It didn't feel like we were lost. It didn't feel like there was no hope. We were relieved for sure, that we were getting there.

When you drive into Pocatello, there is a valley beforehand where the road turns sharply and the houses on the sides of the road are filled with many fields and trees. The valley blocks the view of the city itself but when you start driving through, you know you are close. Another sign—'Pocatello, thirty-two miles' to go. My heart began to race. It wasn't an excitement like finishing a race, but it was an anxious feeling of "it's been so long". We are almost there; Mariah would have some relief. We would finally get to see Dalen; the unknown would be known. I think I drove just a bit faster. I had been going eighty-five the entire way. In Utah, eighty was the normal speed, so I had to go five over the speed limit because I just had to get there. I was in Idaho and the speed level dropped down to seventy-five, but I just ignored it. I now had pulled up the speedometer to ninety. Scott even mentioned; "Aren't you going a bit fast?"

"Maybe, but we are almost there and I just want to get there."

"Well let's get there in one piece," he said.

"I got it." And I slowed back down to eighty-five.

As we were driving, there was more snow appearing on the side of the road. The valley was cooler in temperature and the snow was slowly getting thicker. There was even a bit of evidence on the road. I didn't see any ice and it still just seemed clear, but it did make me a bit more attentive to the road.

9:29 p.m. Sheila "I'm so worried about you. What's going on? How are you holding up? We are just so sorry."

"You know that Dalen won't make it, right? Well, we are about twenty miles away and just want to get there. I don't know what to expect. I don't know what I need to do. I am kind of anxious to stop driving and to see Mariah. I just want to see my son."

"Just so sorry, Sharon. I just don't know what I can do." On the phone, you can tell when someone was crying, and my twin was beside herself knowing that she couldn't do anything to help me. She was devastated at the loss of my son. She was tormented by what I would have to face. I assured her that we were doing well. We just wanted to be there and we almost were. Now we really only had a little ways to go.

"I will call you when I can. Thanks."

The communication picked up a bit in the car. It was like we were all waking up after a nap and had some built up energy that we needed to release. Some of the conversations were on the memories of Dalen and how he made us all laugh. I knew that I would never hear his laugh again. We talked about all the support we had received. The whole trip, we kept reading the positive messages and listening to the heartfelt concerns of our family and friends. All our phones kept ringing with the support and we felt so overwhelmed and blessed.

We kept changing the radio station as Scott always liked country, 80's and rock and roll. Kailee was pretty much the same. I had to have the radio on. I had never liked silence and music had always soothed me. I like to sing to songs too, if I knew them. I like the Today's Hits, and the Easy Listening stations. It has always been an issue when we drove somewhere to where we had said the driver got to choose the station, so there wouldn't be fighting. A lot of the time, the kids would get in the car and automatically change the station which really bothered me. Hence, the driver got to pick. On this trip, that meant I got to make all the decisions. Since I had driven almost seven hours by myself, I thought it was okay to change the station for the others. So, knowing how Scott was feeling, I put on the country station for him. Maria was also just great. She was so supportive and added to our conversation by talking about Dalen in such a positive way. She related many of her memories of Dalen growing up. Her family was one of the only family members that really knew our kids growing up. They were the only ones that lived in California between both our families. Gord and Maria lived in Escondido, California, which was about two and a half hours away from us. We tried to go there a few times a year so our kids could be with their cousins, and I could be with my brother. Family was always a very big deal to me. Gord was, in many ways, my mentor. I pleaded for his opinion many times in my life. And Maria, was just the favorite aunt. She always included our kids in everything she did. She always had special activities for them when we went to their house. Maria was a great cook and extremely talented. She really could figure out almost anything to make and just had a knack for it. I always loved being around her. Gord didn't always communicate when we were at his house, mostly because he was just a very quiet guy. So, when we were there, Maria entertained us. To have them with us at the hospital really meant a lot to me.

9:52 p.m.   Pocatello, ten miles.

'Be still my heart', not really but it was an expression we all knew. It was so weird. When we experience the element of surprise, our body reacts with more blood flowing through it and at a faster pace, usually a smile of anticipation, and the excitement of the unknown, like Christmas morning. This wasn't quite like that. Yet there was definitely anxiousness. Scott and I were holding hands again tightly. I looked at him.

"Are you ready for this?"

"Ready or not, it's what we have to do," Scott stated.

"Then are you ready to do this? I'm right beside you. We can do this. We will handle it the way we are supposed to. I just really feel at peace and just want to see my son. I love you hun."

"Love you too. I'm nervous," Scott replied.

"I think I am a bit too."

We turned the corner and saw the lights of Pocatello. We called Alyssa to tell her we were arriving. She was coming up quickly behind us and wanted to be with the family. I had driven by this town every time we drove up to Canada. We always stopped and ate or filled up with gas. There was a State University in Pocatello, and the population of the church members was very strong. It had always been a nice place for a stop. I knew where the hospital was because of all the trips up to Canada. It was located right off the highway. It looked very new and was quite big, so I think I knew exactly how to get there. The hospital was off to the right of the highway. The exit goes up and then the signs lead you into the parking lot of the hospital.

Here it is. Take the exit. This is it, were some of my thoughts. I looked at Scott and he kind of just had a blank stare on his face. Kailee was ready to get out of the car. We had been driving for a long time and now we finally reached one of our destination. Maria said that if we wanted to just drive up to the door, she would park the car for us so we could get inside quicker. That was very nice of her.

Kevin had called a few times too, and told us what to expect and where to go once we entered the hospital. He told us that Dalen had been moved into the ICU area and was on the tenth floor and that we needed to go to the south end of the hospital. The entrance closest to the ICU unit was to the back of the hospital and the south end of the parking lot. He said that he would meet us outside of the elevators that when we just walked in, they would be down the hall to the first left. I drove into the parking lot and found the way to the south entrance where Kevin had guided us. It was pretty big. Ten feet—keep breathing. It's time. I parked the car and got out. Put my coat on of course, because it was freezing now that the sun had set and it was almost 10:00 p.m. All three of us began walking. Maria took our vehicle to park it. The automatic doors to the hospital opened to greet us. We were engulfed by the heat blast needed to keep the hospital on a controlled temperature.

"Here we go."

The Reality of the Hospital Visit

10:02 p.m. "Hi Kevin." He actually met us outside in the courtyard of the hospital.

"Hi there. How are you guys?" We exchanged hugs with each other.

"Well, we are here." Scott replied. We started walking into the building.

"We can't thank you enough for all that you have done for us and to be here with Mariah is just huge."

We had now arrived at the elevator. Kevin was explaining that the ICU unit was on the tenth floor and that there were a few people up there who arrived to support Mariah. He talked about how our son shouldn't be alive and that he wasn't in very good condition at all. He mentioned that he felt so bad for us and was here to help us however he could. He also expressed how sorry he was for this and that he just...was sorry. We were told to be ready to see tubes all around and a very messed up face.

"Your information had helped us so much. Thanks again Kevin, just thanks." And I heard the bell ring for the elevator to open.

10:05 p.m. We got out and I just wanted to run, but I didn't know where I would run to, so I followed Kevin across a waiting area. I saw some kids hanging out. I wondered who they were and what condition had brought them to the hospital. Then within probably two seconds of getting out of the elevator, I saw Mariah. She ran up to me and I ran up to her and we just hugged and cried hard while hugging as tight as we could hold each other.

"Mom, I killed my brother. I killed Dalen Mom." The hysterical crying that pierces you to hear when a child can't be consoled penetrated from Mariah.

Those weren't the words I was expecting to hear. They stabbed my heart and pierced my soul, but we also needed to reassure Mariah that at no point did we believe she killed Dalen.

"This was an accident. That meant that no one was at fault." She was crying so hard; I could barely hold her up. "No-one was at fault. This isn't your fault Mariah. We love you so much."

Scott and Kevin were just standing there waiting for us to have our moment. Scott hugged Mariah next and said how much he loved her. It was like time was frozen just for that second.

I had a chance to look around at those in the lobby again, and I saw two black kids and two other girls. I thought; '*Oh, are they waiting for a family member too? I hope their story is better than ours.*' Then I saw Aubree, Mariah's friend, and I hugged her and thanked her for coming.

"Of course I would be here. I love Mariah and you guys," was Aubree's comment as we just held each other for a minute. Then I saw my brother who had just walked out from a big door. I went up to hug him. I asked how our son was doing. He held my hands and looked down.

"He's not good at all. I need to prepare you for what you are about to see. There are tubes all over him. His face is really swollen and bloody. You can't even see his eyes because they are so swollen. It's just a matter of time. It's not good. He looks really bad," Gord told us.

We knew it wasn't good. It was hard to hear of his description, but then I think I expected something like that. I was ready to go in. We all started walking towards the big door. Mariah knew the code to get into the ICU area and the door swung into us to open. Within two steps, there was a woman approaching me and she immediately extended her arms out to give me a hug. I realized then that this was Rick's mom. She had come to support Mariah who had spent so much time at their house. Then I remembered that Rick said his family had adopted two black boys from Africa, and the girls were his sisters that were sitting in the lobby. They were there for us. I think her husband was there, but I didn't remember seeing him.

"I'm so sorry for this. I have been looking forward to meeting you, but not this way. I'm so sorry. We just love your family." Sister Hamilton (Rick's mom) was so sad.

"Thank you so very much for everything. You have been amazing to our daughter. I really am so grateful for you and that you're here. We are so blessed. Thank you."

But now it really was time to see my son. I didn't want to talk to anyone else but see my son that was only a few feet away from me. I turned to the right and saw a bed with a person lying on it but couldn't see who it was because the nurse was blocking my view. Then we walked in. There was a very big breath taken. I walked over to the bed and grabbed my son's hand.

"This doesn't look like my son. He's not here," was my first reaction. I knew his body was there, but I just didn't know if his spirit was still there. The reality was that I did know that he was there; he just didn't look like my son. There were tubes everywhere. The nurse said hello to me.

"Thank you so much for all you have done for my son. Thank you," I commented.

I felt a few tears again roll down my cheek. Then I turned to the right; there were people standing in the back of the room. So now I couldn't give my attention to my son again because I needed to be cordial to these people. We shook hands with one man.

"I'm Bishop Nelson. I was Dalen's Bishop at BYUI and this is my brother Frank."

"Oh my, I can't believe you're here. Thank you so very much for being here and for helping my son." I knew that this man had spent time with Dalen. There were some issues that Dalen needed to work out, and he told me how great his Bishop was and how much he liked him. At a church sponsored school, there are assigned Bishops as leaders to living accommodations. Dalen was questioning why he was at school and what his path should be. He needed some council as well from some of his actions that Dalen felt he needed to clear up. So, for this short space of time, this man and my son had developed a very good relationship. It was really amazing that he was there to support Dalen and us. We shook both their hands. Then there was another man. He too, was a Bishop, but the Bishop that Bobby had contacted on the phone while we were driving up. He was the one that would take care of our family while we were in Pocatello. He just said he felt he needed to be there for us. He mentioned his name, but I really didn't remember. It really was surprising that these people were here because of Dalen.[15]

The other Bishop shook our hands and then mentioned that there would be a room for our family at the hotel which was just down at the end of the parking lot from the hospital. There were two queen size beds too in the room and that they would be waiting for us. Who does that? We didn't know these men. They were here serving our family and we were just in awe.

Scott reflected on a text message he received stating that a Bishop DeJones would like to pick up a room at Townsplace Suites by the Marriott just by the hospital for us to stay at for when we needed it. He was told that he could check in anytime and the room was taken care of.

"Thank you so much Bishop DeJones," Scott expressed his gratitude. "Oh my gosh. That is so amazing. How can we thank you for arranging that?"

"Wow, thank you so much. What do I owe you?" Scott asked as he started to reach into his pocket to see how much cash he had or how we would pay him.

"Nothing, you don't owe anything. It's all taken care of. Your friend Bobby was pretty adamant that we take care of you and our desire was to do so. We were happy to help in any way we could. It really wasn't an issue for us." Seriously we just couldn't grasp this. We just walked into the hospital, and now we were being given a hotel room to stay in when whatever we had to do at the hospital was over.

I excused myself for a minute and walked out into the hall and expressed to the nurse my feelings that we didn't really know

---

[15] Dalen's bishop helped Dalen find perspective and guidance in just a few weeks and he would drive to Pocatello to be with my son. I thought that was a great honor for Dalen. This was an amazing man. Then Bishop DeJones that was called by our non-member friend and he was more than taking care of our family. These were men of God, and we were overwhelmed by their love for our situation.

who those men were as kind as they were. I was actually surprised that anyone could come into the ICU and walk into any room. Obviously, the Hamiltons were just in the room before we walked in too. The casualness of the situation kind of rubbed me the wrong way. I wasn't ungrateful in anyways for their kindness; I merely suggested that maybe this could be our family time, and if they wouldn't mind in asking the men to leave, so we could be alone with our son whom we hadn't even really been able to acknowledge yet. The nurse agreed and took care of asking these good men of my wishes. There was an awkward moment when I returned to the room, but I think the men sensed that we wanted to be with our son and that they probably should go. We were so thankful for them and their acts of kindness though, but I needed to mourn and be with my son. They were gracious and said goodnight. They shook our hands again as they were walking out and mentioned that they were again sorry for what we had to endure. We were then able to finally be together as a family and really see our son.

I immediately gathered everyone around, and we held hands as we looked down upon Dalen. We were standing about a foot away from his bed. Mariah was calm, I guessed because she had been there all afternoon and had already gone through all the possible emotions by herself. Kailee was crying a bit as was Scott. Kailee, when in a new situation, didn't always know how to act. This was very good to see that she could figure out the proper feelings to share and to have. She was pretty sad. Scott again was pretty hysterical. He just couldn't get over the way Dalen looked. I needed to find all the strength I could for everyone, and so I stated that we needed to have a family prayer. There were no offers. I thought that Scott should have led the family, but he just couldn't do it, so then I offered it.

We gathered together and held hands. "Heavenly Father, we humbly gather together around our son and brother Dalen." I then began to cry—my first real release of emotion. "We know that we are dedicating Dalen's spirit unto thee. We are so thankful for his life. We are grateful for his worthiness. We are grateful for the lives he touched. We will miss him," a long pause, "so very much. Please protect him. Please allow us to heal and be at peace with his passing.

We pray that this process will be painless, and that Dalen will be taken unto thee quickly. We thank thee for the Plan of Salvation and that we will see and be with our son again. We thank thee for the gift of the atonement from thy son which has allowed all of us to repent and be worthy of thy blessings. Again, we thank thee for the life of Dale:" (again, another pause to gain my composure) "and give him unto thee at this time, in the name of thy son, Jesus Christ, amen."

We stayed there for just a few minutes without anyone moving. Then we all found our place around the bed and began to look into the face of Dalen. He was so bloody. There were tubes going into his body and nose, and out of his head where the tube was put in to drain the bleeding on his brain. You could hear the pump for his lungs going up and down; keeping his lungs inflated, which also kept his heart beating. There was blood dripping from his nose and running down his face. He had on a neck brace and tubes down his throat. There was a cut on his forehead which also continued to drip blood. His lips were so swollen. His eyes were closed, but they were so puffy and bruised. Blood covered his hair. We couldn't see much of his body as he was under a special blanket to keep his temperature at a certain level. I wanted to kiss him or touch him or hold him, but how with all the tubes running into him. I leaned over and tried to kiss his cheek. It was bloody, but he was my boy and I wanted him to know how much I loved him.

"Can I get anything for you guys? My name is Stacey, and I will be the head nurse for your son's care." She and another nurse, who she also introduced us to, were standing in the room monitoring Dalen's meds. "I have never seen anything like that," she said. I think she was referring to our family prayer. "You are an amazing family and I have learned that your son was amazing too. If we can do anything for you, just let us know," the nurse informed us.

"How can we thank you for taking such good care of our son? Thank you. You have done an amazing job. Why does his face look a bit twisted though?" I asked Stacey.

"Well it's because of all the fractures. He has a broken chin. It is actually shattered."

I wanted to know everything about my son. I wanted to know everything she knew about my son. It was like we were all in a trance though. Standing there, watching Dalen and now hearing about the medical conditions that he was enduring wasn't realistic. It seemed like a movie was being shown, and we were standing on the sideline watching it all, but not really experiencing it. Yet reality was staring us in the face, and after an exhale, I was back in the room hearing about the condition of my son that was dying. I really did want to know everything though. I wanted to know the medical conditions and again was in awe at what his body was enduring.

"So we have the brace around his neck to keep his face together. His cheek bone is broken. He has seven fractures on his skull. His chin was crushed. There was internal bleeding, and his heart is bruised because of the shocks he received. He isn't in pain. He can't feel anything. We have his body in the heat bag to keep the organs running properly. Um, he is comfortable. He came very close to dying many times but somehow has hung on. For some reason, he has held on. We will keep him here as long as you want. Again, he isn't in pain." Stacey was very complete in her description of what she knew to be wrong with our son.

There wasn't much else she could say or do. I then knew my prayers were answered, my son stayed alive so that we as his family could be with him when he passed. We just received more information than we had heard the whole way up to Pocatello. Seven fractures on his skull. Wow! Seven! I tried to imagine how he was in the truck to receive all the power of the impact to cause so much damage. They spoke of mostly his head. There wasn't much else said about his body. I didn't think much about that till later.

Scott had to leave the room for a minute. Kailee walked over to one of the chairs in the room that was next to the bed and picked up Dalen's hand. I couldn't even stroke his hair or wipe his cheek because it was so bloody. At one point, I asked the nurse if we could possibly clean up his face just a bit so that we weren't looking at all the blood, both fresh and dried, that covered his face. She was gracious and immediately left the room and quickly returned with some moistened towelettes so she could wipe up part of his face.

10:16 p.m. My phone vibrated, so I stepped out of the room for a minute, but remained just passed the doorway. Dalen was in my view constantly.

"Sharon, have you arrived? Can you give me an update my dear friend? Is there anything I can do for you? I wish I could be there," was the message from my friend Wendy.

"We are now waiting for the process of donations. We will stop the life support they say around 4:00 a.m. when they get all the teams in place. We are at peace though."

"I'm so sorry Sharon. We should never have to see our babies take their turn before us. My love and thoughts are with you," said Wendy.

I then had to excuse myself as the nurse said she had some information for us. I gathered everyone back into Dalen's room. They talked with the family about what would happen with the donor process. The nurse started to explain the situation. I asked if she could wait a minute till I got Alyssa on the phone so she could be a part of it too. She so wanted to be there. The nurse mentioned how there would be a coordinator that would come and walk us through the process. When it would be the time, there would be several other personnel that would be visible. Each would have a job to do in the extracting process. They again would make sure we understood everything. We would have to meet with the coordinator to decide which parts of Dalen's body were to be donated. She also reassured us that the lady was wonderful and that if they could do anything for us, to let them know. We thanked her for her explanation and then she left the room. I believe everyone understood and were okay with what was going to happen. We verified that Alyssa also understood. Sometimes on the phone, conversations taking place near the phone, aren't always heard. We all knew Dalen wanted to be a donor, but here we were talking about it and planning the moves to make it happen. We were all pretty sad with the idea that Dalen's body was going to be pretty much cut up and definitely not look like much of his body when they were done. Mariah had the hardest time with this.

"He's already gone through soo much Mom," Mariah pleas were so hard to hear.

"I know Mariah, but this was his and our decision that we believe is right. It's why they still have kept him alive. No, this isn't easy on any of us, and I'm just so sorry for all that you have experienced. This is so horrible."

"I'll be okay with it because actually I'm happy with the thought of how many people will have a better life because of Dalen."

That witness of Mariah led me to shed a few more tears. When I did cry, there would be just a few tears that would roll down my check, nothing more. It was always a peaceful moment and took just a moment to wipe the tears off. Again, gratitude engulfed me.

The nurse started to clean Dalen up. I watched as she went across his forehead and had to grab another stack of towelettes because her swabs were saturated with blood. Even though some of the blood had been there for a while, and areas were dried with blood, there was still enough fresh blood that could be wiped off that would take a few strokes. There was calmness as the nurse attended to Dalen. I stared into his face. He was so swollen. I just wasn't happy with the blood that kept dripping into Dalen's ear and pooling up and then would run down his neck.

The nurse left the room to attend to other duties. They really didn't have to be over him every minute, so I understood. There were two main nurses assigned to our room. They were pretty regular on giving medications and checking on the monitors. Of course there was a pulse machine. There was also a heart monitor, and IV stands (four) that had the nineteen lines of medications going into our son. There was the heated blanket with tubes running down to help contour to the parts of his body. There were a few beeps and sounds that altered my thoughts, but then I got used to them. Once the signing of the donor papers would be completed, there would be a whole new flush of medications pushed through Dalen. They warned us as much as they could as to what might happen. I stayed by Dalen's side. I just held his hand. I stared into his face and again kept wondering what his process was. Was he aware that we were there? Could he at any point hear us? I knew he knew we were there, but how much of it was he aware of, that we wouldn't know. Did my son know how much we all loved him? Could I let 'my Buddy Boy' know how much I loved him? I loved this boy. I just felt love and wanted to be with my boy.

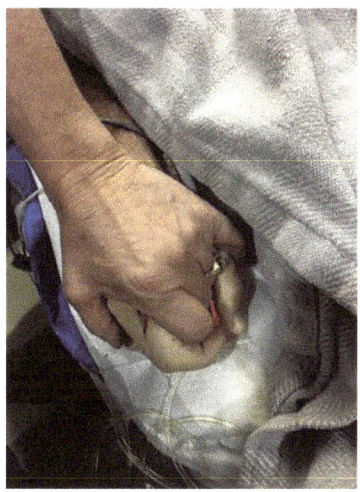

10:25 p.m. We were told that someone would be contacting us soon to talk about the donor process. Every time a person moved into Dalen's room; Scott would come back in from the next room that they had set up for us. I guess it was a good thing that the ICU unit was pretty quiet that night except for Dalen's room. That allowed the room next door to be vacant. As a family, we were taking advantage of that room and trying to have those that could, lie down on the bed they had in there, for a minute and rest. Again, the nurses made sure we had juice and crackers to eat. They knew we all had driven a long way and had endured a very difficult trip. Mariah was trying so hard to relax. She laid down for a minute and then got up and walked around again.

10:38 p.m. "How are the kids doing? I'm so sorry Scott. I'm praying for you guys. Are you with your wife yet?" Scott's co-worker was very concerned and wanted to relay any message he could to his team members. They had all discussed amongst themselves that they would fly up and be with Scott. Scott belonged to an undercover narcotics team. There were ten members and Scott was the Sergeant.

They were all good guys. They did a great job and Scott was grateful to be a part of them. They didn't know what else to do for us but because they were quite a tight group they were very aware of him and wanted to support him. I was very touched by their gestures. They seriously just wanted to be here. They were all willing to drop their lives and to fly up to Idaho to be with our family. Scott reassured them that we were going to be okay. He mentioned that we were currently going into a room to discuss the donor process and that Scott would get back to him. He appreciated the gestures, but we would let them know what was happening as soon as we could. It was such a great comfort to know they cared that much about Scott and our situation. We, in turn, would have to give them the response we could give to everyone: "We were doing okay, and we would let them know of any information when we knew anything". Again, our hearts were full of gratitude.[16]

    10:54 p.m.-Kailee to Alyssa.
    "Alyssa—how much longer?"
    "We are forty-four miles away," replied Alyssa.
    "OK." Said Kailee, that was all that she needed to hear.

---

[16] Scott's whole team was ready to fly up to Idaho to be with Scott. They wanted to be a moral support and to let Scott know how much they cared. We thought of what they would do if they came up and there really wasn't anything that they could have done except to be there. What an amazing group of people.

The Donor Process

We stayed with Dalen for about twenty to twenty-five minutes where we just sat and looked into his face. The family would come into the room for whatever time and then retreat back to the next room. There were small conversations, but nothing really. We just tried to pass the time with some noise. I remained with Dalen and never let go of his hand.

A lady then walked into the room; she was different then the hospital employees because she was dressed in normal clothes. She was wearing a dress, reddish color, I think. We were introduced to LaNae, the representative from the donor center. She mentioned that we would need to have a meeting as soon as possible; in about five to ten minutes to get things going. They had been waiting for a long time for us to arrive and it was now time to move forward with this process.

I just kept holding Dalen's hand. Reality was now that an ongoing process of decisions would have to be made. I kept thinking "Holy cow, that's fast", but then I hadn't realized that they had been waiting for us and this process for over seven hours. They needed to get things going. I had no idea of the involvement that would take place, but I would soon learn all of it. For now, I was standing by Dalen—holding his hand—looking at his face and wondering what his thoughts were during the crash. How much did he feel? Was there time to think or just react? His face was so swollen. He was so bruised. I was good to just stay there and hold his hand. I would get up every few minutes and wipe more blood running down his face, but I was there.

10:38 p.m. LaNae came into the room and asked Scott and I to go with her. As she did, I had to stop for a minute. I felt an almost squeeze of my hand—almost like Dalen was saying "Don't go Mom. Stay another minute." I had been told by the nurses that we might see some spasms or twitches from his body and hands. It wasn't just the body trying to figure out what was shutting down or simply reflexes, which some have interrupted as their loved ones have said they felt their hands being held. I understood that process and I knew that in my mind. This wasn't just an idea. This wasn't just a pass-by feeling. There was an impression made in my hand by Dalen. I sat there for a minute and took in the sensation of Dalen holding on to my hand and not wanting me to go. I actually told LaNae that I would be there in just a minute. I leaned over to Dalen's ear and explained what I needed to do and that I would be back.

"I promise Buddy, I will be back as soon as possible. We need to go and speak with the lady from the donor center. Oh how I love you Dalen. Thank you for your gift. I will treasure it forever. I love you Dalen." I again thanked Dalen for being there for me. I didn't say anything to anyone else, I just said I needed a minute and I think no one even questioned that of me as being Dalen's mom. They allowed me that moment. My son knew I was there! He knew I was holding his hand, and he made a gesture that I knew was all he could do, to let me know that he was acknowledging me. He was there! He was there and I knew it. God had allowed that gift and it was again another miracle in this adventure. I was just so incredibly grateful for that very precious moment.[17]

Kailee was still with Dalen when we left the room, and I excused myself to first go to the bathroom. It was back out in the lobby area outside the ICU unit. Mariah went into the next room again, where they had allowed all of us to rest and relax. It was so late at night and for her to find just a moment of rest would be amazing. The staff just kept bringing crackers, cheese and cookies on a plate for all of us all night long with what juices they could find. We never asked for any of it. We were grateful. It was so sweet of them. I think Mariah felt

---

[17] There are many times in a life of a mother when she knows things of her children. This time, I was given a special gift. Dalen had in some way squeezed my hand. He had let me know that he wanted me to be with him. He was there. My son was there.

she could finally let go just a little. She had been 'a rock' this whole time. She hadn't showed much emotion and did whatever was asked of her. Now she could exhale. She could lay on the bed and just 'vedge'. She felt some relief since we had gotten there. Not knowing again, anything about how long our meeting would be, I encouraged Mariah to lie down and rest on the bed. They had also brought three chairs into the room to assist with the rest of the family's needs. I suggested that they try to eat something and to just breathe for a few minutes.

We literally walked out of Dalen's room, past the nurses' station, which was maybe five steps from Dalen's doorway, and then there was a door immediately to the left which looked like a conference room. The door was opened to us. There was an oval-shaped table with the sides extended out. Maybe ten chairs around the table with four per side and two on the ends. There was a screen at the far end of the table and a small area where they had a coffee maker and some bottled water containers. There was a basket on the little counter with some munchies like bags of chips and some granola bars. LaNae invited us to sit and placed us on the right side of her. She had a packet of papers laid out in front of her on the table.

"I want you first to know how very sorry I am for what you are going through. There is nothing easy about this process, but we need to do it. I'm here to help in any way I can, and we will take as much time as you need. If you need a break just let me know. Know that everything we do will be your choice," LaNae stated.

"Oh, thank you."

LaNae then began. She opened her packet and explained that we were agreeing to allowing parts of our son's body to be extracted and processed. She explained how the process works. Organs, of course, were the biggest issues. It was a very intense process and a timed issue. Then there was the choice of the tissues and soft tissues, muscles, or whatever else we were willing to donate that had to be discussed.

"Okay, so do you think you are ready to begin this process? We know it isn't easy and again we are sorry for the situation of your son, but he is in excellent condition and he will help to save so many lives. This tragedy will bless so many other people and their families," LaNae commented.

"Yes," replied Scott. "We are ready."

LaNae then brought out sheets of paper. Each sheet had itemized lists with boxes to be checked. LaNae started by first handing us a consent form that we were willing to even begin this process. Then we began with the sheet of organs and tissues.

"I know Dalen wanted to donate whatever he could, but he especially wanted his eyes. He felt sight was one of the greatest gifts."

"Okay, so what about the kidneys?" LaNae asked.

"Yes." Scott and I were answering together. Each time a part of the body was mentioned; we looked at each other and nodded in consent.

"Liver?" LaNae questioned.

"Yes." And so on, and so on, and so on.

"We aren't sure if we can use his heart because it's bruised from them resuscitating your son. But we will try if that's your desire." LaNae really was detailed and also very considerate of our situation, but the questions had to be asked and they kept coming.

"Oh, I know it was important to Dalen, but I understand about the heart."

"Would you like something to drink? Can we get you anything?" LaNae was very concerned for our wellbeing.

"A water would be great. Thank you," I responded.

Everyone was so gracious to take care of us and look after any needs that we might have had. They went slow and explained everything very clearly. I'm sure in our state of mind, not everything was retained once explained to us, so they always clarified to make sure that we understood it all.

The lists were so amazingly detailed. It came down to where do you want tissues taken from and how much? It was blood veins from where and how many? Which bones if any? Which skin patches and from where? She named every single part of Dalen's body. It was so intricate. There was so much involvement that I had no idea of. I wouldn't have ever even thought of skin cells, hair for transplants, and any part literally of the body. I was in awe of how the science of medicine had developed so profoundly to attach any part of a body to other persons, so their life would be better and easier. Again, this process was a testament of God blessing his children. We were asked in a very detailed fashion if we wanted the retina, pupil, membranes, or the whole eye donated. That was how detailed it was. They asked about every single vein. Some part as small as a membrane on the eye could be used. We had choices of every part of the organs.

We decided on his kidneys, liver, lungs, eyes, bones in his legs, veins in his legs, and tissues from wherever they needed it. We opted out of the heart because of the time factor. It was just going to take too long to use the heart (five days waiting), and there was only a chance that it would work, but we allowed the heart valves to be taken. This whole thing was still pretty amazing to us, and we were okay with our decisions.

While we were in the room, we got a text from Alyssa. Normally I would have ignored my phone especially in a meeting or if I was with other people, but not today. Nothing and no one were more important than my family, even in the donor center room. I asked for a minute and looked at my phone.

11:04 p.m. **Alyssa's text** "Thirty miles and we should be there."

Scott replied with; "Okay."

We were again directing our attention to LaNae. We were in the room for almost half an hour, closer to like forty-five, fifty minutes. It was beginning to feel like we were there forever. There was so much to go over. It was explained to us the limited time frame too. For example; if we wanted to donate Dalen's heart, he would have to remain on life support for five days to do all the testing and matching, and then, it was only a possibility and not a guarantee that they could use it. I didn't think that was very fair to Dalen. There was no way I was going to wait for five days and just sit and watch my son. We wouldn't even know if they could use his heart because of the bruising from them resuscitating him or not. So, to wait for five days, I didn't think so. We were told that most of the other organs only had hours for them to be transplanted. Tissues and muscles would be frozen and could be used up to years later. That blew me away. The bones would usually be used within a year, preferably within months. I was in awe again at the body and the intricateness of this amazing process. When LaNae got to the reproductive issues, Scott was: "No way! I think you have enough of my son. We are good."

LaNae again, was so gracious to us throughout this whole process. She was gentle and yet professional. She knew that once our meeting was over, there was so much on hers and the hospital part that had to be done to get everything in motion. It was so surreal as to what we were going over. Our son's body would be used for so many things. There was a moment when tears ran down my cheek as I visualized what they would be doing to Dalen, but also so intrigued; I almost wanted to watch how they would do all the procedures. It was explained to us that the second we signed a paper, which we received within seconds of sitting down, stating we were willing to allow the donor process to begin; that the donor center would now be paying for everything. They would take over financially and in any other way needed. Our insurance company was no longer involved. The donor center would pay for flights, cars, medications, instruments, O.R.s, everything that was including the transplants teams and their arrivals. That was amazing too. We learned that additional medicines would be needed because of the donor list now being completed. We were told that we might see some side effects from the new medication. The apparent symptom would be that we would see his blood thinned, which meant he would be bleeding out more, and it would be very visible to us by any cut he had, including the tube on the brain. He could even bleed from his eyes or nose and that we would need to be prepared. As I visualized that, it of course, was worse than what it really would be. I was picturing all this blood oozing out of his body. It wasn't quite like that at all. In fact, it would actually be quite subtle to our view.

We weren't quite finished yet with LaNae. Once we went through the six pages of itemized lists and had all the consent forms signed, we still had more to do. There was a form for every part of Dalen's body that they had hopes to use. It was such a detailed process. This was amazing. I knew that the Lord was helping us with all these decisions and it just seemed like the events went by smoothly.

11:10 p.m. The door opened to the room and a doctor walked in. He announced himself to us and said he was the doctor in the E.R. when Dalen first came in. Now as we were finally getting all this process moving, he came and sat down by us as he talked about how bad Dalen was when he arrived. He talked about the tests and procedures they did for Dalen. He mentioned the CAT scan and that there was major damage on Dalen's brain and that he was pretty much brain dead by then. He talked about the internal bleeding that Dalen had sustained, and that both of his lungs had collapsed. He expressed his condolences for us and still thanked us for allowing our son's body to be donated. He mentioned that it was a hard thing to go through, but so rewarding when we thought of all the lives Dalen's life would alter for the better. He asked if we wanted to know anything else, if we had any questions for him. He asked if we wanted to know anything, anything that might give us more clarity to our situation.

"I'm not sure, but I think we understand it all," was Scott's comment.

"Do you have any questions for me before I leave?"

"Yes—when did my son die in your opinion?"

He paused for just a second. It was almost like I had hoped he would say a few hours ago; or that technically he was still alive, but he didn't. He looked down on the floor. I knew his answer.

"I believe your son died on impact, and that he went quickly."

We paused from all movement or reaction for a moment.

"Thank you." That seemed final and yet so true. My son then had only been kept alive for the family to unite and for all of this process to take place, and then the doctor walked out of the room.

Scott shed a few more tears. It was oh so real to hear his words. 'On impact'. Our son was medically dead and we knew that, but when you see all the tubes and machines and his chest being pumped up and down, it gave you the sense that he was alive. That his body was processing things, however, there was no brain activity and that wasn't going away. Knowing all this information however, did not diminish my moment with Dalen squeezing my hand. The body simply houses our spirits and Dalen's spirit was so very much alive and he let me know that. That moment will never be forgotten.

LaNae graciously asked again if we were okay. We were. We had now finished such a pretty big ordeal. We signed the last document. We took a big breath and exhaled with a profoundness that our son's body would no longer be as we knew it. It was finished. We shook hands and hugged LaNae and her team and thanked them again for all that they were doing for us and Dalen.

I couldn't help thinking about the extraction process. The body had always amazed me, and this whole thing would alter lives through all of the donations. Just very above anything I had ever imagined. Again, I was just so captivated by all the medical issues. In some ways, it was like taking away the reality and pain of my son dying to the ability of seeing the extension of life that would be taking place. Our son would basically be pretty cut up, but in doing so, others' lives would be saved or enhanced. A life could be saved. Those were astonishing words—'a life saved'. For a moment, I thought of all the people waiting to hear of such news that an organ was ready for them or that they could have hope for a better life. I imagined the young people that had been in the hospital for whatever period of time, and that they would now be relieved of those symptoms. This was most defiantly an overwhelming experience.[18]

I had flashbacks of the cadaver we studied in biology class my first year of college. It was amazing how the body worked and everything had such a purpose. I remember seeing the smallest elements of a cell and that a cell developed into tissue that could be used to help another. I remember looking at this body that had been donated to science, and with that, we learned so much. I remember peeling back a skin layer. I remember seeing where the organs would be and what they did. I remember thinking how weird this was, but also amazing. The body we saw was about a seventy-five-year-old female. She

---

[18] When someone sees what the body can do, how it is studied and functions, God can be the only form of creation. It's perfect, every aspect, every cell, it's perfect. I'm so in awe of the greatness of our God.

was a black woman, and her hair was gray. Her body was wrinkled with lines and her skin was tough from the preserving medications. We looked at her legs and the veins that carried the blood throughout the body. It really was amazing. Now I was hearing of the same things I had studied so many years ago except, this was present and from my son's body. Besides the actual organs, which were few, the tissues wouldn't really save a life, but they would make one better. I thought then of the ligament I had put into my hand a few years ago. I never really thought of the ligament coming from someone that had deceased. That never even crossed my mind. It was just; 'yes I'll take the cadaver's ligament'.

I had been so enlightened within this past hour. We didn't know again of how much they would take of tissues and from where, but we gave them permission to take what they needed, and they would tell us later exactly what they used.

We had now finished such a pretty big ordeal. We shook hands and hugged the personnel and thanked them again for all that they were doing. The door was opened for us and so we returned to where the family had been. We went over with them what was going to happen and warned them of the time process. As we were told, this could take a while, but that once everything was ready, that it would happen quickly. We returned to Dalen's room. We were at his side. There was very little time from then on that someone wasn't with Dalen. No way would he be alone. Medications were immediately given to him. These medications were to protect specific body parts and just maintain blood and oxygen levels to the body.

This really was just so amazing. Emotions seemed to be all over the place for my family. We were excited to be together, more relieved than anything. Then it was how awful the experience was. There was fear as to what might happen or at least what could happen during the process. There were emotions of sadness and devastation of course, but also amazement and wonder for the outcome of what we were medically viewing, and the abundance of peace that continued to be with us.

After returning again from the bathroom, I left the family for a few minutes and went back into Dalen's room. The nurses were so very tentative to him and making sure that all the equipment was working properly. They came in at least every half an hour or sooner. I had asked if there were more of the gauzes that I could use to wipe the blood that kept coming out of Dalen's head and rolling into his ear. I could see a difference as they had warned me, from the amount of blood that came out of his body. It seemed to be flowing more quickly. It bothered me a bit. Actually, I was very uncomfortable with it. The nurse immediately went out and brought another stack of gauzes for me. They seemed to be used up quickly. She took a few and wiped down the right side of his cheek and into the ear where the blood just kept pooling. She set them to the left of Dalen's head on his pillow. We were seeing one of the side effects of the medicine. There was blood coming out of every part of his body where there was a visible cut. It was kind of watery and almost see-through, yet it was red of course.

I stood by Dalen and again held his hand. The sound of the machines were so rhythmical and the vision of his chest filling with air and rising and lowering as it naturally would do, was so constant. About every three seconds, there was a rise and fall of his chest. There wasn't an inhale and an exhale. It was just a constant, mechanical movement. The nurses were checking on our needs and how they could attend to us. They were so caring to us and our desires for Dalen.

I never really looked over Dalen's body. They had a blanket-like apparatus over him with tubes running down it that heated Dalen's body to keep the appropriate temperature on all the organs. If Dalen's temperature were to drop to a certain point, it would jeopardize all the tissues and cells. His head was on a pillow and the front of the bed was raised so his head was propped up just a bit. The nurses left, and then I proceeded to wipe his brow, cheek and ear for the draining blood. I stayed with Dalen most of the time. It was now my job to wipe his face and head. I wanted him to know that his mom wouldn't be leaving him. Scott told me later that I stayed there for about five hours. It could have been that long, but I had no concept of actual time. The time kind of stood still.

Scott and Kailee came back into the room. They sat in the chairs that were by his side and one chair was by his feet. We didn't really talk a lot at that moment. We just sat and watched Dalen. Kailee asked if we had heard from Alyssa. We were anxious to see them and knew that Alyssa and Brandon were getting closer. Mariah was lying on the bed in the next room. Gord and Maria were waiting with us as well in the room. So now the wait was for all the personnel to be in place before the extractions could happen. There was no more talk that Dalen might not make it because he was on all these other medications to sustain his body parts specifically. That all these people were waiting with us (Rick's family was still in the waiting room too), was amazing to me. We didn't know what this process would be, but we had support.

My place was standing by Dalen close enough to his head and wiping the blood that continued to drain from his body. I began to look over him from head to toe. The tube on his head was actually bigger than I expected, but the blood would go down the tube and into a pump. You could see how much blood was coming out of his head. The container actually had to be changed a few times while we were there because it would fill up. This wasn't an easy sight to see, but such an essential one. Just thinking of everything that was done to preserve the body of my son, was very overwhelming, and yet very real. We really were doing all of this.

The Wait

11:34 p.m. "Pulling in." Alyssa reported.

"Finally," I sighed.

Mariah immediately went out of the room and stated that she would go get her. Another huge exhale was offered as the last of our children would finally arrive and we would be together again as a family.

The minutes it took for them to park, exit the car, get into the hospital, walk into the elevator, back out again on the tenth floor, walk through the ICU doors and finally into Dalen's room; seemed like an hour. As Alyssa approached the doorway, she was already crying pretty hard. I slightly backed off from Dalen's side as she came into the room and saw her brother. Her husband was right behind her. I hugged her and pulled her in close to me.

"Oh my gosh! My brother!" Alyssa was crying hysterically now. She then leaned into Brandon who hugged her very tightly. And they just stared at him. The only place we could really touch Dalen was his hands because there were so many tubes on him and his face was so swollen and bloody and bruised. The staff wanted his body kept under the heating tubes so his hands were all we could see so we tried to keep them tucked under somewhat too. Alyssa needed to touch him though. She tried to touch his face but then she just couldn't because she was afraid to. I moved so she could hold his hand and then we hugged. She just cried into my shoulder. Scott had moved on the other side of her, and again, we just held her for a minute.

"He looks awful Mom," she stated.

"Yes, he doesn't quite look like Dalen, does he?"

"No he doesn't," as Alyssa cried into my shoulder. "I don't want to do this Mom."

"None of us do, Alyssa. It's none of our thoughts. Let's let Alyssa have a moment with her brother." The rest of the family walked into the next room.

Alyssa sat in the chair and just talked with Dalen. She told him how she loved him and was grateful that he was her brother. She thought of what he would miss out on in life, who he was and used to be, that he didn't look much like her brother. He was so swollen and just didn't look like the happy guy she knew. Yet she strongly knew that Dalen knew she was there. Everyone said he was already gone, but there came a quick moment when Alyssa was squeezing his hand and calling to Dalen, and he slightly squeezed her hand back. She too, knew of muscle reflexes but this was different. She knew Dalen was letting her know he was still there. She knew that he wasn't all there though, and that his spirit was hanging on for all of us. Alyssa then came out of his room and checked on everyone else. She was the big sister after all, and felt it her duty to make sure everyone was okay. We all were concerned for each other and constantly were asking if someone needed anything, or had questions, or was just having a hard time with anything.

11:43 p.m. Kelly Jensen "Sharon, I don't have words that can express my love for you. I can't imagine what you're going through at this time. I'm so sorry. I hope you know we are all praying for all of you."

11:45 p.m. Michelle Cooke "My heart is with you. My soul is with you. Please know that you are loved."

We were all tired. We were all taking turns being with Dalen and allowing others their turn. I generally stayed with Dalen. Scott got to the point that he said he just needed a break, that he couldn't sit there like me and do what I was doing. He said it was just so hard. I actually think Mariah might have taken a nap and maybe Kailee too. It was never for long, but it was helpful.

At one moment, Scott was sitting in the room with me.

"So, can you comprehend that we will be going to a funeral home tomorrow? That is just beyond what I ever thought we would be doing."

"I'm not ready for this. A parent shouldn't have to go prepare for a child's death. I don't want to do this," Scott stated strongly.

"We don't have to honey. Don't worry about it. We will take care of things when we need to."

February 10, 12:18 a.m. I was standing over Dalen and looked at his collar bone that was just outside of the blanket a bit. The nurses had again walked around the bed and were attending to the issues of the medications. They finished their tasks and returned to their station. I was puzzled at what I was viewing.

"Scott, didn't the police officer say that Dalen was wearing his seat belt?"

"Yeah, why?"

"Because there is no mark. There aren't any marks across his body."

"What do you mean?" Scott asked.

"Well, come and look."

We both began to inspect Dalen's body. We lifted up the blanket just a bit to get a better look at his shoulder, and there was no marking of a seatbelt of any kind. I expected to see some abrasions and cuts. We didn't want to expose his body to the cold air, but we wanted to be able to inspect his body thoroughly. We kept the blanket low and peeked through just enough so that we could see. There was nothing. There wasn't a mark. There was no redness at all. It seemed impossible. How could he have gone through such an ordeal without at least, a seatbelt abrasion of some kind? We moved our eyes down to his waistline where the seatbelt connected. Again, there was nothing visible. We were in shock. We just didn't understand this.

I actually had a flashback as we looked at Dalen's chest. He was so proud of his chest hair. I remembered the first time he noticed one. He came running out of the bathroom with a towel wrapped around him and yelling: "Look Mom, look! I have a chest hair." The thought brought a quick smile to my face.

I flipped back to the moment at hand. We had learned that the truck had rolled three times sideways and twice head over heels. So, the truck rolled five times before it settled on the embankment.

With that much motion, how could Dalen not have any physical signs of restraint from a seatbelt that locked itself. We learned they had to cut Dalen out of his seatbelt in the truck and he was pulled out on Mariah's side. We looked again and more intently. There was nothing.

I looked at Dalen again and thought of so many experiences with him: growing taller than his dad, with his feet getting bigger and bigger every year, with his picking a hair style that would make him look older; with his hands and how much he liked to meddle with them. It was a flood of instant images and a lifetime of memories.

I proceeded down his right leg, as that was the side that we mostly stood by. His face looked worse from the left side of the bed and all the machines were on that side as well, so the right side was more accessible to us. Scott was looking with me. We got to his big toe on the right foot. There was blood. That was unique too. Why would just his toe have blood on it? If his foot jammed up somewhere, there should have been bruises somewhere else on his body. We put the blanket down and moved to the left side of the bed. I don't think Scott had ever looked at Dalen from that side. He stopped for a moment and released a big sigh.

"Man, his face sure looks beat up doesn't it?" Scott said.

"Yes he does." And we lifted up the left side of the heated tubed blanket to look at his left foot. It looked normal. We continued up his leg, to his hip and waist. There was nothing. Nothing! How could that be? My son's body was completely intact. We couldn't understand, so we called in one of the nurses from their station. Stacey came in.

"We were told that our son was wearing a seatbelt. Shouldn't there be some kind of marking or bruising on his body?"

"Yes, that would be normal," she mentioned.

"But there isn't anything. We just looked," stated Scott.

"Really? That doesn't seem normal or make sense." She then proceeded to inspect Dalen's body too. "I haven't really looked at him because we were just dealing with the medications." She looked again with us watching on. "I've never seen that. With the trauma that he went through, I would expect a bunch of bruises especially on his shoulder from the strap. He should have some abrasions too." The nurse was as baffled as we were.

The flood of thoughts was intense and rapid. Dalen's body was perfectly protected. He wasn't bruised in anyway. He looked completely normal. All were baffled as to how that could have happened and yet it was true.

"I've never seen a body so prepared to be a donor." The nurse was exactly right. There was a long moment—like a flash across my mind of the perfect condition of Dalen's body and how it would then be able to help so many more people. We were all amazed. The initial reports from the paramedics and the ER staff said that there were contusions in various spots on Dalen's body, but they no longer were visible. I wondered if that meant that his bruising would be on the inside and the nurse just couldn't explain that. She was very much in awe of how Dalen's body looked. She went out and even brought in a few other nurses to see Dalen's body. Everyone was amazed.

"His body was saved to help others," Scott said. "Thank you Heavenly Father. Thank you again."

We instantly understood that God was in charge. My son was passing, but he was so well prepared physically, that he would be saving many more lives than we initially thought. A few more tears ran down my cheek in gratitude. There was just no way to describe our experience. Not one bruise. Not one. It just didn't seem possible, but it was a testimony and a miracle again of God's plan. I said a very quick and humbled prayer of thanks.

We stood there for a minute hugging each other as we realized again the amazing blessing we just witnessed. Dalen's body was perfect. Scott went in to tell everyone what just happened. Alyssa and Brandon came in to check out his body first, and also came to the realization of what we had just learned. They were there for a minute then Kailee also came in. Together they saw his shoulder and chest and that there were no markings of any kind.

"God was really watching over him wasn't He?" was Kailee statement.

"I think he was meant to be a donor." Alyssa commented.

"This is definitely amazing. I wouldn't believe it if I hadn't seen it," responded Brandon. As a paramedic, he had seen his fair share of accidents and bruises. This was a medical miracle. There was a different feeling in the room. There was a warmth that encircled us all. We were overwhelmed again and amazed at God's love for us.[19]

12:30 a.m. After the accident, Mariah in one of her conversations, told Scott about the officer and the report he took. Mariah had told Scott that the officer mentioned that the worst case would be that she could be charged with murder, if that was what his investigation would come to. He didn't think that was the case, but it was an option. That really scared Mariah and I was horrified to hear of it too. That was Mariah's concern and now was Scott's. Yet, like a good dad, Scott said it would all be okay. But then the officer walked back into our room. He was trying to finish his report and needed just a bit more information. I was surprised that he came in at the early hour. He however, mentioned that he had a busy night and was just trying to finish up his reports. We knew what that meant. He wanted to check up on Mariah too and see how she was doing. That was very kind of him. Scott went out of the room to meet with the officer. I heard him identify himself as not only the father, but also a Sergeant with the Los Angeles County Sheriff's Department. The officer reported to Scott his encounter with Mariah. It was determined that they were wearing their seatbelts, and that Mariah wasn't on her cell phone. There was no texting and that all of that information was good for her case. He was trying to finish up his report. Scott expressed his concern in hearing that his daughter could be charged with murder. The officer was very courteous and considerate, and he mentioned that Mariah had asked him what the worst situation would be. He did tell her that it

---

[19] None of the hospital staff had ever seen a body preserved so well as Dalen's was for the donor process. His body was preserved perfectly so that he could bless others' lives.

could be murder, but that his investigation had already revealed that it was purely an accident and reiterated that she hadn't been on her phone in any way and that it really was just an accident.

Scott and the officer discussed a few more details of the accident. With the information he gave Scott, it was very helpful in assisting us with where we could go to check out the truck the next day, to retrieve personal property and items we also needed, get the papers out of the vehicle that we would need and learned of its location. The officer actually ended up being very helpful to our family and especially to Scott where he could accept the accident. If there would have been another person involved, or a vehicle, Scott wouldn't have accepted this. If someone else had injured his children in some way, he wouldn't have been able to just settle the issue. There was no one else around. There was no other involvement. Mariah had lost control and tried to correct her driving and in doing so, overcorrected and the truck rolled. That was it. It was an accident. There was no one to blame. It was an accident.

1:38 a.m. Some time passed. It actually seemed to pass quickly after inspecting Dalen. When LaNae had spoken with us earlier, she had warned us of the time frame and that it might be a long night. She said it would take some time to get things going and to expect that maybe around 2:00 or 3:00 a.m. we would know more. I didn't think it would take that long, but I understood as they would be bringing in teams from Salt Lake area and flying in others from various states. That was amazing too as I didn't think his body parts would be going that far away. One of the teams was coming from Colorado, so I understood that they would need time to fly in to Salt Lake City and drive the two hours to Pocatello. For now, we would be attentive to Dalen and wait.

We mentioned eating throughout the night, but it just wasn't an issue for anyone. At one point, when I went to the room next door, I was also asked if I had eaten anything and that I probably should. I agreed. I took a juice box and that seemed to satisfy me. No one wanted to leave the hospital or to even leave the ICU area. I thought that it was again another blessing that our hunger would be taken away from us so that all our attention could be centered on Dalen.

Even Brandon, who never rejected food, said he was good and didn't need anything. Scott would always eat when it was time to eat. If it was 6:00 p.m., it was dinner time. He didn't always eat breakfast but did every other meal and on time. He had to have a Diet Coke no matter where he went. If he was in a car, there was a drink between his legs. So, no one wanted food. That seemed to be a huge deal to me. It definitely wasn't normal, that's for sure.[20]

Those that could, rested. Those that couldn't sleep sat relaxed and tried to not think about too much. We were all just in the moment, and the moments became hours, and the hours became a night.

Even though we were all together, it still felt like there was a void. We didn't know quite how the night would proceed, but we could only face what would come.

Alyssa and Brandon were also taking turns being with Dalen or resting. There were enough chairs for us all to sit in the next room, so it was a place to be that wasn't far from Dalen.

Of course, throughout our time standing next to Dalen, we would talk to him and express our love and reflect on times of his life. Being brain dead meant his body had no cognitive motion, but his spirit was still with us, and we sensed he knew everything that was going on.

2:00 a.m. Once we knew that Dalen wasn't going to make it; Scott had taken time to review more messages. Many came from his team and his Lieutenant Glen Walsh. The whole team was still wanting to load up their things and be with us. Scott mentioned again that it wasn't necessary. They just felt so helpless. They wanted to do something, anything. I don't think they contacted Scott at 2:00 a.m., but I think that was when he took time to look at his phone and respond back to them. Surprisingly, they responded. They just didn't want Scott to be alone. They listened to Scott though, and didn't come up, but it was mentioned later, that they had regretted not coming to be with us. They were just good guys.

---

[20] Food desires had left our family. All night long, and no one was hungry. All were content.

Being on a task force with the DEA (Drug Enforcement Agency), there was a connection made with the resident agent who was in Boise, who then called one of the special agents, who happened to be in the Rexburg, Pocatello area. He called Scott. We were so surprised because it was the middle of the night. But they wanted to make sure Scott and his family were okay. They were just so kind to all of us. They really made sure we had everything we needed as a family and that we were taken care of. They didn't just ask if we were okay, they asked if we had enough money with us to take care of things. They asked if we needed help with gas. They asked if our well-being was being attended to and by whom. They asked of our lodging. It was just amazing how they took care of their professional family. We were able to let them know that as far as we knew, we had a hotel to stay in whenever we would be finished with the hospital and we hadn't paid for anything yet. Our financial issues so far were taken care of. Such a blessing. The DEA was there to assist Scott. His department was set up so that personnel would always be given aid in such serious situations. Scott explained that we weren't quite sure of the time frame and where we needed to be or for how long, but that Scott would contact him when he knew more. So amazing.[21]

2:18 a.m. The family was pretty quiet. There wasn't much movement from the next room. I assumed that some of the family might even have been trying to sleep. It was definitely needed. I took a brief walk out again to the bathroom and looked out the window from the lobby. It was so quiet outside. The lights weren't all turned on in the unit, so it was dimly lit, which made it feel peaceful. There was plenty of time for your mind to wander, but I really just thought of Dalen. I don't know that there were even times of future glimpses like: 'He won't be able to; He could have; We won't get to see'; nothing like that. I just sat and stared at him. I don't even know that I had many thoughts at all of my own. It was just peace. I wiped his head

---

[21] The department made sure there was someone to check up on Scott. They even sent an agent that resided in Idaho. How amazing and overwhelming for Scott.

and ear for the blood and held his hand. There was no other place for me to be. I just loved my 'Buddy-Boy'.

2:33 a.m. All of a sudden the nurse was hurrying around. There was a monitor that went off. They immediately were taking vitals. I was paralyzed watching their movements.

"What's going on?'" I asked.

"His blood pressure just really dropped. He isn't responding to some of the medicine. I don't know if he can hold on. We are losing him," Stacey stated.

After all that we had been through, that Dalen had been through, the times we were told he wouldn't make it; the lingering on of his body; the perfect preparation of his body and then to be told that he wasn't going to make it. I was having a hard time accepting that. I thought once they were on all these meds for preservation of all the organs and tissues, that he would remain in that state until the extractions would take place. This wasn't good. This wasn't good at all. 'He has fought so hard, please God, please don't let this happen. Please assist him. Help him to hold on. Let him help others by being a donor. We have waited so long. Please help us,' was my plea to Heavenly Father. I immediately went into the other room.

"Hey everyone," I made them wake up and pay attention to me. "Dalen isn't going to make it. His blood pressure just dropped really low, and he's not accepting the medications. We need to say a prayer right now. Come on everyone. I need you to wake up. Dalen is crashing and they don't know what else to do. Please, we need to have a prayer right now. Please let's pray. We need him to hang on till the donor teams are in place. He has come this far."

Gord and Maria joined us as they were in the room too. We immediately bowed our heads and those that were close to the floor knelt.

"Scott do you think you could offer the prayer?" There was a slight hesitation.

Alyssa volunteered; "I will."

"Heavenly Father, we humbly bow our heads before thee. We know that Dalen is trying to survive. We have all been through so much. It has been a very long night for all of us. Dalen has struggled to last this long. We are asking that thou might heed our prayer and let our brother, son, remain alive until all the teams get here and that his body might be used as a donor to bless the lives of so many other people. Please dear Heavenly Father, let Dalen respond to the medications. Please let him be strong enough to hold on a bit longer. Please Heavenly Father, please hear our prayer. We say these things and ask with all our hearts in the name of Jesus Christ, amen."

"Oh thank you Alyssa, that was beautiful." We all got up and I quickly returned back into Dalen's room. The nurses were still trying to get his body to respond to the medications and have his systems regulate. They were pushing medications in like crazy. It was a flush of lines being checked and tested and shots, one after another, being given.

It was about one minute later and: "Wow, it looks like he is doing just a bit better. I think the medications are starting to work again. He's responding."

A few more seconds went by: "I see a regular pulse. This is good. I think we got it." The nurse had no idea that our family just had a prayer, but there was no doubt in my mind that our prayer was answered and answered immediately. Dalen was still alive and responding well to the medications. What a fighter Dalen had become.

"Thank you our dear Heavenly Father. Thank you so much." I expressed my thought vocally. Some of the family had followed me back into the room so they knew the news; but I ran back and told the others that he was responding. You literally could hear a relief from everyone. What an amazing experience of faith and prayer.[22]

2:48 a.m. The pharmacist came into the room from downstairs. He wasn't quite sure of our situation and was pretty anxious to hear of the story that would cause the need for so many medications at one time.

---

[22] God had shown us a miracle. He had preserved the life of our son and just because he could. He had given us a bit longer to honor and love our son. God had made the medications work and his body accept the treatment and within a minute. That is a miracle.

"I need to check what's going on here. I'm checking on why you need all these medications for this person? There are an awful lot of them, and you seem to be pushing them through pretty quickly. I just need to make sure we aren't duplicating anything and that all the medications are all really needed."

Stacey responded: "He is our donor candidate. He has lost a lot of blood that we keep pushing back into him, but we needed the meds to keep him going. We almost lost him for a bit. We haven't asked for more than we need. He is responding very well to them now, and things are progressing."

"Okay, then I will keep filling the prescriptions. It just seemed like so much for such a short time period. I just needed to double check. That's all I need. With his weight and physical conditions though, he is pretty intact. So, I guess it's all good." And he walked back out of the room.

They all continued on with their duties. Every time the nurses came in, they checked the machines first. They checked all the IV lines and made sure they were all working properly, all twenty-three now as lines were added once the donor process began. They would check his heart rate and oxygen level. The head nurse would always stop for a minute by Dalen's head and wipe more blood from him as it drained out of his nose, or forehead, or ears. She made sure he was taken care of. I so appreciated that. I resumed the position once she left the room. Dalen didn't just appear to be a body to her, but someone's son. He was my son, and she treated him that way.

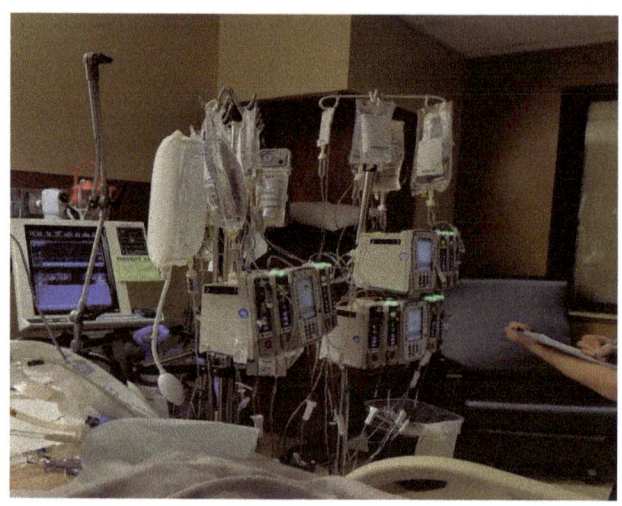

    The nurse was working on Dalen's right side where I normally stood, so I walked around to the left side of his bed. The other nurse went out to get more medication.

    The view of Dalen from his left side was worse. You could see more of how bruised and swollen his eyes were. You could see more tubes, and he just looked more beat up. His left hand was kind of in a fist position. I had to pry his hand open—pull just a bit more to get his hand to open enough so I could grab his hand and hold it. I wasn't sure why it was stiff. Maybe because of poor circulation and the many hours that his hand hadn't been moved caused some of the stiffness. I wouldn't allow any other reasons to be expressed to me. His hand was stiff because of lack of movement. At least I couldn't see blood dripping out of his ear from this side. His ear was more pressed into the pillow so maybe he was bleeding, and I just couldn't see it. You could tell his cheek bone was broke—it just looked a little off. The neck brace they put on Dalen was doing its job. So I was holding Dalen's hand and just thinking: *'Are you okay Bud? Do you know I'm here?'* I spoke to him. "I love you so much. This is just so sad. Do you know I'm here?"

    Again, I knew that a body responds in different ways to medication, and it had only been a few minutes from the last dosage so that could have explained what happened next. But it wasn't the explanation of what really happened.

Scott came into the room and said, "The girls had a question for you."

"Okay. I'll be right there," and I went to let go of Dalen's hand when again I felt a squeeze. It startled me. I gasped at what was occurring. Scott asked if I was okay. I assured him I was. Did I really feel that? My son just squeezed my hand again. It was as if he was saying: "Yes Mom, I so know you are here, and I love you too." It seemed so profound to me. I think a tear or two rolled down my cheek.[23]

"I'll be there in a minute," was my reply to Scott. I stood there in awe. My son heard me. It wasn't a twitch. It could have been a reflex but not to a mom. I held his hand and stroked his arm. I just kept repeating: "I love you Buddy Boy. I love you so much." And then I just stood there. A few minutes passed, and I felt it would be okay to leave Dalen for just a few minutes, so I left the room to attend to my family.

3:02 a.m. It's a unique mental scenario sitting over a hospital bed and looking at a loved one that you know will be passing soon. There was calmness, peace and a unique quietness. I don't think I have ever experienced anything like it before.

Everyone respected the situation. When they would come into the room, it was almost like a whisper was the form of communication. The discussions in the room were about what everyone was feeling or whatever they wanted to talk about—especially Dalen. They talked about his physical condition and memories of him. The nurses would ask us about Dalen and what he was like. We discussed his sports and his abilities, especially with volleyball and how much he loved it. We talked about his mission and how he touched so many lives. It was good to talk about him, but still it was all in the past. That phrase, 'the past', was never my friend.

We knew Dalen was in a good place and knew where he wanted to go, at least spiritually. He wasn't sure of a career path, but he knew how to keep himself close to Heavenly Father. The family talked

---

[23] I had asked Dalen if he heard me. The only way he would be able to let me know was through his squeezing of my hand. Such a tender mercy—a moment to never forget.

about his last few months and how Dalen was figuring out where his path was going to take him. We were happy to reflect on his four months since being home from his mission, and that he was happy with whom he was. It was good to talk about him.

Other times, it was just quiet except for the machines which sounded like a metronome keeping perfect time for a pianist, as they were so consistent. It allowed me to reflect and pray. With it being the middle of the night, we were tired but more of a mental tired. We all seemed fine physically. I didn't know if anyone got a nap as I pretty much stayed with Dalen. At one point, I walked into the other room again just to check on everyone. Mariah was on the bed lying down. Scott was in a chair beside Kailee who was in the other chair, and Alyssa was sitting on Brandon's lap in the third chair. I saw the crackers and juice on the hospital tray that was in the room. All the lights were on high. You know how you can have the room lights; the overhead lights; or the under lights which were dimmer. The room was with the bright lights on. I think everyone wanted to stay awake just in case something happened. I heard conversations of Dalen and their memories. It was funny to listen to some of their stories.

"So what's going on in here?"

"Not much Mom. We are all just talking about our memories of Dalen and how he made us laugh." Alyssa sounded tired even though she didn't look tired.

"That's nice. Is everyone okay? Do you need anything? The nurses keep asking if they could get us anything."

"Yeah, we know," replied Scott. "They just asked us too."

"Maybe some of you should get a nap. We really don't know how long this thing will be. I hope it's soon."

"Yeah, me too. This waiting is hard." Even though Mariah was lying down, she was completely awake.

What would this night bring? How long would this really take? Would it be an easy process, or would it be more of an emotional thing? I was hoping for an easy transition because I didn't know how much more the family could take, especially Mariah. The hours ticked on. We were all demonstrating so much strength and peace. We definitely were given those amazing blessings.

3:25 a.m. "Do you think something will happen soon?" I asked Stacey.

"It really just depends on when they can get all the teams together. There is a team for the kidneys, another for the liver, a team for the tissues, and another for his bones. So, to get each team member in place is a big process. I'm sure you are tired so you should try to rest. They really are doing all they can. It's just a waiting thing. Your son's body is stable and doing well. So we can't do anything but wait."

"Yes he is stable. I think we are getting tired. I don't think I could rest though."

"That's totally understandable. Your family has been through a lot. Again, you have been amazing. I just have never seen a family handle this type of situation like yours has. It has been an honor for me to be around your family and their strength. I just can't imagine going through this."

"Do you have any children Stacey?" I asked.

"Yes, I have a little boy. He's four now. It's hard to see him when I work twelve-hour shifts, but my husband and I work it out."

"That's what you do as a parent, anything you can for your child." And I rubbed Dalen's forehead again, to catch some dripping blood.

"If you want to take a break, I will stay here with your son."

"That is really nice of you. I just took a minute to check on everyone, but maybe I'll take you up on that and take a bathroom break."

"Of course, go ahead. I won't leave him."

I walked down the hall. Again, I crossed the hallway and headed out of the ICU unit to the bathroom. Gord and Maria were in the room with everyone else and had decided that they would be going home. They didn't see much reason to stay, so they were saying their goodbyes to everyone. We met at the door to the room.

Gord spoke first. "I don't think we can do much more here and we are getting tired. I think we will head home."

"Are you sure? It really has meant a lot to me to have you here. You know there is a room over at the hotel for us that you can go use. We won't be there for a while it looks like. We are waiting for the different teams to get together. Why don't you go over there and go to bed?"

"We thought of that, but prefer our own bed. Do you want us to stay?"

"I mean yes, but I also understand. This could be a really long night. We know our son will die; we just don't know when. I don't know what to tell you."

"So why don't you just call us when things happen. We can come back if you need us to, and we aren't that far away." Maria was a voice of reason. I knew that if I asked them to come back, they would, but I also didn't feel that we would need them to return.

"You have been amazing. Thanks again for everything. It really did mean a lot to me that you were here with Mariah, Gord. Did you want to say your goodbyes?" I wasn't sure if I was referring to the group or to Dalen. To say your final goodbyes to a family member was a thought that I was coming to see as so very real. Gord said that they already did. They hugged me and both held me for a few extra seconds. It felt very comforting.

"Sorry again sis, that you have to go through this. Just not a fun thing for sure.

"Thank you again. Thank you so much. I love you."

"I love you too, Sharon." Gord was my hero once more.

"Yeah, you know we love you and would do anything we can for you." Maria was the angel to us all, taking care of everyone while I was attending to Dalen. I didn't really have to worry about them because I knew Maria was there. I was just so grateful.

"We will go to Rexburg tomorrow to take care of everything, so we will see you on our way back. We don't know the time frame yet as to what has to be done or anything, but we will let you know when we know."

"Are you sure you want to do that now?" Maria asked.

"Yeah, I think so because we are here and it would be easier to take care of it now instead of coming up again to do it later. I know we will need to clean out his apartment and then whatever we need to do with the school. I think it will be the best to take care of things now. We might be a few days."

Scott and I had had some conversations while we were together watching Dalen, as to what needed to be done next. It came down to contacting a funeral home. Getting in touch of the school to see what we would need to do to close out Dalen's apartment and his semester. We would need to get whatever was left out of the truck and make some intense decisions. So, giving the information to Gord and Maria was now a verbal process confirming previous decisions we had made. My mind was just in overload. I had to think of future plans, but also just wanted to stay in the moment and make sure my thoughts stayed with Dalen.

"Okay, do you have clothes and everything? Do you need anything?" Maria again was addressing the needs of our family.

"No, I think we all have enough clothes for a week. We didn't know what to expect, so I had everyone bring a few days of clothes to change into. I think we are good, but thank you. If we need something, we will just buy it."

"So just let us know what is happening. We will see you in a few days then."

"Thanks again Maria." And we hugged once more. Gord was right there too for another hug.

"Love you guys." They took another gaze into Dalen's room and then turned away and walked through the ICU doors. They walked around the corner to the elevator. I followed them. I watched them wait for the elevator to open and then the door closed, and they were gone. I could see out the window in the lobby. It was so dark outside, but then it should have been as it was about **3:30 a.m.** There was very little movement outside. In fact, you couldn't see any cars on the highway and the few that were in the parking lot, looked like they had been there a while. The snow was glistening as the moon wasn't full, but it gave off enough light to see the ground covering. It seemed like we were the only ones in the hospital as it was so quiet. At least the floor we were on was very quiet. I walked back into the ICU unit after going to the bathroom. We had to knock on the door each time we left the ICU unit to be allowed back into the area. One of the nurses from the station would come and open the door for any of us that chose to go to the lobby. It was just a minute and then the door opened for me to return.

3:53 a.m. LaNae had come into the room again. Everyone joined us to see what she had to say. She mentioned that the teams had all been notified and should be here within the next hour or so. She mentioned again some of the process that would take place.

"So there are four teams coming. Each team has their own agenda. Once they are here and Dalen is removed from the room, they will first take his kidneys and liver and then switch teams. The bones and tissues will be extracted after. They will let you know when they are done and you will have full knowledge of everything. As a donor family, we offer you handprints and finger prints and as many as you want for family members. Do you think you would like something like that?"

"Yeah, I would want one," said Alyssa.

"I think that would be a great idea," I remarked. We looked at Kailee and Mariah for their responses. Kailee shook her head yes, but I don't think Mariah was really sure because there was no answer from her.

"Mariah, do you think you would like a fingerprint?" I asked her again.

"That would make me feel better," she finally replied.

"Okay, then I will get things ready and we will make sure that happens before they take Dalen away," LaNae responded.

"Thank you so much again, LaNae. You have been so kind to us and have helped us through this whole thing."

"My pleasure, even though this isn't an easy thing to go through, you all have made our jobs so easy. I've never seen a family that made this process so easy. You have been amazing. It has just been great to work with you."

"Thank you." And she walked back out of the room.

"Why would you want his fingerprint?" asked Scott. He couldn't understand that this would be all that we would have of Dalen. It would help to us remember him and carry a part of him with us. He thought it was kind of a freaky thing, but we all reassured him that it would be a comforting thing. The rest of the family then walked back into the room to wait. It seemed that the speaking was a bit louder. It was like we felt that things were going to happen now. It wasn't an excitement but an eagerness to see how things would take place. It was an ending to all the waiting. It was as if we were all getting ready, and so the volume of their voices seemed to increase just by the slightest amount. It wasn't like yelling or anything like that, but the speech was quicker and just a bit more energetic.

I continued to wipe the blood from Dalen's head. I wondered if this part would ever stop but then I realized that when the blood stopped dripping, my son would die.

I have never liked the word *dead*. It was harsh and final. It was an end of no return. It sounded so terminal to me. Instead, I would generally say 'someone passed', or 'they have moved on', or 'their life ended.' I never liked the term *loss* either. "Sorry for your loss." That was like-lost. My son wouldn't be lost. We knew where he would be and what he would be doing. I understood the statement though, as we would be losing time spent with our son. The mortal time period would now be gone. I got it, but I just didn't like the terminology. However, I was thinking and talking about when my son passed and what we would have to do. My son was going to die, and it was the end of his physical life. And it was getting closer to the time that it really was going to happen. We sensed it. We knew it.

Scott came back into the room, he just sat and held Dalen's hand.

The Dreaded Time Arrived

4:27 a.m. As a family, we thought it was needed that everyone got their time to say their goodbyes. We knew that things would be happening very soon. When I was thanking the nurses that were in the hallway, the girls and Brandon went in. I'm not sure if they had individual time or if they kind of were just all together. We didn't know how long everyone would want, but since we had been there all night, we kind of already had our moments. I walked back into his room after what I thought was sufficient time for them. You could visually see heartache. Alyssa was crying pretty hard. Kailee was just staring at Dalen. Mariah was holding on to Alyssa's hand. Brandon was standing behind Alyssa and Mariah with his arms around them both. They were all standing at the foot of his bed, which surprised me. I thought they might like to be next to his face. But it really didn't matter—what mattered was that they had their time.

"Have you all had enough time?" I asked.

"I think so Mom," said Alyssa. So now it was Scott's turn.

"I just can't do this," and again he was flooded by emotions. "How do I say goodbye to my son? How do you say goodbye?" He was holding Dalen's hand and leaning over him. "Bye Buddy", which not only made his tears continue to flow, but was joined in by all of us as we watched a father say goodbye. It was very touching. There were sniffles from everyone. Scott backed out, and it was now my turn. I held his hand and looked at his face. There were a few tears streaming down my cheek. Reality really had sunk in now that this would be the last time I would get to see Dalen in this life. I just wanted to kiss him all over, but couldn't again, because of the condition of his face and the blankets needed to keep his temperature controlled. They would be taking his body away very soon.

"I love you so much Buddy Boy. You're my Buddy Boy! Goodbye Dalen. Goodbye for now!" And I kissed his hand and wiped more blood out of his ear and off his forehead that had puddled since we had returned to the room. "My boy, my boy." There was a shock that ran through my body. Was it possible? Was I really feeling another squeeze from Dalen? I again couldn't deny what I felt. There was for just the slightest of moments; I mean the slightest of movements, a very weak and soft impression on my hand. Dalen knew how much I loved him. He knew how much our family loved him. He now wanted me to know how much he loved me. It was him saying goodbye to me. Again, a calmness overcame me, and I was engulfed with peace. It was as if I was hearing; "l love you Mommy. I love you. I love you."

And then it was time to go.[24]

4:30 a.m. A group of persons started to form in the hallway. They all had scrubs on, so of course we knew they were some of the teams that needed to make arrangements. It was almost an excitement as we had been waiting for so long. There were some brief communications between them. We went out into the hallway and were introduced to most of them. They were all so nice and very respectful to us and our situation. They each mentioned their names and what their duties would be. It was described where they would be in the room and what would happen. After shaking their hands and saying thank you, we sensed that our time to begin this process was very close at hand. Once Dalen had passed, we would need to move out of the way and let them do their jobs. They made sure we understood that and that we were okay with their requests. Of course we were. We wouldn't want to stand in their way by any means. One nurse was so very young looking. She was red headed and had her long hair in braids, which of course made her look younger. It was explained that they would have to switch Dalen to another gurney. Two men

---

[24] Dalen found a way to let his mother know one more time, how much he loved her. There was a movement from his hand while I held his hand. He brought me peace and what an amazing gift he gave me. I knew he loved me. After all this time, and my son was still waiting around for me.

were there for that. One was wearing black scrubs and the other blue. When I looked around, there appeared to be colors for various teams, but again that could have just been my viewpoint. They all had the surgical drapes on with their hair up in a hairnet, and shoes covered as well. This was going to happen.

Our little red-headed nurse explained her duties. She would be the nurse in charge from here on. She would be monitoring how the drugs would act once the plug was pulled to make sure all organs and tissues and whatever else, would be okay. There would be another nurse recording exactly the same thing, so there could be no mistakes.

Another nurse was just to watch the temperature on the blankets while traveling—again to preserve everything properly. There would be a doctor that would shut off the machines and then she would tell us when there was no longer any sign of life. Once that occurred, her job would be done. The teams would take over from there. It seemed that the whole family had, of course, joined in as well as a few more personnel from the teams that had converged. The kids all knew and understood what was going to happen.

We signed the last of the papers stating that we now consented to what would be happening and we relinquished all responsibilities of our son's body to the extraction teams and the hospital. We needed to wait just a bit more for a few more team members, but there were already an extra eight people ready to do their jobs. We met them in front of the nurses' station. I thanked them all again and shook each hand. I knew the seriousness now of all that would take place. I excused myself and went back to Dalen as did the family. We knew that this would be the end of our physical time with our son.

4:35 a.m. LaNae came into the room, "I think we are almost ready. If you are okay, we will do the prepping of the teams for donations. I'm ready to take his prints."

She had construction papers in her hand with also a tube of acrylic black paint. She poured the paint into a bowl and then took a paint brush and painted Dalen's hand with the paint. She was then ready to make a print and asked the colors of paper we would want and how many.

"How many would you like, do you think?" she asked.
"Could we have five of them? I think that would be enough."
"Are you sure that is all you want?"
"Yes, I think that will do and then the fingerprints, right?"
"Yes, I will do them next."

LaNae made the firsthand print. Not the best, but there were others entering the room, so there might have been some pressure to get them done, so it was a bit smudged. I offered to help. The second one was better. The prints were made of his left hand, the one that was a little stiffer to open. We got the right amount of ink on Dalen's hand and as she placed his hand on the sheet of paper, I helped to push down the knuckles and palm to make the print look better. The prints were made. She cleaned up Dalen's hand with some towelettes and tried to get all the paint off. There were a few tiny spots of paint still on his hand which I saw after. The personnel said it wouldn't matter that much, but it mattered to me. I wanted my son to be clean. I cleaned up the rest of the paint. A few more people were in the room. Two nurses were again checking the machines. They asked our family to join them outside for just a minute.

We walked outside of Dalen's room and joined them in the lobby in front of the nurses' station. The head nurse then began to explain what would happen.

"This is _____. She is in charge of the organ transplant team." There were four other persons with her. "This is _____ and she is assisting with the tissue donations with her team members."

So now there were nine other people that would be taking care of Dalen. There was so much information and again they were all very gracious to us. The nurses said the complete team would be there in just a few minutes.

Our family went back into the room. It had been explained to us when they would be standing in the room and what they would each do. One would keep track of the monitor. One was checking on the vitals. One would assist with the transporting. Others were there for the extractions. We met a doctor that would be overseeing the procedures. So, everything was now in place. LaNae was cleaning up her things. Two persons had clipboards to document everything taking place. The pages of prints with Dalen's hands on them were lying around trying to dry. Some of the prints were on the bed, some on the table they have in rooms to set your plates of food on, and one print was on a chair. LaNae still needed to collect the fingerprints and then would have to excuse herself. LaNae and I were both on the left side of Dalen. The nurses all started doing their things. There was a lot of movement in the room. I wanted to say; 'Can you possibly wait a minute so we can get these fingerprints?' as I felt LaNae's stress in trying to get them done, but I didn't say anything, we just kept working to finish them. She got about ten prints altogether.

"I think I have everything I need," she commented.

We finished cleaning up Dalen and gathered LaNae's things. She had the paints there so just a bit more of emotion as we all picked different colors that we wanted and started to then paint our own hands. We each placed our fingerprints on a page where Dalen's print was in the center and all of ours were on the outside of his. That print was for me. It was so cool.

A couple more people came into the room with the gurney to transport Dalen. LaNae was just finishing up. She said she would only be a minute to get things ready for us. She left the room. The family was just finishing cleaning the paint off their hands and the gurney was being pushed to the right side of Dalen. Tubes everywhere. I kind of ended up in the middle of them.

"Is there anything I can do to help?"

"No, I think we have it taken care of," said our red-headed nurse. The two transporters were releasing breaks on the bed and lowering the side rails. Nurses were turning off some of the machines. There were two machines placed between Dalen's legs. One was his vitals, and one was maintaining some of the drugs continuing to be pushed into Dalen.

4:48 a.m. The sides of the blankets were folded up onto the bed and draped on Dalen. Four persons each grabbed corners of the sheets so they could lift and transfer Dalen. Everyone shuffled into positions. So things were all set. Two were on one side of the gurney and two were on the other. One person was at the head of Dalen to pick up the slack when they slid him over. "On my count—ready—3–2–1." And they lifted Dalen and slid him over onto the other gurney. They had to be careful with all the tubes and made sure everything was stabilized. They put everything else where it needed to go. The heating tubes were now powered by a monitor between his legs. The extra gurney was taken out of the room. A quick look let me see the blood pools on the sheets of his bed, but most of the blood was from the head area. We sensed the urgency and knew that our time was very short.

There were now about twelve people in the room besides our family. There was a reverence in the way they spoke. The two team members with clipboards were ready to do all the documentations needed. Everyone was there except an actual doctor. She had stepped out to handle something. Everyone was just kind of standing back and out of our view. They looked at our family who were all standing at the feet of Dalen, and just watched the whole process. I was again at his head, wiping some more blood off.

5:00 a.m. The doctor came into the room. She was a lady with long brown hair. She had a very soft voice and was kind of short in stature. She immediately listened to Dalen's heart with her stethoscope.

"Are you the doctor?" I asked after she backed off from Dalen's chest.

"Yes I am. I'm Dr. _____. I will be here to make sure everything is okay. Are you ready for this?" she asked us cautiously.

How would anyone ever really be ready for what was going to happen? Yet, we were calm and reserved. Our family had now moved out of the way and to the back wall so the rest of the people, including the hospital staff, could be where they needed to be.

I asked: "Can I stay here?" I was holding Dalen's hand.

"Of course," said our nurse. "You are just fine."

"Thank you."

"Just to remind you that once we turn off the machines, it usually takes about five or six minutes for the body to shut down. Everyone in place?" was a question presented to the teams by the doctor. "Okay, here we go." She listened one more time and then reached up and shut the machine off that was sustaining life for our son and brother. Alyssa and I both looked at the clock: **5:02 a.m**.

I returned my eyes towards Dalen. We stood in silence. There were tears from some of the family. I was in a trance looking at Dalen's face. Sniffles were being heard from the back. The two nurses with clipboards would make some kind of marking on their papers every thirty seconds and then about every minute. They were watching his blood pressure to see how far it dropped and how fast. Our son's chest was no longer moving up and down. The oxygen pump was no longer moving up and down. Now nothing was moving on any of the four machines that were in the room. We couldn't see the monitors between Dalen's legs so we couldn't see his blood pressure drop. All activity was now being monitored on the two machines, and they faced the medical personnel instead of the family. I totally understood why, they had to see and verify what was happening, and to protect us.

The room was still silent. They were so respectful of everything. I glanced over to Scott. I wanted to hold his hand too, but I wasn't going to let go of Dalen's. Alyssa was crying. Kailee wiped her eyes. Scott was staring and Mariah was standing as if she was there, but not able to relate to what was happening. Pretty sure she was numb.

5:04 a.m. Everyone was still quiet. We watched in amazement at the natural process as a body lets go of life. I would take a glance around the room every once in a while and looked at the faces in the room. Of course my family was devastated. But the personnel also appeared to be moved by the event. They had very somber expressions on their faces. I saw one nurse wipe a tear from her cheek as well. Heaven was opening its doors. You could sense the enormity of the journey Dalen was taking.

5:05 a.m. The doctor, who had backed up a bit, moved forward again to listen to Dalen's heartbeat. She looked at the monitor but said nothing. If seemed forever from one minute to the next. Again, there was reverence and silence from those present in the room.

5:06 a.m. The doctor moved forward again to listen to Dalen. It had now been just four minutes. She looked over at the monitor and again stepped back.

5:08 a.m. It seemed almost like time stopped and we wanted it to move. We were ready now for Dalen to go. It seemed to be passing so slowly.

"Shouldn't something be happening?" Scott asked.

"Well normally yes, but each person has their own timeline. His pulse is still at sixty-five, so it might take a few more minutes." The doctor explained again the process. That the body starts at one point and realizing that the blood isn't being pushed anymore, it tries to compensate for it. And it keeps trying to make things work. For the blood to flow through the body takes a bit for the pulse to be sensed with all the pathways.

"Of course, it's Dalen," Mariah commented.

"Yup, that would be him," Kailee stated.

The conversations broke through the anxiousness of everyone. It was like we all exhaled for a minute. The tension seemed to be released from the statement.

"It's okay Buddy,—you can go. Let go Bud, it's time to go," I said as I leaned over his head and whispered in his ear. I remained there for just a minute.

5:10 a.m. Again, the doctor listened to Dalen's heart rate. The nurses made their little markings. Our family looked around. Their stances changed as they shifted their weight around a bit.

5:12 a.m. "Come on Dalen, just go." Scott was almost commanding him and making a statement like: "Here we go again—another Dalen moment". This one was so very different though and we wouldn't ever have one again. The family seemed to agree.

"Yeah, Dalen, just go already." Mariah stated.

"It's ok Buddy, you can go." This time I made the statement out loud.

Another motion from the doctor, I guess she had learned that we wanted to know of his state, so she responded: "He is progressing as his heart rate is now at thirty-five. It really shouldn't be too much longer."

You could sense the anxiousness of our family. We were all like—'Okay Dalen we said goodbye, we've waited, it's time and you can go, just go.' We were so ready. We almost needed him to go. It was becoming awkward just standing there and staring at what was happening. He had held on for at least fifteen hours and had surpassed all expectations. The nurses were all still standing with their bodies almost at attention and again were in a silent mode. Their arms were crossed in front of them and most of their heads were bowed. They were so respectful as they honored our son's body. They were so respectful of us and our families' states of mind. I was in awe of their almost humbleness towards this process. It was so amazing to me. The spirit was very powerful in the room. Again, I knew heaven was so close.

"Say hi to my mom Bud. We love you Dalen. We love you."

5:16—FLAT LINE.

The doctor was immediately responding to turn off the machine so we wouldn't hear the sound of the monitor and no life. She listened for a pulse. When she removed her stethoscope, she merely shook her head as if to say, 'Yes—he's gone', without any actual words. No words were expressed by anyone. We knew what it was.

"So do you pronounce him?"

"No we don't." replied the Doctor.

I thought that was a very unique response, but I would again learn why later.

"Okay—so time of death, **5:16 a.m.**" I pronounced him.

We stood literally for just a second. "Mom, it took fourteen minutes—that's Dalen's number." Mariah gave us all the new insight.

"Yup that was his number, his favorite number. His football and volleyball numbers too." Kailee was informing all of us present of some history to the number.[25]

"Bye Bud. Love you," Alyssa said.

I leaned over and kissed his hand. "Oh I love you Dalen," as I offered one more kiss, and this time it was on his forehead. Within seconds, we had all backed away and the teams came into positions. We knew to walk out of the room. We stood all together in a line. Then they wheeled Dalen out of the room and passed us. They were in motion. They moved quickly. We could only watch as within seconds; they were pushing him through the ICU doors.

And he was gone.

---

[25] The staff had never seen a person take so long to pass. Dalen's favorite number 14 was a very significant one and it meant the world to our family to share the same number. We all were in awe.

It's Finally Over

5:18 a.m. We stood in the hallway of the ICU unit on the tenth floor of The Portneuf Hospital and knew our lives were now altered for eternity. Our son had made it. He would be in a happy place and a peaceful state of mind. He would be with loved ones. Now it would be up to us to live our lives in such a way that we could live also with our son, forever. We would have to do all we could to live our lives and be obedient, humble, and righteous in following our Savior as Dalen did. A few nurses that remained behind as they worked the station, asked again if they could do anything else for us. Stacy was no longer there as she had previously announced that she would be assisting with the extraction surgeries. They all were just so kind to us. I had given Stacey my phone number as she said that she would let me know when they were done with everything. I just didn't think that was a normal response to our situation, but it was such a generous gesture. So, we were now conversing with our second nurse and a few others that had joined us.

"Your family has just been amazing through this experience. We have all commented that we haven't ever seen the strength that your family has demonstrated. We wish you all the best through this tough ordeal."

"Oh thank you and thank you for all your service to our son. We really appreciate the amazing care he received."

There was another nurse standing there that I had seen at the desk throughout the night and would express a few phrases of cordial conversation as we passed: "Excuse me, but where is the closest bathroom?" She pointed outside the ICU door and explained that it was just to the left of the lobby.

"How are you holding up. It's been a long night," I enquired of the nurse.

"Yes it has, but we should be asking how you are doing."

"Good thing it was a quiet night, so we got all of your attention." And she would smile.

At this moment, she was standing behind me and was rubbing my back as the procession took place. She then gave me a very big hug.

"I'm sorry for your loss." That was the first of thousands of expressions we would hear about the passing of Dalen.

"Again, let us know if we can do anything for you," she insisted.

"Thank you," and I hugged her again.

Alyssa responded, "You have all been so good to us. Thank you."

Mariah—"Yeah, thank you."

Kailee—"Thanks."

Scott—"We are very grateful to you all. Thank you. Please express our gratitude to the other nurses as well."

We all seemed to glance at one another with the unspoken knowledge that it was time to pack up our things and take care of whatever we needed to. Purses were grabbed. We cleaned up the room that our little family had occupied. LaNae again came out of the conference area with a few more things for us. She explained to us that some pertinent decisions would have to be made pretty quickly. The hospital would only hold Dalen's body for a short time, so we would have to have a mortuary picked out so he could be transferred soon. LaNae handed us the final papers that Dalen had now been taken into surgery. There were a few pages with Mortuary information, some other areas where we would very soon need to focus our attention with some of the decisions that would come quickly into our minds. It was a little guideline of 'what to do next'. We appreciated this very much.

We all had our things. LaNae hugged each of us and presented me with a manila folder that had all the hand and fingerprints in them. What treasures we were just handed. The fingerprints she put into charms for us.

"I don't know how to thank you for everything. I know it was a very long night for you," LaNae commented. "I'm just so thankful for the way you have helped us to help you."

"You have all been so great. Thank you for the dignity and respect you have shown us through this." Scott expressed his gratitude as did the girls and Brandon too. Now it was our turn to walk through the ICU doors and face our new world.

We stopped by the bathrooms to breathe for just a minute and let those that needed to use the facilities take advantage of them. It was kind of a release for us. As we got into the elevator, there were comments made of how kind everyone was to us. That they treated Dalen and us very nicely, and we talked about how tired we should be, but weren't really.

"I think that we will all crash when we get to the hotel."

"I know I will," Mariah said. She had been through so much more than the rest of us. Would we ever really understand what she had to endure? My heart will always ache for her pain, and the pain that I couldn't ever take away from her no matter how much I wish I could.

As we walked out of the doors on the bottom floor, we were flooded again with the heat from the entrance doors. I looked back up at the tenth floor and the lights in the hallway that were visible. Seconds of reflection passed through my mind and what had transpired in a short period of time—altering our lives forever.

Scott got into the driver's seat. He was ready to drive again. Alyssa and Brandon got into their vehicle and said they would follow us. We started to pull away from the hospital's parking lot. We went back up around to the front of the hospital and the road veered to the left. It was done.

What to Do Next

The hotel was literally just down the hill and even on the same street as the hospital, about one quarter of a mile away. It was the building next to the hospital.

"There it is," said Kailee who would always be the first to point out landmarks and even the obvious to the rest of us.

"Wow, that was pretty close." We pulled right in front and parked. I went in to register us.

"Good morning," stated the attendant. "May I help you?"

"Yes, there is supposed to be a room for us. Our son just passed away and someone had made a reservation for us. I'm not sure what name it would be under?"

"Oh yes, we were expecting you. Aren't you the Grahams?"

"Yes we are." I was surprised that she would know about us, but then maybe there weren't that many people whose son passed away recently.

"We have your room ready for you. Two queen-sized beds—right? And we are very sorry for your loss."

"I think so and thank you."

"Everything is set up. If you just go past the lobby and turn right, your room will be on the right-hand side of the hallway not too far down. If you park here (pointing to the map on the counter), it will be by your room and the entrance is right there."

"Thank you so much." I signed the necessary papers and we were finished with our business. I walked outside and explained to the family about our room and where about it was located. We all gathered our suitcases and proceeded to the room.

It was a nice room. It didn't really even matter to us though, because everyone was so exhausted from the experience and we all just wanted a bed. We set things up, putting suitcases in places that would still allow room for Mariah and Kailee to sleep on the floor. Each bed had four pillows, so we were good there. There was a note on the counter from the Bishop who had gotten the room for us. "We hope this helps. Please let us know if we can do anything else for you."

"That was just so very thoughtful."

We read the note while we also were inspecting the amenities in the fridge. There were sandwiches for us and milk to drink. '*Who does that?*' were our thoughts. They were just so kind to us and took care of every need they could.[26] We were very tired but also knew we needed to express our gratitude to our Heavenly Father as well. We all knelt down for family prayer. Then it was time to go to bed.

At that moment though, realizing how tired we all were, no one wanted to eat. All decided that they would eat the sandwiches when they woke up. I said I needed to ask the desk a question and would get more blankets while they all got ready for bed. I went to the main lobby.

"I'm sorry to bother you. I saw that check out time is 11:00 a.m., but would it be possible to have a later checkout? We have been up all night at the hospital where our son just passed away." It was a different person attending to the desk from when we checked in.

'Of course, don't even worry about it. I'm sorry for your loss.' There it was again: "Sorry for your loss". It was a phrase that I would come to acknowledge but would never be my favorite usage of words.

"Thank you. I don't know when my family will wake up, and we have to go to the mortuary and make arrangements. It would just be nice if my family had a place to stay. Would it even be okay if we stayed till maybe one or two? I really don't know how long things will take."

"It should be okay—let me just check."

She was gone for just a quick minute. I looked around the lobby, checking out the décor. It was a usual lobby where there was a rack of

---

[26] The first gesture of amazing kindness was presented in the way of a room to sleep and sandwiches to eat with milk to drink. This was so above anything we could have ever thought of.

pamphlets explaining various points of interest. There was a fireplace with a few couches next to it. I guess they could use it in the winter. I liked the colors of teal and browns they used for accents. It was tiny but nicely decorated. She returned.

"That will be fine. It's not super busy right now so you can take all the time you need. Don't worry about it at all."

"Oh thank you so much. That is very kind of you." And I then asked for a few extra blankets and towels. She mentioned that they would be delivered to our room shortly. I walked back to the room. Everyone was on their phones reading all the messages that were pouring in.

> **Facebook post: Feb. 10 @ 5:35 a. m. "We took Dalen off life support. We had to wait for them to prepare for his body to donate kidneys, liver, tissues, and bone. His life will save another. Love you buddy-boy. Thank you everyone for thoughts, prayers and support. More details to come."**

It only took seconds and we were inundated again with love and support from everywhere and everyone. It amazed me how quickly the word spread. Alyssa started reading her messages. She read a few and then Mariah read some of hers. Scott read some and Kailee joined in too. It was so overwhelming of the outreach we received.[27]

> **I was always uplifted by Dalen's happy fun loving spirit and constant smiling face. I am blessed for his presence in my life. Love and prayers.**

---

[27] We learned very quickly of the intense and proper way the internet can be used. The world was responding to our family and at a very difficult time for us all. We were overwhelmed with support and love. This again was a testimony of the proper way that technology could be used for good. The response really touched us all. It really did give us strength and comfort.

The thoughts and prayers just kept coming. We had to decide to actually stop reading them all for a minute so we could get some rest. I made the family actually turn off their phones. We were overwhelmed with love and truly were engulfed with support.

We all continued to read messages for about 10 minutes. The blankets had been delivered during that time, and I made the beds up for the girls.

> **5:45 a.m Alyssa's post.** "February 10, 2018 @ 5:16 a.m. I said my final goodbye. My brother is my hero and I love him forever.
>
> You will be missed dear bro. Families are forever."

5:48 a.m. Stacey (Dalen's nurse) sent a text message: "Closed and everything went well."

My text-"Thank you again for everything. What was donated?"

Stacey's text—"They did do heart valves. Tissues and bone were not taken before the unit called us back up. IDS should let you know what all ended up being gifted.

They have closed up from the organ donations. They continued with tissue extractions after I left. I was just not able to stay and confirm what they used.

My text—"Thank you again so very much."

> **Mariah's post: 5:54 a.m.** "Dalen passed away February 10, 5:16 a.m."

> **Kailee's post: 5:58 a.m.** "February 10, 2018 5:16 a.m. I said my final goodbye. Age 22. My one and only brother is and will always be my hero and I love you forever. You were a great pal.
>
> He was able to donate his kidneys, livers, cells, bones and tissues. You will be missed dearly brother. Families are forever."

"So, let's have family prayer."

We all knelt down. Scott offered the prayer. He expressed how much love we had for our Heavenly Father and Dalen. He talked about our gratitude for all the support we had been shown, and for the doctors and nurses who had cared so well for Dalen. He expressed our love for all of our family and prayed for peace and comfort and that we would be sustained through this, which we were feeling and felt of immediately. We said amen, hugged and exchanged our love for everyone as we always had with a kiss. The girls didn't like me kissing them so I would always just kiss their cheeks. Dalen never minded kissing his mother.

"We will be getting messages for a while so let's put our phones away and get some very needed sleep," I suggested. We all agreed. Our day was finally over.

"Good night everyone," (even though it was early in the morning). "Know how much I love you."

"Good night Mom, love you too," replied Alyssa.

Kailee and Mariah expressed similar thoughts.

We all positioned ourselves in our beds with the hopes that we would actually get to sleep, and we tried to allow our eyes to close and our bodies to rest just for that purpose. 'Good night' even though it was 6:23 a.m. For the first time, our family would no longer wait for Dalen. Our family would consist of our three girls and Brandon. There was such a huge void. Yet again, we were engulfed with so much love and support. The angels were attending to us. Our God lives and was showing us of His love and mercy for us.

7:14 a.m. President Taylor (Dalen's mission President). How we love you and are praying for you at this most difficult time! Love, Brian Taylor. We love our Elder Graham...as does his Savior, perfectly.

We received calls from our Relief Society President (the women's organization in our church). They were already planning to make arrangements for housing people who would be coming and of course food for whenever we needed it. We were so inspired and humbled of all that was happening because of this event.

8:25 a.m. Of course I didn't sleep much. It was daytime, and there was light even though the curtains blocked out so much of the light. It only took a crack for me and if there was any light, I was up. I knew that everyone needed to sleep, so I tried to be quiet and just lay there for a bit. I knew there wasn't really any place to go, so I just laid there. I didn't want to move too much in case I woke someone else up. I looked again at my messages from Facebook, texts and Instagram posts. I kind of placed my blanket over the light of my phone so the glare wouldn't bother anyone. I was so overcome with gratitude for all the prayers and good wishes. I just laid there for about half an hour before Scott started to move around.

> —Our hearts are broken. Praying you can handle the complex situation.
>
> —Such broken hearts. Forever our hero for saving others. Dalen was such a truly great man. What a pleasure to know him. Loved his strong and unwavering testimony. I am just so sorry. Always here for you.
>
> —I can barely read through the tears. I am so sorry yet know you and the family will find comfort in each other, the Lord, and fond memories of Dalen. Please know I am here for you. Just ask.
>
> —Our hearts are broken for you. Life is so precious! He was a faithful valiant young man. We are so sorry for your loss. Love, prayers and hugs to all of you!!
>
> —I can't even imagine your pain, please if there is anything we can do for your family, please let us help. I'm so deeply sorry for your loss. He is with God now. Rest in Peace you sweet young man.

—Dalen was my son's companion for a couple of transfers. He was an amazing young man! He wrote me a personal email thanking me for my son. But it was I whom was grateful. He taught my son so much. I am so sorry for your loss!

—I wish I could say this to you personally and give you a hug. Although I did not know your son personally, I know he had an extraordinary mother so he had to be pretty incredible. I was also able to feel his testimony and strong spirit through his posts as a missionary that you shared. May your family be blessed with the comfort and strength you need as you go through this most difficult trial. Take comfort in his goodness and the wonderful gift he was to so many right to the end. And thank heaven for the gospel knowledge of eternal families. I love you Sharon.

—You taught Dalen to love the Lord and serve others and he became an amazing young man. We hope you can find peace and comfort during this difficult time. We love you Graham Family!

—I have never met you but am friends with Scott from years ago. My heart is just breaking for you both. But I wanted to tell you that as a mom of a child who received sight from organ donation, I wanted to thank you for your decision. It's so hard for my son to accept that someone had to pass on for him to have a better quality of life. But he is so grateful, every day. Know that even though this is more than anyone should be asked to do it means so much to so many that you would share him to help a stranger live. And it looks and sounds like

he was just an incredible young man. So many will benefit from having parts of his goodness inside of them. Thank you.

Before I had gotten out of bed, I looked through some of the information LaNae had given us. We knew we needed to contact the mortuaries. It was about **8:40 a.m.** Scott and I decided to get going. We would let the kids sleep.

We both knew that we had a lot to do, so he was waking up knowing that we needed to make some appointments especially with the mortuary. I got up first and showered. I knew that Scott wanted to sleep for just a bit more, so I let him. The decisions coming seemed to be big ones, but also what needed to be done. We needed a mortuary but didn't know which mortuary we would be using. While he was showering, I would try to figure out locations and a plan to visit some of them.

Scott usually showered longer than I did. I was getting ready, so I could easily pull my hair back and put on some makeup and would be good to go. That was what we did. While I was in the shower, Scott posted his feelings:

Scott's post-Facebook 8:50 a.m.-My beloved son Dalen Scott Graham passed away at 5:16 this morning from injuries sustained from a car accident. He was loved and admired by his family, friends, and pretty much everyone he came in contact with.

Thank you everyone who has reached out to my family in our time of need. He was 22 years old with a bright future ahead of him. He recently returned from a mission he served for The Church of Jesus Christ of Ladder-Day Saints. He served well and was an ambassador of the Savior."

The kids started stirring as they heard Scott and I get ready. I told them all to go back to sleep. Alyssa was waking up. We were whispering with each other in hopes that the others would get back to sleep. We told her that we were going to go visit the mortuaries.

Scott had finished showering and was getting dressed. I left some money on the counter. "If you guys get hungry before we get back, there is a store just over there (pointing outside and to the left of the room), where you can get something for breakfast. And there are sandwiches in the fridge too."

"Okay, we'll be fine. Do you want us to go with you?"

"No, I don't think you need to. We will see what needs to be done and let you know."

"Okay."

The mortuaries would be open at 10:00 a.m., so we wanted to get there and start the whole process. Alyssa would call us later when everyone woke up and we would be able to let them know more of what we were doing. She agreed and rolled back over.

> **Facebook 9:22 a.m. Kailee's share of a cousin's thoughts. "Feeling so, so sad today. What an unexpected thing. I can't even find the right words really. How grateful we are for eternal life, and the knowledge and comfort of a beautiful life after death. I always admired my cousin for his positivity and love he showed to everyone. He will always be remembered for that, his true love for others and the gospel. What a great legacy and a wonderful guardian angel. Absolutely cannot stop thinking about his family. So much love is being sent to you all right now. So many great, funny memories of childhood playtimes."**

9:40 a.m. From our paperwork it showed where the different mortuaries were located so we wanted to be there early to get things taken care of. We looked over the list and really just guessed at which mortuary we wanted to try. Scott picked a name he liked, and we put the address into the GPS and headed out. It wasn't far, and we were there at **10:02 a.m.** It was open. It was a huge place. As soon as you walked in, you saw what looked like a chapel. It had to have seating for two hundred people. It was very big. Having never been in a mortuary, I didn't know that they would hold services there as well as all the preparations for the funerals. I know when Mom died, we had one of the viewings at the mortuary, but I learned they house the funerals too.

We couldn't find anyone. So, we started walking around. There were several different rooms. One to the immediate right was full with all kinds of coffins. I wasn't quite ready for that yet. It was very weird to think that was why we were there. To put our son's body in a coffin, reality hit for sure. There were displays like at Lowes kitchen area where there were no walls but different angles of displays. We saw plaques, coffin padding, monuments, program displays. It was very pretty and so much more than we had ever thought of. There was track lighting and cherry wood wall enhancers. But we couldn't find anyone.

Scott started to walk a bit behind the display rooms. We found the embalming room. We closed that door quickly. There was an area like a courtyard, and in one room there was a window where we actually saw someone outside. We followed the direction he was going hoping we would meet up with him.

We finally greeted each other. Scott said, "Our son just passed away this morning and we need to take care of things I guess."

"I'm busy for just a minute, but I'll be back with some information. Please excuse me and look around."

We had already spent about ten minutes trying to find someone. So we said 'okay.' and continued to look at caskets. Wow, they were expensive. This whole new world was becoming real very quickly. Prices were now visible, and the reality of this expense and the costs involved were of course, never thought of previously. We waited and waited. Scott was getting frustrated and said, "Let's go. This is ridiculous." I agreed: we started out and got to the steps of the parking lot. The man came out to get us.

"I have time now if you would like to come back in."

Scott said, "It's okay. We just didn't want to wait any longer. Thanks." And we got in the car and left.

"Well that wasn't very good service," was both of our expressions.

"Yeah, let's try one of these other places."

We drove to another address. Scott didn't like the way it looked.

"I remember seeing a sign off the freeway. Let's go find that one."

"Okay, where was it?"

"I saw it when we drove in last night," Scott said.

"Do you know where it was?"

"No, but I think I can find it." It caught his eye and so he thought it looked good, and he remembered where it was. We backtracked from the hospital and went down the freeway and got off on one of the earlier exits. We drove around for just a bit and sure enough, Scott figured out how to get there. We didn't even know the name of the place, but it was right there so we parked and started to go inside. There were quite a few cars in the parking lot. We thought that meant it was a popular place. We learned quickly of another reality. There was a Hurst right by the front door. We thought that was just for advertisement. Wrong again.

We opened the door and stood in the lobby where we heard voices. When we turned to the right—there was a funeral taking place. We felt really bad and definitely were there at the wrong time. I never knew funerals actually took place in a funeral home like I mentioned previously, but here we were in the middle of one. We tried to sneak back a bit when a gentleman came over to great us.

"Hello, would you like to sit down?" and he pointed to the assembly too.

"Oh no, we aren't here for that. Our son passed away this morning and we are here to make arrangements. We didn't know we would be interrupting a funeral. We are sorry."

"I'm so sorry for your loss. I would be happy to help you. Come over here for a minute so we don't interrupt the funeral."

We took a few steps into the hallway.

"I would love to help you. But I obviously can't at this moment. This can't be easy for you and again, I'm sorry, but do you think you would be able to come back at 3:00 p.m.? We have another funeral to take care of, but then we would be able to give you all of our attention. I'm really sorry again that I thought you were here for the other funeral, but we can and would love to help you."

The lobby and halls were painted yellow, a very calming color. It kind of had the appearance of a house built in the 50's, old antique looking pictures and frames with little lights on nightstands and deep cherry wood rails on the staircase and all the picture frames on the walls matched. It was very comforting. There was a guest book to sign that had a dish beside it that had some mints in it. The hallway we stood in led to the bathrooms. It was just very comforting there. We felt good. Scott agreed to coming back as he shook hands with Jared, the owner of Colonial Funeral Home. He introduced us to his beautiful wife, and it was discussed that we would return later today. They were just so cordial even with another funeral in progress. Scott and I both felt that this place was the right place, but that we probably should go as not to do any more disturbances to the other family. I excused myself for a minute and went to the bathroom. Again, I noticed the pictures on the hallway as I walked to the bathroom. They were of peaceful scenery. There were plaques of comforting words like: 'A loved one never leaves you—they just have a different view.' 'The Lord will send his angels to attend you.' It felt right. We again thanked our host and walked back out to the car.

"Do you think that that was normal? It just seemed amazing to me. It was so simple and right," I asked Scott. He concurred.

We started to drive back to the hotel. We talked about what our plans would now have to be for the day. We would go check on the girls and think of breakfast even though it was almost **10:30 a.m.** We needed to go and check on the truck and take out any personal items we could. We wanted to drive by the spot where the accident happened too. We also thought we should take care of Dalen's apartment which meant we knew we would drive to Rexburg today. There was a plan now and a time period. And we had the day to take care of it all.

We needed to start heading back to see if the kids were up yet and get the rest of our day moving. We arrived at the hotel and actually saw the kids out in the street coming back from getting something to eat. They were in the parking lot right in front of the cars, so I knew they didn't go very far, if anywhere at all.

"Hey there, what's up?"

"We were getting hungry, so we were going to look for something to eat," replied Alyssa. Mariah was walking with them.

"Where is Kailee?"

"She is still in the room. She wanted to sleep some more."

"Ok. We have some things that we need to do now so I guess I will go and get her up. Do you need more money for breakfast?" I inquired.

"No, we got it. Thanks Mom."

"Maybe you could get something for all of us, just something light."

"Sure thing," Alyssa said.

We went into the hotel and passed the front desk. They asked how we were doing. It was a different attendee.

"We just got our room about 5:35 this morning. Our son just died and I was wondering if we could get a late check out." I wasn't sure if any of the kids wanted to sleep more, but I wanted to give them the option. I didn't know if they would want to come with us to see the truck, the accident place, and the funeral home.

The clerk said: "Oh yes, I'm sorry about your son. I heard about the accident from the news. You can have the room as long as you need it. It will be fine."

"Thank you so much," and I turned to walk down the hall to our room. Kailee was lying down. We told her that we were going to go see the truck and the accident place and that we thought she should get up as we wanted everyone to be there together. I kind of changed my decision of letting them sleep as I walked back to the room because I thought it would be for the best if we all went.

10:12 a.m. We got word that our niece started a GoFundMe Account.

> **Facebook 10:30 a.m. (13,000 + views)**
> **"It is with deep sadness that I share with everyone a tragedy that has deeply affected the LASDMotorsports family. This morning,**

Sgt. Scott Graham, our organization's founder and president, said goodbye to his son Dalen, who tragically passed away due to injuries sustained in a car accident last night. The Graham family is strong, resilient, and true to their faith. We know the Graham family will endure. Everyone's continued support, prayers, and thoughts through this tragedy I'm sure will provide the family with some comfort and help ease the pain of their loss. Dalen was 22 years old. He was bright, funny lighthearted and full of life. He had his whole life ahead of him. Although Dalen didn't share the same passion of racing as did his dad, he was often there supporting him, helping the team, helping others. Dalen was proud of his dad and thought highly of his dad's racing accomplishments. Everyone who knew Dalen enjoyed his company. He was loved by his family, friends, and those who knew him. We will miss Dalen at the track, at the car shows, at the get-togethers. Although he may no longer be there to join him in body, he will always be there with us in spirit.
Rest well Dalen.
Bob Furman.
LASDMotorsports.
Desert Racing Team.

Alyssa, Brandon and Mariah returned not very long after that. They found doughnuts and milk for us. When they returned, there was a bit of noise with the talking that would make Kailee get up for sure. It was agreed that they all wanted to go with us. So then we waited for them to get ready and ate the little breakfast we had. We still weren't really hungry, but the doughnuts were quite filling.

It took about an hour for everyone to get ready. It was also decided that we would probably check out because we didn't think we really would come back once we left.

Scott received another call from his team members. They were just so worried about him. One asked our plans and if we knew what we were doing.

"Yeah, we are going to look at the accident place, see the truck and get out what we can and then we have a meeting with the funeral home at 3:00 p.m. We also decided that we will head to Rexburg and clean out Dalen's room." There was a pause on Scott's end of the phone as he was listening. "We will probably stay in Rexburg tonight and tomorrow." Again a pause. "No that isn't necessary, no not really." Again, a pause. "That would be wonderful. It's really not necessary, but we would greatly appreciate that. Thank you."

When Scott got off the phone, he said that Glen Walsh (Scott's Lieutenant) wanted to put us up in a hotel in Rexburg and that he would take care of it. He told Scott he would get back to us with the place to stay at and let us know of the reservation. He was very adamant that he did this for us. We were so very humbled. Really we could have taken care of the room, but what an amazing gesture. We all again felt very grateful.

"Wow, that is really cool," Mariah said.

"Yeah, that is way cool," Alyssa replied.

"Another blessing for sure," Kailee added to the conversation.[28]

We continued to pack up our things because it was decided that we would do what we needed to and then head straight to Rexburg. Three and a half hours of sleep after such an emotional event was kind of tough, but we also felt and knew we needed to resolve some things so why not get them done?

Scott again had communicated with the officer that was on the scene at the time of the accident. He knew where the car had been taken, and we were given a time to meet with the man there that towed

---

[28] Glen Walsh had been in contact with Scott from the beginning. He did all the research and found a place for us to stay and for as long as we needed to be there. There was an amazing gesture and very humbling that he wanted to take care of our family in that way.

the truck and could let us into the storage area so we could get whatever we needed out of the truck. The appointment was for **1:00 p.m.**

There of course would be a fee to pay for the towing of the car and also because it was impounded. We didn't know how much, but either way we needed to take care of it. That would give us time to go to the location of the accident first so that was where we were going.

We decided to take one vehicle since we had to come back at 3:00 p.m. to meet Jared at the funeral home. That meant that Mariah would have to sit in the back of our Durango. She was okay with that.

While traveling with our young kids, we always had to assign seats for them because they always fought about who got to sit where. I came up with what I thought was a pretty good solution. During the week, one child would have the 'shotgun' seat the whole week. Since there were four weeks in every month, it worked out really well. That child would get to choose the movie watched for Sunday night popcorn and a movie.

because everyone would get their turn. I was surprised when Mariah volunteered for the back because that was never anyone's favorite place, but since she was the youngest, it kind of made sense too. Actually, Alyssa said she would sit with her too so that was an even bigger surprise, but it also was logical because Brandon was a big guy and needed more leg room. He and Kailee sat in the middle row, and I pulled my seat way forward to make sure Brandon had enough room for his legs.

11:10 a.m. We left the hotel room after I went to the front desk and now explained that we would be checking out. We knew we needed to go to Rexburg and wouldn't know when and if we would return. I thanked them for their kindness though. We loaded up and started out after a family prayer. We usually had a prayer before we travelled, so it was a normal thing for all of us. We started to drive towards Blackfoot to where the accident was. We were getting so many messages again of love and condolences. We also learned through the texts, that Dalen's story was in the papers and also had been on the Utah news. That really surprised us. The accident was in

Idaho so why would Utah show the story? I thought it was so strange since surely Utah would have enough of its own news. We kept getting messages from people we didn't know. The news—how the heck? We didn't have any interviews. How could the news show our story and why in Utah? I understood why Idaho told the story, but I didn't think that it was such a big story to be told in two different states. Maybe because Dalen had only been home from his mission for four months and was a student at a church college. Maybe it was told because of the donor process. Whatever it was, I was surprised. This was amazing. I went on line to try and find the stories. I found one. It was about the accident from the police report.

EAST IDAHO NEWS

Update: California man severely injured in 1-15 crash. Idaho State Police report Mariah Graham, 18, of Los Angeles, California, was driving a white Chevrolet S10 south on Interstate 15 near milepost 92 when she was involved in a crash.

Police reports show Graham drove off of the left shoulder of the road and then returned to the road, where her vehicle began to rotate. Graham suffered minor injuries.

The passenger, Dalen Graham, 22, was severely injured and transported to Portneuf Medical Center via air ambulance. Both occupants were wearing their seat belts.

Original Story: Blackfoot—Idaho State Police are responding to a one-vehicle rollover on southbound interstate 15 exit 93 to Blackfoot. The crash occurred just before 2:30 p.m. Friday.

Where It Happened / The Truck

11:53 a.m. We drove on and were approaching signs showing Blackfoot was getting closer. Mariah seemed okay, but of course I was very worried about her. We were coming into Blackfoot. We thought it would be best if we drove into town on the one exit that we knew of and get some lunch. So, we drove into the McDonalds.

Lunch took about half an hour. While we were there, I received a text from a lady in our ward. She was in Rexburg visiting her children that were going to school there. When she had heard of the accident, she went and put some flowers on the sight. This lady not only knew where the accident occurred, but was thoughtful enough to think of laying flowers down for us. I thought again how kind people were being to us and what incredible efforts of love were being displayed. We were all touched.

We all knew that we needed to get going so we loaded up again in the car and drove down the highway. We were paralyzed at the mile markers. The next exit was #93 and we drove past it to find a place to turn around which was exit #92. Now we were on the right side of the road. You could see Mariah cringe. I didn't know if she would be able to handle this or not. We drove past the '92' mile marker and saw where some things were skewed around. We were all staring at the side of the road. Scott pulled over.

"Are you okay Mariah?" I asked.

"Yeah I'm good."

Alyssa commented: "This is so unreal. I just don't know how to feel.

"Me too," said Kailee. "I guess we'll know when we get there."

"It's right here. I see it." Scott announced.

I could see some pieces of debris at the spot. I was fixed on that spot. I thought how small the embankment looked. How could the truck have rolled five times? There just wasn't enough room. There was no decline on the roadside. It was pretty smooth and flat. The little hill was about fifteen feet from the road, and again didn't look that big. It was hard to imagine the force needed for the truck to roll both head over heels and sideways. We pulled over to the shoulder and came to a stop. We all started unbuckling our seatbelts and opening our doors.

"You don't have to come out Mariah if it's too hard for you." I tried to be sensitive to Mariah's emotional state of mind.

"Yeah, I think I will just stay in the car."

"Okay honey. Do you need me to stay with you or would you be okay if I went out?"

Scott and Alyssa had already vacated the car and were walking over to where the accident happened. Kailee was waiting to see what I was going to do.

"I'm okay—go ahead." Mariah stated.

"Are you sure?"

"Yup—I'm okay. It's just a little too soon."

"Okay, I'll see you in a minute. If you need me, just call me back."

I proceeded to close the door and started walking towards the accident spot. It hadn't even been twenty-four hours yet, and we were asking our daughter to relive again the accident that took her brother's life. This was just overwhelming to think of. I prayed for Mariah to gain the strength she would need to proceed with what we felt was necessary for the rest of us to do today. How could she not be engulfed by everything related to the accident? It had to be playing over and over in her mind. Would she be able to think of anything else? I'm sure she saw again and again and again; the truck rolling, and hearing Dalen yelling to gain control; and feeling herself upside down; and reliving it again. There was a very somber feeling as we all started to look around and see what we could find. Scott found some window stripping right by the road. It was pretty disfigured in shape. I immediately saw the flowers and expressed gratitude again for our friends. They were yellow daisies, again, how sweet. I picked them up and smelled them. It was pretty cold outside. There was frost last night, but the flowers weren't frozen.

Alyssa and Scott were up on the embankment seeing the indents in the ground where the truck would have flipped. They were figuring out what would have happened. We all kind of walked over by them. Before I got there; Mariah had exited the car and was walking back towards us. She only had socks on her feet, so she was walking cautiously. Brandon noticed her and went over to get her. The next thing I saw was Mariah getting a piggy-back ride from Brandon. He brought her over to us and she then looked at the debris from her position near the side of the road.

"I think this would have been where they landed." Scott was pointing on the dirt that had been indented from the impact. "You can see footprints from maybe the people trying to get Dalen out." We knew they couldn't get him out from his door and had to cut him out to pull him from Mariah's side. Dalen's side would have been closest to the road. I looked a bit to the left and saw a gray crate which probably had some of Dalen's supplies in it. I saw a blue cap that I had no idea what it would have been until I kind of made a motion to pick it up and then realized it was Dalen's baseball cap, and it was saturated with blood. Pretty sure he was wearing it backwards, which he always did. That made Scott mad every time. Dalen just liked how it felt, but to Scott it was a sign of the gangs, and he didn't like his son looking like some gangbanger. To Scott, it was wrong. I tried to keep the family away from that spot by pointing out other things, especially for Mariah who was still on the side of the road. Brandon kind of edged himself over, so he could look at the area as well. Mariah wasn't wanting to get down. I called Scott over.

"Scott come here. Look what I found."

"What is it?" he asked.

"It's Dalen's ball cap."

I then pointed to the ground and where it was laying. It almost looked like it had been there for a while just because it kind of blended in with the ground. In reality, it was because Dalen's cap was saturated with blood that actually stuck it to the ground after the freezing temperature during the night. It had been twenty-two hours since the accident and the blood had not only dried but maybe froze a bit during the night. Either way, we had to tug a bit to get the cap loose. Scott released a big sigh of unbelief. Alyssa came over and looked. She never likes anything to do with blood, or hospitals or the smell of sick people. I was surprised when it appeared that she was the one searching through everything. She needed to get all the pieces together that she could. She scoured the area for anything she could find. There was a toothbrush. Some wrappers of some candy were off to the right a bit. Kailee was pretty quiet, but also had a need to search for a few more items. Someone had picked up their suitcases and the emergency backpack that were in the truck at the accident. Didn't know where any of that ended up. There wasn't much left there. Kailee found a sock. I found another blood stain on the ground—I made sure that my evidence again wasn't visible to Mariah. I took a look to the right. She was hiding her head in the back of Brandon who was still carrying her and staying kind of back a bit.

I knew Mariah was rehearsing all that she had gone through. What was said between her and Dalen? How could she not feel responsible? And how could I take any of those feelings away from her? Then I saw her motion to get down, and she was walking around just a bit.

"You okay sweetie?"

"Just pretty real." There was a big sigh from Mariah.

"I know. I'm so sorry. So where were you when they got Dalen out?" I asked with hesitation in my voice.

"I was over here I think." She walked up to the embankment area where Alyssa was investigating the spot. "They wouldn't let me see him. There were about four cars pulled over here (pointing to the road) and I was over here (pointing to a spot to the left of us)."

"Where did you find the phone?"

"Um…it was closer to the road. I got out and looked for a phone, so it wasn't too far away." She walked off a bit.

I realized that the blood spot where Dalen's cap was, was where they laid Dalen once they pulled him out. It would later come to my understanding that that was also the spot where they would try to resuscitate him. That was where they lifted him onto the gurney and moved him again into the ambulance. There was a lot of blood in that area. Mariah said all along that he was bleeding mostly from his head and that there was a lot of blood-my son's blood. I wondered if he had any understanding or feelings of any of the accident. We all continued to walk around each with our own little space. Mariah was now very quiet again. Brandon had united back with Alyssa. There was a very slight breeze blowing. It wasn't freezing, but there was coolness to the air. I found a gum wrapper and some soap pieces. There were a few pieces of toilet paper too. That seemed weird to me, but I guess Dalen wanted to be prepared. I again walked over to the flowers and picked them up to smell them again. I laid them back down again as the memorial marker.

We had been there for about ten minutes and even though it wasn't really cold outside, it was cool.

"I'm getting cold so I'm going back," Mariah said. She wasn't wearing a coat or shoes.

The rest of us weren't quite used to the weather temperature being from California and Vegas. We all had our coats on and seemed to be okay.

"Me too," said Kailee.

Alyssa was still looking around. Brandon was just waiting by the side of the road. I was just watching. We weren't going to rush anyone. If they needed to stay longer, we would.

"I think I've seen enough," replied Scott. He had pretty much analyzed the whole area and had come to his conclusions from all of the evidence from his investigation as to what happened.

I just walked slowly around the area looking here and there, picking up some trash. I walked over to Alyssa. I took a few pictures as did the girls. These pictures would forever show the altering event of our lives.

"This is pretty unreal to see. Are you okay Alyssa?"

"I think so Mom. I just wanted to find something of Dalen's."

"Well, it's pretty cleaned up. Sorry sweety. Are you about ready to go?"

"Yeah, I think so." I started walking back with Alyssa when Brandon joined us and grabbed Alyssa's hand as they continued to walk back to the car together.

We had all made our way to the car and were warming up. Our conversations were reviewing our findings and our thoughts. Scott took a moment before he decided to drive away. We all just stared at the spot. I didn't want to leave, but I didn't want to stay. It was time though, to move on, so we did.

12:40 p.m. Scott had the phone number of the man that towed away the truck. Scott called him to tell him we would be there in about ten minutes. He said he would meet us there and gave us the address.

It wasn't that far away from the accident to where the truck was, so we knew we could take our time. We drove into Blackfoot. I only knew where one exit was and that exit had the Wal-Mart and the Howard Johnson Hotel off it, as we had stayed there once when we were too tired to keep driving on one of our trips up to Canada, and of course the McDonalds too.

It was time to go and find this wreck yard. We drove around for a bit. Scott thought he had the right place but couldn't see any vehicles on the lot. We drove on but were going slow as we were assessing our whereabouts. I pointed out a fenced in place with vehicles in it. Scott drove to it. We were all looking.

"There it is," I said as I pointed to the truck.

"Where?" asked Scott.

"That white truck on the last row."

"I don't think that's it." Scott commented.

"Yeah it is."

We pulled over parallel to the chain link fence. We got out of the car and stood looking on. We walked around the corner of the fence to look at the truck head on. Could this really be our truck? Tires were flattened or not even on the truck. The roof was crushed in. The whole thing looked tilted. All the bumpers and tailgate were thrown into the back of the truck. It was a bit freaky to see. Mariah was just staring at the truck.

It was only a few minutes before this man appeared. He was actually a little abrasive as he mentioned that he didn't like to come on Saturday. We apologized. He also stated that he usually only gave a few days for people to get their stuff and that after a certain time they would be too late. Well, we knew we would probably be in Rexburg for a couple of days, so we had to get our things out now. We thanked him again for letting us look through the truck and get whatever we could find. We drove over to the truck. We all got out and immediately started checking things out.

First close view let us see Mariah's side. The bumpers were ripped off. There were scratches along the side of the vehicle where the truck had skidded on its roof. One back wheel was totally crocked like the axle was twisted. Two tires weren't even there. We looked in the windows that were smashed out. You could see glass everywhere. Scott started looking inside. He checked the seats, the dash and the floor. The rest of us kind of walked around to the front of the truck. When you looked at the roof, it was slanted. Mariah's side was fine. Dalen's was completely crushed in. We could see how he was crushed instantly. I walked around to his side and looked at the door. You could see how something was dragged across the window as the blood was scrapped along. It was over the top near the door frame of the window. I didn't want the girls to see it, so I tried to stand in the view when someone was on that side.

We could reach in, and we tried to find things. I saw Dalen's pillow and backpack. His pillow was turquoise blue, so it was pretty visible. But it was way jammed in there. We tried to move the seat a bit so we could get the items out. We pulled pretty hard. Scott was with me and he was trying to move the seat more, so I could move things around. The backpack came out. I started again to grab the pillow and everyone said we didn't need it. When you looked in the passenger window, which of course was shattered out, you could see how easily it would have been for Dalen's head to hit the roof. There wasn't much room. He was 6'2 with maybe an inch of space above his head. There was glass everywhere. We opened the glove box that was cracked through, and pulled out whatever was there, insurance papers and the manual for the vehicle. Scott had just spent so much on this truck to spoof it up for Mariah, to make it the best he could and that meant it had to look good too. It was her Christmas present. We had put on new tires, new stereo, new suspension. BJ didn't like the bumpers, so he just whipped something up in his shop. BJ was Scott's engine builder and could fabricate almost anything. So, the truck looked so cool. Both bumpers were sitting in the bed of the truck and weren't too badly damaged as they flew off with the first roll. One was bent but not too bad.

Alyssa found a part of Dalen's shirt under some of the rubble in the back. It was Dalen's favorite sweat like hoodie. He wore it everywhere. It was in the last pictures we have of him when we took him up for school after his friend's wedding that we all went to in Bountiful, Utah. It was short sleeved, but he wore it all the time. I so wanted that hoodie. It was in pieces. They had to cut Dalen out of the truck and cut off his shirts so that they could put the heart paddles on his chest when they had to shock him. There was just a strip of material now. Not quite sure what happened to the rest of his shirt, though. Alyssa picked it up. I don't know what happened to it after that. Brandon was inspecting things over and trying to dig through the stuff in the bed.

We all walked around again. It was just so freaky to think what Mariah was doing during the crash and now what she would be going through seeing the truck. This poor girl. She was just so amazing through this ordeal.

"Can I take this?" Alyssa asked while holding up the remnant of material.

"Of course," said the man. "You can take whatever you want."

I even made the comment that it was too bad we couldn't take the bumper back. We didn't try to get the stereo, which was brand new. We didn't take anything out of the truck. BJ could have fixed whatever we took and found a place for them on another vehicle. It wasn't until a few days later that Scott wished we had taken out the stereo since it was a really nice one. There wasn't much else to look through. There were scraps of metal in the back. There were all kinds of car parts. It was so unreal. Mariah at this time went over to the driver's side and just stood there for a minute. You just knew that her flashbacks were flooding her memory. The front window was hardly even cracked on her side. You could see where Dalen's head hit on his side. We asked Mariah if she was awake through the ordeal or if she blacked out at any point.

"No, I was awake the whole time. It was like slow-motion though. Dalen was yelling at me to get control and then I remember him throwing his hand in front of my chest and pushed me back as we started to roll."

I held my chest as she started to describe what had happened. It sounded like my son was trying to save his sister from whatever he could.

"I remembered feeling the truck roll and then it rolled again. I could see us rolling. When we finally stopped, I tried to figure out what happened. I asked Dalen if he was okay, and I kept yelling his name. He didn't respond, I knew I needed to get out of the truck. I struggled to get out. I ended up crawling out."

We were all standing around her by now. Alyssa went to hug her, but Mariah pulled away.

"This is horrible, can we leave yet?"

"Yes we can. Anyone else need more time?" Scott asked.

We were all very aware how real this was for Mariah, and we were very sensitive to her. We all took our last pictures and started to walk back to the car. The man reminded us again about getting everything we wanted because they would be taking the vehicle to the salvage yard on Monday, and they wouldn't let us come back. We suggested again that we had everything we wanted to take. We thanked the gentleman again for opening the gate for us. Scott extended his hand and shook the man's hand. We loaded up into the car.

"Wow, that is amazing how you walked away Mariah. I just can't believe you weren't hurt more," I stated.

"Yeah, me too."

"You could so see how you were protected," Alyssa commented.

"Yes, but why? Why was I spared?" Mariah questioned.

"It wasn't your time Mariah," Scott said.

"But why was it Dalen's?" she asked.

We couldn't answer that. Scott started the Durango and we headed back to Pocatello to find the funeral home. We were all pretty quiet on the way back. Someone would make a comment just to try and change the mood. Of course the radio was on, and that helped to ease the situation a bit too.

"I'm okay," Mariah kept reassuring us all, that she was okay. I believed her. She has always been a strong girl. The whole family was handling all of this so very well. We weren't hysterical at any time. It was so devastating though to see that truck. It really crushed my heart. Yet again; so profoundly grateful that the life of our daughter had been preserved. God's plan wasn't completely understood, but after seeing the truck, there was a very definite purpose for Mariah to accomplish. She was protected. Her life was spared, and she would learn of the reason why. Dalen was crushed instantly. I could see how he wouldn't have felt much. I wasn't quite sure how his chin was crushed. The headrest caved in on Dalen's head. In flipping, he would have been jerked around pretty good. The whole body of the truck was twisted.[29]

We knew instantly as we did in the hospital, that it would now be our calling to testify to everyone of God's power, to see the reason that Mariah was meant to live, that she literally only had a very little bruise on her eye and a sore shoulder. We all knew it instantly, that as sad as Dalen's passing was, we knew of the atonement and would now testify of the life after death with all that needed to hear of our witnesses. Seeing the truck made it very apparent that God was in control from here on and had been.

As we drove back, Mariah was talking and made mention that Dalen held her back. She repeated it again and again. "Just before we started to roll, I remember Dalen throwing his arm in front of me and pushed me back."

"He was trying to save you Mariah."

"I think so, but why would he do that and not save himself Mom, why?"

There were questions that we just couldn't answer again. But there was a stronger presence of what happened. Some tears rolled down my cheek again as I pictured my son trying to protect his sister. It took about half an hour to drive back to Pocatello. Scott knew exactly where the exit was and where he saw the billboard of the funeral home. It actually seemed pretty easy. We got off the highway and turned a corner and then saw the facility. We drove into the parking lot. This time, it was almost empty.

---

[29] Mariah shouldn't have walked away from the accident. She should have had more injuries. There wasn't much logical sense as to her not being hurt more. We had to rely on the evidence that God had protected her and preserved her live, that she had more to do.

> Facebook 2:35 p.m. Ali and Jordyn Jepperson—"Graham family, we can't imagine what you are going through at this time and hoped this would be a way to help relieve some stress. We love you guys. Gofundme/DalenGraham."

That was such an overwhelming idea of our niece. We were so amazed how quickly the funds started coming in. About every hour Alyssa would update us on the amount. We were blown away by the generosity of others. We were more than blessed. There was $600.00 within the first hour of posting. We were just so blown away.[30]

> Facebook 2:45 p.m. Alyssa—"Everyone keeps asking what they can do. My cousin set this up and I just wanted to share. Thank you all for the love and support."

> Kailee's post—"Cousin started this in way of support to the family. Thanks-for all the love, calls, posts, messages etc, and support in this time. If you want to help, you can just keep the prayers going."

> My post—"My niece wanted to help and didn't know what to do so she set this up. What a sweetie. We aren't asking for anything, but it's her way of trying to help.'

---

[30] A GoFundMe account was set up by our niece Ali and Jordan Jepperson. So honored and blessed.

The Funeral Home and Making Arrangements

2:52 p.m. Sitting in the parking lot, we again asked everyone if they wanted to go in and that it might take a while, so it would probably be the best choice. They all had agreed anyways that they wanted to be a part of this.

We walked into the door and were immediately met by Jared, the owner. He was probably 6'4 or 6'3. He was a big guy. His wife came out to introduce herself to us as well. After the introductions, the family was escorted into their conference room, and we were all asked to take a seat.

"Does anyone need anything before we get started?" Jared explained that as sad as this process was; that it could be a very peaceful experience and he would be there to walk us through the whole process. He opened a drawer and pulled out a packet of information that would help us understand what was to take place.

"So to start, you need to first understand that we will contact the hospital and have your son delivered here, but that is only if you choose to use our facility. You do need to decide though because they won't hold his body for long. They usually only keep the bodies for a day or two."

"I think we agreed after we met you this morning, that we would be very grateful if you could help us with our son's funeral." Scott commented.

"Okay—so we will make the arrangements. Some things that you will need to think about; what papers would you like to have the obituary in and what cities they are in."

"Oh, I never thought of that."

"You don't have to do anything right now. We will go through everything, and you can make decisions later."

Jared started first, of course, with different options. There were the platinum, gold and silver options. There were like six different plans to choose from. It meant the padding was thicker, the coffin was more ornate, the coffin was made of a heavier wood, the package included the program print out, guest books, and thank you cards. It would be based on the amount of money that we were willing to spend. We automatically went with the just about the middle range. We never discussed how we were going to pay for anything; it wasn't even an issue. We were going to have what we wanted and would take care of whatever we needed to later. For now, it was to choose which plan we liked and go with it.

We spent about an hour and a half with Jared. We talked about what kind of program we would like. We needed to figure out a program and get it to Colonial (the name of the funeral home), so they could fill in the spaces on their template and we could get the programs printed. He asked if we had any pictures of Dalen. We all started looking through our phones and tried to pick the ones we liked best of Dalen so we could give them to Jared before we left. Several options came up and we all had our favorites, but when we thought of which ones would look best on the program, we were able to get our suggestions down to a minimum. We could have pictures on just one side or both sides of the program. We chose both sides.

Jared gave us an outline that we could use as a guide to help with talks from whom and when; musicals if any; and where and when and and and and. We immediately gave suggestions as to what we all would like for the program, and I started making notes. Our suggestions made it sound like it would be a nice program. It wasn't getting exciting, but a lot more uplifting to talk about what we wanted in the program. We would get to share our testimonies with so many nonmembers that we knew would be there. Jared asked what Dalen would be buried in.

As members of The Church of Jesus Christ of Latter-Day Saints, we are buried in white clothes we wear in our temples. We knew Dalen would be dressed and buried in his temple clothes. Dalen's white pants were the ones he used on his mission. Missionaries are dressed in white when they would perform baptisms for someone—to represent purity. We also knew that we would be going to Rexburg to clean out Dalen's room, so we would be able to get Dalen's temple clothes as he had them with him up at school. We would be able to drop them off to Jared on our way home. Jared was a member of our church too. That was comforting as it wouldn't be an issue for him to dress Dalen in his temple clothes. That was just another blessing and was very calming for sure.[31]

"That would be great and help us out a lot. We have clothes here if you need them."

"No, I think we would like him buried in his own temple clothes. He loved the temple and rejoiced in the knowledge that he could go. The temple meant a lot to Dalen."

"Okay, that will work out for us then," Jared stated.

"I really think this picture needs to be on the front cover," Alyssa suggested. She had been looking the whole time for the one particular picture that she liked. It wasn't my favorite at all, but the family all agreed so it was fine. It was one she found of Dalen's head. It was just of his head. I thought the eyes were a bit squinting, but again the family liked it and so, it didn't matter if we used the picture. Another decision made.

Jared asked us about who would preside at the funeral. We needed to figure out when to have it and where. We needed to think about whom we wanted to speak and if there would be any musical numbers. We needed to think if we wanted a viewing or not.

The casket would be closed of course because of the extractions taken from Dalen. But the viewing would be to greet the family. We needed to think about transporting Dalen and where we wanted to bury him. Of course, I instantly started planning things out. There would have to be some discussions from the family as well, and their views of course were important.

---

[31] With Jared being a member of our church, there was no issue with dressing Dalen for the coffin. Jared would respect the clothing as we would hope for. What a comfort.

Jared spoke about the burial. Again, we really had no thought of the 'where' before. Jared explained that Dalen would have to cross five state lines: from Idaho, Utah, Arizona, Nevada and California. Each state had their own requirements, and it would be very expensive to cross them. He explained that he would have to check out the California requirements for us and would let us know. At first, it just seemed normal that we would have Dalen buried in "Eternal Valley" in Santa Clarita by our house. That thought was really only for a second though.

"Scott, why don't we bury Dalen in St. George. That way he would be where we will eventually live and we could go see him there."

"That's a really good idea." Scott said.

"That makes sense Mom," Kailee said.

"I like it," Alyssa replied.

So, the first decision of Dalen's funeral had been made. We knew the where. Dalen would be buried in Washington County Utah. Jared liked the idea too. It would be easier for him as well.

"Well, that will be a lot easier," was Jared's insight.

We talked about having a coffin in California. I wanted people to have something to say goodbye to. I had been to funerals before without a casket and there was just a hole. I didn't want that to be. I didn't want people to think he was cremated which I strongly disagreed with even when family members have expressed that as their finial wishes. So that was also a thought that we needed to process. Scott wanted a casket too. I think we all did.

We needed to change the mood for a minute. Jared asked if we would like to see the coffins now. We all said yes and began to push our chairs back to get up.

Unlike the other funeral home, the cassettes were in the back—not just in the open. I liked that better. It made it more sacred. It was a very weird sensation though walking in the room. It wasn't like the excitement of a candy store for a child, but there was a bit of wonder as to what we would pick. There were some really expensive coffins. Jared explained about the thickness of the padding and the different woods used. We all just looked around. But then it was the 'ahha' moment. There was this gray-blue cassette. It was perfect. Not super fancy but classy.

"I like that one," as I pointed to the back left of the room. It was mounted on the wall.

"Oh, that looks nice," Alyssa responded.

Kailee was pointing to a different one. "How about this one? I like all the padding on the head."

"I don't really like that color Kailee." Scott said. It was almost a red color. It was pretty dark and heavy.

Brandon commented: "The blue one looks more like Dalen," and that was it. The coffin had been decided on. That fast and that was it—we decided on a coffin. It literally took us about six minutes. We didn't discuss the cost, the padding, the extras, because we didn't need anything else.

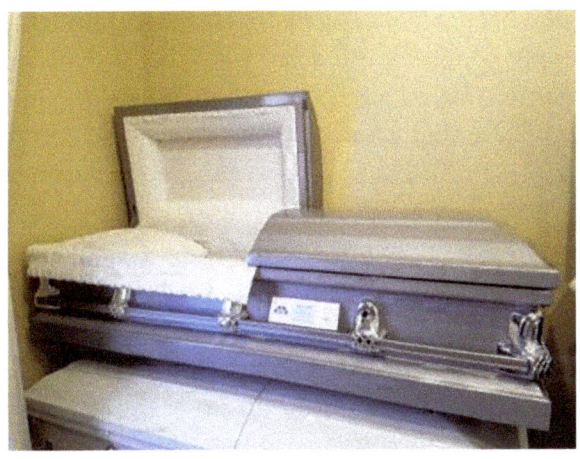

"Well, that was done quickly," Jared commented. "I don't think I've ever seen a coffin chosen that quickly where everyone liked it. Nicely done. This is a good one. It's about in the middle of our price range, but its padding is very nice, and I think you will be very happy with your choice. How easy was that?" Jared even sounded surprised in his voice from our decision and how quickly the coffin was selected.

"Yeah, that was pretty easy," Scott replied. Don't think that has ever happened with our family before that we all agreed on something that quickly."

There was a room off to the right of us.

"What's in that room?' I asked.

"That's where the embalming tales place and where we prepare the bodies to be put into the coffins. Would you like to see it?" asked Jared.

"Yes, I would."

"No mom, we don't need to go in there." Alyssa was adamant that we didn't go in the room.

I wanted to know how they prepared a body. I wanted to see the tools they used. It seemed fascinating to me. Jared explained it as almost a sacred thing. He always felt like heaven was right there. He mentioned that his job was to prepare that person for when they would be received into heaven when the resurrection would come. That was a very comforting thought. It still didn't take away my curiosity though.

The resurrection, to members of our church, is a joyous event. We strongly believe that when a person dies; as the scriptures state; they go to a place called the spirit world. We are with loved ones. This is a probationary state. All will be taught the gospel of Jesus Christ and will have the option to accept the gospel or not. We will remain in this state until Christ comes to the earth again. At that time, the graves will be opened and the bodies will reunite with their spirits. We will then change our physical state and we will be reunited with our bodies in a perfect form of immortality and will then live forever. Our bodies and spirits will be together forever. Our bodies will function perfectly. We won't have disabilities of any kind or health issues or any form of infirmities. It means God's promises to his children will be fulfilled, and we will have the chance to live with Heavenly Father and our families together forever. That is one of the ordinances we perform in the temples—we are married not just for time, but for all eternity. Death doesn't separate us. And God won't have any issues of putting our bodies together after deterioration from death. So, Dalen will be dressed in white, the symbol of purity and worthiness. He will be dressed for the resurrection.

We walked back to the table and sat down again.

"Since you will be coming in a few days, we will settle everything then. I have your pictures and kind of know what you want for the program. I'll have my wife start with the outline. If you can just get me the information as soon as possible, that would be great." Jared continued to explain the process to us.

"If you need them before Monday, I can email it all to you," I stated.

"No, Monday will be okay."

"Okay, I will have everything ready for you by then."

"So, what else do we need to go over right now?" Scott asked.

"I think we are good. You have all the information and we have made some of the important decisions, so I think we are on a good track. What else can I do for you guys?" asked Jared.

"Are you kidding, you have been amazing. How can we thank you?"

We had discussed about guest books and how many I would need. I asked for four—one at each door when people came in. We talked about thank you notes and what we would like them to say and that we would need a lot. Of course, I was very willing to pay for the added ones. We talked about the newspaper articles and where we would like them published. It was just so amazing. We had been there for an hour and a half. It was an hour of information, decision making and comfort. It was a very sweet experience. We were just so grateful again for the incredible manner that Jared walked us through a very tough situation. How blessed we all felt again. It was as if we all left uplifted. That probably wasn't a normal reaction to planning out a funeral. But we felt really calm and good about the decisions we had made. We all expressed our thanks and each shook hands or hugged to say our goodbyes. When we walked out, we were all in amazement as to what had just happened. There was no way that God wasn't guiding us along this path. We were meant to be with Jared and his wife, and they were meant to be our coordinators.[32]

---

[32] I have never heard of a funeral planning as being a sweet experience, but this was. We were all together with our thoughts, Jared was more than amazing and we had complete peace.

"Is it supposed to be that easy?" Alyssa asked.

"It just seemed almost natural," Scott said. "They made it very easy for us, that's for sure."

"I think it helped that we could make a few decisions and not just leave things up in the air either. It was like we helped them by answering their questions and making decisions to help them get things moving along. It really was an incredible experience." In the car, everyone talked about how good they felt.

We knew that we had to get Alyssa and Brandon's truck that we had left at the hotel and then we would drive to Rexburg to further our arrangements for the day. The whole way back to the hotel, there was constant positive conversations. It was amazing.

> **Facebook 3:30 p.m. Mariah's post** (while we were planning the funeral, she had a few moments by herself) **"I am lucky. I am lucky my brother, my best friend, my favorite man, was protecting me and ultimately gave himself up for me. This is not easy and will probably be the hardest thing I will ever go through. But Dalen died a hero. He was already my hero but today he became a hero known to the world when he donated his body to save others. I will continue to live my best life with my brother always in my heart. He will continue to be my best friend. With every thought, and action, I will do my best to please not only Dalen but God. Thank you for all the prayers and thoughts."**

We immediately started talking about when we should have the funeral. We knew it needed to be on a weekend to allow family travel time, especially my family that would be coming from Canada. We decided together that the funeral would be the next Saturday, the seventeenth of February. Now we needed to get a place first and then we could get the word out and make the necessary arrangements. So of course, within the church, if there is an issue that needs attention from the church, it goes through our Bishop.

"Hello Bishop. How are you?" I asked.

"I'm good. But the question is, how are you guys doing? I was meaning to call you but didn't want to bother you. Are there any plans made yet?"

"Actually, yes. We literally just decided that we would like to have the funeral next Saturday. The issue is that our building isn't big enough. So, I guess the Stake Center would be the best place. Would you be able to check on that for us?"

"Of course. Is there a time you are thinking of?"

"Probably the viewing from 9–10:45 a.m., with the funeral at 11:00 a.m. We think that will work out. Can you let us know if that is possible?"

I happened to know that for funerals, they usually have precedence over other issues that take place in our buildings. These buildings are big and usually can house one thousand persons plus, when necessary. We weren't thinking in any way, that there would be that many, but that there would be a lot of people there. So, we would wait a bit for the Bishop to make his calls and see if he could get the necessary arrangement done.

4:15 p.m. We got back into the car. Our day would go along much in the same way; messages, reading them out loud and gratitude that just kept increasing. It was very humbling. We were hearing from family, friends of mine and Scott's, and our kids. We heard from mission associates of Dalen's. Friends of our girls would write on my posts and people I didn't even know were sending messages as they mentioned that they had heard of our story on the news and in the newspaper and felt they needed to send us their thoughts.

I would later contact all the news media that covered Dalen's story to get a copy of their articles. We weren't just in the newspapers but also on the news. We all took turns reading whatever messages we received or articles that had been broadcasted. The girls were able to pull up the articles on their phones for me to see. I was like: "How the heck do they get all this information? None of us were interviewed." It all came from our posts. In some way that was amazing how quickly the information was received around the area and even the world. We got messages from literally people all over the world. Scott's brother mentioned that he even saw something about Dalen's accident and he lived in Chicago. 'There was no way'—we all thought, but it was true. Dalen's story of passing was heard in Chicago by Scott's brother. That so surprised us. We weren't sure how he heard of Dalen's accident, but he had.

Idaho State Journal

LDS—Living
ISJ
Colonial Funeral Home Newsletter

All stated something similar to:

"Dalen Graham, a BYU-Idaho student, died Saturday morning, Feb 10, due to a car crash that took place Friday on I-15. Their car veered off the freeway, then returned where it began spinning and rolling. The vehicle overturned and came to rest on its roof off of the right side of the road. After being cared for in the ICU at Portneuf Medical Center, Graham's family decided to take him off life support on Saturday. His sister Mariah only sustained minor injuries. "We had to wait for them to prepare for his body to donate kidney, liver, tissue and bone. His life will save another. Love you buddy boy," replied Dalen's mother. The 22 year old recently returned missionary from California was in the passenger seat while his 18 year-old sister, Mariah Graham, was at the wheel near milepost 92 in Blackfoot. "Dalen was a true disciple of Christ. He carried the

light of Christ where he went and everyone could feel his love for them as well as God's love through him. He would always tell me how much he loves me and wants me to be happy. Chloe, his girlfriend, reported. Both Dalen and Mariah were wearing their seat belts when the crash occurred. The 15 interstate was temporary closed.

Wait—"Whose Chloe?" a question that would later affect dramatically, our lives.

Messages That Altered Our Lives

4:25 p.m. The messages continued throughout the day. There was one in particular that made me cry the minute I read it. This was one of the reasons Dalen wanted to donate whatever he could—that someone else's life could be better. How we hoped for that to be the outcome.

> **Sylvia McKee—"I am so sorry and heartbroken for your great loss at this time. Right now I am sitting in the hospital room at IMC in Murray Utah and my son, who has been on dialysis for five and a half years, is about to receive a kidney transplant that will give him a new life. May you find comfort in knowing that your selfless decision to donate is bringing life, hope, and joy to many others. One of those could be my son.**
>
> **I pray you all will be blessed for your great selfless gift of life to others and find that peace that passes all understanding in your time of deep grief."**

I responded immediately: "Oh my gosh, thank you so very much. We will be praying for your son as well. I know my son's organs went into the valley. Wouldn't that be something if your son received my son's kidney?"

"That would be more than amazing. My son's last name is Graham also. I will IM you

later. We were asking who the donor was. They told us we could go through the social worker, but that they couldn't tell us who the donor was."

This woman instantly was connected to me. I wondered how she had heard about Dalen. Through a text message, she said that she saw our story on the news.

4:30 p. m. Brandon and Alyssa got into their car and they were going to follow us into Rexburg. We were about forty-five minutes away. The miles didn't seem too bad this time, maybe because we were all together and the messages were just so amazing, or maybe just because we had a different mindset.

The whole drive I was looking through the packet Jared gave me as we were starting to make arrangements. Scott was driving now so I could go through all the information that we had received. It didn't seem long to get a small outline for the funeral. There was talk of where to have it. We knew that we would need a big place. Our stake center would probably be ok. So, I called our bishop again to see if he had heard anything yet. He would have to get back to me with the information. He still hadn't heard anything. We had decided on the prayers and that the girls would all talk about their memories. Alyssa was on the speaker phone to help with the decisions as well.

I had another thought of something that we also needed to do and that was take care of Dalen's housing; I called his housing complex to ask if we could come clean out his apartment. I had to look up the apartment name on google to get the number; but I knew the name of the complex and the hours that the manager would be in the office. I made the call. They were so gracious to us.

"Hello. My name is Sister Graham and my son lived in your complex."

"Oh my gosh, Sister Graham, we are just devastated about your son. What can we do? How can we help you? We are just so sad at what happened," she responded. It sounded like she was a bit in shock and having a difficult time expressing herself.

"We were wondering if we could come and clean out Dalen's apartment. We will be in town taking care of his school things. It would just be easier for us to take care of this now than to have to come back in the near future. Would that be a possibility?"

"Of Course! How can we help? What can we do for you?"

"Nothing, we are good. We just want to get his things. We think we'll be up there around 7:00 p.m. tonight. Would that be okay?'"

"Oh my gosh, of course. I will have the guys out of the apartment so you can have your own time."

"Seriously that won't be necessary. We will be fine. It shouldn't take us long to clean things out. It really will be fine. We won't mind if the boys are there. I would actually like to see them."

"If that's what you want. We just want to make this as easy as we can for you."

"Thank you so very much. It's so kind of you."

"We are so sorry for all of this that you have to go through," she commented.

"Thank you again. I guess we will see you later."

Everything was just so natural. It seemed normal. It was the next thing to do so we arranged it. I had to remember that it had only been twelve hours since Dalen passed away. This whole thing just left us all in a sort of time warp and we were all just there watching it all happen.

4:49 p.m. Response from Blake Hudson (my nephew).

"At times like this the inescapable failure of words to capture the sadness and grief I feel is a reminder of the shortcoming that any condolences can offer. I shed tears for the Graham family, as they've lost a son and a brother. Until the very end, Dalen was a shining example of the joy and happiness that the gospel of Christ can bring to this world and individuals alike. Many people when experiencing a crisis like this crumble under the sheer agony and pain.

The Graham family has always been a bastion of faith in Jesus Christ and his gospel. Scott and Sharon, you should know that both you, and especially your children are and have always been true examples of how faith in the gospel isn't just something you believe, but it's something you are, and it shines for everyone to see. I've never been so proud, and our family always speaks so highly of Kailee. She's grown so much and has surpassed anything we could possibly hope she could become. We all truly love her. Alyssa's smile and pure charity towards others is a gift to this world. She has inspired me numerous times that I can be trying a little harder and loving those around me a little more. She has so much to give and selflessly does. Mariah, as well, as always been such a ray of hope and sunshine. At a time when others her age are consumed with themselves and their image, I've noticed she's very aware of those around her. A quality nurtured through her study of the Savior and his teachings; I have no doubt.

One dear sweet Dalen is no exception. Dalen's optimism, positivity, and light were always apparent, he was, and is, an unwavering rock of faith. The scripture in Alma comes to mind: "Yea, verily, verily I say unto you, if all men had been, and were, and ever would be, like unto Moroni, behold, the very powers of hell would have been shaken forever; yea, the devil would never have power over the hearts of the children of men."

Dalen is my Moroni. As Moroni bearing the Standard of Liberty, I knew what Dalen stood for and where his convictions landed.

> It's my shame to bear that a moment so tragic as this is what is awakening my soul to its lack of light. I've been experiencing a faith crisis for some time now. It's been a burden on me, my family, and undoubtedly those around me who may have noticed a change. I've felt as those wandering through the mist of darkness; often clawing forward for something to grasp hold of. That changes today. I know and I've always known what makes me happy. I'm happiest when I'm following the teachings of Christ, loving and serving those around me.
>
> This passing is tortuous. Let us be reminded that if you have kind words to say, even if it's just saying you love someone, be vulnerable and do it. Life is precious and short. To quote one of my favorite poets, "know that love is a vulnerability, but not a weakness, love is the volunteer that raises it's hand and steps forward without needing to be rewarded, love is an occurrence that functions in reverse because the only way to be wealthy with it, is to give more of it away." Here's to you Dalen."

This post, of course, caught us off guard. I was surprised to hear that my dorky son affected his cousins. That they saw him with a spiritual strength that I knew of but didn't expect the extended family to see and know of. This was amazing and totally blew us all away. I knew then that Blake would need to speak at the funeral, if nothing else, to read his post. Dalen's passing caused the power needed for someone to change their hearts. We were just so very blessed. Our God was so good to us.

Seriously: Planning for a Funeral

I immediately read Blake's post to the family as we were driving. I sent it to Alyssa who was driving behind us so she could give us her opinion too. Conversations were constant between our vehicles. Alyssa was on the phone when we all agreed that Blake's message would be good for the funeral. What a thought, we agreed on another issue for a funeral—my son's funeral. A funeral: where we pay tribute to a family member that has passed on. A funeral; a final goodbye. Wow, a funeral—a funeral for my son Dalen.

I pulled out the form that Jared gave us, and I began to fill it in.

I started calling people that we wanted to participate at the funeral. My first call was to Blake.

"Hey Blake, this is Aunt Sharon."

"Oh my gosh. I'm freeking out about Dalen. I can't believe what has happened. We are so upset and sorry. I don't know how to feel. Is there anything I could do for you? What do I do?"

"Blake, Dalen's funeral will be next Saturday. Do you think you might be able to come? Of course, we know it's a long ways and we understand with work and things. We are just asking. And if you think you could come, well, we all just read your post and were wondering if you would mind speaking at Dalen's funeral and reading your post.

To know that our son helped to change your desires was huge for us. We would really appreciate that. Could you let me know?"

"Of course, I would love to be there and talk. I would be honored. I just don't know how to get through this. It really hit me hard." Sharon.

"Blake, we have no doubt. We have no fear. Let Heavenly Father help you heal too. You can call me, and we can talk. I'm here for you. Let me help you if I can. I'm sorry for your hurt. It will be okay Blake. It will be okay."

"So how are you guys doing?" I asked.

"We are pretty good. Things are just getting planned so we have lots to do which helps. We have so much support and are overwhelmed by all the love. Thanks for asking."

"Thanks Sharon."

For some reason, none of Gord's kids ever called me Aunt Sharon. I always wished they would, but when they became adults, they just never did. Blake mentioned that he would be more than honored to be there, and that as soon as they heard, they were making plans to come down. That was very cool. I really had no idea how many people were altering their lives to be with us for Dalen. Blake and his family were one of them.

I dialed another number. "President Taylor, this is Sister Graham. My husband and I were just talking and we were wondering if there would be any way that you would be available to come down for Dalen's funeral and possibly speak on the plan of salvation. There will be about three hundred plus non-members there. What a great opportunity to maybe hear of some of Dalen's mission experiences. It will be next Saturday in California and would mean the world to us."

"Oh Sister Graham," and there was a pause. "There would be nothing more that I would love to do for you. I love my Elder Graham so very much. I just love my Elder Graham. Let me check my schedule and I will get back to you but know that I will do everything I can to be there. Thank you so very much for asking me. That would be an honor." There wasn't a hesitation at all on his desire to be there.

"Oh President. You meant the world to my son. You guided him, inspired him, and helped him with the repentance process. You saved my son. How can I ever thank you? Thank you President Taylor."

"Sister Graham, know how much I love you too. We will pray for your family through this ordeal. Let me know if I can help in any other way. Again, thank you so much for the honor."

"Of course. You are so very welcome."

"I will call you as soon as I know my schedule." he said.

"Okay, talk to you soon." was my reply.

President Knowles called. He said that he just got a call from the Bishop and that there was some issues with our Stake Center. There was a wedding Saturday night, and they were told they could have the church Friday and Saturday to decorate. That was a bummer. I asked if funerals took precedence. He said normally, but with us expecting so many people, it would have been okay if we just needed the chapel, but we would need the cultural hall too. With that many people, it just wasn't going to be possible. We talked about the Santa Clarita building, but that really wasn't my choice. He then suggested the Lancaster Stake Center. That was perfect. I loved that building. He said he would call right back after he spoke with them over in Lancaster. That was pretty exciting. It would be a perfect place.

I called my dad.

"Hi Dad."

"Hi Sharon. I'm just so sorry for what happened. I know what it feels like. I'm just sorry."

"Thanks Dad. Do you think you would be able to come down? If you do, we were wondering if you would say the closing prayer for the funeral."

"When is the funeral?"

"We are trying for this Saturday. I know it's a long way and not much time. I just would love it if you were there. I will have to let you know the details when I know more."

"Well let me know as soon as you can, and we will start making arrangements here. Your sisters will probably want to come down too."

"Okay, Dad. Thanks. I love you."

"Love you too."

"Talk to you soon."

Dad was quiet about the issue, but said he would try to be there. I thought for sure, that my dad would understand some of my feelings because of our similar situations with mom passing away a year ago. Things didn't really happen that way, but I would learn why later.

We hesitated to call George, Scott's dad, because we knew they would be uncontrollable, but we wanted them to know how we were and our desires for him to say a prayer at the funeral. Scott's dad was very upset and emotional on the phone. He was in shock. He and Trish, who we always heard in the background or on the other line, were hysterical. They were crying pretty hard. They both just kept crying and saying they couldn't believe this. They were devastated. I assured them that we were really doing good. I couldn't console them, but I reassured them that things were good for us. We were taking care of things and moving along. That we felt so much peace and that we were just being so incredibly blessed. There was a moment when I asked George if he would say the opening prayer. He said he would.

We were getting closer to Rexburg. I kind of knew to ask the ladies in our ward to play the music and lead the songs but I could take care of that later. The program was becoming real.

Thoughts were coming in of what kind of musical we would want. A few names came to my mind. We discussed them as a family and made some choices. Now I would just need them to agree.

There were calls made to the organist, and the conductor. They said they would help.

We called another very good family friend Eric. Alyssa and Eric went to high school together. They were casual friends. Eric wasn't a member of our church and knew about it, but showed no interest.

Alyssa invited Eric over a few times with some of our pool parties that we had. Eric came. They started talking. Eric started asking questions about our church and why we were the way we were. He knew Alyssa didn't drink or smoke or party in the normal sense. He wanted to know why Alyssa was happy. Their discussions led to more gospel discussion. Eric joined our church and his brother joined quickly after. We adopted them immediately. We became their 'Mormon families'. Their dad wasn't really around in their lives, but their mom was a very sweet lady. She supported her sons' decisions but really didn't want anything to do with the church. She and I became very good friends. Eric served a mission for the church as did his brother Matt. They always allowed us to be a part of their lives. They were both married in the temple and of course we were there.

Eric was like Dalen's big brother. He was 6'3, so he was tall but also very skinny. Dalen and Eric were just fun to watch when they were together. So, Eric was very much a part of our family and was the perfect person to read Dalen's life story. Dalen loved Eric and Eric couldn't have loved Dalen anymore. I later learned that Eric had such a hard time when Dalen passed away, that he had to drop out of his semester because he just couldn't focus on things. He really couldn't understand why Heavenly Father would take Dalen, but he trusted his reasoning and would use his faith to accept it.

"Hey Eric, how are you?" I sensed immediately that he wasn't doing very well. I heard the raw emotion in his voice and that he was traumatized.

"Um, I'm not doing very well. I can't believe this. I'm just really struggling with this. I don't know what to say."

"Oh Eric, I'm so sorry you're having a hard time. Know how much we love you. We were hoping that you would do us a favor. Do you think you could read Dalen's obituary for the funeral? I will have everything written out for you; you just need to read it. Would you be able to do that?"

There was actually a long pause. He couldn't contain himself. He didn't know how to respond. I assured him that if he thought this was too hard, that it would be okay if he didn't think he could do it.

"No, I really want to do this for you. I just don't know if I can. Of course, I will help you though. I will do whatever you need. I will do it for you." Eric stated.

"That would really mean a lot to us. Also, we would like to know if you and Matt (his brother) would be honorary pallbearers? What do you think?"

"That would be an amazing honor. Of course. Thank you."

"Okay, I will let you know more in a few days. Thanks Eric. I love you."

"I love you too." And I heard him holding back the tears.

Facebook 4:58 p.m. Michelle Van Ornum—Dalen's Jr. High School Math Teacher "This morning we got the devastating news about a former student Dalen Graham who passed away after being in a car accident with his sister Mariah. Jake was so excited when Dalen came home from his mission and so proud that he could say he knew Dalen. Dalen was 'buddies' with all of the little kids in the ward and always made them all feel like a million bucks. Mariah Graham was a sister queen with Kenzie and set such a great example of love and enthusiasm for life!

She is physically okay from the accident, but I pray for her to feel the love of our savior as she tries to make sense out of his tragedy. As their story unfolds, I am immediately reminded of the loss of my brother. Each detail of their story, so closely mirroring our own story. Please add the Graham family to your prayers tonight! The loss of a son, brother is unimaginable and the new normal of life they will walk is, I am sure, turning their world upside down. Life is sooooo short!!!! Burdens in life seems pale in comparison! Love and hug

> our kids closer tonight as I know I will be! Love to all of my friends and family who took the time to read this and share in our lives!"
>
> 5:03 p.m.   "Hello Sharon, this is Bobby. I just want you to know that I've done the necessary work for you guys so that you won't have to pay for anything. ALADDS and POPA will be giving you some money. The Sheriff's Relief Association will also give you assistance. I think they each will give you $5000.00. So get whatever you need, take care of the funeral and get what you want. Don't worry about a thing. If you need more money, we will find it. You will not have to pay for anything. Do you understand me, you will not pay for anything! Just know that it will all be taken care of."

Another phone call from Bobby and Gina. They just kept blessing our lives.

"Oh my gosh—how is that possible? How does this just happen?" I was overwhelmed. Scott understood that while I was on the phone that the agencies were going to help us. He didn't know how much though. He knew that they would offer something as they always had when there had been a tragedy within the department family, especially with a death.

"Thank you so much Bobby." I started to cry, and I think he could hear that in my voice. "Thank you so much. This is amazing. I'm just so shocked by all this support."

"You are very welcome. Just take care of whatever you need. We will talk to you soon." And he hung up.[33]

---

[33] The donations that were being collected to pay for the entire funeral and burial of Dalen were so amazing. Everything was being taken care of so we wouldn't worry about anything. Amazing for sure.

"Scott, they are going to pay for everything. Bobby has arranged for everything to be taken care of. How do we thank them or even accept this?"[34]

"That's what they do." He paused for a moment. "That is so amazing." He was crying too. There was more than an overwhelming sense of aweness. The attention everyone gave to us was just more than words could express or our lives could comprehend. We just couldn't seem to handle all the blessings. They were so profound.

We did nothing but read our messages as we drove.

We received a phone call from the Stake President. He had told us of the problem in trying to find a place for the funeral and mentioned that they checked on the Stake Center in Santa Clarita but it was booked. He again said he would try for the Lancaster East Stake Center. I mentioned that would be my choice for sure. It would be perfect. I knew the building well as I had assisted with a Creche exhibit for years. That was a display of nativities, and they were from all around the world. We had had as many as 1200 nativities on display in past years. I was on the committee for over 12 years. Again, I was relieved and excited to get to use this building. This would be perfect.

Within the hour, we heard back from President Knowles and he said that everything was cleared for the Lancaster Building. I would be able to have access Friday at 8:00 p.m. to set up, and it would be opened at 8:00 a.m. on the Saturday. That was good news. It really was the perfect place. We now had a funeral destination and the time.[35]

---

[34] Bobby was not just taking care of us; but completely taking over all our worries.
[35] Our Stake President did what he could to find us a building even out of our Stake, for Dalen's funeral.

Surprise or Another Miracle

5:10 p.m. We received another phone call.

"Yes, this is Sister Graham."

"Really, that would be wonderful. Of course, we would love to be there."

"That sounds good. If you could send us the address we will be there. Thank you so much."

"Okay—you aren't going to believe this one. That was the President of BYU-Idaho President Erying's secretary. She had heard that we were coming to Rexburg and so she was asking if our family would like to join the president and his family for dinner tomorrow. His secretary mentioned that they really just wanted to get to know us and express their condolences and were very hopeful that we would consider seeing them at this time."

"What, that is amazing," Kailee replied.

"Wow, that is very cool. Oh yeah, the Hamiltons (Rick's family) also wanted to know if we would come for brunch in the morning when we woke up. There wasn't really a specific time, but they just wanted to offer us something. I love them." Mariah commented.

What was happening? These people again, reaching out to us and knowing that we were coming to Rexburg. We were amazed. The president of the school seemed pretty unreal. Gratitude just doesn't express the true feelings we were experiencing.

5:30 p.m. There wasn't too much time that went by before we got another phone call.

"Is this Sister Graham?"

'Yes,' I replied.

"This is the secretary of President Erying of BYU-Idaho again. We just want you to know how sorry we are for your loss again. President Erying was excited to hear that you were willing to come for dinner. He would really like to know how he can help your family at this time in any way." she stated.

"Oh my gosh. That is amazing. I really can't think of anything. We were hoping to come tonight to Rexburg and clean out Dalen's apartment. What else would we need to do at the school?" I enquired.

"If you would like us to clean it out, we will be happy to do that for you," she mentioned. "As for the school, you just need to close his classes and that should be it," commented the secretary. She had the most soothing voice.

"We actually had it planned that we would clean it out tonight. Thank you for the offer though. We are doing okay and feel that we need to do this and since we're here, why not get it done. As for his classes, we wondered what might need to be done. I think we can plan to stay till Monday so that we could take care of whatever we need to do."

"Okay", are you sure we can't help you?" she seemed eager. "Do you need a place to stay at, or food to eat? Can we help you in anyway? The president has a few homes in town. I'm sure you could stay at one of them if you needed to," she offered.

"I really don't think so but thank you so very much. We were going to get a hotel."

"This is just so sad. We are all devastated. President Erying just wants to help you out in any way he can. We in no way want to infringe on your time. He just wants to make sure that you're still okay to have dinner with him tomorrow. That is the least he could do for your family."

"Scott, President Eyring's secretary is on the phone again. She is just checking that we are still on for dinner tomorrow and wants to know if they can do anything else for us. He wants to put us up in one of his houses. He really wants to take care of us however he can. He just wants to be involved with our family on a personal level."

Scott agreed that we were doing fine and that there really wasn't anything else they could do for us but we appreciated the offered.

Scott was as shocked as I was at what was occurring. We all sensed just such a big awareness of this situation. They wanted to ensure that we were okay. They personally wanted to be involved with our family. It just seemed like we couldn't hold in the support no matter how many baskets we tried to fill. They were all overflowing with love, support, blessings and peace that carried us through it all.

"What the heck?" Kailee commented. "That seems unreal."

"It is unreal Kailee. This is just amazing."

I asked the secretary where she would like us to meet.

"Let me call President Eyring as he has two houses, and I will call you right back. Would that be okay?" she inquired.

"Of course. Thank you so very much. There are six of us. Would it be better if just my husband and I came?"

"Of course not. He would love to have your whole family, and I'm sure he would say to not worry about it at all." she said.

"Wow, that would be amazing. Thank you so very much. This is incredible. I guess I will wait for your call."

There has to be at least three thousand, maybe even five thousand students at BYU-Idaho. The President was asking to have dinner with our family and express their condolences of the passing of our son, a student at their facility.[36] We had no way of knowing if this was normal or not, but we knew it felt incredible. We were all in shock just a bit. It seemed like such a huge gesture for our family, and their outward concerns were for both Dalen and Mariah. How very blessed we were.

We continued our drive into Rexburg. The ground was covered with more snow than we had seen the whole way there. It was cold, but not freezing outside according to the temperature gauge in the car. It seemed like we were making pretty good time. The radio was playing country music of course, not my choice but Scott's. We

---

[36] President Eyring heard of our son's death and wanted to make sure our family was doing okay and offered anything he could do. What an amazing gesture for our family.

could see the town of Rexburg in our view. We were almost there. My phone rang again.

"Sister Graham. This is _____, President Eyring's secretary. He was wondering if 6:00 p.m. would be okay for dinner. He would like you to come to the President's house if that's okay, and I'll send you the address."

I looked over at Scott and kind of whispered to him, 'They would like us at 6:00 p.m., would that be okay?" He nodded yes.

"That sounds perfect. We will see you there. Thank you again. Please thank President Eyring for us too." She said she would, and we hung up our phones. We just started driving into town and the lights actually were just coming on. The messages were penetrating through our phones and didn't stop.

> **Facebook 5:35 p.m. Katrina Duvalois**
> **"Some things hit me more acutely. Today my thoughts are revolving around Scott Graham and his family. The tributes to Dalen Graham from family and friends is touching and heartbreaking at the same time. The words from my favorite movie ever keep popping into my head, "Each man's life touches so many other lives. When he isn't around, he leaves an awful hole, doesn't he?" That hole will never be filled. We just adjust."**

Our Evening Unfolds

We got into Rexburg and decided to get something to eat first. Alyssa was driving right behind us. The roads were clear and we made good time. We found the hotel and it was very close to a restaurant, so we went to eat. We ate at Applebee's. It's a good restaurant and they have a nice selection of food, and everyone pretty much got what they wanted. We were okay. We discussed some of the phone calls we had received and the expressions of love we were feeling. Alyssa was pretty amazed too after hearing of the dinner invitation with the President of BYU-Idaho. We seemed to enjoy ourselves at dinner. It was almost like we weren't there for anything but to enjoy our time together as our family on a dinner date. Then it would hit us that we were only there because Dalen had passed away. The conversation wasn't all about Dalen, although there were mentions of him the whole night long.

I think we also pretty well lined up the funeral. A lot of decisions being made today and they were coming smoothly and as if they were meant to be. We ran over the agenda during dinner.

ORDER OF SERVICE

Family Prayer:	**Scott Graham**
Prelude/Postlude:	
Chorister:	**Vivian Oswell (Primary teacher of Dalen's)**
Accompanist:	**Helena Hathaway (from our ward)**
Musical Selection:	
Invocation:	**George Graham (Scott's dad-grandfather)**
Life Sketch:	**Eric Lewis (We introduced Eric to the gospel. He was a big brother to Dalen, and we were his 'Mormon family'.)**

Speaker:	??? Hopefully—President Taylor (Dalen's Mission President, recently released and living in Salt Lake)
Musical Selection:	Pam Castagna (Special Ward member to Dalen)
Accompanist:	Helena Hathaway (from our ward)
Speaker:	Memories from the Girls-Alyssa, Kailee, Mariah
Speaker:	Blake Hudson (cousin)
Closing Remarks:	Stake President
Musical Selection:	
Accompanist:	
Benediction:	Art Hudson (my dad-grandfather)
Dedication of the Grave:	Scott Graham

Pallbearers:

Brandon Stirling (brother in law)	Jordan Castro Friend—played volleyball	Riley Bunker Mission Trainer-Friend
Paul Crapo (cousin)	Chris Shelton Mission Trainer-Friend	Frankie Lindstrom Friend

Honorary Bearers

Eric Lewis (friend)	Bryce Hudson (cousin)	Jordyn Jepperson (cousin)
Matt Lewis (friend)	Kyle Hudson (cousin)	Justin Jepperson (cousin)

Dallen Hudson (cousin)	Timothy Robinson (cousin)	Brendon Jepperson (cousin)
Blake Hudson (cousin)	Thomas Robinson (cousin)	

    The hotel was across the street from the restaurant. It was the Embassy Suites. It was really nice. We walked into the lobby. It looked pretty nice inside. Actually, it was really fancy with contemporary style décor. There of course was the sitting area, and you could see where they would have the breakfast too. The front desk was green marble with a few offices to the right. There were the luggage stands near the door when we walked in. It was funny too, because you felt a gush of heat when you walked in, so the temperature outside wasn't carried into the hotel. Scott went to the counter to register. Again they knew our story and were expecting us. They expressed their condolences.

    We went upstairs to the room. It was beautiful. There was a sitting area, a little fridge and an eating area. There were two queen sized beds. There was a closet and both the closet, and the bathroom had one very unique thing about them, the doors were etched glass which meant when you turned the lights on—it wasn't see through, but it was very evident where you were. The room was just beautiful. We knew it had to be pretty expensive too and it was all covered by Scott's Lieutenant. Again, we were just so thankful. We arranged ourselves. Scott and I had the bed near the window. Alyssa and Brandon had the inner bed. The couch was in a c-shape and had enough space that both Mariah and Kailee could sleep there and be quite comfortable. There was a hide-a-bed on the long side of the couch too. We weren't in the room very long because we had an appointment to go to Dalen's apartment at 7:00 p.m. and we were close to that time. So, we unloaded our things, and settled in for just a few minutes and then left for Dalen's apartment.[37]

---

[37] Mark Reyes—Scott's Lieutenant, had wanted to help us so badly and was gracious as he paid for two nights of the hotel for our family.

6:45 p.m. It was time for us to go over to Dalen's apartment. Alyssa had offered to bring their truck because we could load up all his stuff in the back and they had a cover. That sounded like a good idea, so we again took two vehicles. We drove over to the apartment. Dalen's truck would be there too, so there would actually be three vehicles there which meant we would have plenty of space to put his things in.

We got to the apartment building, and I knew exactly where to go as I had just dropped Dalen off not to long ago when he first arrived for his semester. We walked up the stairs to the second floor and opened the door and turned to the left. Dalen's room was on the immediate right. We knocked on the door. It was opened to us.

"Hello, Sister Graham. I'm _____.

"Hi, how are you?" as we extended our hands to shake them with one another. There were five young men standing in the kitchen with three young ladies. One person was the manager of the apartments that was so kind to me on the phone.

"I'm _____ the apartment manager. I just want you to know how sad we are and very sorry for Dalen's passing."

The room was pretty somber. You could sense that they didn't know how to feel or what they should say or do. We all introduced ourselves as Dalen's family and shook all their hands. They again asked if we needed them to leave so we could do what we needed to alone as a family.

"Of course not—this is your place. We're the ones that are intruding. If you're okay we're okay. So, Dalen wasn't your roommate for very long (five weeks into the semester) but did you get along?"

"Dalen was the best. We got along really well," said one of the roommates.

"He was the funniest guy. No matter what was going on, he always made us laugh," replied another.

"I was his actual roommate, and he was by far the best roommate I had ever had."

"That is very cool. I'm so glad you got along. He mentioned you all often and said how much he enjoyed living here so thank you all. That is just great. Umm maybe we should start in his room if that's okay. I think we just might like to get things done. Thanks again for everything."

We were led to Dalen's room by Will, his roommate, and we all just looked for a second. Not the messiest of rooms which surprised us at least for Dalen's side. He wasn't the cleanest of guys. Dalen kind of had things in their places. His bed wasn't made but his floor was picked up. There weren't many clothes even on the floor which was so not normal for Dalen. He had to be constantly reminded to pick up his room when he was at home. Then we looked over at his desk. The room wasn't huge but with the six guys in there, it was a bit crowded. It of course, was a dorm style room and this was housing for college students. Two beds, two dressers, and two desks side by side. That was it and that was all the room there was.

"Look Mom," Kailee said. There was a beautiful bouquet of flowers and a note from the apartment managers. That was just beautiful. There was also a basket full of traveling things. There were granola bars, and nuts, some hand wipes and traveling pillows. There were little packages of tissues that we definitely would need. There were note pads to write some of our thoughts on and pens included. There were some bottles of water and some packages of mints. They had thought of everything. How incredibly thoughtful they were for this gesture. It was so amazing what they had put together for us in such a short period of time. We just felt so cared for.[38]

I went back out to the kitchen area and hugged the manager again.

"That was the sweetest thing you could have done for us and the flowers are just beautiful. Thank you."

"You're welcome. It was the least we could do," she said.

"Well, it was just so sweet."

Again, I returned back into Dalen's room. Everyone was just kind of looking.

---

[38] The flowers, note, basket and reverence the apartment manager gave to our family was heartfelt.

Since his bed wasn't made, it was pretty easy to just start pulling things off. The manager had brought us a few boxes and large trash bags to help us pack things up too. Just such a kind gesture, but it really helped. I pulled out Dalen's suitcases from under his bed. Dalen's bed was lifted so most of his storage was under his bed. There were a few crates pulled out and I said: "Okay, let's get started," and we all just kind of did our thing from where we were standing and started packing.

We looked over at his desk area. His scriptures were open. There was an alarm clock on the desk with a canister for pens and highlighters. He had a few books to study from. There were pictures of his family and him on his mission on the wall. He had his missionary plaque and his mission flag on the wall as well.

In some stakes of our church, when a person decides to go on a mission, they are given a plaque for the missionary. On the plaque is the missionary's name, a place for a personal picture, another place for the favorite scripture of the missionary and a map of the actual mission location. These plaques remain in our church buildings for the duration of the mission and then are presented to the missionary when they honorably return. It's a great symbol of a huge accomplishment. It was nice to see Dalen's plaque on display in his room. He could look at it every day and remember his accomplishment.

There was a picture of Christ over where his head would have laid on his bed. Scott made a very profound statement: "Nothing seems out of place. It seems perfect."

What an amazing tribute to Dalen. We would hope that our son would make Christ a big part of his life and to see his set up on his desk, it was a very comforting display. He was doing good things. It was nice to see.

Alyssa, Brandon and Kailee started cleaning out his closet. Mariah was still pulling things out from under the bed. Scott started taking his bed down and pulling the sheets off. They got stuffed into one of the trash bags. The roommate guided us to the dresser and Dalen's two drawers. It wasn't hard to figure out what things were Dalen's. We took his clothes and put them in his suitcases. The dresser was cleaned out. I packed everything of course. I felt it was easier than just throwing things in. All his shirts were folded and pants and whatever I could fit in. The rest we did shove into the bags, crates and storage bins Dalen had. There were enough bins to get all his items packed. He had a backpack where I put all his desk items in and they fit well.

As the girls were looking at some of his clothes they were packing, they were talking about the event they might have seen Dalen wearing them at.

"Oh, I hated this shirt," Mariah said. She held up his neon orange t-shirt.

"But wasn't that his favorite one?" Kailee asked.

"Yeah, I think so."

Alyssa pulled out some casual dress shirts I had given him at Christmas. "Look Mom, the tags are still on."

"That sounds like Dalen." There were often times when I thought he liked a shirt I gave him, and it would sit in his closet hung up and never worn. There was a very relaxed tone with all of us. We weren't having fun, but it was in no way a horrible experience. One of the other roommates brought us some more large trash bags. That made things even easier. We really didn't take long. We tried to lay things in instead of shoving things in. The bags and suitcases filled up pretty quickly. It maybe took us ten minutes to clean out Dalen's things. I went into the kitchen with a box and asked where Dalen's things were. The girls did his bathroom. Scott and Brandon stated that they would start taking things out to Brandon's truck. By the time they started walking through the kitchen, the roommates all offered to help if we needed it. So, they all grabbed a bag or suitcase and headed out to the truck. It was pretty smooth. It actually went very quickly. While I was doing the kitchen, I asked the roommates that remained how they were doing. I inquired about their personal, emotional wellbeing. I wanted to make sure they were okay and if we could help them in any way. None of them felt like they could talk so I led the questions.

"So how much time did you actually spend with Dalen?"

"We all kind of hung out, but it wasn't all the time," one said.

"Yeah, if we were around, we would eat together," another one said.

"Dalen just always made us laugh. It didn't matter what we were doing he made us laugh."

"He did like to make people laugh. In just his short time, we have seen how many people Dalen touched, and many comments were of how he made them laugh and taught people how to have fun, no matter where they were."

"I can see that. He seemed to enjoy his life," replied his roommate Will.

It was pretty amazing how Delany knew we were going go to be there as she had seen our posts and asked if she could come see us for a few minutes. We had met her in January as a friend of our son's was getting married January 6th in Bountiful, Utah. Dalen was one of his groomsmen. Dalen had it arranged that Delany would be his date and then the two of them would drive up to Rexburg for the beginning of the winter semester to start. Delany knew Dalen on his mission. After his mission, he had convinced her to go to BYU-Idaho for school so they could be together. Dalen could convince many people to do things he wanted done. He just made them all see that it was good even if the good, was for Dalen. I assured Delany that we would love to see her through our text messages. We thought she was still his girlfriend until we had read the comment from Chloe in the newspaper as she was being Dalen's current girlfriend.

Dalen had talked with me that he had thought of breaking up with Delany because he just felt they weren't good together. That was a bit scary for me. He said he was just questioning their relationship. I knew it was an issue, but didn't know it was a reality. I also knew he was interested in another girl (that also happened to be from Texas where he had met both these girls while on his mission) but had no way of knowing that Chloe was the girlfriend already. That too was a characteristic of Dalen—he got emotionally attached really quickly to a girl, but he could also move on very quickly and that wasn't always comforting for me. He loved having a girlfriend and he was a very devoted boyfriend—even if it wasn't for very long.

Mariah received a call that Rick was on his way over and would be there in a minute. Within a few seconds, the doorbell rang, and it was Delany, Dalen's old girlfriend that he broke up with just two weeks earlier. She was friends with the roommates and it wasn't unusual that she would come and hang out before the breakup. She heard we were there and wanted to see us. I walked over to her and hugged her. She broke down in my arms. I felt so bad for her. This sweet girl had just lost her dad and brother to a traffic accident one year ago, as her brother was going to attend BUI-Idaho and her dad was driving him up to school. They were killed by another car accident, and now her boyfriend too. Someone else she cared so much about had been killed in another car accident. That was pretty hard for her to take. I just held her for a minute. I sensed her crying so I held her some more.

"I'm so sorry sweetie. I'm sorry for the breakup and the heartache you have at this time."

Scott and Brandon walked back into the room while I was hugging Delany. Scott walked over first to Delany and hugged her too.

"We want to make sure you are okay. What can we do you for sweetie?" I asked.

"I don't know. I don't know how to handle this. I don't know." She pulled out of our hug and wiped the tears from her eyes. "This is just really hard. I just don't know what to do."

"Well, we will do what we can to make you feel better. Dalen was a good guy and I know that your feelings were real for him. I know that you just broke up but that doesn't mean that your feelings stop."

"Yeah, we want to make sure you are okay." Scott reassured her.

"I will be. I'm struggling pretty badly. I actually think I'll go home. With all this, it's just really hard. I think I might need some time to process and heal. Thank you."

No one really heard our conversation, but they saw her raw emotions. Scott came over and hugged her again.

"So, are you ok?" he asked.

"I will be, thank you." Delany replied.

I felt very badly for Delany. This couldn't be easy for her. The poor thing: I knew she still loved Dalen and I did feel sorry for her. And in her mind, her dad and brother died while driving to school and now an ex-boyfriend died while driving. What a trial for her. However, I knew that Dalen wanted to move on with his relationship with this other girl and had done so. It just wasn't an easy situation for sure.

7:30 p.m. The DEA agent came to check on Scott while we were cleaning out Dalen's apartment. Scott walked out of the apartment, and we didn't really think much about it until he walked back into the room a few minutes later with a representative from the DEA's office of the Sheriff's Department. This man's duties were to check on personnel that were experiencing trauma. He wasn't from Los Angeles but LA had made the connection with the DEA office from Idaho that put this agent in contact with Scott. There had been some communication with this agent throughout the day, and it was previously decided that he could come and meet up with Scott at Dalen's apartment. He came in and introduced himself to us as Eric. He mentioned that he wasn't just there to check on Scott but to make sure that our family was okay as well. He was there for a while. What a nice guy. He was very pleasant, and we all made the situation as positive as we could. I was just so grateful for the care given to my husband from strangers, yet the departmental family. He hung out and asked questions as to how we mentally were doing. He specifically made sure of Scott and his well-being. He was there to inform the DEA of whatever we needed, and whatever assistance they might be able to give to our family. He proceeded to check in with Scott for the next three to four days. He really wanted to know that things were being taken care of and that Scott was okay mentally. What a power of support.

"Do you guys need anything, anything at all? Can I get you food or warm clothes or I know you have a place for tonight, but if you need anything, I want you to call me, a toothbrush or money for gas or whatever you need. I'm not far away and I want to make sure you have what you need." It was just so overwhelming how this made us feel. Scott was so very grateful. It seemed that everyone cared for us and our family. We were very gracious of their thoughts and actions.[39]

"I think we are all okay," Alyssa replied.

---

[39] The Sheriff's department would take such care of their personal was so overwhelming.

"Yeah, I don't need anything," Kailee said. As prepared as Kailee was, she seldom needed anything when traveling. In fact, there were times when we cautioned Kailee from bringing too much because she was prepared for everything that could happen.

Scott reiterated that we were good and that it was just really cool that he was there checking up on us.

"Would you mind talking over here with me Scott for a minute?" He made a gesture to move to the front room area so he could converse with Scott on: 1) his personal condition, and 2) Scott's family condition in private. Eric was in shock of how he saw our family reacting to this situation. He just kept saying: "You guys just seem to be doing so well. I don't see you devastated or overcome with emotion. It's very unusual. I still want you to know that we will help you however we can and maybe later things might hit you harder. Either way, I'm here for you and will check in on you from time to time."

We were so astonished that through Scott's department, he was being cared for by a representative in Idaho who just happened to actually be in Rexburg when we needed him. He didn't just call Scott, but personally visited with him and checked on our entire family. This really just doesn't happen I don't think. We were so taken care of as a family, and we knew that God was taking the lead.

There were three of the roommates sitting in the little front room off the kitchen because they didn't want to be in our way. Two had gone out with Scott to the truck, but when they returned; we congregated around the island in the kitchen as I finished packing. They all simultaneously just talked about what a good kid Dalen was.

"He studied his scriptures every day." Will said. "We talked quite a bit about what he was studying, or questions he had. It helped me to keep up my studies too. It was pretty cool."

"Awe, that's something a mom likes to hear. So do you have any questions about Dalen, that we could answer for you?"

"So, what actually happened if you don't mind telling us?" asked the manager.

Mariah was still cleaning the bathroom, so I felt it would be okay to answer the question and that was good as I didn't want our discussion to bother her. "Our daughter was driving and kind of lost control and then she tried to compensate and overcorrected herself and the truck flipped. It rolled five times. Scott had rejoined us from his private conversation.

"Dalen's head was crushed instantly." Scott commented.

"According to the doctor, Dalen died on impact and was brain dead due to the crush he incurred on his head, but he still had a pulse, so they kept him alive, and his body was perfectly preserved for him to be a donor."

Mariah walked out.

"We actually have made contact with a lady whose son we believe will be a kidney recipient." I tried to divert the conversation just enough to protect Mariah.

"Yeah, it has been very humbling to hear all the comments about Dalen touching people's lives." Scott added.

"To us, our brother was just a dork," Alyssa said. Everyone laughed.

"He was just our goofy brother," Kailee commented.

"Yeah, so to hear of all the things he did or how he helped someone, we had to think—*That's my brother?*" Alyssa replied.

I finished with what I could do in the kitchen. We didn't worry about any of the food in the fridge. We actually left all his food and just took his kitchen items. Now we were all in the kitchen. Some of the conversation returned with the roommates in the kitchen.

"Dalen really helped us all. He even helped me plan my proposal," said Will. "Congratulations. That's so exciting for you."

"Thank you. Dalen was a big part of it." The girl responded.

"That's so cool." Alyssa replied. It brought a bit of light to our situation. The entire visit was really uplifting. We felt gratitude to the boys for being Dalen's friends and we were just grateful they would let us take care of this stuff within such a short period of time.

"Yeah Dalen helped me plan everything. He was pretty excited for us."

"Of course he would be."

"He really wasn't here a lot because he was either at his girlfriend's until they broke up a few weeks ago, or he was playing volleyball," stated another roommate.

"He loved volleyball, that's for sure." Everyone agreed on that point.

"I didn't really spend a lot of time with Dalen and I'm sorry for that," said another.

"You don't need to worry about that."

"We just had different schedules, but he always was smiling. He always tried to make us smile too." The roommates all concurred.

We decided as a family that we didn't want to interrupt their evening anymore and that it was probably time for us to go. It was an obvious time to say our goodbyes. I went up to everyone and personally hugged and thanked them.

"For whatever you're going through, here is a mom's hug. Maybe it will help." And I would hug them as I would hug my son.

"So just in case you need a mom's hug, I'm here," and I would walk over to another roommate and hug them.

Will and his girlfriend were kind of standing in line waiting for their hugs. We had learned through our visit, that Will had served his mission in California and actually had served in the area where our dear friend Bobby and his wife Gina lived. Will was 'their missionary' as people called the missionary that would teach them the gospel of Jesus Christ. Bobby and Gina never converted, but they had a very deep love for the missionaries and especially Will. It was amazing that we had a very common friend that we both loved dearly. I had to get a picture with them and send it to Bobby and Gina later that evening. And they were more than ecstatic.[40]

"Come and get your mom's hug too. Congratulations again. I'm sure Dalen is very happy for you. Thank you for being such a good roommate to Dalen. He loved you."

"I really loved him too," Will replied. "We were supposed to get engaged last night but after hearing about the accident, we just couldn't. We also thought that Dalen wouldn't want us not to get engaged, so I asked her today thinking that would make Dalen happy for us."

---

[40] It wasn't a coincidence that Bobby and Gina, who had taken care of us so profoundly, knew well of Dalen's roommate and loved him deeply. It was of divine intervention.

"Of course he is happy for you. We hope your happiness continues. If you happen to remember Dalen once in a while for helping bring you together, that would be cool too."

It was just so hard to constantly talk about Dalen in the past tense. 'He loved'—he still loves, so why didn't we talk that way? I was conscious of the words I used. I didn't use the word died or dead. Those were so very harsh to me. Instead, I chose passed on, not even passed away, but just passed on. *'He loved'; 'he liked'; 'he had'*; everything was now in the past. And yet our son had passed on; on to the other side and was totally at peace as were we. I would come to accept the lingo used for a person that no longer lives. It really would be a part of the rest of our lives.

We thanked everyone again for all their kindness and the beautiful flowers and basket of goodies. We said goodbye again as we all walked out with our arms full of whatever we needed to carry out. Dalen's truck had been left in the parking lot because he and Mariah were coming down to Vegas in Mariah's truck. We filled up what we could inside of Dalen's truck. It was pretty full. We put some things into Alyssa's car and also a few things into mine. We didn't want to leave things in the bed of his truck because we didn't know if it would freeze tonight or not, or how severe the weather would be. We got it all in. His truck was really full, but I wouldn't say it was stuffed because we had stuff in all three vehicles. Since it was February, it was way dark outside and it was cold. It wasn't freezing, but the temperature was definitely dropping quickly so we were glad that we got all his stuff inside the vehicles.

We drove back to our hotel. We had asked Mariah if she wanted to go to her apartment or stay with us. We encouraged her to stay with us, but that it would be her choice. Again, when we thought of everything that had transpired—it had only been fifteen hours since Dalen passed on and about thirty hours since the accident. It was still such a new experience and there would be constant adjustments that we would have to make. We were very aware and concerned for Mariah's mental state. I just had no idea what her thought process was and how she was really doing. She seemed to be okay when she was with us. We all seemed to be handling this ordeal pretty well. We were positive and felt that we were okay. We needed to be witnesses for the atonement and the peace we have felt when things were given to God, and we let him lead. Things just happened. We couldn't explain them, but we were so very grateful for them.

> **Facebook 8:30 p.m. Friend of Dalen's** "Appreciate the everyday little things, today is a prime example. We never know when the last time will be when we see someone's smile, feel their touch, hear their voice, or receive communication from them for the last time. Be kind, do your best, and never hesitate to share your love, all the other little annoyances of daily life will pass better if you feed the positive and take the rest in stride. Dalen was an extraordinary example of this from a very young age. His earthly body will graciously help save others, and his soul will shine above in a greater place."

8:32 p.m. We had just gotten back to the hotel. We were there for maybe ten minutes when there was a knock on the door. When we opened it, there was a box of very special cookies that were delivered by the hotel personnel. There was a note: "We just wanted you to know that we were thinking of you. Love Maddi and Mason." The abundance of love was so overwhelming. Maddi was a young girl that grew up in our ward. She was a year younger than Kailee and a year older than Dalen. We loved her family, and they were very good people. The family had moved to Highland, Utah a few years ago, and Maddi was attending BUI-Idaho with her fairly new husband. For her to know where we were and that we were even in Rexburg was so amazing and yet, they found us. Look what technology had done, how many people knew of us and what was happening. We were so overwhelmed.

9:00 p.m. We had learned more of the articles written about Dalen and his accident in the various newspapers.

Idaho State Journal
Feb. 10, 2018

BYU-Idaho Student severely injured in Interstate 15 crash dies in Hospital day after wreck.

A Los Angeles man who attended Brigham Young University-Idaho died Saturday morning as a result of injuries he suffered in an Interstate 15 crash in Blackfoot on the day before.

Dalen Graham, 22, was pronounced dead at Portneuf Medical Center in Pocatello, where he was airlifted after suffering severe injuries when the 1998 Chevrolet S10 pickup he was a passenger in overturned on Interstate 15 Friday afternoon.

The driver of the pickup, Mariah Graham, 18, also of Los Angeles, suffered minor injuries in the crash, state police said. Mariah is Dalen's sister and Dalen was a student at Brigham Young University-Idaho in Rexburg.

The crash occurred around 2:30 p.m. Friday while Mariah and Dalen Graham were headed southbound on the interstate in the pickup. State police said, "Mariah Graham drove off of the left shoulder of the road and then returned to the road, where her vehicle began to rotate. The vehicle overturned and came to rest on its roof off of the right side of the road."

State police did not say what caused the pickup to initially leave the left shoulder of the interstate.

Both Mariah and Dalen Graham were wearing their seat belts when the crash occurred, state police said.

An online fundraiser has been set up to help the Grahams pay for Dalen's medical and funeral expenses. To donate visit https://www.gofundme.com/dalen-graham-medical-funeral.fu

LDS-Living
Feb. 12, 2018
BYU-I Student Taken off Life Support After Car Crash

A day before his sister's birthday, a BYU-Idaho student was taken off life support afte he ws involved in a car crash on I-15.

On February 9, Dalen Graham was with his sister Mariah when their car veered off the freeway, then returned where it began spinning and rolling. After being airlifted and cared for in the ICU at Portneuf Medical Center, Graham's family decided to take him off life support on Saturday. His sister Mariah only sustained minor injuries.

"At 5:16 we took Dalen off life support," Dalen's mother, Sharon, posted on Facebook. "We had to wait for the nurses to prepare for his body to donate kidney, liver, tissue, and bones. His life will save another. Love you Buddy-Boy. Thank you everyone for thoughts, prayers and support."

The following day, Sharon posted a sweet message about Dalen's sister Alyssa, saying, "Knowing that this isn't an easy time for our family, I would like to direct my thoughts first towards my eldest daughter whose birthday it is. Oh Alyssa, what a treasure you are to me.

You are a determined young lady who when you allow it: your spiritual strength is ginormous. Know how loved you are. Know how blessed you are. Know that you're my favorite oldest daughter. HAPPY BIRTHDAY ALYSSA. Let there be some happiness today just for you."

Through this difficult experience, Sharon Graham has said her family has been overwhelmed with love and support.

SCROLL—Idaho
Feb. 12, 2018
Car Crash on I-15 Kills BYU-I Student

Dalen Graham, a BYU-Idaho student, died Saturday morning feb. 10, due to a car crash that took place Friday on I-15.

Kailee Graham, Dalen's sister, stated in a Facebook post that her brother was taken off of life support at 5:16 a.m. 15 hours prior, he was involved in a severe car crash around 2:30 p.m.

"For him being my only brother it's hard to think I won't have another brother," Kailee said. "All my sisters have been saying about how we can't say we have a brother. It won't be the same. He loved us, respected us and always had a smile."

His mom, Sharon Graham informed in a Facebook post he was airlifted to Portneuf Medical Center, where his kidneys, liver, tissue, and bone were donated to help others.

"Dalen was genuine, always happy and loved people," Sharon said. "He initiated a conversation to know that person."

The 22-year-old recently returned missionary from California was in the passenger seat while his 18-year-old sister, Mariah Graham, was at the wheel of a white 1998 Chevrolet S10 south on Interstate 15, near milepost 92.

The police stated the vehicle drove off the left side of the road then came back to the freeway, where the vehicle started to rotate. The truck rolled and landed on its roof on the right side of the road.

A witness of the accident Margaret Lynn Anton, said in a Facebook post that she called 911 before the vehicle stopped rolling.

"The loss of a life is always tragic, especially a life so young," Anton said in her post. "Please, if you have the means, consider donating to this family to help them cover medical and funeral expenses."

According to the 'gofundme.com,' over half of the family's $10,000 goal has been raised with the help of nearly 100 donators.

"Dalen was a true disciple of Christ," said Chloe Howard, Dalen's girlfriend and a freshman studying special education. "He carried the light of Christ where he went and everyone could feel his love for them as well as God's love through him. He would always tell me how much he loves me and wants me to be happy."

Sharon said she would always get calls from people from Dalen's mission saying what an inspiration he was to them.

"My brothers and sister in the work of the Lord, he truly is there, he answers our prayers," according to Dalen Graham's instagram post. "He wants to guide us! Yesterday I

prepared to go to the temple, I had questions that I wanted answers to. I was praying beforehand, listening to hymns while I walked there. I got my answers, I got my direction."

We were very surprised at where these papers received their information, but I guess that once it's posted on the internet, it can be used for other publications. We didn't object, but we also didn't know about them. We also didn't know about this Chloe girl and that she was supposedly Dalen's girlfriend. I was informed later, that the day he broke up with his girlfriend, he called Chloe and asked her to be his new girlfriend. Nothing like wasting time there Dalen. I guess he met Chloe while he was serving his mission in the Dallas Texas Mission, and they had kept in casual contact afterwards. So, I guess they did know each other and were actually boyfriend and girlfriend for a whole two weeks. In Dalen's last post, his question of going to the temple was: "Should I marry Chloe or let her go on a mission and then marry her?" We were a bit blown away by this news but couldn't do anything about it. Chloe would come to be a very special person in our lives, and we would love her as I guess our son did too.

We were starting to settle in the room. Everyone was preparing themselves for bed. It hadn't been that long and there was another knock on the door. It was a bouquet of flowers that were sent for Mariah. Some of her friends again found out where she was and had waited for the flowers to have been delivered when we arrived back at the room. This was just so overwhelming. The thoughtfulness and consideration of everyone around us just didn't seem to stop.

I set up the girls' beds on the couch and pulled out the sofa bed that we didn't know was even there when we first went into the room. I put the sheets and blanket on the bed and it was ready to go.

"So, who wants the bed, there's enough room for both of you."

"I want the couch." Kailee said. That made things easy.

"Okay I won't argue—I'll take the bed." Mariah seemed content with that. Mariah hadn't seen Rick all day. We knew he was on his way over for a bit. The rest of the family were getting themselves ready for bed. Some changed clothes. Some, like Scott, got under the covers. I was putting things away—my clothes which I never liked leaving in a suitcase. I put the suitcases under a bench or in the closet and just tidied things up a bit. Rick had spent about an hour with us. During our time together, he had asked again if we would consider having brunch with his family in the morning. His mom wanted so badly to help us in some way. She really wanted to do something for us. Since it would be Sunday, and we had already decided that we would go to church with them; breakfast or brunch was an easy choice. We graciously accepted. Rick commented that his mom was grateful that we accepted her invitation within the seconds that it took him to text his mom.

Alyssa Brandon were sitting on their bed and Kailee and Mariah were sitting on the couch. We just kept reading and listening in amazement of the persons that had taken the time to send us messages. We kept hearing of this person that altered lives; helped in any way; spiritually led them; and the devastation of his passing and it was all about Dalen. Again, we just naturally took turns and would read from Instagram, Facebook, texts and actual phone calls. All of us had hundreds of messages. It was very overwhelming.

Scott commented: "This is what social media is used for and this is how it should be used. This is good, it's all good."

"Isn't it amazing how fast the news has spread and who knows about it? It's just amazing." I commented.

"I know I'm blown away," Alyssa said.

"Me too," said Kailee.

"It really is just so amazing," Scott mentioned.

> **—I was so touched to see Dalen's post Wednesday of his testimony of being guided by the Lord when we go to the temple. Dalen was such a light in this world who always shared the gospel because he loved to do the Lord's work. I am very glad I have known such a wonderful guy since I was a little girl. Dalen, only 22 years old, he will be forever remembered.**

—It is so unreal seeing that your gone. It's so hard for me to try and explain how much of a brother you were to me. You inspired me and many other people to do great things. What I would do to play one last game with you by my side! I'll always love you! Love Kailee.

—Heaven gained an amazing angel. Life is short and we never know when the Lord will call us home. Dalen was ready.

—Dalen, you were one incredible man, always putting others before yourself and wanting the best for everyone in this world. You had a great impact in my life and you never failed to check up on me. In disbelief that your gone, my thoughts and prayers go out to your family.

—While I don't know your family, I live in Utah and heard your story on our local news. I just want to say what an inspiration you are with your strong testimony of our Lord and Savior Jesus Christ. His light shines in you and my prayers are with you and your family. May he bring you peace, comfort and love.

—I want to offer my sincerest condolences on the passing of your son, Dalen. I didn't know him but my son, Adam does and told me what an amazing young man he is. You and your family are in our thoughts and prayers.

It was time to go to bed. I grabbed my pajamas and went into the bathroom to get changed. When I came out from the bathroom, everyone was already in bed, and they were still talking about the messages. We read the news articles again. We listened to all these amazing words of comfort and support. It was actually a very spiritual experience. Many of the words would bring tears to our eyes.

One message I received touched my heart very deeply as we were sitting there on the bed.

> —"Hi, I didn't know Dalen. I was one of the first people on the scene of the accident and tried to help stabilize Dalen. I'm very sorry for your loss. I have done a lot of thinking these last few days about Dalen and your family. I had an uncle who passed away shortly after he returned home from his mission. His patriarchal blessing said that he would continue to be a missionary after this life. I can't help but think that Dalen is also continuing the work of the Lord in the spirit world. D & C 138 we read: 'He beheld that the faithful elders of this dispensation, when they depart from mortal like, continue their labors in the preaching of the gospel of repentance and redemption, through the sacrifice of the Only Begotten Son of God, among those who are in darkness and under the bondage of sin in the great world of the spirits of the dead.' This scripture brought me some peace as I thought of your son."

As we kept reading these inspired words, many times we weren't just overwhelmed but humbled. Many of the words would bring tears to our eyes. We gathered the family together to have family prayers. Since Scott was already in bed, the rest of us went to his bed side and knelt down and Scott leaned forward. Alyssa offered the prayer. Again there was so much gratitude expressed and our love for Dalen, our Savior, and all that we had been given. We shared our goodnight kisses on the cheeks, and everyone got into bed. I made sure they were comfortable before I turned out the lights. I could see they were still on their phones. They continued to talk about comments from family, our friends and we were floored by how many comments we just kept reading; from people that never met Dalen but had been inspired by him or they were expressing their condolences for his passing.

Since Ali and Jordyn had set up the GoFundMe account, Alyssa was constantly updating us on the donations being offered. It was very humbling.

"Mom, you wanna see this!" There was great excitement in Alyssa's voice, so I walked over to her sitting on her bed.

"What is it?"

"Look Mom!" and she pointed to her phone.

I gasped. "What-how is that possible—what the heck?"

"What is it Mom?" Kailee asked.

I started to cry—again meaning just a few tears rolled down my cheek: **10:32 p.m.** "There is over **$5000.00**—What—how is that possible? What is going on? This is just so overwhelming. Who are all these people that are contributing? How do we know who to thank and how do we thank all these people?"

"What?" Scott's voice asked in shock. "How could there be that much money already." This couldn't be normal. We couldn't contain the abundance of support we were all feeling. All of us cried in gratitude. "Thank you Heavenly Father, Thank you!" We paused for a moment, it was just very still and quiet. We all just reflected on what was happening.

I usually was the last to get into bed because I could see better in the dark than Scott and I was the mom, so my kids needed to be safe before I could relax. I don't know if there would be any sleep that night, but we were in a comfortable and beautiful room with our loved ones around us, so it would now be up to us if we slept. Our day would finally be over. One day down. One day down.

February 11, Alyssa's Birthday

A tough day for Alyssa in particular, as it was her birthday. Of course, I was awake before 4:00a.m. It was hard to just lay there and not wake up the family, but I got up and went into the closet space they had. Although the doors had etched glass on them and kind of shone through when the light was on, it was a quiet place. I posted about Alyssa and scrolled to find pictures I had of her on my phone.

> **Facebook 5:15 a.m. 'Knowing that this isn't an easy time for our family, I would like to direct my thoughts first today towards my eldest daughter whose BIRTHDAY it is. Oh Alyssa, what a treasure you are to me. You are a determined young lady who when you allow it, your spiritual strength is ginormous. Know how loved you are. Know how blessed you are. Know that you're my favorite oldest daughter. HAPPY BIRTHDAY ALYSSA. Let there be some happiness today just for you.**

Would she ever be able to enjoy her birthday? It was for her that Dalen and Mariah were driving. We were all going to meet in Vegas to surprise her for her birthday and spend the weekend together.

I was again looking at messages and still the flood of concerned friends and family for our wellbeing. It was so very comforting. I set my phone down for a minute and knelt in prayer. It seemed easy to talk to Heavenly Father and express the absolute pureness of gratitude for all that we had been given, for the love we felt from Him and others, for the care that was given to us; for the safety of all of us;

and for the abundance of blessings that had been poured over us. The peace we were all given was greater than anything I had imagined. We were literally engulfed by it. We had sadness but not devastation. There was calmness in our voices. We felt strength in our fibers and seemed to pursue our course with no hesitation. I was very comforted during my prayer.

It was some time before the rest of the family woke up. I let them sleep until I felt they should get up and get ready. I was reviewing over in my mind all that had transpired in the last day and a half and how our lives had been altered forever. I could see in my mind's eye, fragments of Dalen's life and all the memories that I wanted etched deeply into my memory so as to never forget. I looked through all the pictures on my phone to see how many I had of Dalen. I looked through all my videos and so wanted to find anything that would have his voice on it. That wasn't as easy as I thought it would be to do. In fact, it was a struggle to find them. I had pictures of his mission because that was the last space of time that was recorded. He loved his mission, and we were so proud of his accomplishment. So, I found a few videos. One was of him and Mariah driving. Both were dancing and jamming to: "I Love Rock and Roll" and it was perfect as to their personalities. Loved it.

The other one was a message that was sent to Mariah, but I copied it off her phone. It was Dalen on his mission. It was supposed to be him expressing how much he loved Mariah and how they were best friends. When I listened to it, it just made me laugh because: 1) it was in Spanish, which Mariah didn't understand. I did as I served my mission for The Church of Jesus Christ of Latter-Day Saints in Bolivia some thirty-five years ago and have taught English as a Second Language (ESL) for over twenty years. I could understand much of Spanish that was spoken, and I could still speak it although some of my vocabulary had been limited with the lack of use over the last few years. Dalen and I quite often would speak to each other in Spanish, and we were reading our scriptures together every day in Spanish. Actually, we would read our own scriptures, but we were both in the same area. That way we would have some conversations about what we had read and it helped us both with our Spanish.

2) The video was mostly talking about a new sweat jacket that Dalen had purchased, and he was saying: "Don't I look good? I look so good in this jacket! I know I look good. Anyways if there's anything you ever need, just ask me and I will be there for you. Don't I look good in this jacket? I'm so handsome. Yes I'm good looking!" and it just made me laugh. Of course he ended by saying he loves her and "peace out". What a character, but it was Dalen.

Some time had passed and I heard the group stirring. It was time for them to get up. I wasn't sure who wanted to shower or not, so I quickly jumped up and got in so they could have their time after. Sometimes, we use showers just for cleansing. I just stood there with the hot water running down my head. It gave me more time for reflection. It was comforting. Kailee was awake and then Alyssa and then Mariah. It was like they all had an alarm clock inside and they went off at the same time.

When I got out, the family had pretty much woken up and were walking around or looking at their phones. Our phone lines really were like lifelines. They gave us so much comfort and we were amazed from where the comments just kept coming from. It really was such a blessing. We took our time getting ready as we didn't need to be anywhere till 11:00 a.m.

> Facebook 8:00 a.m. "We are just more than overwhelmed with all the texts, IM, Facebook thoughts, prayers and uplifting remarks. Just know that I want to hug you all and thank you. For any traveling for Dalen's funeral, especially out of state and country; although I won't have beds for you all, I want to see you at my house during the day. Just know that. We are so overwhelmed."

My thoughts of course were very focused on Alyssa. Would she ever want to celebrate this day again? I hoped so. I hoped she would reflect on Dalen but also know that he wouldn't want her to be sad on her birthday. Would she carry guilt that again they were driving to be with her? I was so worried for her. How could we make this day special in any way for her that she would accept? I didn't have these answers yet, and I wouldn't know what to proceed with until she related her feelings to us, and then I would be able to analyze her state of mind. She said thank you when we wished her a happy birthday but also stated: "I don't want anything done for my birthday today. I don't want to remember it's my birthday. This isn't a birthday I want to remember."

We agreed to her wishes. Still, it was her birthday no matter what was said.

Kailee went into the shower next.

> Facebook 8:12 a.m. Brandon's post-"She doesn't want this because she doesn't want the focus on her right now, but I'm doing it anyway. Happy birthday to my wonderful wife Alyssa Stirling! She is selfless and kind and has the biggest heart. She is an amazing strength to her family and everyone around her. When you see her smile you can't help but have one yourself. Marrying this beautiful woman was the best decision I ever made. I love you Alyssa."

Facebook 8:15 a.m. Kailee's post—"Although it's a hard time right now, it's still my older sister's bday and would love to wish her a happy birthday even though she doesn't want it. I love you and am grateful to have an older sister.

Facebook 8:17 a.m. Scott—"We would be honored for all our family and friends to attend our son's funeral and celebrate his life with us. Funeral services for Dalen Scott Graham will be at The Church of Jesus Christ of Latter Day Saints, Sat. Feb. 17, viewing at 9:00a.m., with service at 11:00 a.m. Address; 44330 27th St. E Lancaster, Ca."

Our Amazing Sunday Day

The messages began early. I was receiving thoughts from **5:00 a.m.** on. It surprised me how many people were online, on my lines of technology, to express their thoughts and concerns. Sister Bennett (our Relief Society President in our ward) was trying to arrange housing for family that might be coming for the funeral. This was so weird, talking about who might be traveling and from where. We were discussing the family dinner after the funeral and how many we might expect. We were beginning to get a head count of those expressing their desires to be with us. It was going to be a big deal. Time frames were discussed. The family dinner was going to be at **2:00 p.m.** in our building in Agua Dulce. We were planning for one hundred and fifty people. That too, sounded amazing as there would be that many family and friends that would have traveled to be with us.

We were learning quickly that everyone felt they needed to do something for us. There really wasn't anything for them to do. They wanted to help. They wanted to take whatever sadness they could from us. They wanted to make our situation better. There were offers to feed our animals. People wanted to offer their homes for us. Food was being organized for when we arrived back home. "Please let me know how I can help", was repeated over and over.

Some of the greatest words of advice we received, were presented by our Bishop to Scott when he was driving him to the Burbank airport: "*Everyone mourns in a different way. Let them have their time.*" What I learned from that was that our family was strong. We had handled this ordeal well and positive. We had moments. Some have cried more than others. Some have been a bit quieter in their responses. Some of us felt the need to talk about Dalen and his passing and express our constant gratitude for the miracles that had transpired. Now we were noticing others that were mourning. Others felt that they were falling apart. Others seemed to need our comforting words or hugs. Others couldn't think of anything else but to find something they could give to us that might help our needs. Whatever it was, everyone mourned in a different manner. So, we learned to accept whatever was being offered. It was what they could do to help them feel better about this devastation. We would shake hands and say thank you for their good wishes. We would be united as a family and stand as witnesses of our Heavenly Father's plan of the next life. We would accept flowers, food, houses and transportation if that would help someone else process. We felt empowered by love.

> **February 11, 10:43 a.m. Kathy Blake (my cousin)** "I know you're probably overwhelmed so, I promise after this text, I'll try not to bother you for at least 45 minutes. I had a dream last night that I wanted to share with you. Dalen and Mariah were in heaven standing with Heavenly Father. Heavenly Father was explaining to them what their life would be like when they came to earth. He talked to them about the family they would come to and the work they would do here. Heavenly Father turned to Dalen and told him that a time would come when he would be called home to do a work critical in the building of the Kingdom of the Lord that only Dalen would do. Then Heavenly Father turned to Mariah and explained to her that she would have a huge role in helping her brother get back to Heaven. He knew that it would not be easy, but He chose her because of her faithfulness and strength. They both told Heavenly Father that they were willing to do whatever He asked of them. Heavenly Father then expressed the

> deep love He had for them and promised that their family would be blessed far beyond what they could imagine for their obedience and faithfulness. That's all I can remember. I wanted to share it with you while it was still fresh in my mind. We are continually praying for you and your family. Love you."[41]

"So powerful! Thank you. One of the best stories ever. Thank you so much." I said.

I knew immediately after reading this message, that Scott and I would have to speak at the funeral and share this, as well as our thanks for everyone and everything.

Scott wasn't quite on board yet, but he would come to agree with me. We had to express our thanks.

Everyone was getting ready for church. Rick came over to be with Mariah and to escort us to his family's house. Alyssa was getting hungry which was normal. It seemed like her and Mariah could eat almost at any time and when they were hungry, they meant they were hungry now. The cookies were on the counter from last night, and there were a few munchies from all of us driving up which we took out of our vehicles. They found enough to calm themselves for a minute.

"Mom, check this out," Alyssa stated. Again, I was looking at her phone screen and there was now just shy of **$9,000** in the 'GoFundMe' account. I just couldn't believe that. It really blew me away. Why were so many people being so kind to us? We really didn't think that many people knew us or considered us friends. It was so overwhelming. They truly did care, and we were being cared for.

"My mom said things are ready if you want to go over early," Rick commented.

"I guess we could leave early. How much more time would everyone need to get ready?"

"I'm good," Alyssa said.

---

[41] The insight my cousin had in her dream presented an understanding to us all—it almost seemed like this was in some way, God's plan.

"I'm ready," Mariah said.

"Let's go," was Kailee's thought.

"Okay—then let's go."

Usually on a Sunday morning, I would have all four of the kids ready to go to church. We would all be cleaned, dressed and prepped, and still have to wait for Scott and this was the same scenario. Scott was doing his hair and still needed to get his socks and shoes on, so we waited for him again. Rick took Mariah in his truck and the rest of us went in our car. We followed Rick to his parent's house.

As we drove up to the community and looked around, it was in a very nice area. The homes had nice sized lots and they looked pretty big. We didn't know a whole lot about Rick except his dad was a professor at BYU-Idaho and his mom was mostly at home, but also heavily involved on the city council. We knew they had adopted two boys from South Africa and that Rick had some sisters, but not really any other information more than that.

10:40 a.m. We walked into the Hamilton home. They were so very cordial and gracious and welcoming of us into their home. We came in through the garage which led directly into the kitchen. It had a big island and lots of cupboards. It was very opened. Her decorations were of family pictures and contemporary style décor. The colors were beige based with black granite tops on the counters and they had cherry wood cabinets. It felt very homey. Their table was long. It had a bench on the back side and then there were six chairs around it. We stood in the kitchen for a minute and talked briefly. Sister Hamilton was very concerned for our wellbeing. She wanted to make sure we were good. She was very kind. You could see a bowl with a fruit salad, there were mini sandwiches and pancakes with all the trimmings. There was whipped cream, two types of berries, syrup, butter and peanut better. They had things set up in a buffet style for us.

"Should we offer a prayer?" Brother Hamilton suggested, to which we unanimously bowed our heads and folded our arms. Sister Hamilton offered it. She made mention of our trial and petitioned the Lord for comfort on our behalf, that we would be able to make it through this event. She prayed for us to have strength and to see all those that loved us. It was beautiful and appreciated. And of course, she blessed the food. So now, it was time to eat.

Of course, they let our family dish up our plates first. Brandon said he would be last which he usually did because then he wouldn't have to worry about taking too much, but that he could also take what was left since he could usually clean up the food. So we dished up our plates, I took some pancakes and fruit. There was a quiche she had made also, which I took just a very small portion of as I felt my plate was pretty full. I didn't have to have butter, but I put some strawberries and blueberries on my pancakes, squirted some whipped cream on the top and poured syrup over it all so it was dripping onto the pancake. We sat down one by one. We all waited to eat till our hosts also sat down with us.

"Go ahead and eat. You don't have to wait for us." Sister Hamilton commented.

"We're good. We can wait," Alyssa responded.

"Well, it isn't necessary, but nice of you." Sister Hamilton tried to encourage us all to just eat.

It only took a few minutes for us all to have our plates and sit down. Rick was actually, one of seven kids and we all fit around the table or island by choice. We started to eat. There was normal conversation of: "Oh this is so good."

"Thank you so much.:"

"This smells and looks so great."

"Thank you for having us over."

Conversations continued amongst us. Sometimes it was between the whole group (probably 90% of the time), and then there were a few of side interactions going on. It was very comfortable. We talked about our jobs and careers. We talked a bit about our families. They were very hesitant to say anything about Dalen. I broke the awkwardness.

"I don't think I thanked you for being at the hospital Friday night. That was so amazing and it was so comforting to know you were there with Mariah, that there was another mother to take care of her."

"Oh, it was no problem at all. Of course, we would be there," replied Sister Hamilton who asked that we call her Tisha, to which we obliged her.

"What time did you actually leave the hospital? I don't think I knew, nor did I thank you."

"You did thank us. We left before midnight. We stayed for a bit to make sure you guys were okay," Tisha replied.

Dalen had been over to their house I heard on several occasions, so they knew him and all his quirkiness. They said he made them laugh all the time.

"Oh, that was so kind of you."

"But how are you all doing? You seem like your fine and doing okay. How are you doing that? We expected this to be so much harder than it is," Tisha stated.

"We are good," Alyssa said.

"Yeah, it's weird, but we are all okay. It's not easy. but we are good." Scott commented.

"It's like we know to comfort everyone else. We really realized early in this process that this was our calling. Because we had resolution with Dalen's passing, it would now be our turn to help others with their mourning. We really were okay."

They seemed surprised of our state of minds. We didn't know that we weren't acting normal. It was just what we were doing.

Our conversation was good. We laughed and shed some tears, but really just enjoyed ourselves. It was a very pleasant experience.[42]

I looked at the clock and it was approaching **12:15 p.m**. We knew that church was at **1:00 p.m**. so we still had a bit of time. My girls got up to help clear things. I was kind of stuck in the middle of the bench so I had asked if they could help. Mariah—who was very used to being there, was too casual. She said she didn't need to help because the other girls could do it, but she repented of her ways and helped. Everything was either downsized into smaller containers or thrown away because there wasn't enough left of the item. Brother Hamilton was the biggest coordinator on the cleanup. He said it was his job.

Once the kitchen was cleaned, we walked into the family room and sat for a few minutes. The Hamiltons talked about the family

---

[42] The Hamilton family was not only kind to us but they were the beginning of our healing.

pictures on the walls, and we learned a bit more about the personalities of each child. It was just a very pleasant visit and we felt very comfortable being with them. Our conversations were as such that everyone was included and contributing. It was a great brunch, with good company.

At home, we live about ten miles away from our church. When church starts at 9:00 a.m., I like to leave by 8:40 a.m. so we get there on time, get our seats and have a few moments to mentally prepare ourselves for the services. Generally, a ward meets together and there are three separate meetings. The first seventy minutes were for the Sacrament portion. This was the main reason we went to church, to renew our covenants of baptism by partaking of the sacrament, which consists of bread and water. We follow the example of the Savior when he gave bread and wine to his disciples and called it the sacrament. In our covenants we promise to keep his commandments and always remember Him. We then are promised by our Savior that we will have His spirit to be with us. The bread represents the body of Christ. The water represents the blood that Christ shed for us and our sins. There are specific prayers offered on the bread and water and then as a congregation, we get to partake.

When there are more than one ward in the building, they share rooms. Generally, we would meet in what we call the chapel first, which also happens to be the biggest room in our buildings. We sit with families. Our ecclesiastic leader (Bishop), sits in the front of our congregation on the stand with his two councilors that help our bishop with the affairs of the ward. The sacrament is passed to the congregation. Those who are worthy, partake. After the sacrament part is completed, there are generally two or three speakers chosen out of the congregation with a previous notification. Their goals are to inspire the rest of us to be better and learn about our Savior.

After Sacrament, we divide into various age-appropriate groups throughout the building and attend Sunday school. While we are in the chapel, another ward might be finishing up their Sunday school lessons in the other rooms. So, when they finish, the rooms are vacant so our ward then resumes our classes, and another ward might be meeting in the chapel. There are two hours between each ward in a building where the population of the church is great. One ward would start at 9:00 a.m., one at 11 and then one at 1:00 p.m.

Sunday school is of course, where we learn the gospel. We are in classes with an instructor and study the scriptures.

The third hour is where the children are in primary from ages three to eleven. We have singing time, play time, and time for lessons. The youth from twelve to eighteen are in mutual classes. They have more spiritual discussions again divided into age groups and sexes. Girls meet together and the young men meet together. The Ladies attend Relief Society, and the men participate in Priesthood. Again, we discuss the same topics but with specific insights to men learning of the priesthood power and how to be servants for God. In Relief Society, which is the world's oldest women's organization in the world, we are instructed on how to be better mothers, show charity; enrich family blessings and do good to those in need around us. The ladies learn of our roles as partners to our husbands and how to guide our families as the nurturers in our homes.

Sundays are days of uplifting, visiting with others and fulfilling ordinances. There are no paid positions in our church. Everyone has promised that we will dedicate our time and talents to the building up of the kingdom of God. That means that we accept callings from our Bishop who either feels inspiration to put someone in a position for them to grow; or for that person to help others grow. They can last for all varied periods of time. For example, I have been a primary teacher (eight—eleven-year-olds) for about a year. Prior to that, I was called to be the chorister during Sacrament. I held that position for almost two years. Our classes are all directed from our church headquarters, which resides in Salt Lake City, Utah. So, no matter where we go in the world, we know the lesson for that day. We are given manuals with lessons in them, and they are specified to the date and are our guidelines. It is actually really neat knowing that my kids in our three different states, would be studying the same topics and that we could discuss the ideas expressed in our wards with each other.

We believe all our callings come from our leaders praying to the Lord. He waits for inspiration as to who should fill what calling. Revelation is when Heavenly Father lets us know of His desires. We accept our callings as that—the Lord has called us to that position for that time.

Sundays are a day of rejuvenation. We get to renew our baptismal covenants through the sacrament; then are edified through lessons taught. I love Sundays. They are simple days and are supposed to keep things centered on Christ in all we do.

A month ago, our prophet, President Nelson, announced a change in our Sunday meetings and took our services down to two hours instead of three. With our church being worldwide and now more members outside of the United States than in it, there was a need for a change. The doctrines will never change but policies have over the years. Distance, finances, time and availability were all factors that would help those that lived throughout the world. So now we have two-hour services: Sacrament is only one hour, every week. Then the 1st and 3rd weeks we would have Relief Society and Priesthood. The 2nd and 4th weeks would be Sunday School classes. Today was only the second week with the new schedule for us all.

We walked into the building. There is never awkwardness in one of our buildings even when we are in a different city or country. It's a comfort and so we went in and found our spots to sit down. The Hamilton family sat near the front on the first two pews. It was interesting because everyone had heard of our situation and of course, they had seen Mariah there before, so were very saddened and almost reverent towards us. Sister Hamilton introduced us to some of her friends.

"This is Sister Graham, Mariah's mom and her family." They would cordially greet us and shake our hands.

We took our places. The music played and the service began. The opening song kind of shocked me as it happened to be Dalen's favorite. How unique was that? We were visiting a ward that was singing our son's most liked hymn. I found a sweetness while partaking of the sacrament. I felt of the atonement of our Savior. I knew that my son had been received by a hug from our Lord and that the work was moving forward. The speakers today were talking about missionary work and how important it was. They mentioned too that our missions don't just end with this life but carry on. I thought again how appropriate. I felt great comfort and was grateful to have been there. The girls had another view. Alyssa and Mariah especially, were showing that they were having a hard time that Dalen's favorite hymn was played. They didn't want to hear about missionary work on the other side even though we knew the plan. They were a bit uncomfortable with it all. Kailee seemed okay. Scott was listening, but his head was down most of the time too. I felt bad for the girls' struggles.

It was time to attend our next meeting which meant we would move to another room. This week we would happen to be in Relief Society for the sisters and Priesthood for the brethren. This change had only been announced a short time ago, so we were all still adjusting. I was actually grateful for that because I was in need of the sisterhood and desired to feel of their strength. We walked into the room again with some introductions. The chairs were placed in a circle, also a new change, to help everyone feel more included and not just receiving instruction, but became participants in the directed discussion. They had only done it once before, so it took a minute to turn all the chairs around. I got to sit with all my girls which I always loved. Most of the ladies again, knew of our story and that our son had passed away just yesterday. I found that amazing too because Dalen was a student at the college, but that didn't mean that everyone in the town knew of the accident, but I guess they did. You could tell by their faces that there was almost a shocked look first that we were there, and then what they could say to us. Again, we were introduced as Mariah's family, which was sweet. They knew Mariah and Rick were dating and we were with Rick's family, so it wasn't too hard to figure out. Now we were the family whose son just passed away. There was almost a hush from all the sisters when they heard it announced who we were.

We start every meeting with a song and a prayer and again we were surprised as another one of Dalen's liked hymns was sung. I felt a tear roll down my cheek. The prayer was offered, and they mentioned our family and that we be granted peace, very humbling for sure. The instructor then began to lead her topic which was: "How to handle adversities and trials". How appropriate for us. With all of us having trials, she wanted to focus more on how to not just endure them, but to endure them well. She did very well on keeping the discussion on helpful suggestions with various issues. Of course death of a loved one was mentioned, as was physical issues or financial situations or marital problems or children. But somehow the comments returned to someone passing. I felt very inspired to relate my testimony on the subject and the experiences we were going through. I raised my hand and the instructor called on me.

"I was in no way expecting to say anything today, but I felt strongly that I should. When we understand the spirit, we are guided in different points—what to say—what to feel—what to think. We are always guided by the Holy Ghost."

The Holy Ghost is a member of the Godhead. But unlike Heavenly Father and Jesus who have bodies as tangible as ours, the Holy Ghost is a body of spirit. His purpose is to testify of truth. You feel your heart race maybe, or there becomes an excitement inside your body. You feel the need, or prompting to talk about what you're experiencing. It might be that an issue presented just makes sense. All these and more feelings are witnesses of the spirit. It's like a burning from within. When truth is there, a witness of the spirit can be born and so we testify.

"We learn of who the Holy Ghost is because it's through him we can know our Father's desire for us. I think most of you know that our son was the one that passed away yesterday from a car accident. It has been a very difficult but amazing experience. We have felt the guidance from the Lord the whole way. As bad as a death is, I can honestly say that everything has been absolutely perfect. God hasn't just comforted us but guided us. We knew of His plan all our lives, but now we are asked to live what we know. My advice to get through this kind of trial, literally let God take the lead. We have learned that tender mercies are different then miracles. Mercies are when we have asked for something and petitioned the Lord. I've lost my keys. I can't find my book. I don't know where to go. Please help me. And God answers our petitions because He loves us. Miracles are when you just let go, maybe because you just can't do anything else, but let go and let God lead. This is when He magnifies His love for us, and our understanding becomes so enlarged as to who we are."

Alyssa also felt the need to bear her testimony or to witness what she knew to be true. The spirit was strong with her. "Yeah I would like to add to what my Mom said. This isn't easy in any way, but we knew right away that we as a family would now have to testify to those around us. Heavenly Father has been right there with us. We have felt of Him and know that He knows of our situation." Alyssa bore her testimony. There was silence for a few moments as I think people might have been reflecting on our words. I felt the power of our witnesses.

We believe as members of our church, that there is no doubt or question of life going on after we die. Death is a separation of our bodies with our spirits for a time. Our spirits never will die. When our Savior comes again, he will release the bands of death and our bodies and spirits will be reunited to then live forever. We have no question as to where Dalen is and what his work will be now. He will be a missionary to all those spirits who haven't heard of the gospel of Christ yet. There is no doubt. There is no fear. There is no guessing. We know.

Yes, there are trials, and they are so hard. When we understand God's plan, not that the trial is easier, but we are given assistance and guidance through them. I know the ladies in that room knew of our convictions. It felt pretty amazing for the need to bear witness of God's love for us.

Other comments were made in the class as they continued. "I don't know how you are able to express such strong feelings," one lady commented.

"That was incredible," responded another sister.

"Sisters, I'm sorry. I'm not meaning to come across as boasting in any way, but we all know in our family that God loves us and is sustaining us." I stated.

There were a few minutes left in the class and the instructor concluded with her testimony and another witness that God was there. He wants to be in our lives and will help us all along the way. The class came to a close.

I have always believed in Heavenly Father. I have always known that I was his child. Sometimes, I haven't believed I was of major importance, but I have always known of Him. His plan of happiness is to have all of his children return to him and live with our families forever with Him. So that was our goal, to live our life in accordance with God's laws that we could be worthy to receive all that Heavenly Father has for us. And now as a family we just knew that our position in all this, was to testify of what we knew and where Dalen was and what he was doing. We felt blessed, so very blessed.[43]

Many ladies came up to us after and expressed how much our words helped them. Others expressed their condolences. It was a good meeting. Church was the right place to be. We went into the hallway of the building to wait for the rest of the family members so we could leave.

We said our goodbyes to the Hamiltons and decided to go to our room at the hotel, for those that would want to take a Sunday afternoon nap—an important part of Sunday for my family. That was a tradition in our home. We would go to church in the morning. Come home at noon. Eat lunch and then take naps. When our kids were little, Sundays were a bit crazy so I told them that they could do anything they wanted to do in their rooms as long as they were quiet, and it wouldn't bother anyone else. Our kids would play for a bit but then lie down and eventually would fall asleep. It then became routine that our quiet time ended up a nap time. Mariah was all over the idea and Alyssa merely stated that she was ready. So, we went to the hotel. Everyone went straight to their beds. Quiet time had begun.

When I looked over from my bed, everyone was still on their phones reading messages. They all shared some of them for the few minutes, but then I mentioned: "If you want a nap, you better take one or you won't get to because we only have about 2 ½ hours before we needed to leave for President Eyring's house."

I think I even fell asleep for a few minutes which didn't happen hardly ever. It felt good. When I did wake up, I laid there trying not to move too much to wake anyone else up. I kept reading messages on my phone.

---

[43] Bearing a testimony isn't always easy, but when we have learned what the promptings are it is important to bear that witness because someone else needs it. Alyssa and I were blessed to bear that witness. It was amazing.

Dinner With President Eyring and His Family

5:00 p.m. I started waking everyone up so we could get ready and freshen up before we went to President Eyring's house. We were expected to be there at **5:30 p.m**. We weren't quite sure what to wear. They said we could be casual, but would that be the same casual as a President of the university would think? Scott said we should dress in our Sunday clothes which meant suits for the men and dresses for the girls. The Eyrings actually lived in Rexburg, but as President of the university, he was offered 'The President's house' to live in if he chose. It was on the east side of town where you could tell the houses were huge and each had some acreage with them. We found the house through our GPS.

"Holy crap, that's a big house!" Scott exclaimed.

Alyssa quickly responded: "WOW!"

"This looks like a house a president would live in," Kailee gave her insight too.

There were huge rocks in line with the driveway and built into the design of the landscape. Because there was snow on the ground, we couldn't see quite how big the boulders were, but it was nice. The porch was also very big. We all stood on the steps. Scott knocked on the door. It only took a minute, and the door was opened by Sister Eyring who immediately invited us in. The house was huge. The entryway was almost the size of a bedroom. Looking straight ahead was the living room. It was still decorated with Christmas decorations. There was about an 8ft tree with red and silver ornaments on it. Some garland was still hanging on the mantel. There were two couches.

When you looked to the left, there was a formal dining room with a table that was set up for ten people to eat at. That made sense since there were ten of us. The wood was a cherry wood, and the setting was beautiful. The table was set with stoneware plates and crystal glasses. It was very nice.

You walked through an archway and then into this huge kitchen. I first noticed the island that had to be about twelve feet long and five feet wide. It had black granite on all the counter tops. The cupboards were all white. There were two sinks and two big ovens and two conventional ovens. There was a microwave. Two warming drawers that was really cool. Looking straight ahead from the kitchen was the family room where a sectional sofa set was there and a huge TV screen. It was of earth tone colors in décor.

"We are so excited to have you here." Sister Eyring said as we were walking into and through the house on a tour. "We are just so sorry for what you are going through."

You could tell that this would now be our normal, learning to talk about Dalen in the past tense. How to help others that didn't know what to say, to avoid the awkwardness seemed to be our task.

"Oh it has been difficult, but we have been so blessed," I commented.

President Eyring was now greeting us. We shook hands and he looked into our eyes; "I'm just so sorry. This must be horrible for you."

"We are doing okay. We are very blessed and it's still pretty new," Scott replied. "But we are okay."

He asked the names of our family members and introductions took place as we had now moved towards the table after setting our coats on the couch in the living room.

"You must really like Christmas to still have your tree up." Kailee stated.

"Well, actually with President Eyring being the president, they give us this house to live in. We really live in our other house and just use this one for when dignitaries come, or special reasons come up. So honestly I really forgot we hadn't taken things down yet. It looks okay, so I haven't worried about it, but I probably should find the time," Sister Eyring replied. We all laughed which felt good too.

They had two boys and they looked pretty young. I think they were twelve and fifteen maybe. But President Eyring looked exactly like his dad who happened to be the first councilor to our prophet of our church. He really could have been a twin (younger of course) to his dad, talked like his dad and even laughed like his dad. There was small talk asking what Scott did for a job—if I worked, where our kids were at in life. Sister Eyring asked if we were hungry and said that things were ready if we wanted to sit down so we could eat. Everyone made a motion to where they suggested we sit. I followed her into the kitchen.

"Wow, this is big!"

"Yes it is. It's actually too big for me. I think that's why we live in the other house."

"But it is very beautiful." I stated.

"We are so grateful to have you here." Sister Eyring said again as we were walking into the kitchen. She opened the warming drawers. They were so cool. Inside were stuffed chickens and broccoli with mashed potatoes and a salad came from out of the fridge. I helped her dish up the food onto beautiful serving trays. It was just amazing.

The food was placed on the table and we all took our seats after some guidance from Sister Eyring as to where she would like us to sit. President Eyring bowed his head to offer the blessing. Usually a blessing on the food is just that, we bless the food that our bodies would receive nourishment. We thank Heavenly Father first and express our gratitude for what we have to eat. Then we close our prayer in the name of Jesus Christ as he is our mediator for the Father. All we do is in His name. Along with the blessing on the food, President Eyring mentioned our family and our tender situation. He asked that we would have peace. He asked Heavenly Father to send angels down to attend to us. He spoke of Dalen's testimony and that he was in thy care. I felt as if I was receiving a personal blessing. It was amazing. The spirit was very strong there. We had peace and comfort again. We began to dish up our plates.

"This has to just be so hard;" President Eyring stated. "How are you truly surviving this ordeal?"

"Well it is actually pretty amazing. Right from the start we have known as a family that we had been comforted and that we now needed to comfort others."

Scott added: "It's not like you plan for this. I didn't plan on my son dying but we are just doing what we think needs to be done."

"But how are you doing so well?" Sister Eyring was very concerned for us.

"I've learned a few lessons in the short time since Dalen's passing. I had come to know the difference between tender mercies and mighty miracles. A tender mercy is when we plead with Heavenly Father. We've lost our keys and we pray to find them. We're not sure what career to do, so we ask. We need help with where to live. God loves us so he answers our prayers. Miracles are when we let him lead. And our lives have been so blessed because of that. We just didn't know that how we were acting and feeling wasn't normal. It's not easy to say that our son has passed on, but the moment he died, everything had fallen into place. We have been comforted and guided and so abundantly blessed. It's just been absolutely perfect," I commented. This would be my new phrase. Everything transpiring had been perfect, completely guided by God and filled with peace.

"Wow—that is amazing," stated Sister Eyring, "that you could be that strong."

"We don't think we're really strong. We just know that we all feel we should help everyone else through this." were Alyssa's thoughts.

The conversation continued on. There was discussion about our family, what Dalen was like. That's where the girls contributed a lot. It was actually kind of fun until again we realized the reason for our visit. Besides that, we all enjoyed ourselves. I sat next to one of their boys and we talked about their likes and passions and some of their goals for the future. One liked to play basketball and wanted to get really good grades. The other boy like playing musical instruments and wanted to be in the band. They liked X-box games and hanging out with their friends. All around the table we had our own little vignettes and very often the discussion would unite us all back together again.

The food was so delicious. It was just a really nice evening. We had already been there about an hour. We were finishing up with our dinner and Sister Eyring mentioned that we had dessert coming too. All my girls immediately got up together and started collecting the plates and clearing off the table. Everything was brought into the kitchen. I tried to get my girls to start washing the dishes, but Sister Eyring wouldn't let us.

"Oh no, I don't want you to do the dishes. You are our guests and we can take care of it," she replied.

"We don't mind helping," Mariah said.

"It would be our way to say thank you for the lovely meal," Alyssa said.

By now, everyone was in the kitchen and we were handing the plates off to the person rinsing them. At least that way we could stack them and kind of clean up the counter space a bit. She had two types of pies for us to choose from, apple or cherry. That was perfect because everyone in my family liked one or the other, of course with an ice cream scoop too. The desserts were scooped out and again we returned to the dining room with our treats in hand and to our seats. It was just so nice to be there and to feel and see of their concern for us and to see the state of mind that we were all in.

"Well, this has just been such an amazing experience," President Eyring stated. "I didn't know what to expect or the mental state of everyone, but your family has been amazing. You have inspired me. We are so grateful for all of your sweet spirits. This has been a very enjoyable evening. So thank you."

Again, we were standing near the entry way, and we had to get some pictures. They were such a neat family and we felt so honored to be there. We all started hugging each other and expressing our gratitude. We learned about them and them us. We talked about Dalen and felt blessed. We were seeing miracles and learning that Heavenly Father was leading us. I doubt if many people would get to say that they had dinner with President Eyring and his family, but then again, maybe they do this for everyone in our situation. Either way, we were blessed. And of course, the circumstances weren't normal, but it felt normal to be there. They were just so inviting and as awkward as we might have thought the dinner would be, it wasn't.[44]

We said our thank yous one more time, and we loaded up into the car.

"Wow, that was really nice."
"I loved that chicken," Kailee replied. "It was so good."
"I'm pretty full myself," Brandon added.
"Yeah, I liked it too," Alyssa responded.

Mariah mentioned how she liked that we all laughed. She liked that there wasn't awkwardness. We were told by President Eyring that he would have his secretary check upon us tomorrow. They knew that we would be closing Dalen's schedule for school. He told us who to contact. He reiterated a few times that if we needed anything, that we should let him know and that he would help us however he could. It was again so overwhelming the reception we had been given. We all were very grateful. Driving away left us all talking of what a good experience it was. We talked all the way back to our hotel about how outstanding the Eyring family had been.

---

[44] We got to spend time with the President of BYUIdaho and his amazing family. They blessed our lives. Mariah's Apartment.

Mariah's Apartment

Mariah had commented that she needed some things from her apartment.

"So why don't we go there and we can do movie and popcorn. You do have popcorn, don't you?"

"Yes Mom, of course I do."

"Are you guys up for that?" Scott asked.

"It's better than just sitting in the hotel room," Kailee said.

"Okay, then let's go there." And we did.

Growing up we would have Sunday school in the mornings on Sundays and then we would go back in the afternoon for the Sacrament meeting. With the growth of the church and the convenience for many, they consolidated the meetings. For my family, we would have hot chocolate and toasted cheese sandwiches after church meetings, and then we would watch '*The Wonderful World of Disney*' as a family. I loved Sunday evenings growing up. After Scott and I got married, he didn't want toasted cheese, nor would hot chocolate be appropriate in California where it was quite hot for most of the year. We agreed on popcorn. But it couldn't be any popcorn—no microwave popcorn for sure. So we had to have hot-air popcorn and not just margarine but real butter. It was agreed and so one of the traditions for our married life began. We even converted some of my siblings and my parents to the popcorn.

So Sunday night, **7:00 p.m.** we knew where we were and what we were doing. Since Disney wasn't always available, we would watch a Disney or family movie. I loved this time. Kailee usually was the hard one to get to watch a movie with us. Her Autism meant she didn't like to sit in one area and especially not doing something. So I would pull out a game she liked and while the family was watching the movie, she and I would play our game. She learned to be a part of the family. She never really liked just sitting there, but she would oblige. I was grateful that my kids wanted to keep it going too. So to Mariah's house we went for her to get some things, and our movie and popcorn.

When we arrived, none of her roommates were there. We had seen her place before, at least Scott and I had when we dropped her off for school in January. The other girls hadn't. It was actually like a house. So of course you walked in and the kitchen and family room were always the first things you saw. The kitchen was very big.

There were several cupboards and every one of the roommates would have at least four cupboards which wasn't the normal for a college house. Then to the left was the family room. This house even had a gas fireplace. There were two couches and a coffee table in the middle of them. It was pretty good sized. You walked down a hallway and actually saw four bedrooms, but they only used three as rooms. The fourth they made into a study room.

So, two girls went to a room. The first room was right off the family room where two sisters actually stayed. Then down the hallway and the study room was next, bathroom and across the hall, two more rooms. Mariah's room had a couple of family pictures on the walls and some plaques with quotes on them. She had an American flag on her wall. All the beds were raised on blocks to allow for more storage space under the bed. I kind of liked seeing the jean quilt and other blankets I had made Mariah, that were on her bed. All my kids had a crocheted blanket and a quilted jean blanket and then just a regular blanket I had made for them. Quilting was a joy for me and even though I never seemed to have spare time to do as much as I would like, I did get a few completed every now and then.

Mariah's scriptures were on her nightstand and since they put the desks in the spare room, the bedroom seemed to have a lot of space. There was another bathroom at the end of the hall and then even a garage that was also the laundry room, but all the girls could use it for storage and there were shelves for food as well. What a find. This was a cool place to live at. Mariah got along with her roommates, but mentioned that she just never saw them very much.

She was always with Rick and his family. We encouraged her always to make time for her roommates, to have maybe Sunday dinners together and to make them a part of her college experience. I still have contact with a few of my college roommates.

"They are still a part of my life," Mariah said between school, work and Rick, that she didn't have time for anything else. It was what it was—still a nice place to live and it was right next to campus. It was just so easy and convenient. We walked in and toured the place and then there was a knock on the door. Most of the family had picked their spot in the family room to sit down in. Mariah answered the door. Two young men in white shirts and ties were there. Normally that would be a description of the young missionaries that would be preaching God's words. These however, were what we call 'Home Teachers' in our church. Within the men's organization under the direction of the priesthood, the power to act in God's name, they were assigned to families or in this case of a university, assigned to a housing complex. They were to monthly visit their assigned persons to make sure that things were well. These two young men were fulfilling their callings and mostly came to see if they could help Mariah in any way. They sat on the couch and offered their condolences. They asked a few questions about Dalen, but were mostly concerned with Mariah. She of course said she was fine. Externally that view seemed truthfully, but we had no idea how she was handling things internally. I'm sure her thoughts were consumed with the events that had transpired. Since she wouldn't talk about her feelings, we could only assume she was okay. These young men were very well representing themselves as servants of the Lord. They asked repeatedly if they could do anything for Mariah and she reassured them that she was okay.

"Well if you do need anything, please know that we are here for you and will help however we can," they replied.

"How sweet was that?" Alyssa asked.

Mariah commented that she had never seen her home teachers before but these young men mentioned that they just received their assignment today and so they came. We all shook hands as they left and thanked them for their concerns.[45] What a blessing to know that young men were fulfilling their priesthood responsibilities and that my daughter was being checked on which was comforting to a mom.

The door opened again, and the sister roommates came in. They went straight to Mariah and hugged her. "We are so sorry Mariah." And they just hugged. Mariah soon introduced us to them. She reassured them of course that she was doing okay. They expressed their condolences. I think they weren't quite sure what else to say, so they retreated to their room.

I received a text from a young man that a few months earlier had been a missionary serving in our ward. He was following all our Facebook posts and knew we were in Rexburg and asked if he could come visit us. "I just felt like I needed to see you." He was almost pleading for our time. I invited him over to Mariah's, and it was less than ten minutes and another knock on the door, and there was our Elder Smith. As a missionary they are only allowed to shake your hands, but when the door opened, he just came right up to me and hugged me. He broke down.

"I just had to see you. Dalen meant a lot to me and especially because I love your family," said Elder Smith. I hardly ever heard of this Elder's first name. As missionaries, to show respect, they are referred to as Elder _____ or Sister _____ for the girls. Elder Smith had met Dalen through Mariah. He took it upon himself to check on her occasionally as he had spent a lot of time at our house when Mariah was still in High school and knew her pretty well. It wasn't out of the ordinary that when he heard of the accident that he would have a strong need to make sure Mariah was okay. He was holding a small 2 x 3 picture of Jesus Christ that he said he had been holding on to since the accident was known throughout the campus. The information was almost instantaneously known. Everyone knew and everyone knew Mariah or Dalen and that Mariah was driving. That had to be hard for her too-how well known her story was. Elder Smith handed me his picture.

---

[45] Assignments are given to members, but they don't always fulfill them. These young men weren't just checking on Mariah, they were genuinely concerned for her wellbeing and offered whatever they could.

"Here, I really want you to have this. I just felt that you needed a picture of Jesus Christ with you," he hugged me again.

"Thank you so much Elder. That is way special. I don't remember your first name even. I guess I don't have to call you Elder anymore except you will always be our Elder."

"It's Collin," he stated.

"Oh yeah, now I remember. Well come on and sit down with us. We had just been standing in the kitchen barely past the door. He went over and hugged Mariah first.

"I'm just feeling so bad for you and I don't know how I can help but whatever you need, I'm here for you." He was crying as he spoke with Mariah.

"Thanks," Mariah said. "But I'm doing okay." That became Mariah's standard response; 'I'm okay'. How could she be or was she really? We had all just been carried with so much peace and comfort that maybe Mariah really was okay. Oh how my prayer was that she was okay, that she would be given the strength that we all felt and if needed—to lean on us. Scott got up and was waiting to say hello and was offered a hug too.

We all sat down and talked about where we were in life; how his school was going, how Scott's job was going and of course there was a discussion about Scott's race car. Mariah and I walked into the back as we were still on a mission to make popcorn and watch our movie. She showed me her food storage shelves. My daughter could eat for a few weeks if she actually ate the food she had. We found the popcorn and went back into the kitchen. The conversation seemed enjoyable.

Again, there was another knock on the door. This time it was the manager of Mariah's housing. There was a young couple that lived in the next apartment. They saw that people were home and had hoped that Mariah might be there as they also wanted to check on her. Again, they came in and shook hands as introductions were made.

"We didn't know you would be home, but since we didn't see you at the memorial, we hoped we would find you here," the tall blonde young lady said.

"What memorial?" Mariah asked as the rest of us now also had desires to know the answer to that question.

"Over at Dalen's apartment complex," the young man answered.

"They had a memorial for Dalen. They just arranged it today and announced it in his ward. I think they were expecting thirty to forty people maybe, but there was probably closer to eighty people there," she said.

"What? What memorial?" I asked.

"It was really nice, everyone just gathered around in the lobby and everyone just talked about Dalen and how sad this was. Everyone mentioned how Dalen just made them happy."

"That's amazing!" Alyssa replied.

"If we had have known, we would have gone over. That would have been amazing to hear." I commented.

"You would have gone over?" she asked us, questioning our desires.

"Of course. We would have loved to have heard what they had to say about Dalen."

"Some of the kids were from Dalen's ward, some played volleyball with him, some were from his complex and didn't even know him but wanted to learn of him."[46]

Kailee responded, "That is really cool."

"Yeah, I would have liked to have heard that. What time was it at?"

"Seven," the young lady responded.

"It just barely ended. If you'd like, I could have some of the volleyball guys come over," the man replied.

"Really, that would be so cool."

"Ok—I'll text them." Both her and her husband were sending messages and time went pretty quickly as about another ten minutes later and there was another knock on the door. All conversations up to that point were of our day and especially dinner with President Eyring and how special that was. The young couple agreed that that would have been an amazing experience. But now I wanted to know what happened at this memorial.

Over a year later and we happened to receive a recording of the memorial and the beautiful thoughts that were shared for Dalen. They were very touching.

---

[46] Dalen's complex would honor him with such an event—a memorial, amazing.

Aria Apartment Fireside for Dalen

Stories from memorial.

Zach Lambson Dalen and I would play tournaments in Utah, and other places. Even though Dalen wasn't on the team, he was a part of the team. He came down. We like to video ourselves and get highlight videos. But one of the things he did for us was tirelessly make videos for us. Every single play. He would press play, then pause, and play and pause. Again, being the type of person that he was, he contacted Darin, like before he even got home from his mission, asking about our team because he wanted to play. I don't know Dalen as well as many of you do. I just had the opportunity to be with him and acquaint myself with him. To see the type of person he was. The positive person he was. The positivity is something I think is really important to remember about him and something that we could try to emulate. I never saw him without a smile on his face. Honestly. Other than that, he was a good guy.

Chris Garcia Dalen was on my club team or my rec team last semester. We were the underdogs. Didn't make it very far. It didn't matter what the score was, Dalen always had a smile on his face. I remember writing on his mission and he would be discouraged, but he was always trying and just doing his best. That's what he did here, just smile. Trying to make sure that everyone was happy weather you knew him or not. And that's something I will remember, is his example.

Brock Peniata I've known Dalen for a while. Before, after and in between his mission and his time serving as a missionary for the

Church of Jesus Christ of Latter-Day Saints. We're here to cherish moments and to celebrate his live. He was exactly that. I've often thought, like Zac said, he was always smiling. Dalen was always celebrating life. He was one of the people that I know when I would run into him, I know he would be in a good mood. I know he would be enjoying life. Every opportunity that I had to speak with Dalen he let you feel that. And I mean, to say I was jealous of his outlook of life, his ability to enjoy himself, and just be happy. A lot of the people that are here, are fun people. We have a lot of fun together. But can we say that we live life to the fullest, but I know for a fact that Dalen did. And I also know if you were in this spot, I know he would speak on behalf of all of us. I just love him very much.

(A young Lady) Dalen was in my religion class last semester. He was the coolest kid ever. He always had a smile on his face. He was always happy. He was one of the funniest guy ever. Last semester, he came over a couple of times because I did his hair. He really liked his hair done right. He was really a great guy. And as you were saying, I do know that for us, even if he didn't know us, he was the type of guy that would give you the shirt off his back. And in the short time I got to know him, he really showed that to me. You knew exactly how much he loved the Savior. He LOVED Jesus Christ A LOT!! And in class he was not afraid to bear his testimony or anything. And he was just a really amazing guy. I definitely know he's here with us right now, cause the spirit is so STRONG. I love him.

Dalton Homer I'd like to share a few words. So, I had the opportunity to play volleyball with him last semester and this semester on the co-ed team. This semester was very interesting because the moment we got back from vacation and came back to college, he would call me every single day. He's like: "Hey let's go work out. Let's go play volleyball." His love for volleyball was so deep. But then there was something really interesting. He would call me every day every afternoon. He's like: "How was your day?" and he was genuinely asking and concerned with "how was your day going?" One issue, we always talked about the gospel. One thing was that he always spoke about the spirit. He said one of his goals was to always have the spirit with him. I just thought it was beautiful just the way he would always mention the spirit. That's something that I'm really striving to keep with me too.

Chad Farnsworth I talked with Dalen twice this week. I didn't know it would be the last few times. On Wednesday, I went running to try and keep up with all these people and try and stay in shape. And uh after I went running, Dalen popped up. I see him running around the track. So, I started running too. I started to talk with him a little bit after words, actually he started talking to me because I was out of breath. Seriously, and immediately after, well standing there, I'm still trying to catch my breath and he started asking about my life and how things were going. And what am I doing with myself. You know from the moment I ever met him; he always had a smile on his face. And he always knew what he was doing with his life. And just like earlier, volleyball was such a big part of his life and being part of our family. You know while we were up there he's like: "You know I really shouldn't be here right now." And I'm all 'why'.

"Well, I went to the doctor, and he told me I'm working out too hard and getting in shape way too quickly and somebody is having a little bit of a problem with that." But what can I say, but volleyball was his life. I could totally understand that. That makes total sense to me. And then I started to think of who he is as a person. And the type of person he is: is he goes all the way. Just hearing of his accident made me think of his life. And I don't know what he was like as a missionary, but what I can imagine is he was one that was 100 % all the time. 100% obedient and went all the way throughout his whole mission from day one today-two years later. And just thinking right now that he's gotta finish that. He's gotta continue doing that missionary work on the other side. Because of how good of a person he is. He's only been home like for 6 months and look at how he has affected us all. And I can appreciate that. He's somebody that can really know the family around him. He really is that guy, that smile and always come up to every single person and want to know exactly what's going on in your life. What's going on with you and what are you doing with yourself. And then the next time you see him; I saw him the next day on Thursday, and we picked up our conversation from Wednesday. We just kept going on and I might have forgotten what we talked about, but he just kept going. I just love that cause he's just one of those guys that makes you feel loved all the time. And he cares about every single one of us.

Cody Wong I knew Dalen for a little while. I met him in my Sunday School and that I think something special that everyone has mentioned upon when sharing their testimonies about him and that was how passionate he was about everything. It was to the point where I'd say the majority of us in this room were envious to the point of knowing how passionate he was about volleyball or school or Jesus Christ or even being just too in shape for all of us. He uh, if anything the way he stood out to me was just how passionate he was about everything and even his life. Like I don't think there's a day in Dalen's life where he thought he was just wasting his time. I meant he could have been sleeping but he could have been dreaming.[47]

So now there were nine other persons that walked in the door. They introduced themselves and again more handshakes were exchanged. It was kind of cool that all these kids came over. They played every night with Dalen. I really found that hard to believe that they played that often, but they did. Things were making sense to me as every time I called Dalen after or near **9:00 p.m**. and he was hurrying to get off the phone because he had to go play volleyball. There were times when Saturdays weren't as strongly participated in. They had self-made teams. Of course, Dalen was on the underdog team. They had very little skill levels according to Dalen trying to describe those that had been picked for the other teams, which left the not as developed players for Dalen's team. Dalen volunteered to play with this team because he wanted to help them. About then was when I was quite frustrated with him because I thought he could put more

---

[47] For Dalen's complex to honor him was more than we could comprehend—so inspiring.

effort into his studies and homework instead of playing volleyball. I thought it was a joke and that it was just an excuse to not do schoolwork. Of course, I was very wrong.

"Have you done all your studying bud?"

"No Mom, but I can do it tomorrow after class. I have to go play Mom. I'll call you later."

I had many repetitive conversations with Dalen about volleyball. Now I was learning that it was all true. They would start at 9:00 p.m. and play till 10:30 p.m. and Monday—Friday. This was my son's addiction. He had to be there. It didn't matter to Dalen if he won or not, he just wanted to play. Dalen would take members aside and help them with their skills. He made it fun for them. We were just told over and over again that Dalen just made things fun.

We found chairs for everyone and we all sat in a circle from the family room that extended through the kitchen. There was one other couple sitting by the couple we had already met, one very big Samoan man and two other girls and two more guys that were there. They didn't quite know what to say. So I helped out again.

"So is there anything you would like to know about us or Dalen and our family, or maybe tell us about your relationship with Dalen."

One young man spoke to us first. "How are you really holding up so well?"

"Well, we don't know how to do anything else. This isn't easy, but we all have felt that we are good," Scott stated. "We had felt right from the first few moments after seeing Dalen, that our job would be to comfort others and testify of what we knew. It's not easy seeing your son and knowing he's brain dead. We had to go through the donor process and that wasn't easy. Then watch him take his last breath. It hasn't been easy, but we have been so blessed through this. It's really been amazing."

"Yeah, everything we do just seems to be guided by Heavenly Father so we can't really complain," Alyssa commented.

"Wow, that is amazing," was one of the responses.

"So what would you like to know about our Dalen?" I asked.

There was no hesitation. Questions started immediately. They wanted to know what kind of a kid he was. They wanted to know what he did during high school years, what he liked to eat, his favorite trips, what some of his dreams were for growing up, what kind of missionary he was, to name a few. It was amazing. The whole family talked about Dalen.

The girls loved to talk about Dalen. They loved to talk about the pranks he pulled on them or how he comforted them. They discussed how he was sensitive to all of them and their needs. The group agreed that they could see many of these characteristic in him. They all mentioned how sensitive he was to them as well. It was expressed that he could just visit with you and within minutes you would be crying with him. He gave great advice and really seemed to care about them. Again, we heard that he cared for the 'one'. He would take the time to teach someone how to serve better or what they should do in a particular position. We heard of him constantly laughing or smiling and making everyone around him feel better. "He was the best."

The young Samoan man said he had a story to tell us. "Your son scared me to death."

"What the heck. You are twice his size so how could he scare you?" Scott asked.

"I know. But you could never just say 'hello' or 'hey dude' and walk by. You knew that when Dalen greeted you and said 'hello', he would ask how you were and would expect an answer. Not just a 'good' and walk by. There was a time recently that I was struggling a bit. I wasn't reading scriptures or anything, and I just didn't want to have to report to Dalen. So he scared me to death. I didn't want to admit my issues and I didn't want to stop and talk to him." We all laughed because we could visualize that clearly.

"And sure enough, one day there was Dalen and he looked me right in the eye. I couldn't avoid his eye contact. He said, 'Hey Dude,' and motioned to give me a fist pump. I told him I was good and he asked me, 'How's your scripture study?' and I couldn't lie or walk away. I felt frozen in my tracks. I couldn't move. Dalen put his arm around me, and I told him I was struggling with that. Dalen told me that he would help me if I needed it and would read with me if I wanted him to. He told me I knew what to do and that I needed to correct it right now. He hugged me and" (there was a little pause as he was getting chocked up), "and said he loved me and I felt it." The 280 lb Samoan man cried.

Again, we heard from the group how Dalen did that with everyone. You couldn't just say 'hi'. He really wanted to know about how you were doing and you couldn't walk away. The girls all commented that they could see their brother doing that because he was the one to always make sure they were good too. He was the sensitive one, and he always hurt if someone else hurt. He really did try to carry their pain.

Another of the young men talked about how he didn't want to play volleyball, but Dalen said he would help him and spent personal time with him before everyone else came and helped him with his serves. "I wouldn't have been on the team if it wasn't for Dalen, in fact, we wouldn't have had a team if it wasn't for Dalen."

"My boy really did love volleyball. In fact, he would rather play ball than do anything else. I really don't know if he did any homework even though he said he did." Everyone laughed. "I tried to believe him. I would ask him almost daily if he was keeping up on his studies and that he had to put as much effort into that as he did with volleyball." I remarked.

"Yeah, but we all know he didn't do that." Scott commented.

It seemed that all our discussions were showing what a good guy Dalen was. We knew that with all this, Dalen affected a lot of people that we had no idea about. We learned that Dalen was never seen walking on campus that he wasn't carrying a Book of Mormon. He didn't just have one in his backpack; he held it visually in his hand. And when he acknowledged someone, he always asked them if they were reading The Book of Mormon. We learned that he knew a lot of people. He didn't just greet people, but had to know about them personally. They talked of his sense of humor and that he always seemed happy even if he was troubled; he had a smile on his face.

In turn, they learned about Dalen as a kid and all the crazy things that happened. If he broke something it never seemed to bother him. It was just "Oh well, it's not that big of a deal", even though it might have been especially to us his parents, a big deal. He dented the fenders on the truck, the camping trailer, and the horse trailer. In fact, we wish he would have felt bad sometimes about some of his accidents, but it just didn't seem to bother him. It wasn't in his character.

Mariah commented that most of her scares were from Dalen. He pushed her into a puppy crate and the gate prongs poked through Mariah's lip, and she had to have a plastic surgeon fix it. She spoke of the cut over her eyebrow when again he pushed her into a brick wall at the church during a baptism when the person was changing their clothes after they had been baptized. She had another cut above her eyebrow. We literally had it super-glued together by the hospital. There was a scar on her arm, another on her leg, and it just became funnier as she kept pointing out, as Mariah called it-'Dalen's handiwork'. We all were enjoying our evening so very much.

All of these young kids really loved and respected Dalen. Elder Smith remained with us too. I was just blown away by hearing of the type of man that my son had become. I knew he had a very good heart, but to just hear again and again the care that he gave to others; really amazed me. I knew Dalen struggled to try and figure out where he really belonged and knowing that he was only at school because we told him he needed to be there. There was a good influence around him. You could find people striving to live the gospel and returned missionaries who were yearning for the closeness of the Savior that they felt while on their missions, but they were there in this area and could talk about their mission experiences and remember all they felt. We knew how powerful that support was to a returned missionary. I knew Dalen hated school and would attend a class a few times and then drop the class which would frustrate the crud out of me. He did waste so much time. Instead of taking a full load and work his butt off to study and progress scholastically, just wasn't what Dalen wanted to do. He didn't know what kind of job he wanted to do. He didn't know what path he wanted to take. So our advice was to try a few things and see which ones fit him, but that still meant going to school and studying and it just wasn't his thing.

Our discussions led to comments from the others: "I guess that's where Dalen got his sensitive side from" or "I see where Dalen got his funny side from". Scott responded, "Yeah from me—naturally." I remarked.

Mariah interjected with: "I think we can all see who he takes after and of course it's me."

I learned that Dalen had another ulterior motive; he was there to inspire others. This was so huge to hear and see. My son was meant to bear witness to them. He was there to let others know they mattered. My son did good. He loved everyone. He encouraged them. He knew of them, and he was happy for the most part. What an amazing blessing to me. With all the contention on school, life choices, and lack of follow through, focusing on classes; trying to get a job to help support himself and him not caring, it seemed so insignificant now at this point in time. Now I was treasuring the words I was hearing being expressed about our boy. Our son made a difference. Our son was a righteous man. Our son served others. Our son loved all around him.[48]

We spent over two and a half hours together talking about Dalen. It was so amazing. We were laughing, learning, rejoicing, crying a bit and being uplifted in the life of our son. We had all been edified and not really wanting the night to end. There naturally came that point though that these kids needed to get home.

"Thank you so much for sharing your son with us," the first comment came. "Thanks for telling us about him. It makes a lot of sense now seeing your family and where he got his spiritual side from," was another comment. "That's all her," Scott said while pointing to me which was also a surprise because he usually wouldn't relay a compliment like that to me in front of others. It was nice.

"This has been amazing. I'm so glad we came over," one of the girls replied.

---

[48] For Dalen's complex to honor him was more than we could comprehend – so inspiring.

It was like the feeling you get when something you have aspired to comes about, but even more exciting than that. It was like working three hours outside in the heat and jumping into the pool clothes and all, because you were so hot and yet that elation of being in the pool was amazing. The high of the highs were so very strong and we just didn't want this feeling to end. That was how we all felt and yet it was almost **10:30 p.m**. and they did need to get home.[49]

Mariah gathered what she wanted, and we left her apartment. We entered our vehicles and proceeded back to our hotel. Again, we were involved with catching up on the messages from the evening. Since we were in two vehicles, we waited till we were all together in the room before we read the majority of them.

The goal had been reached with $10,000 in the GoFundMe account.

Seriously, that just seemed so unreal. We were so in awe—again, who were all these people and how could I thank them. I could read

---

[49] Having all these young adults offer us their time and be in Mariah's home and hearing of the good from our son, was just amazing. Our cup was definitely flowing over. Our God again, was so good.

their names and how much they contributed. One family in our ward, whose children are all married except one, all contributed, which just blew me away. One son, actually wasn't active in the church, but his comment was: "I know this young man knew what truth was." It was very humbling to hear. We saw people that donated $5.00. That touched our hearts as much as those that contributed $100.00 or even $200. 00. It was so overwhelming. There were people that we didn't even know, but they heard of our story and contributed. Old teachers of Dalen's were supporting us. It truly blew us away.[50]

We heard from Dalen's Bishop. He called to see how we were doing. He said that today there entire meeting was everyone talking about Dalen. He said it was amazing how many people knew him. He also spoke of the memorial they had and how amazing it was. I would come to learn latter that everyone in the ward wrote a letter or note about Dalen too that we wouldn't receive for a few weeks. School had only been in session for five weeks and there were so many students that wouldn't know a lot of people. I know that in college wards that's usually not the case, because they always had activities to help them connect with each other in a short time. So, if you wanted to get to know people, the platform was prepared to do so. But still, five weeks and I was just floored by the outreach of people that knew our son.

11:00 p.m. It was after 11:00 p.m. and we were spiritually rejuvenated. It was emotionally draining too, but so rewarding. We got ready for bed and knelt to say our family prayer. Brandon took his turn. His words again were of gratitude for all we had received and the pouring out of so many blessings. The atonement had become so very real to all of us. Again, I went around and turned off all the lights and was the last to get into bed. It felt like the TV show '*The Waltons*' from years ago when one person said goodnight and they in turn said goodnight to someone else and so on. You could hear the rustling of the blankets as people were settling into their positions.

---

[50] $10,000 was raised. How were we to accept this miracle? Everything was taken care of. Everything!

Then it was quiet. I laid in bed and just reflected on our experience. Was this really happening? Our son had passed away from a tragic accident. Our family had united together, and we were hearing and feeling nothing but support and love from everyone. My son was gone. He really was gone. I loved my Buddy Boy. And now my speech about my son was all in the past tense. I hated that part of my life that was now a fact. A tear rolled onto my pillow.

3:10 a.m. I usually have to get up during the night to go to the bathroom. It's very annoying because I don't always go back to sleep. I would lay there and get restless, so I usually ended up on the couch. In the hotel though, the only really quiet place I could go to was in the closet. Again the door was mostly etched glass and was kind of bright, so I was worried about waking someone else up. I sat on the floor. I was again reading more messages. It was surprising that comments were being sent at 2:00 a.m. or 1:30 a.m. People were so upset about Dalen's passing. I re-read the emails and texts and then I had a breakdown. I just started crying. I was trying to be quiet, but I understood the power of this reality—my son wouldn't be saying my name anymore—I wouldn't hear his 'Hi Mommy' in his high little voice. He couldn't hug me, bother me, frustrate me, laugh with me, or physically love me. I broke down. I felt abandoned by him. It wasn't a cold feeling just a real deep realization of my new normal. I had to get some toilet paper so I could blow my nose, which meant I had to go into the bathroom. I turned off the light in the closet and grabbed some toilet paper to wipe my tears and blow my nose again, trying to be so quiet. I then got into bed and had to crawl next to Scott. I woke him up. I needed him to hug me and hold me. I broke down again a bit more once he had his arms around me. He held me tight. I was crying but still trying to be silent for the others. No words were spoken, but my tears seemed to be very strong for me. I had a tendency to cry pretty easily and always when I felt the spirit. I cried when I got frustrated, but I never cried uncontrollable or hysterically. I felt a bit out of control at this time and it was so hard to try and cry in silence. I was worried about everyone else hearing me and I so didn't want that.

I felt a person on the other side of me in the bed. Alyssa heard me crying. She got up and snuggled in bed with us and was rubbing my arm to console me. I guess you could say that it was my time to have a hard time, so I took my few moments.

I whispered to Scott and Alyssa, "My Buddy Boy is gone—he's gone!" I felt Alyssa's tears on my shoulder too. "My Buddy Boy is gone away from me. He's gone." We stayed there for just a few moments. I was able to take some deep breathes and regained my composure. I really just felt the need to keep breathing and then it would be over. I was calmed now.

Alyssa asked: "Are you okay Mom?"

"Yes, I think I am. Sorry that I woke you." I just had to let it out. We spoke in a very soft whisper.

"It's okay Mom. That really is the only time you've had a break down and it's okay. I've been crying the whole time."

"Thanks again Alyssa, I love you sweetie. Thank you for showing your concern."

"Of course Mom, I love you too."

"Good night Alyssa."

"Good night Mom," and she went back into her own bed.

Scott asked if I was okay, and I expressed that I was. He then rolled over into his position to go to sleep and I tried to find mine. My prayer now was that I could relax to get some sleep tonight. I guess I just needed the night to be over.

Taking Care of Dalen's School Stuff

February 12, 6:30 a.m. I was again up first. It was about 6:30 a.m. and I went to the bathroom. Again because of the close proximity with the family, I was trying to be quiet. I snuck back into bed and grabbed my phone. There were already messages and emails appearing. It was just so amazing. So, I pulled up the covers and laid there in bed so I could use my phone, but the light wouldn't bother anyone because I had the covers up over my head. I laid there for what I thought was awhile. Everyone was still asleep, so I got out and went into the closet again and knelt and said my prayers. My heart truly was just full of gratitude and peace. I just had been overwhelmed by all the thoughts, prayers and condolences from so many people. Their words were such a comfort not to just me, but to everyone.

8:30 a.m. People started getting up. McDonalds was just on the corner of the street, but the hotel also offered breakfast. Scott wanted McDonalds. We all decided to walk there. Again, with it being winter and quite brisk in the morning, once we got outside, we started to walk and realized that maybe we should drive. We all laughed at how we forgot that it was winter and that meant in Rexburg, it was cold outside. Pretty much anytime we went out to eat, Scott's all 'So you know what you want?' when we hadn't even read the menu. That's partly because every time Scott went somewhere, he got the exact same thing every time. Dinner at Black Angus meant rib eye steak, baked potato, sour crème, chives and butter, with a green salad and Thousand Island dressing. At Jack in the Box, it was a sourdough Jack burger, no fries and of course a large Diet Coke, easy ice always. At McDonald's for breakfast, it was three pancakes with sausage. Every drink he ever got would be Diet Coke with easy ice and keep them coming. But the rest of us needed a few more minutes to decide. We made our decisions and breakfast was ordered. At the table we went over the plans for the day. First and foremost, we needed to take care of Dalen's schooling. We had already closed his apartment. Now we just needed to clear his semester and figure out any financial issues. We were going to stop at the funeral home in Pocatello with the rest of the arrangements for the funeral made and give them to Jared on our way home. Then we would drive on to St. George and stay there for the night.

9:15 a.m. Scott and I were getting ready to leave for the campus. Everyone else was quite content to just sit in the hotel and relax. We really didn't think it would be very long, so we agreed they didn't need to go. There had been previous phone calls with the Dean of Students as that was who we were directed to. His name was Kipp and he was so very nice. As we walked through the building to his office, it was almost like everyone knew who we were. Of course, that was just our interpretation, but it did feel like people knew of us and knew of Dalen. We walked up to Kipp's secretary's desk and introduced ourselves.

"I knew who you were. We are all just so devastated by all of this and want your family to know we are praying for you," the secretary commented.

"Oh thank you so much. We have felt the power of all your prayers, and it has been amazing!"

"We are just really humbled by everything," Scott stated.

The secretary pointed to Kipp's room with a gesture that was where we needed to go. We took the gesture and sat ourselves down in his office. I was to the right of Scott in front of the desk. Kipp wasn't right there but was on his way. He was taking care of another emergency. We sat down and looked around at his office. He had pennants from BYUIdaho. There were a few family pictures on his desk and one on the wall. He had a football in the corner of his desk. There were plenty of books on the shelves, but they were mostly guidelines as to how to be the Dean of Students and educational points.

Kipp walked in. He was a big man—probably 6'2, maybe 240 lbs. He was a big guy. He was bald and was wearing a shirt and tie and was clean shaven. He looked maybe a bit like he might have come from the islands, or that his ancestors did. We shook hands as we were introduced and again sat ourselves down.

"I just can't imagine what you are going through. This has to just be so hard." Kipp stated.

"Well, it hasn't been easy, but it's been incredibly amazing as everything has just fallen into place, and we have been overwhelmed by all the support. The school has been great to us too," Scott replied. "Yeah, we heard there was even a memorial over at Dalen's apartment last night. That was so amazing!"

"Oh yeah, I had heard about it. I couldn't go because we were helping with another emergency, but I heard it was well attended and really good," Kipp said.

I was so surprised that: 1) he knew about the memorial, and 2) that he knew what happened there.

There was just a quick moment of silence as we were refocusing.

"We wanted to make sure that we could close everything we need to for Dalen and make sure that he didn't owe any money."

"So, here's how it works. We delete Dalen from all his classes. His transcript will look like it did before this semester began and I will check, but I'm pretty sure, we will reimburse you for his semester." He was pulling up all of Dalen's information on his computer while he was talking with us.

"Well, that won't be necessary. We need to pay for whatever schooling he had, and he did live here for six weeks and so we need to take care of his housing too."

"We know he wasn't here long, but he was here," Scott contributed with his thoughts.

Kipp flipped his computer screen around so we could see Dalen's information. We could see exactly what he was supposed to be taking and what he really ended up with. That goofball dropped below twelve credits, which I told him not to do for insurance purposes and for the school to have him as a full-time student. Our insurance gave discounts if the student was fulltime. Dalen had now eleven credits. I knew he dropped a class just a few weeks ago, but I didn't know it dropped him below the twelve-credit mark, by one credit—agggg. He would have had to be full time with a 'C' average for our insurance to give a good student discount.

"*Cha-ching, cha-ching*. Again, even when this kid isn't alive we still have to pay for some of his choices," Scott said, and we all laughed about it.

Kipp said he would have his secretary look into this situation for us. He left the room for just a minute to talk to her.

When he came back in, he continued discussing with us how this would work. The school would send us his transcript in about three weeks. That it would show a withdrawal of courses because he's not here. He got a phone call and had to excuse himself.

"Of course, don't worry about us, we will be fine". There were just a few moments before he returned.

"I'm sure as the Dean that you constantly have issues with students." I suggested.

"Well, actually this was about another student that died yesterday."

"Oh my gosh, I'm so sorry. How is the family?" I enquired.

"Well, it's a very different situation as it was a suicide. It is just so different than Dalen's. His was an accident and such a surprise. His was devastating. This other young man's was just sad. It was a young man that was struggling. He just couldn't get how to study and struggled. He was getting tutoring, and so from the school point of view, we thought he was doing better, but then it's only one thing that sets them off—a breakup, a failed test, no friends, or just not following the word of wisdom and the guilt gets to them. It's just so sad. Any is too many, but it is becoming more and more common. So, for Dalen we are grateful for the atonement and where he was spiritually. For this young many it's just all devastating," Kipp stated.

"Oh, his poor family. That would be really hard. We are just so blessed how Dalen passed."

"Yup, if there would have been another car involved or a drunk person, I wouldn't have been able to accept this so easily, but it was just an accident. That no one else was involved was a huge issue for me. That made it so I could accept it," Scott added.

Kipp then shifted his thoughts to Mariah and what some of her options were. She could back out of the semester and take an incomplete. It wouldn't be a fail, so she would be able to continue her education when she returned. We knew that Mariah would need some time, but we didn't think she should withdrawal from her semester. Mariah would just have to let her teachers know of her wishes and then they could help. Kipp mentioned that most of her classes could give her allowance to work on-line and keep up with her studies if that was her desire.

"I think she will need at least a couple of weeks if that would be okay. But I also don't want her sitting at home doing nothing."

We just didn't like idle time for our kids. "Yeah, I think a bit of time is all she needs and then she would just continue her semester. I don't want her just sitting at home either," Scott stated.

"That would be amazing. This can't be easy for her in any way," commented Kipp.

"It isn't," said Scott. "That is why I think she needs just a bit of time. We will have to ask her what her thoughts are though. Is there a time period that we could get back to you?"

"Well, yes. We really can't leave too much time because she doesn't want to lose her credits. We probably need to know as soon as possible, at least by the end of the week." Kipp informed us.

"Oh, that's no problem. We will have an answer as soon as we can for you. Thank you for your counsel though, about her options. We will definitely let Mariah know of them." I replied.

"Of course, and if you have any questions or issues or you forget what we talked about, you can call me any time. I really mean that. I want to help however I can."

Once again we felt of Kipp's concern and consideration for our family and the situation. We thanked him for all his care, and his personal attention to our family. We basically had cleared up everything that we needed to do. We could have probably handled this from home, but we didn't want to. We were done. His apartment was cleared out and all his school issues were resolved. We had options for Mariah, and all had been settled.

We again expressed our gratitude to Kipp for his time and all his care in regard to Dalen. We began to walk out of his office and his secretary, and the other two ladies there, again expressed condolences and best wishes for our family. How blessed we were. What a contrast too as we talked about this other family and hearing that their son hung himself in his bathroom. The horror of what the roommates would go through, along with the lost feeling that the family would have to endure, it was just profound to me. I couldn't even understand how they would be feeling and how their meetings with the school would be so different from ours. I again was overwhelmed with gratitude for my son's life and the kind of life he lived. He struggled at school. He had lots of stress with tests and homework. It very easily could have been my son that killed himself according to the pattern that was increasing on campuses across this country. Why was it that one thing went wrong, and these kids think killing themselves was the best solution?

There are hard times in life. There are struggles. We are supposed to have trials. It doesn't mean end your life now. May I also say that I understand depression completely though. I was there, and my depression lasted for years. It wasn't just a one moment, or issue that led my thoughts to taking my life. It was a very long process to get that deep into the depression. I looked at Scott's gun many days as it rested on our closet shelf. I understand not feeling of worth, or fitting in, or just tired of struggling. I guess, my luck was that I actually looked and asked for help. That meant that when someone offered help, I accepted it. That is probably one of the biggest issues with depressed people: they don't see the help they are being offered. The loneliness is bigger. Doctors wanted to put me in an institution as I was so depressed, and I needed major medical care. Our insurance then played a part in our decision as they wouldn't cover any of the cost, and so I ended up going to a friend's house for a while to heal. I was so depressed. I couldn't give an answer to a question. I couldn't handle my kids. I felt like I wasn't a good mother, and they would have been better off without me. I was constantly finding ways to avoid people or choices. 'Don't ask me today if you can play with a friend.' 'I don't know,' became my response for everything. There was so much that led to my depression and it was a very dark time in my life. But it was over a period of years, not like today where one incident leads these kids to the suicide thoughts within days or hours. I learned how to get out of depression and live productively. I learned I am of value and can contribute to society. The proper medication helped. Constant prayers helped. Accepting help helped. Admitting I wasn't feeling normal helped. Changing my environment helped. It took me three years to believe I had any value to God and myself and that I was of worth (even just a little). I was so grateful my life changed. I truly could empathize with depression though. And I could now help others because of my experiences. Once you have experienced something, in some ways we become an expert on it. If I cooked something new and it didn't turn out, I'm an expert on what not to do. If I have a root canal, I can give my opinion to others of what to expect. If I have a child, I know the pains of labor. If I repent of a sin, I testify of the power of the atonement. That's why we are all important. Through our life experiences, we can help others. I understood depression fully, so I could take my experience and knowledge learned and give it to another. I have helped friends a bit with their depressions because of my trials. What a blessing to be able to help others, to make their lives better if possible. With the kids today though, it was just so sad. I felt so bad for this mother and that forever she would carry that; "What could I have done more of? Or been better at?" Or even, "How could I have seen the signs?" My heart ached for her. Suicide had just become such an easy out. Just so final.

10:02 a.m. Scott and I again were very humbled as we walked to the car. We had made contact with the girls to see where they were at and what plans they might have. Mariah wanted to get some things from her apartment and then they all just wanted to 'veg' a bit. We were okay with that. So, we drove back to the hotel and headed up to the room. It didn't look like there was a whole lot of movement from when we left. I encouraged them that we needed to get up and get our things together so we could start to head back. We had talked with Mariah about what the school had said and what she wanted to do. They had asked if she was going to back off for the semester or stay. She said that she wanted to stay at school and go ahead. We all concurred that that was a good choice for her. We told her that she could take a couple of weeks and just see how she was doing, but that we would let her instructors know so they could plan for her work to be done independently. I agreed too that she needed to keep busy and how much better it would be for her then just stay at home with us. We knew that she would need at least this week off and maybe more time. We contacted Kipp and let him know of Mariah's decision. He was very surprised that she wanted to stay in school, but was also very supportive and again reiterated that at any time if she was struggling or felt overwhelmed to let him know, and they would work with her to help her through. Kipp said he would have his secretary take care of informing her instructors as to the plan and get the class assignments put on-line for her so she could do the work anytime, at least in the next few weeks. That was just so amazing how much they were willing to work with Mariah and help her complete her semester.

 Mariah agreed that she would do her best, but to give her at least this week, and we all agreed. Actually, everyone was pretty surprised that she would come back home and return to school as quickly as she planned. We were proud of her for being willing to try. It wasn't going to be easy to focus, but none of this was easy. Mariah seemed relieved when we seemed to resolve her situation. Alyssa agreed that Mariah needed this time and Kailee was just shocked that she would even want to come back to school. She had a job, a boyfriend, friends, roommates and a scholastic schedule to maintain. With the funeral date known, it was also figured out that Rick would come to California for the funeral and that Mariah could come back to Idaho with him if she was ready. That seemed really fast for us, but it was a possibility. Time would tell; time would tell.

> **Facebook Feb. 12, 11:00 a.m. (Scott's post)** We would be honored for all our family and friends to attend our son's funeral and celebrate his life with us. Funeral services for Dalen Scott Graham will be at The Church Of Jesus Christ of Latter Day Saints Sat. Feb. 17th at 9:00 a.m. for a viewing, and service at 11:00 a.m. Address: 44330 27th St. E. Lancaster, Ca.

Messages kept going through all our phones. The love and support was very overwhelming. I really was just surprised at all the people that knew me or Scott, or Dalen or my girls and just felt compelled to express their condolences to us with their love, prayers and worries expressed for our family. I felt much love and that was a very warm feeling.

> —You are so much braver than us. We couldn't have done what you have.
> —I'm so glad your family is feeling the love. Our continued prayers for you all.
> —Dalen was a friend of mine from **Especially For Youth** (a youth group that meets for a week at a church school campus during the summers. They are grouped in families and given enlightening opportunities to develop their testimonies of the gospel through motivational activities and inspirational speakers. They come home as valiant warriors.) **He was so much fun to be around. He kept in touch over the years and was really a great example to me.**
> —Your strength amazes me! I know this is so very painful for your family, but I also know your testimonies will help you make it thru all of this. Dalen was a great young man, and he was prepared to meet his Savior and start his new mission.

—Our thoughts and prayers are with your family. Just read this in one of the LDS news courses online. May your son RIP and all of you have peace and comfort. Warmest greetings from Australia.

—So much love to you and your family at this time!

—Alyssa, you may not remember me, but you touched my heart when my family met you while you were serving your mission. I want to thank you for sharing your testimony. My family has been through some similar events since we met you.

—God will take care of you. He is real and angels are real. We all need friends and loved ones helping us from heaven. I know your brother will do this for you! Lots of hugs and prayers for you and your family.

11:05 a.m. We really didn't have anything else to do in Rexburg. Mariah's things were fine in her apartment so we could just leave that whole situation. Everyone else was ready in their mindsets, to pack up and start heading out. The goal was to stop at Gord's house, now three and a half hours away, and regroup from there. We would pick up Kailee's car and would continue on to St. George which was about five hours further; or we could stay at Gord's for the night. Alyssa and Brandon would take their vehicle. We were going to leave Dalen's truck in Rexburg for Mariah to have when she came back up to school. We were able to leave it at Rick's house. Of course we emptied everything out of it and put the supplies into ours and Alyssa's vehicles.

We picked up the hotel room and packed our bags. We all were ready to leave. I grabbed the flowers from the apartment. Mariah grabbed her flowers from her friends and the cookies were now gone. Scott double checked everything, and we were done. It was a perfect room and our needs were met. We opened the door to leave and were met by Rick and a couple bags of Subway sandwiches. His mom wanted to take care of us before we left and thought we might be hungry. What a blessing. We again were overwhelmed by the fact that our needs were met and these people knew exactly what to do for us. We took a minute to check out the sandwiches and everyone chose their particular one. We decided to eat them so we went back into the hotel to eat in the breakfast area. They were so very good. Each one kind of got what they liked too.[51]

12:05 p.m. We reminded everyone to drive carefully, which I had done ever since the time they all got their licenses. I rehearsed those words in my mind and remembered saying them to Dalen and Mariah, so what happened? Why weren't they careful and could it have been any different? A question that never would be asked again, but the remembrance would still be there.

We were on the road again, but this time the anxiousness was gone. The weather was again cold but not freezing like it could have been. It wasn't snowing and the roads were clear. I asked Scott if he wanted to stop at the accident place one more time before we left Rexburg and he said no, so it would be to just drive through. I almost wanted to stop and kind of say a goodbye, but again, it was important to listen to everyone's concerns and determine what would be the best for all involved.

1:03 p.m. The line marker on the side of the highway showed 90. I looked at Scott and Mariah to see if they were okay. We were coming into the accident area. Mariah said she was good. Kailee and I instantly changed our conversations too.

"We're getting close Mom." Kailee would usually announce the obvious.

"I know Kailee. Are you okay? Do you want to stop, or do you need anything?"

"Nope, I'm good," Kailee replied.

Mile 91.

---

[51] We received a variety of sandwiches, but each one was what someone would have chosen in our family. There was no way they would have known what we liked and they were only being kind. So amazing.

Mile 92. We were the front car with Brandon and Alyssa behind us. We automatically slowed down. Scott was driving and he couldn't really look out, but I took as much of a glance as I could get. I saw the flowers and some of the dark spots of blood on the ground. I saw the indent on the embankment where the truck landed, and the ball cap filled with blood was still in the dirt. A huge exhale again came over me in realizing all that had transpired in such a short period of time. Just two days—it had only been two days. We passed the markers between the 92 and 93 miles slowly. We moved on.

Final Preparations

Knowing that Pocatello was still about twenty-five minutes away, I actually wondered how we would all handle passing the hospital especially for Mariah. Every bit from here on would only bring horror to her. At least we were all together and our attitudes were good. We would have to stop at the mortuary and turn in Dalen's temple clothes and give Jared the final points for the funeral program.

Passing the University on the right side of the road and looking directly forward gave you a view of the hospital.

"Mariah, are you okay?" I enquired.

"Yeah, let's just go past this place though." Her voice was strong. She wanted to pass this quickly.

"I agree," Scott replied.

We all gazed off to the left and stared at the hospital. I actually looked back and rehearsed all that took place on the tenth floor of the Portneoff Medical Center and the ICU unit and how our lives were altered forever. The next exit was where we got off to go to the funeral home. Scott pulled off and again found the mortuary. He parked and we all went inside.

Jared greeted us cordially and asked how things were going.

"We got all of Dalen's things, cleaned up and it went really well." Scott proceeded to inform Jared of our events.

"I have his temple clothes," as we were ushered into the planning room where we were before. We started to talk about the funeral and I gave Jared the outline I had completed.

Jared had some information for us. He told us first, that Dalen was now in the back. He gave us the papers to process his death certificate since he was out of state. Then as we were talking again about having to transfer Dalen across four states lines and that it would be a huge process with each state having their own requirements, we were seeing that it would be a huge expense. I really was concerned that we might not have a coffin for the funeral. I wanted one there mostly for people to have their final goodbyes. I never liked when you would go to a funeral and they had nothing representing the deceased. I wanted people to have their closures. We talked a bit again about how expensive it would be and that we might look into renting a coffin in California. While we mentioned that, Kailee was already looking online to see what it might be. Jared had his contacts too and was able to give us some options. It was crazy how expensive a rented coffin was. So that created a hesitation on our part. In California, it would be about $2,500 or more just to rent a coffin for two to three hours. We of course were surprised. Jared had an 'aha' moment.

"What if I lend you a coffin? Yeah, that would work," he stated.

I think we were all in shock for a minute. Did we really hear what we thought we heard?

"What do you mean?" Scott asked.

"Well, I was just thinking. I could lend you a coffin and you take it home for the funeral. It would actually be cheaper for you than to rent one in California. I've checked that out for others and the cost is outrageous."

"You want to do what?" Scott's voice was in amazement. "Why would you do that for us?"

"I just think it would work. We would just have to figure out how you could get it," commented Jared. "Would you have any way to transport the box?"

My mind was racing as I thought that our Durango wouldn't have enough room.

"Would it be visible?" Scott asked.

"No, it's in a box," Jared replied.

"Actually, we left Dalen's truck in Rexburg. We could go back and get it and it should fit in the back with no problems. It's a long bed," Scott commented.

"Oh my gosh. That would be amazing," was my surprised response.

My mind again was racing with the understanding of what was just offered to us. Who does that? Who loans a coffin to travel across three other states so a coffin could be used for a funeral? We would then just exchange the empty coffin when Jared would drive Dalen down for the burial. This way, we would only have to pay to cross one state line into Utah. Again, was this real? This was just such a miraculous solution. Jared was such an inspired man to help us out in this way. We were all very humbled by his gesture. He said that he had never done anything like that before, but he just felt it was a good idea. We weren't sure why he was being so kind to our family, but we weren't going to deny his amazing offer either.

"Jared, that is just one of the most amazing things that you would do for our family. How can we thank you enough for that?" Scott commented.

"I don't know. It just was the logical answer," replied Jared.

"Thank you so very much. Thank you," and the rest of the family concurred.[52]

We went through the whole funeral and had made all the decisions we needed to. Jared would put together the program and then send it to us by email so we would get the programs printed off. Scott had mentioned that the department does tons of printing and maybe they would be willing to help with the printing of the programs. Again, we were just overwhelmed by Jared's gesture and kindness. We offered to pay something for this exchange, but Jared denied us the chance. He just kept saying it was meant to be. He felt inspired to offer this to us and who were we to deny him that.

So Brandon and Scott would drive back in Brandon's car back to Rexburg to get Dalen's truck. I would take the girls, and we would head to Gord's house and meet up there. First, I wanted to see my son. Jared said that he was the only one in the embalming room. We could take all the time we needed. He also mentioned that we might not want to see him and for sure that we would only see the cloth draped over him. He wouldn't let us actually look at his body. There was a lot of him that no longer existed.

---

[52] The idea that we could borrow a coffin, pass four states, and have something to display for Dalen's funeral just wasn't usual. He would save us thousands of dollars. He was so gracious to us at this point in our journey. This couldn't be normal, but it happened.

"Do you girls want to go in?" I asked.

Kailee was immediate: "I do. I want to say goodbye. We will never see him again."

"I'm not sure," Alyssa said.

"Okay—well you decide, but I'm going in. I agree with Kailee."

"I would like to go," Scott added his two cents worth.

Jared first got up from the table and led us to the entry way where the coffin displays were and then we turned to the right and went down a little hallway. Jared opened the door to the room. It was a good-sized room and stainless steel was everywhere. It was just like you see in TV. Maybe ten (or a few less) cupboards of stainless-steel doors all in a row were at our view. If a door were to be opened, they would pull out a body on the table and preparations would take place for embalming that body. At that moment, Dalen was the only one in the room, but he wasn't behind any of the doors. He was positioned at the back of the room. We walked toward him.

Jared explained while pointing to an area to the left of us, that that was where they would embalm the bodies and drain all the fluids. They would prepare the body by clothing them and doing the makeup touches that would be used for an open cassette. The hair had to be fixed. Many times the families were asked if they wanted to take care of that part. Not an option for us.

"It is actually a very spiritual experience. They are so peaceful. I don't know their hardships of life or any trials. I see them at peace and give reverence to them. I do what I need to." Jared explained his thoughts on a very different side of what a body goes through for a funeral.

We saw Dalen's body lying on a gurney under a white sheet.

"That's your son," Jared confirmed.

"How do we really know that? Can't we see him?' I pleaded.

"I promise it's your son." Jared reassured me. "I promise it's him."

"You don't want to see a shell. Think of it. Look, see how where the legs should be it is lower. They took out the main bones in his legs and the veins. They opened up his chest and took out his heart valves." Scott related the evidence that we could also see from just looking on the outer lining of the sheet.

"They do very well to sew them up and make the body look as normal as possible. Sometimes, they just use staples, but mostly they do close up whatever they can with stitches. But yes, he doesn't look much like your son." Again, Jared was being informative for us.

"That's okay. I don't need to see him," Alyssa replied.

We were all standing on the one side of him. I just wanted to touch his body somewhere. I wanted to be reassured that it was my son, but I guess I had to believe in Jared's words. My curiosity wanted to know how it was all done, but I had to let it go. Alyssa and Brandon and Mariah walked out first. Kailee wasn't far behind them.

"Bye bud," Kailee walked out.

I was hesitating for just a minute.

Scott asked: "Are you okay?"

"Yup I just wanted a minute to say goodbye," I stated.

I stood there for a minute. There was Dalen's body under a sheet. This was all that was left of him. He had fought so hard. He had done so much for so many others. Here was my boy—'my boy'. Scott started to leave and allowed me just those few seconds to say goodbye for this lifetime to the body of my son.

"Oh how I love you Dalen. Goodbye my Buddy Boy." I was so tempted to reach out and put my hand over his hand, but I didn't. I respected the situation and walked out of the room. This room was the last memory I would have of the last physical place I would see my son prior to his burial. We all gathered again in the conference area.

I grabbed Dalen's temple bag and we went through it to make sure it was all there. Also, I took everything out of the bag to give to Jared the necessary temple clothes and so that I could keep the bag. At one point, I hesitated. There was a part of the clothing that I actually had made for Dalen. It took me a long time and had hand stitching throughout it. It was a treasure to me and my son. For just a second, I was thinking: '*Oh I made this for Dalen.*' I announced that to Jared. He sensed my hesitation.

"Would you like to keep this?" and held up the garment. "You can keep this. I have others that we could use."

That was a possibility. It was only for a second though, that I had the thought. I had made this item for Dalen when he first went through the temple and then he took it with him on his mission and it was part of his temple clothes. We believe that in the resurrection we are raised in the robes of the temple, and I want to see Dalen with his clothing and not someone else's. Nope—I didn't want to see anything else. The choice was made. I handed over the item to Jared.

"Are you sure?" Again, Jared wanted to make sure that I wouldn't regret not taking the item.

"Yup, I'm good, thank you," and it was then taken from my hand.

Scott and I now knew that we would have to finalize the finances and to take care of everything that wasn't resolved yet. Bobby had previously called and talked with Jared about the finances unbeknownst to us, and had it arranged that $5,000 would be charged to ALADS directly and the rest would go to The Sheriff Relief Association which all members of the department are entitled to receive aid from when necessary. We saw zero transactions. The whole burial would be paid for except for the cement plot. The casket, embalming, transporting, taxes, certificates issued for the different states, programs, thank you notes and delivery of Dalen's body to Utah, were all taken care of. Everything would be covered financially. It was all cleared. Again, our awareness of all this being handled was just so unbelievable and yet very real.[53]

It was time to leave. Again, Scott and Brandon said goodbye and left to get Dalen's truck back in Rexburg that Scott would then drive back home. They would need to be back in Pocatello before 5:30 p.m. as the mortuary would then be closed. The girls loaded up into the Durango and we would meet again later that night in Syracuse, Utah at Gord and Maria's house.

I tried to reflect on our trip and see if there was any part that was out of the ordinary. It wasn't. There was mention of what music to listen to or if we were tired or how the road conditions were. All

---

[53] Everything had been taken care of financially. We hadn't paid for anything and were told that we wouldn't. This was so ginormous, truly more than blessed.

were asked if they needed to eat anything or wanted a drink. We were about two hours from Gord's house. Maria had asked if we would like to stay for dinner. I previously had said we weren't sure where we would be and not to worry about us, but now things were different, and we would be there waiting for Scott and Brandon so dinner would be a nice offer.

2:48 p.m. Here is Dalen's eulogy for the newspapers. What do you think?

> Dalen Scott Graham born November 28, 1995 in Thousand Oaks, California. His death occurred Feb 10th, 2018 @ 5:16 a.m. in the Pocatello Portneoff Medical Center in Pocatello Idaho after a tragic truck accident. Funeral services will be at the Lancaster East Stake Center for The Church of Jesus Christ of Latter-Day Saints at 4330 27th St. E. Lancaster, California. Viewing will begin at 9:00 a.m. followed by the serves at 11:a.m. Friends and family are welcomed. Dalen moved to Acton when he was 6 years old. He went to the local schools in Acton and in High School he played on the football and volleyball teams. He's had a few semesters at Brigham Young University Idaho in Rexburg, Idaho. He had served a mission for The Church of Jesus Christ of Latter-Day Saints in the Dallas Texas mission where he returned 4 months ago. Dalen loved people. He loved life. If you knew Dalen, you knew he was always happy. He loved the ocean. He was the kidder of the family and best friends with his sisters. He loved to tinker and take things apart although he couldn't always put them back together. Dalen can't be replaced and won't be, but the solace is that we believe

our family is eternal and will be together again after this life. So now, it's up to us to get there. We love you Buddy Boy.

Alyssa—"Sounds good Mom."
Kailee—"That's good."
Mariah—"Yup, it's good."
Scott—"Yeah I like it."

The afternoon went on. Within a few minutes of each other, the girls all posted their feelings about Dalen-pretty amazing and so heartfelt.

Facebook Feb 12 4:30 p.m. (Alyssa's post) I have been neglecting writing this post. As we were making more arrangements at the funeral home, I was asked to look for good photos of my brother. This one spoke to me in so many ways (and actually makes me tear up every time I see it). And then the picture of Christ, is one I carried on my mission. It's how I picture Christ greeting my brother when they meet. And the last one is a quote I thought was fitting. They all go together really well. I love my brother probably more than anyone will really know. He was such a stud. I always would say whoever got my brother was really lucky. Little did I know how lucky I was to be his older sister. He was always so happy and made you smile even if you didn't want to. He was a quirky spunky sassy pants and yes he was obnoxious sometimes, but those are what I remember most.

He was a friend to all and really just lived life to the fullest. He lived worthily of the gospel and just loved God So much it just became him. We've had so many wonderful conversations and just so many memories. I will miss him not being here. I will miss him telling me to do so much better. But I want to share a thought I had. He WILL BE there to protect my children in heaven. He WILL BE there to all the important life events. He WILL BE forever and always my brother who looks out for me and will never leave me alone. I love you @Dalengraham so much more than you will know. Thank you all for so much support and love. I'm so grateful for the upliftment I've had. I'm grateful to know of Heavenly Father's plan that FAMILIES CAN BE TOGETHER FOREVER. I'm grateful that I have such a close family. I'm grateful I don't have regrets about my brother. I'm grateful that the gospel is amazing and God is in the details of our lives. I'm grateful that the spirit has been so strong and that it hasn't stopped being so strong.

I'm grateful that my family is all worthy to feel that love and to be in the temple together. I'm grateful for the power of prayer. I'm grateful for the scriptures. They have been just so much more of a comfort. I love my Savior #foreverfam. I love my family. I love my brother and I'm so grateful for all the blessings that have been given to me and I'm so grateful I have my own personal guardian angel that actually knows me really well. In the name of Jesus Christ, Amen.

Facebook 4:32 p.m. Kailee's post Been thinking a lot about what I will miss most out of my brother. Has been a very hard one to figure out. But some things have come to mind. Growing up he was my sibling I spent most of my time with. Doing things we both loved together like videogames, Nerf wars, Air Soft wars, Lego building, going on adventures, dirt bike riding. Really, just being outdoors, collecting the rocks on our hill, making forts, and just doing random things that 99% of the time were very childish and just stupid funny things. As he has grown up and away from home, now his spiritual side was amazing and how he always had a smile. No we didn't talk much but was just a little snapchat checkup was how we talked this last little bit, but where he was willing so send me things of either being with Mariah to doing volleyball, I was able to see it daily. He loved his volleyball, which I had fun when I could play with him or go to a BYU game with him. You were a true brother to me and will be missed. I love you Dalen Graham.

Facebook 4:35 p.m. Mariah's post. I have been spending my time going through as many photos as I can find with me and Dalen. He always said we were homies since day 1 and it couldn't be more true. I took our amazing friendship for granted. I did not realize how close we were until a few months ago when he got off of his mission. We only grew closer every day since he moved up to Idaho and joined my new life.

4:50 p.m. Bryce's thoughts—(cousin, also within minutes of the girls' posts) **It has been a heavy and sad weekend to hear of the passing of my cousin Dalen Graham. He was a 22-year-old man that was taken all too early in** a car accident. My thoughts are with the entire Graham family as they go through this hard time. But I wanted to share a little bit about what I knew of Dalen.

Dalen was a young, enthusiastic, athletic, and talkative person. A faithful church member and the perfect match to an ideal child. We didn't grow up very close together, but did see each other on occasions like cousins and family do. But if I have to be honest here, I always liked Dalen, but there was always something that slightly annoyed me about him. Not that I didn't love him or want to see him, but there was something that was consistent every time I saw him that caught my attention. And it wasn't until this accident that I was able to pin down exactly what it was.

The thing that bugged me was that he was always so happy. Not just a normal level of happy, but the overly excited type. This annoyed me because I figured life can't be as good as he made it out to be every time I saw him. Like 'dude' you can't be that excited Sharon put you in timeout because you didn't finish your food…or that excited you just drove 700+ miles to get here for dinner…or that excited and confident to leave everything you know and go on a church mission…or that excited to be drenched in rain in your suit. But it turns out that you CAN be that excited, all the time. Wherever he was, whatever he was doing—he saw the good in enjoying that very moment. He gave that moment and experience 110% of his focus and attention, and he loved every second of it.

As mentioned we were never very close growing up, but after Dalen started his mission, he reached out to me a lot while he was away from home. He would ask my opinion on subjects and for advice on things he had never done before. He genuinely looked up to me and was proud to say he knew me and was a relative to me. I took these emotions for granted while he was here with us. But now more than ever, I know he is holding me accountable for my actions and watching from above. I will continue to try and inspire you Dalen while you look down on all your friends and family, and I will try to live my life with half as much happiness as you carried around with yourself. This dang kid was too happy and excited about everything!!! Who would have thought? Little did he know the impact he had on others, and the influence and example he set for me!

Heading Into Yet Another Miracle

I kept receiving messages. Several were from Sylvia who had been informing me about her son's surgery and how he was doing. She so wanted to meet me. She asked if there might be a way to come to the hospital. I knew that we would drive right through Murray on the way home so of course, I told her I would be there. I was very excited to see her. I knew that Dalen's organs had gone into the Salt Lake Valley and Murray was in the Valley. I knew that his organs had been transplanted Saturday evening. I received that information from the Donor Center. It just so happened that the Murray hospital was the only transplant hospital in the valley. I also learned that there were two separate transplant operations that night and both were from a male donor, and they were kidney transplants. How could this not be Dalen's organs? I knew it was and Sylvia knew it was. We both, more than, felt it.

What a miracle that I would know and get to meet Dalen's kidney recipient within forty-eight hours of their surgeries. When I spoke with the donor center, they mentioned more than once that we wouldn't have any way to contact the recipients until they were ready first to show interest of meeting us. I strongly disagreed with that. I believed that the donor's family should have the choice of meeting. I didn't want to meet them to boast about my son or glorify my son. I wanted to meet them to see that their lives would be better, that they would be able to have better health. I wanted to see them enjoying life, and I strongly disagreed that I couldn't do anything till they contacted me first. We were told that it could take years before we would hear from any of them. I could only write a letter with very specific details—no last name—no address—no mentions of where we lived—no information of how our child passed-just that I would like to get in touch with them. That was protocol, but that wasn't our story in any way. I was going to meet the man (I learned that he was fifty-four years old) that Dalen's organs would alter.

I let the girls know right away about the possibility of meeting Sylvia and her son, and they didn't seem very excited or even interested at all.

"What do you mean you don't want to go—why not?" I eagerly asked.

"I think it's weird Mom. I don't want to meet somebody that has a part of Dalen's body in them. I might later but not now. Don't get me wrong—I'm grateful Dalen was a donor, and I know he's blessing lives but I'm just not ready." Alyssa was pretty adamant that she didn't want to go.

Another issue was that we all decided that we just wanted to keep driving. We had an agenda for tomorrow and we wanted to get to Scott's mom's house which was still five and a half more hours from Gord's house.

We stayed at Gord's house for a bit. I hardly even remember the drive. It was calm and clear. There was communication with everyone and we heard of Scott retrieving the truck and where he was. Of course Maria fed us. She was a good cook and we always just enjoyed being with her and especially after her being with us in the hospital. She was an angel.

About two hours after eating, Scott and Brandon arrived and there was a box in the back of Dalen's truck that would be the borrowed coffin. While Scott and Brandon were driving, they had made arrangements with Brandon's dad who lived in Alamo, Nevada, which was north-west of Las Vegas. They would meet up with him in the morning near Glendale and bring the suburban up for Brandon to drive. That way the box wouldn't' get wet and it would be a little more concealed. So, Scott wanted to leave and start off to his mom's. Mariah wanted to go with her dad. I had told them of my meeting with Sylvia and they too, thought it was so very cool, but that they weren't ready yet. That stunned me. How could they not be ready? This man's life was being altered because of our son. They were going to live better.

Our son would be thrilled and these people were so very grateful. Their lives were forever going to be different. I was beside myself with excitement. Alyssa and Brandon would follow Scott in their car and Kailee would drive her car down that we had now picked up from Gord's. So again, we would all drive separately but remain in contact. Nothing was going to stop me from meeting Sylvia though, nothing. God had so directed her to me and me to her. I couldn't deny this miracle and wouldn't want to. I wish my family would have wanted to come, but again I couldn't alter their way of thinking. We loaded up and started to drive toward St. George, Utah.

6:30 p.m. We all left at the same time from Gord's house. We wouldn't be all together, or I guess really it was just me that wasn't going to be with them. We would meet together again at Scott's mom's house. There we would leave Kailee's car again, but that would be normal since Kailee was renting a room from her grandma so she could save money to get into an apartment. She had been living there for about six months. So sometime tonight, we would meet up with everyone. I didn't know how long I would be able to visit or would want to visit with Sylvia and her son, but I guessed that I would be at least an hour or so behind everyone. Of course, we would be on our phones making sure everyone was doing good and driving safely.

Sylvia had given me the address to the hospital and how to find her once I got there. The drive seemed pretty quick. I couldn't believe that all of a sudden, I was driving past Salt Lake City and heading through the valley. At one point during this evening, I had communicated with LaNae about this.

"Well, we can't tell you anything other than we know Dalen's organs went to the Salt Lake Valley."

"Doesn't that seem amazing—that this lady got in contact with me and her son could have received my son's kidney?"

"That would be more than a miracle for you to know that and especially this fast. It just doesn't happen. I can't tell you anything until the recipient acknowledges they want contact, but if you happen to put 2 and 2 together, you might be able to figure it out," was LaNae's response. That kind of gave me insight that we were on the right path. This was possible. This was God's design. It really was going to happen—I was meeting my son's recipient and within such a short time period. Had this ever happened before? It sure made me question this process. I was beside myself with excitement.

LaNae was saying what I very strongly believed. She couldn't tell me exactly what I wanted to know, but in a way she did. With adding the 2 + 2, I had the answer. I was going to meet my son's recipient and it had only been two days. So overwhelmed again with this experience guided by God's direction.[54] Sylvia had been guided to get in contact with me and we both just knew it. There were a few tears of gratitude and excitement as I was approaching the area by Jordan. I asked one more time if any of my family wanted to join me as we were within a few miles of the turnoff for the hospital. I was on my own.

GPS was right on. I drove to the exit and the hospital was there on the left hand side of the highway. It was a pretty big complex just like Sylvia had described. I was now understanding why she said I would drive in and pass the first two buildings and then head to Building 'V'. I kept thinking, *'Should I have brought something to give to this mother? Was there a protocol for something like this?"* I really had no idea.

7:05 p.m. I was a few minutes late which caused just a moment of anxiousness, but it quickly was replaced with pure excitement. I found my way into the parking lot. I had to drive kind of in a 'C' shape to get to the right building. I got out of the car and started to walk in. The automatic doors opened. The lobby was in soft green and earth tone colors and décor. There was a wall of plaques with sponsors' names and a desk to the right for volunteers to give assistance. They weren't there anymore as it was after normal hours. I looked at the wall guide to show me where to get the elevators and found the tenth floor which in this hospital, that was the transplant

---

[54] Sylvia was meant to contact me and I knew my son helped her son with a new kidney and to find all this out on my own and so very quickly—had to have been God's plan. There was no question in my mind that this was meant to be. Thank you Heavenly Father. Thank you so very much. Seriously, think on this.

unit. My heart started to race. There was just such an excitement. I had no idea what to expect. The elevators opened and there was this lady waiting there that didn't even ask my name. As soon as she saw me in the elevator, she ran up to me and hugged me.

"You have to be Sharon." Excitement was in her voice too.

"I am, and you must be Sylvia."

"Oh my gosh, I'm so grateful to you and so sorry that we have to meet this way." Sylvia had an accent that you could determine immediately. She was from Ireland. It was just so cute, and she was so excited. She was about 5'9 or so. She was taller than me, that's for sure. She was a very thin lady with red hair, but her smile was amazing. I loved her voice.

"How is your boy?" I inquired.

"He's tired but doing okay." We started to walk down the hall to her son's room. It was about three doors down and on the left side of me. The rooms were only on one side of the hall. There were windows all across the right side. The rooms were pretty big. They were all private rooms with a bench under the window and I saw the recliner chair that would turn into a bed for a family member that desired to stay. I knew that chair from when Mariah broke her femur bone at the age of three, and I stayed in the hospital with her for a couple of weeks and got to know that recliner style very well.

I saw four other people that all came to the door to meet me. Sylvia's daughter named Debbie and another daughter with her daughter. Then there was this really tall and very skinny guy that was introduced as Sylvia's husband. His name was Chris. They were all crying when they hugged me. Then I was able to see the bed where the patient was lying down and I met Gary Graham. He was so much older than I expected. I really was surprised. There wasn't ever a mention of age or size or personal details when previously talking with Sylvia. I just assumed that as young as Dalen was, that his organs would go to a very young person or even a child to give them a whole life to live. This wasn't the case. Gary was fifty-four years old. He was a very small man. Physically he didn't look healthy. He had on a baseball cap and seemed pretty out of it. In our mind, we think: *okay a transplant—goes in and they are good*, but there is a long time for the new body to accept the organ, and it takes a process. So, he really looked good for just two days after surgery. He was smiling at me. I went over and shook his hand and introduced myself.

"Hi, I'm Sharon Graham, Dalen's mom."

He shook my hand.

"We can't believe we are meeting you," Sylvia said.

"I can't either. How did you know to contact me?" I asked.

"I saw your story on the news and my daughter" (motioning over to Debbie) "was 'Mom you have to contact her. You have to let her know.'" Sylvia was trying to give me all the details.

They had received a call about 10:00 a.m. Saturday just after Dalen passed, saying that there was a possible donor. They hurried and got things together and went to the hospital to wait. They knew that Gary would die soon without a new kidney. He had been sick his whole life with kidneys, intestines, bladder and stomach issues. At one point, his stomach was growing outside his skin. He had only half of his intestines. He has just had a rough life. He had a kidney transplant from Sylvia, that was good for sixteen years, and so this was the last time they could do the surgery. If this didn't take, he would have kidney failure. I was so mortified to hear of how much suffering this man had gone through and yet he was fifty-four, so he had done a lot of fighting for his life. All of his family came from Ireland because of Gary.

When he was a child, his mother met the missionaries for The Church of Jesus Christ of Latter-Day Saints. They had several visits. Sylvia joined the church. They informed her of Children's Hospital in Utah and that they wouldn't turn down anyone. She came. No money, no place to stay and only her clothes on her back, but she came. She was taken care of, and Gary was immediately accepted into the hospital. They have resided in the Salt Lake City area ever since. Sylvia had five children. Her husband was very abusive, and she needed to leave to save her life and her children. What a huge amount of faith this woman had. I sensed it immediately. Through the hospital, she was provided a home to live in. She found a job and began to provide for her family. They felt so blessed to have such good medical opportunities for Gary.

This poor man had suffered for so long and this mom has dedicated her entire life to her son's health. He had been on dialysis for the past five and a half years. That meant that three times a week, Gary would go to the hospital for a four-hour treatment, every three days. Then he would repeat the cycle. That just blew me away. The never-ending struggle to live a healthy life was very profound. I was so humbled by Gary's will to fight for his life and all the suffering he had gone through. Dalen's suffering was almost none if he died like the doctor said—on impact. Here this man had suffered for fifty-four years. I just couldn't comprehend it. There was always another complication that would come up. So, Gary had a total of sixteen years of dialysis with the two kidneys. Sixteen years—can you imagine that? The anguish of this mother and the faith waiting to always see a better life for her son was unbelievable.

Gary didn't say much. I was a bit surprised. I thought he might have been, "thank you so much, I'm so grateful". But he was pretty medicated up. I really didn't understand about the recipient's process, but Sylvia and her family explained a bit more to me. The kidney basically falls asleep and can take a few months to wake up and begin to function again. This person goes through a very serious surgery in hopes it works to have a better life, but won't know if it takes for months. That means continual hospital visits every so many days to again, see that everything else is functioning and working well. Since Gary already had another kidney, it would function at 100% until the other one kicked in. The problem with Gary was that his other kidney was already weak. Gary would be in the hospital for at least two weeks waiting to see if urine was being produced and how much. It was a pretty big ordeal for him, but he was so willing and hoping for a donor. The older you get, the lower you are on the donor lists because they do look for the younger people first to give them a longer life whereas an older person can at least say they have had a life.

"So how are you feeling now Gary?" I asked.

"I think I'm doing okay. I'm still in a lot of pain, but it seems better already."

"Oh my gosh, that just sounds so amazing and I'm so grateful to hear that."

Sylvia proceeded to tell me a bit more about Gary and all that he had gone through. I was in tears for his suffering. I just kept thinking how hard it was for Dalen to pass, but it became very much of the minute thing. Here, this family had suffered for his whole life with medical issues. Their pain was never ending. I felt so very grateful and humbled—so humbled.

"So would you like to know anything about Dalen?" I had to correct them on how to pronounce his name. They called him Dallin. No biggie.

"Oh yes. We would love to know everything. We were just afraid to ask. This is so hard to think that your son had to pass away for mine to have a chance at a better life. We just can't imagine your pain and how sorry we are, but how grateful we are too," Sylvia responded.

"I would love to hear about your son," Debbie added.

"We have had so many miracles through this process, but with you contacting me, that is probably the biggest. This is just amazing. We see very clearly God's hand as he is leading us," I responded.

"We have prayed so hard for so many years for this—you have no idea," the other daughter commented.

"Well, let me tell you about Dalen. He was, is" (I caught myself again of talking in the past about Dalen). "He still is twenty-two years old. He was up at school in Rexburg going to BYUIdaho. He had served his mission for The Church of Jesus Christ of Latter-day Saints first in Ecuador. He came home with a knee injury after four months and didn't go back out for eighteen months. He was re-assigned to Dallas, Texas. He finished his mission and had only been home for four months before the accident. He loved baseball."

"I do too," Gary stated.

We talked for a few minutes about what Gary liked. It was funny how we were trying to instantly find connections with Dalen and Gary. Did they eat the same things? Did they like the same things? Did they have similar interests? I was surprised that I almost expected some things to be similar when, in actuality, there wasn't really any reason they should have things in common. Baseball was Gary's favorite sport. He liked to be outdoors and went camping as often as he could. He enjoyed doing things with his hands. I laughed.

"Dalen liked to play with things too and take them apart. The problem was that he couldn't figure out how to put them back together again. It was always an issue with his dad."

Everyone laughed. It was just surreal that I was sitting in a hospital with someone that had received a body part from my son that had passed away two and a half days earlier. We were laughing and learning about each other. I was just so excited to be with them. I wish my family could have been there too.

Sylvia told me a bit more about their family history. She mentioned that she was from Ireland which wasn't hard to tell from her accent. I was sitting in a chair right by Gary's bed. Their family was all standing around the bed, and we were interacting with each other like we were family. All were laughing, or asking questions, or just finding ways to get to know each other. Gary started coughing for a minute and the room instantly changed in attitude to that of taking care of him. Sylvia got him some water to drink. She was mentioning how he was still pretty drugged up and then he would have a hard time talking too much. Sylvia's daughter's checked if he was due for more medication or what they needed to do to make him more comfortable. During that time, Sylvia pointed to the bed tray and asked me to look what she had Gary write down.

"Look at this," she insisted. "I made Gary write this when he heard you were coming."

It was a piece of paper about a 5 x 7 in size and it read: "My kidney is going to work perfect!" That was so cool. It made me cry. Sylvia wanted him to say something in case he was too out of it when I was there. The family talked about Gary's life and all the struggles he has had to endure physically. We kept switching back to Dalen and how he lived his life.

"Dalen always wore his baseball caps backwards which drove his dad crazy."

"Gary always wears a baseball cap too." His sister added to the conversation.

It was crazy how things were coming up that we were finding similar between the two. Generally, they were both happy. They loved ice cream and pizza. They liked to be outdoors. They took things apart. They didn't really like school, but they endured. Dalen loved volleyball and Gary loved baseball but they both followed their college teams faithfully.

"Don't be surprised if Gary starts having unique cravings. When I gave Gary my kidney, he started to like eating nuts which he hated before. So that led to a whole bunch of questions about that experience and how it affected both of them. Gary had one amazing, dedicated mom for his wellbeing. She literally would do anything for her child. So, they asked of some things Dalen liked. I had to think for a minute because there wasn't really anything that stood out.

"Dalen liked food period. He would pretty much eat anything. I know he liked triple decker peanut butter and jelly sandwiches," I replied.

"What's that?" the granddaughter asked.

"That's when you put peanut butter and jam on a piece of bread. Then you add another piece of bread and one more layer of peanut butter and jam. You put a top piece of bread on and eat away."

"Oh," Sylvia's granddaughter said as you could see her trying to visualize this. She was about fifteen years old and so I knew she could figure out what I had just described.

"He liked to play video games and would be on with several people that he never knew, but he was good friends with all of them through gaming."

"Oh, that sounds nice," Sylvia said.

"Here, I have some pictures of him. Would you like to see what he looks like?" (Again, I was aware of the tense I used. I almost said he looked, but I didn't.)

"Of course," was one comment I heard.

"We really wanted to know everything about your son but didn't want to ask because we didn't have any idea how hard this might be on you," was another comment.

"Please don't worry about me. I'm just so excited to be here and this is amazing. I'm not saying that I wanted my son to die, and it wasn't easy, but I'm not thinking that way. I'm thinking that your life might be better now."

I pulled out my phone and went to the file on my gallery of Dalen. Most of the pictures were of his mission as that was the most recent event in his life. I also had some pictures in my family file. I searched through them and selected a few of Dalen and the girls, and they learned a bit about our family as I did about theirs. They seemed excited with their new knowledge. Then I just handed over my phone and let them browse through the pictures at their own speed.

Was this really real? Was I really in a hospital talking about my son and knowing he no longer lived, but that his kidney was now a part of not just this man, but his family's life too? It seemed so surreal and yet I was very much right in the moment. It was like we were best friends.

Gary was hurting. Sylvia made sure he was looked after and gave him some more medications. I was leaning more about a transplant operation and what Gary's body had to now go through to adjust to the kidney. It really could take months. I had no idea. A person that was so severely sick was so willing to go through the pain and adjustments for the HOPE of a better life. I was very humbled by the life Gary had lived and was overwhelmed and awed of this whole process.

I talked about how strong of a testimony Dalen had and that led to inquiring about Gary's activation. I knew his mother was a very good member of the church. Sylvia said that Gary wasn't really active. He had had some hard times. I told him that he was given a new chance of life and that he needed to think about that. Dalen wouldn't be happy knowing he gave his life to someone that didn't care about the gospel especially if they did at one time. I asked if he would go back to church and try and be a bit more active. It kind of broke my heart to hear that. Here my son was in such a good place spiritually and this man didn't care about his spiritual side, but knew better. I just hoped: 1) that Gary would get better and 2) that he would think of his blessings and want to let God know of his gratitude by being obedient.

I had been there for about an hour. I could see that it was wearing on Gary. It was time to go, but not until we took some pictures.

This experience had been so overwhelming. Sylvia had been guided to me and I in turn had confirmation that Dalen's kidney went to Gary and would change his life for the better.

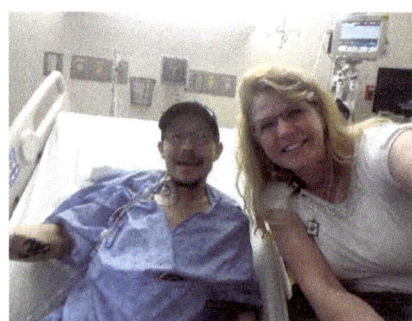 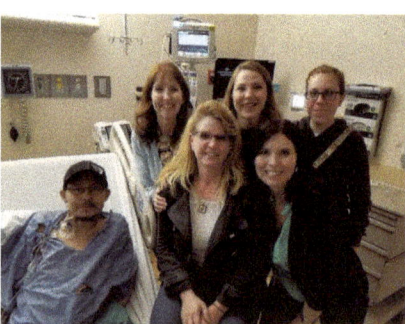

Through some of our discussions, I had learned about another kidney transplant operation that took place the same time as Gary's, and that the man was next door and was the recipient who also happened to be an older man.

"Come on Sylvia, Let's go visit him. Let's pretend we're candy strippers or just see what surgery he had and go from there," I suggested.

"I know that he's an old man. I saw him walking the halls when Gary and I were walking. He had white hair and was kind of a big guy. He didn't look very happy, but then maybe he was in pain like Gary. We didn't talk, but the nurse told me what his surgery was and they have to keep transplants persons together because of all the extra care they need," Sylvia informed me.

"Oh—wow, that just really surprised me. I just didn't envision that an old man would receive my son's kidney. I guess I was just expecting someone younger.

"Well, he's pretty old and grumpy. Gary tried to say hi and ask how he was feeling and he just walked off," Debbie said.

"Well, that isn't going to work. Dalen liked everyone and would talk to everyone. He will have to change that for sure," And we all laughed.

I began to go around the room to say goodbye to everyone. It was a very tender moment. They just kept thanking me and the tears flowed from all of us. It was amazing.

"We are just so grateful for your decision to have your son donate his body," Debbie commented.

"Yes, thank you so very much" the other daughter said.

"We just love your son so much especially after learning about him. He was such a spiritual young man. I hope that Gary gets these desires from him. He will come back to the church, I know he will." Sylvia mentioned will all her faith.

"Well Gary, I'll tell it to you straight. If my son has given you another chance for a better life, then don't waste it. He knew his Heavenly Father loved him. He knew his Savior atoned for his sins. He had a strong testimony and loved to share it. Please don't let his sacrifice go to waste. When he greets you in the next life you're not gonna want him asking you, 'What did you do with your new life? Did you waste it?' I know my son will be watching over you. I just hope he's happy with your choices in life that will affect him in the next life." I felt Dalen's spirit very strong. I knew he wanted me to bear his testimony.[55]

"Me too," Sylvia agreed. "You have to get your life together and remember who Dalen was and that he's your example to follow and your angel to guide you."

"I will," Gary said. And he smiled at us both. I believed him. He wanted a better life. He wanted to be happier. He had motivation now to do it. "Thank you so much."

"Thank you again," they all announced. "You have answered so many of our prayers," Sylvia added. "I have a question for you that I don't want to offend you with. We were wondering if you would mind if we came to Dalen's funeral. We so want to be there for you."

"Are you serious? That would be just amazing. We would love it. Let me know for sure if you're coming and I will find a place for you to stay at. That really would be awesome. I would love it. We have

---

[55] Look where I'm at—a hospital bearing testimony of my son's testimony—REALLY!!!!!!!!! And with Dalen's kidney recipient. This was crazy.

to keep in touch. Sylvia, you have my information. I would love to hear how Gary is doing and of course will add my prayers to yours."

"You are just so amazing. I know God sent you to us. Our lives have all been altered for the better. I just love you. I really do." Sylvia was like a best friend. We felt so close to each other. "Oh how I love you too." And we hugged again. Sylvia said she would walk me out.

We got to the door of Gary's room, and I looked back at a miracle. It was quite the picture that I would hold forever in my mind. Sylvia and I began to walk down the hall.

"I really want to go and see if this other man received Dalen's kidney. It sounds like it had to be him."

"Well, there were only two transplant operations that day. The other man was first and then Gary." Sylvia informed me.

"And I know that Dalen's kidneys went into the Salt Lake Valley."

"This is the only hospital that does transplants, so it has to be."

"Maybe we could go find a nurse and ask them. But I doubt they would tell me anything—Let's just go and see." We turned to walk past Gary's room and head to the next room, but then fear overtook both of us. "What if he doesn't want to meet me?"

"I don't know why he wouldn't, but I guess he could."

"I just want to know so badly. Could you imagine that—meeting both recipients within forty hours. That would just not be heard of. I know it has to be this man. I know it." But like so many decisions in our lives, we let the possibility of fear control us as did this one. "I guess maybe I shouldn't bombard this man. He might not want to meet me." and we turned and walked back past Gary's room again and headed down the hallway. I've since learned that this man would have loved to have met me that day. That choice altered my life for the next year of which I regret. But like anything, we have the right to make a choice, but not the right to choose the consequences of a choice.[56]

---

[56] I knew in my heart that the man next door was the second recipient of Dalen's kidney. I was directed to him. Truth is truth even when we don't listen. I had found both recipients within forty hours of their surgeries. I found them.

I was leaving the hospital so full of blessings, warmth, and love that I would be okay and they would be better. Sylvia just kept repeating how much she knew I was meant to be in her life and thanked me again and again and again. We truly did love each other instantly.

"You are my God sent sister and I will always love you." She hugged me again as we were now at the car.

It was very cold outside, so we didn't want each other to be out too long so our goodbye was quick. We were arm in arm and huddled a bit when the cold air brushed beside us.

"Oh I'm so glad I came. This has just been so amazing. I'm so grateful to you."

"I have to take you all the way to your car. You are my sister now, and I love you."

"Isn't this amazing? You were inspired to contact me and in return we have been blessed to meet each other and know that your son has my son's kidney. I do love you Sylvia. I will call tomorrow to check on our boy." One more big hug, except this time there were a few tears from both of us. Once again, our God was so good. He puts us where we need to be, and he just blesses our lives over and over again if we let him. I'm just so in awe of it all.

I got into my car and started it up. I had to let it warm up for just a minute. Sylvia wouldn't leave till I did. The faith of this woman was just amazing. I was so inspired by her. I began to drive out of the parking lot. I remembered that it kind of curved around so when

I was out of sight from the building that Sylvia and Gary were in, I pulled the car over and bowed my head.

"Heavenly Father, I don't know how to express the depth of my gratitude for this amazing experience." I proceeded to rehearse with God what had transpired. I just couldn't contain myself and there were a few more tears that rolled down my cheek. This time I was actually crying with joy and gratitude. So, in awe—my heart was so full.

I called Scott to see where everyone was at and then to describe my experience to him. He was happy for me, but just didn't need to have the same result. He was good just knowing that I knew for certain, where our son's one kidney went and how so many lives had already been altered. He was grateful to hear of my experience. He explained where he was at and that the others were right behind him. I would be just shy of two hours behind them. And so the night would continue on.

More Driving to Come

8:30 p.m. I started to drive to St. George which was about four hours away from where I was. I was very adamant that my family not take any chances of driving and being tired. Scott and Mariah were driving together in Dalen's truck. Kailee was following them. Alyssa and Brandon were also close to them and again we were in contact with everyone the whole way. I was the last to leave the valley, and even though I was behind them, I was very much awake and aware of everything. I had my trail mix or nuts to eat if I needed help staying awake. In my previous prayer, I also pleaded with Heavenly Father to guide my family and to let us all drive safely.

I knew that the roads were pretty clear once I got out of the Salt Lake Valley. It had snowed since we had last driven through, but again everything was clear and I was grateful.

My mind just reflected over and over again of our last three days and where we were at. I kept thinking that if I couldn't stop thinking about Dalen's passing, that how could Mariah not think about it. Hers, of course, would be of the accident and all that she went through. How I continued to pray for her and that her memories could be filled instead, with the mighty miracles that our family had experienced instead of the horrific event she had experienced. "Heavenly Father, please give her peace."

The family had all stopped to eat together. That would take about an hour which meant I was that much closer to them. I liked that a bit better. We were all making good time and again knew that we were being blessed.

It wasn't that the drive was a blur, but we had driven it so many times and had our landmarks along the way. Once you got out of the valley and about to Nephi, it became more desserty looking and fewer cities. Again, the snow on the sides was glistening in the fields, but the roads were clear.

9:40 p.m. "Okay, I need to know where everyone is." I exclaimed through our group texting. "I'm just past Nephi coming close to Fillmore."

"We are in Beaver." Scott and Mariah replied.

"I'm right behind dad." Kailee said.

"We are right here too, mom." Alyssa included her input.

"Yup, we just ate so are good to go." I know the text came from Scott's phone, but I was pretty sure Mariah was doing the texting. Scott really hated texting.

"Well good. So, we are about thirty-forty minutes apart." I also knew that I drove a bit faster than Scott. The speed limit was 80mph in Utah and I would normally go 85. Kailee would too, but since she was driving with the family, she would stay with them. Scott on the other hand, would drive me crazy when he drove in Los Angeles. He would speed, dart in and out of traffic, tailgate who ever wouldn't get out of his way and always said how stupid the drivers were. But in Utah, he would drive seventy—seventy-five. It drove me crazy and didn't make sense to me. At least do the speed limit—right!!!!

"Honey, do you think you could drive a little bit faster so we could get there in five hours instead of seven?" Remembering that; he also stopped about every 1-1 ½ hours to go to the bathroom. An example of our trips: from our daughter's house in Vegas to our house was about 4 1/2 hours normally. When I went with Scott, it was like 5 ½-6 hours at least. You had to stop and wash the truck at the truck stop. We had to stop to fill up with gas because he didn't ever do that before we left. We had to stop to eat because we couldn't eat in the car. So, it all added up and with kids, it was frustrating because they would get tired of taking so long to get somewhere and I agreed. When the kids were little; it was eat, pee and gas up all at the same place because Scott would just stop whenever he needed to relieve himself, but the rest of us weren't given that offer. That was how we did things, but now he would stop to eat, and not like that place or the gas wasn't the price he liked so he would try to find another one, and not always on the main pathways. We would eventually make it to our destinations though, so I guess it all worked out.

My music kept me entertained and the miles seemed to be melting away. It was peaceful and quiet. Not really much going on, but we all just kept going. Going through Beaver, there were light snow flurries. I didn't want it to get any worse, so I offered another prayer for our safe travels and clear roads. From there on in the drive, you went up in elevation as you got closer to Cedar. If there was going to be snow on the drive from Salt Lake City, it would be in the Valley and Cedar area. It was snowing, but not really sticking which I was very grateful for.

10:15 p.m. Cedar was coming into my view and it was snowing harder, but again, it wasn't sticking and so it made the road a bit wet but nothing else. Of course I slowed down whenever it was snowing. I was being careful for sure. What a blessing. It didn't last very long either, which was even better. So, I stopped for a stretch and again checked in with the family. They announced that they were about ten minutes outside of St. George.

"Very cool. I guess we will see you soon."

"Okay dear, drive carefully," Scott commented.

"I am. There were snow flurries by Cedar but nothing really so it's all clear."

"Yeah, that happened with us too, but the road is clear the rest of the way," Scott informed me of the view ahead.

"Okay, thanks. See you soon. Love you."

"Love you too. Drive carefully," he stated.

Cedar to St. George was about forty-five minutes away. Cedar could get a lot of snow and St. George was a desert. It kind of starts one end of the Grand Canyon. Lots of red rocks and it can get very hot in the summers. I was in no way expecting any issues with driving past Cedar. I just kept cruising through.

11:12 p.m. I was driving into my mother-in-law's house. We had to drive through her gate and go in through the back door to the house. My mother-in-law's house was very ornate. She collected Bernstein bears, dolls and had them placed all throughout her house, but it was not cluttered at all. They were so strategically placed with maybe a book in a doll's hand, or a chair to sit on, or plants in between them, but it was very nicely done. I walked past the laundry room and kitchen where I saw Mariah and Alyssa getting something to eat.

"Hey girls, how was your trip?"

"Good Mom, how was yours?" Alyssa asked.

"It was so cool to meet Gary and his mom Sylvia. I think you actually might have liked to have met them."

"Oh well, I'm okay that I didn't." Mariah said.

"Where's everyone else?"

"Downstairs."

"Are you all set up for sleeping arrangements?"

"Yeah. Kailee and I get the couches and Alyssa and Brandon will be in the other room." Mariah informed me. Kailee gave Scott and I her room which normally would have been where Scott and I slept before Kailee moved there.

"Okay, I think I'll head down. You guys coming?"

"Yup, just getting a drink," Alyssa replied.

I walked past the dining room and one of the family rooms. Turned left and came to the staircase and front entry of the house and past the formal living room and dining room and went downstairs to see the rest of the family. Kailee was already in bed. She usually was the first one to go to bed. When she was growing up, it was almost funny that if it was 8:00 p.m., Kailee was in bed. It didn't matter where we were, she would go to bed, even if it meant hiding behind a couch to go to sleep. Brandon was on the couch in the downstairs family room watching TV. They were all just settling in. Scott came out of the bathroom and greeted me.

"So let's call everyone down for prayers so we can get to bed."

"Okay," and Scott yelled up the stairs for the girls to come down.

"Coming," Alyssa said.

Kailee kind of woke up so she joined us. Brandon took his turn. We were so tired and yet so blessed. Another day had come to a close. Thank you Heavenly Father. Thank you.

This is the Right Place

The agenda for today was to find out about a burial plot and what that would entail. Alyssa and Brandon had made arrangements for his dad to bring them the suburban so we could put the coffin in it, so it wasn't quite as conspicuous. They would meet Ross, Brandon's dad, in Glendale which was about halfway between Alamo and St. George.

Scott and I got up and ready. We were pretty sure that the government building would be open around nine so that was when we planned to be there.

We had discussed that we needed to go to the county building. We left the house about **8:45 a.m**. and drove into town. We thought we remembered where the building was because we had driven through downtown a few times over the years. Scott also had to take his mom there once, so he thought he would be good on directions. We were heading toward the freeway and back into town and got off on St. George Blvd which was the main street through town. We found the building after only one wrong turn. Parked, exited the car, and walked into the building. It was a brick building about four stories high. We found where we needed to go. We walked in and introduced ourselves.

9:04 a.m. Scott said, "We are wondering what we need to do to find information about a burial plot."

"Okay. Is it for you?" the receptionist asked.

"No. Our son passed away Saturday, and we would like to bury him this Saturday."

"I'm so sorry. That must be so hard for you. Let me get someone who can help you," she stated.

We remained at the counter for just a minute while she went to go find someone to help us.

"Hi, I'm Mary and I understand you need a burial plot," Mary replied.

"Yes we do," was Scott's answer.

"Which cemetery were you thinking of?" Mary asked.

We had no idea that there was more than one cemetery in St. George.

"We have no idea. We didn't know there were options," Scott stated. "We own land in Washington and wanted to bury him by there."

"Okay, except that is a different county. You will need to go over to their building," Mary informed us.

"Could you give us the directions?" Scott inquired.

"Of course." She actually drew us a little map and told us exactly where to go. She was very nice.

"Okay, so that didn't work out very well," Scott commented as we walked back to the car.

"It's not that bad. I just didn't know how many cemeteries there were here."

"Yeah, me neither."

We drove down the main street which ran east and west, to the main crossroad that ran north and south, called Red Bluff. It was a ways down the road, but then we were in this whole new area. It actually looked like a very old part of town, and then all of a sudden there was a park and two very nice-looking buildings about four stories high, which were the government buildings for Washington County. So again, we parked, exited the car, and walked into the building. There was a key log right there. We looked for the registration office because that's where we thought we should go. It was just to the right of us. We walked in and asked if this was where we would buy a burial plot "Actually, you are close, but this is the construction registry. You need to go out the door and up the stairs and it will be the door in the corner to the right," the receptionist said.

"Okay, thank you." And we walked up the stairs. "Well, we are getting closer," Scott said.

"Yup."

9:08 a.m. We reached the top of the stairs and read on the door Washington City. We were in the right place. We walked in and there was yellow paint on the walls. The desks were all of a cherry wood color. There was a huge metal clock on the wall to the right with pictures of the surrounding area adjacent on the walls. We walked up to the counter. I always found it interesting that when we see a counter, we automatically lean on it. It happens in a bank, at a restaurant, or wherever, that we lean against the counter or set our purse or drink on it. Scott immediately leaned on it. A lady came out to greet us.

"Hi, my name is Scott Graham, and this is my wife Sharon. Our son just passed away a few days ago and we were told this is where we go to get a burial plot."

"I'm so sorry for your loss, but you are in the right place." She immediately pulled out a packet of papers from under the counter. "Well, this is basically all the information that you will need." She began to explain the process to us. Everything about the actual burial had already been planned with Jared. This literally was just picking the plot and paying for it. She told us that it wasn't a hard process, but that our main thing was to pick out the spot.

"Okay, so where do we go to find it?" Scott asked.

"You're really close. Go back out to the main road and turn left. You will take the next left on 300 N and as you come up to the cemetery, turn right and drive through the cemetery. You will actually be in a new area. It's behind the baseball field. I will have our plot engineer meet you over there."

"Well that sounds easy enough. Is it okay if we go over there now?" Scott asked.

"Of course. We will contact our engineer right away."

"Thank you."

We left her office with our little packet of paperwork and a map of the cemetery showing us what was available. It was a pretty new area, but the spots on the outside of the cemetery near the tree line were all taken. The middle was empty though. Her directions were right on and within just a few minutes we were there. It was weird that a main road ran through the cemetery and not a road in the cemetery. We drove through and saw the baseball field to the left. There was a really nice boulder arrangement on the landscaping of what we learned was the new cemetery. There was a rod iron fence around the area except for the open area where you walked through to go into the cemetery. We started walking around. We noticed tombstones which we never had really looked at before. We looked at how names were printed and what information was on the headstones. We were learning quickly. We walked with the map to see what places were available. We kind of wanted something as close to the edge as we could get, that maybe the shade of the trees would reach Dalen. I thought it was interesting on the thought process, to pick the best spot: maybe in the shade, or maybe on the outside; or maybe over here or there. Would it really matter? Actually it did to the family. His body would rest there, but of course his spirit wouldn't be there. It was important to get the spot that we felt was right. It was also interesting what people were allowed to put by the tombstones. I had never seen anything like it before. There were wreaths, solar lights, pictures, twinkle lights, fans and team pennants. For some, it looked like almost a contest of who could crowd the grave sight the most. We actually laughed at some of them, trying not to be disrespectful. Scott and I just looked in awe. We walked around slowly.

"It's very quiet and peaceful here," Scott said.

"Yes it is, and I like how it's set up. You can see the mountains and I like the rocks and trees around the edge."

"Yeah, it's really nice." Scott was looking around.

We were trying to figure out spaces. We just walked and looked around. We would stop every once in a while and just look around from where we were at to see if we like the spot. We started to narrow down our choices. We didn't like the north end. It was too open. There was no one buried there yet and no trees or rocks. It led us again to more of the south end. We didn't want to be right by the gate either because of it being the traffic route. So, we walked slowly but a bit eastwardly and kind of got the feel for the space. We pulled out the map again. We saw a row where there were a few spaces together. I tried to see if there were any number 14 for plots available, it wasn't, but that ended up being a good thing because we didn't like where 14 was. I found a place and I liked it.

"What do you think of this area?" I asked Scott.

"Umm, I actually like it." Scott was a few feet away from me, so he walked to be beside me. "Yeah, I like this spot."

"Me too. It feels good."

We were there for maybe ten minutes or less, when a government truck drove up.

"Oh, the guy is here."

"Wow, that was fast." Scott explained.

Introductions were made and handshakes were given.

"So how does this work?" I asked the man.

"Well, you decide where you like and I can tell you if it's available," he answered.

"Okay, we kind of like this area right here," as I motioned with my hands a circular motion of the area in front of me.

He looked at the map he had and because he knew the spacing of plots, he commented: "Well, if you move about six to eight inches to the left, you will be in the exact spot."

"Are you serious! That is amazing. Really this is the spot?" Scott and I were both a bit stunned that we could be that close to where the spot was that we wanted for Dalen.

"Yup, you are good to go if that's what you like." The man confirmed.

"Oh my gosh. This is so amazing. We are in the right spot. That is so cool."[57]

That was pretty amazing with the open spaces around us and that we were actually on the spot we liked, and it was decided. It was that easy. It was actually exciting to see how simple the process was and that we felt we were led to the spot, and it was done.

"Well, that was probably the easiest placing I've ever done," the man stated.

The man said he would radio it back to the office of the number we wanted and all we would need to do was go and pay for it. Wow, that was easy.

---

[57] In choosing a burial plot, we were within inches of the place where our son would rest in this life. "Yup, and he said we were good."

Scott and I walked out hand in hand. Through most of this ordeal we were very attentive to each other mostly to make sure the other was okay.

"That was pretty painless," Scott stated.

"That was pretty simple."

9:37 a.m. We were back to our vehicle. We retraced our driving track and returned to the government building and up the stairs to the department in the corner.

When we walked in, the lady that had helped us before, was there and greeted us. She said that Tracey was the lady in charge and would be able to help us out with the rest of the things that we needed to do.

Tracey was a bit older than the receptionist that assisted us earlier. She greeted us and again gave her condolences.

"So did you decide on a plot?" she asked.

"Yes we did. We would like D-8. I think that was the one the guy said we could have." Scott informed the lady of our choice.

"Did the engineer meet you out there?" she inquired.

"It was actually really neat. We were walking around and kind of found the spot we liked. When the guy came, he said to move about six inches to the left, and I would be on the exact space. We thought that was another miracle we witnessed. We have been so blessed through all this," I commented.

"That is actually very amazing," the lady responded. "For some people, this is such a hard part of this process because it's so final."

"Maybe it will be when we actually bury our son, but this was easy, we were at peace and it was quick."

Through some of our conversations they learned about Dalen—that he was twenty-two and just home four months from his mission and that he was attending BYUIdaho with his sister. We mentioned a bit about the accident and then how blessed we had been.

I explained the knowledge I had gained about the tender mercies and the insight into the mighty miracles like finding his plot which was another miracle. Both the ladies agreed with us and they too, had tears in their eyes when we explained what happened.

It came time to pay.

"Are you ready to pay now?" Tracey asked us.

I took a deep breath because this is where I had heard people 'freak out' with how expensive everything ends up being. You have the plot, the cement case, the permit and it usually is a lot. I was expecting her to say the cost to be within $1,000(s) and not really knowing how much but thinking of between $3-$4,000.

"How would you like to pay for this?" Again, Tracey asked us.

"We will be putting it on a credit card if that's okay."

"That would be fine. For many people we offer a payment schedule too if that would make it easier." She took the card from Scott. "That will be $400.00 please."

"What did you say?" Scott and I had to question.

"How could it be that low?" I inquired.

"That's our normal price, I promise," Tracey reiterated the cost.

"You're kidding, aren't you?" Scott and I just couldn't grasp the low price. "It's like $2,500 in California."

"Well, not here." Tracey reassured us that $400 was all it would cost.

"If it's that cheap, we should buy our plots too. That way we could be together with Dalen."

Of course, that in no way, was our thought with the start of the day. We weren't even thinking of us or our future.

"Well, we actually could do that, couldn't we?"

"Yes and I think we should. We are here. We would be next to Dalen, and we can afford it." We had in our mind set aside $1,500 for what we thought might be close to that figure, we were under the budget and now would be getting three plots. Tracey brought out the map and we began to look. We knew that there were several spaces to the south of Dalen and a few to the north or above him too. It was so easy as there were three spaces right next to Dalen. They were right there. Again, it was that simple. We thought that was pretty amazing and again another miracle. It was just right there.[58]

---

[58] When we chose Dalen's plot, we were blessed to know that we would be right next to him.

10:10 a.m. Okay, that was a very weird concept. First, we were buying a burial plot for our son and that was different enough, but now the thought to begin the process of buying Scott's and my plots. We were buying our burial plots. That was just so very weird and yet it was so cheap that we had to. How could we not? It just made sense to us, and the plots were available. We could have Dalen in the middle of us as there were plots on either side of him; or pick the two plots to the right of his. Scott and I only needed a minute to decide that we would like to be next to each other, so we chose number 9 and 10. It was done. It was really awesome. We had Dalen's plot and now ours too. They were paid for and everything. We knew we had the funds from the amazing donations given to us as well. To find the exact spot for Dalen was amazing to us, but then to be able to afford all three of our plots was so unreal. Could it really have been that easy? Yes, and it was.

I was told by Bobby not to pay for anything, but we didn't have all the money exactly yet from the donations, so we just charged it to our card and still felt it was all good.

We hugged the ladies and said thank you again as we walked out of their office.

"Can you believe that?"

"Nope, that was pretty surreal," Scott stated.

"We just bought our burial plots—that's insane. That was in no way my intention today."

"Mine neither, but it just worked out perfectly," Scott stated.

"Yes it did."

We got into the car and started to head back to the cemetery. We wanted to see now where we would be buried. We walked right to the spot. It was perfect, absolutely perfect. We walked through the gate again and right up to the space. There was a tombstone on plot 11 so it was easy to count out where we would be. Cool! So amazing for sure.

We drove back to Scott's mom's house. We were almost excited. It was actually kind of exciting how it all worked out. We were in the car for maybe thirty seconds when I got a phone call from Bobby and Gina. They of course wanted to check in on us and find out what we were doing.

"So how are you today, and what are your plans?" Bobby asked. "I should have all the financial stuff done today so you should have the money by tonight."

"How can that be? That's so fast." I put him on speaker phone for Scott to hear.

"Well we need to get things taken care of right!" Bobby said.

"Yup, I guess so."

"So what are you guys doing?" Gina asked, as we were on their speaker phone as well.

"Well, we actually are just leaving the register's office. We just found Dalen's plot and are at the cemetery as we just paid for it. It was a pretty cool experience."

"Wait a minute. You did what?" Gina was almost shouting at us. "You did what?" she asked again.

"We just bought Dalen's plot," Scott replied.

"What are you not getting that you aren't supposed to buy anything? We need to take care of this. We didn't want you to have to worry about anything." Gina sounded serious but almost to a funny part.

"Well, we didn't know Gina. We just did what we needed to do."

"Hi Bobby," Scott interjected." What's going on?"

"Well, you weren't supposed to have to pay for anything." Bobby repeated.

"We didn't know that Bobby. We had to get it done and didn't really think about it," Scott replied.

"It happened pretty quickly. Actually Bobby, it was kind of cheap, so we even decided to buy Scott's and my plot too."

"What, wait a second. Now say that again," Bobby asked.

Gina was all: "UH UHHH. Oh no you didn't. You're not supposed to do that." Gina was a very animated person with a ginormous heart.

Scott and I looked at each other and shrugged our shoulders. What did we do wrong? We had to take care of things, so we did. That was all it was. We didn't know what else to do.

"Well, have you left yet?" Gina asked.

"Yes," I replied.

"Well, go back and get a refund." Gina and Bobby were both telling us what we needed to do and they were adamant.

"Why do we need to do that Bobby?" Now Scott was questioning.

"Well, because we had it planned out all along that we wanted to pay for Dalen's plot," Bobby stated.

That totally surprised us and after all that they had done for us.

"Are you serious?" Scott asked.

"Yes, you are so going back and will get a refund," Gina said.

"Well, we have already left and it's okay Bobby. We can take care of this," Scott stated.

"I want to. We want to take care of this, so we need to figure it out." Bobby again was persistent.

"Okay Bobby. Let me call the office and see what can be done." Scott reassured them that we would try to get this changed.

"We don't want to pay for you of course, but we will take care of Dalen's," Gina insisted.

"Okay Gina. I'll call them right now." Scott reassured her.

10:24 a.m. The conversation with the registration's office was that of surprise. They had never really heard of someone wanting to pay for a plot that was already paid for. Again, how amazing was this. They consented after it was all explained to them. So, Bobby was to call them and they would call Scott to authorize that we were asking for a reimbursement of $400 to our account and that we had also authorized Bobby and Gina Harris to pay for Dalen's plot.

Not knowing when the finances would be in our possession, we went ahead to pay for Dalen's plot, but the Harris' wouldn't let us. Again all was taken care of. This truly couldn't be normal but it was absolutely perfect.[59]

We actually pulled the car over for a minute during our discussion with Bobby and Gina. Scott needed to call Tracey back at the registration office. We were just blown away.

"Can you believe this Scott?"

---

[59] We were so overwhelmed with any of the finances that we received but the payment of Dalen's plot was so unexpected.

"No, not really, but then again, it's Bobby and Gina, so I guess I shouldn't be surprised," Scott said.

I texted the girls and let them know again of a mighty miracle and how blessed we were as a family. They all expressed their gratitude. It really was just so unbelievable that's for sure.

We drove back to the house and made preparations for the next task at hand. We wanted to show the girls where the plot was and then go and check out getting a headstone. They hadn't moved too much yet that morning, so while they were getting ready, I was cleaning our beds and putting away our things. We weren't loading things up yet in the cars, but were just getting things ready.

Alyssa and Brandon had returned from getting his dad's suburban. They said it didn't take long at all, but then we had to transfer everything into the suburban from Dalen's truck, remembering that we had filled Dalen's truck previously with all his stuff. Then when we were going to leave his truck in Rexburg, we divided all the boxes into Alyssa's car and ours. Now with the suburban, after putting the coffin in, we loaded up all of Dalen's things. It was pretty full, but it meant the rest of us would have a little bit more room for our travels.

11:30 a.m. I received a pretty special message that I immediately shared with the family. It was from Sylvia—Gary's mom in West Jordan. She sent a picture of me meeting Gary and her family there. It was amazing.

> **We love you love, love, love, you so so much. Words cannot express my deep feelings for you, and all of your family. Yes it was an amazing experience to meet you and I felt like I've known you forever after our meeting.**
>
> **How are you all doing today? Gary apologizes for being so out of it last night. They had given him some strong pain medication plus the medicine to help him pass gas. He said he was very uncomfortable with the gas pains, and he was afraid that it might happen**

while you were there, and he would be embarrassed. LOL. You are a WONDER WOMAN. I wouldn't be surprised if Dalen is approving of all your doing. You are such an inspiration to me. Thank you.

That was so nice to hear, and I was also rejoicing because of our meeting. We would never be separated from each other. We had such an amazing experience. I so appreciated her and all that she had gone through. She was one amazing woman and a fighter.

Of course Alyssa was getting hungry, so I decided to make some lunch first and made everyone sandwiches before we left for the cemetery. Scott's mom always made sure she had plenty of milk and chips and always the flavored chips that we liked. There was usually turkey, roast beef, and sometimes ham meat selections for lunch. It was an easy process, except I just forgot if Brandon liked mayo and mustard and if Scott only wanted mustard. I thought it was funny, but I was pretty good at fixing the kind of sandwich that each one would like. 'Go Mom' as I tooted my own horn. As mothers' we felt the need to cater to our family. I never felt it was a big deal if someone wanted ham or turkey, mustard, mayo, or relish. I didn't feel to put out by making what they would like, and I was pretty good at remembering except for Scott. I just kept forgetting if he liked mayo on one side and mustard on the other. Actually, what I really learned was the type of meat determined the condiment he wanted. And Brandon, well, I just hadn't made too many sandwiches for him, so I still had to ask what he liked.

We were all conversing again like we normally would. Conversations were light hearted and we were joking around like a normal family does. For the most part, we were a normal family until the conversation went to the experience in buying the plot and how amazing that was and how normal that then made our situation be.

We all loaded up in the Durango. Brandon, because he had such long legs, I would insist that he sit in the front. Mariah and Alyssa sat in the back, and Kailee and I were in the middle. We drove over to the cemetery.

"What the heck! Look at those headstones and all the decorations," Alyssa commented.

"I know. It's weird huh."

"Wouldn't see that in California, that's for sure," said Scott.

"They have everything out here. Why?" Mariah inquired.

"I guess it helps the families feel good. I don't know."

"Well, we won't be doing anything like that for sure," Scott stated.

"No way. It's all just way too much." Mariah was adamant.

We all agreed. It was very different to see wreath stands, lights, flowers of course, fences, pictures, chimes and ribbons. It was a bit much for me and definitely was the topic of conversation by us all that Dalen would NOT look like that ever. We agreed. So we drove through the cemetery and past the ballpark. That changed some of their views as they didn't really like the old cemetery, but they really liked the new area. We walked through the entry way.

"Oh, this is kind of cute," Kailee said.

"Cute, how can a cemetery look cute?" Mariah questioned. It wasn't abnormal for Mariah to question Kailee. In fact, Mariah was sometimes pretty hard on Kailee. She didn't have a whole lot of patience with her.

I thought this area was cute like Kailee, but it was a cemetery. Some parts just looked better than others.

"This side is really clean. It's not very big, so it kind of is cute."

They had these big red boulders and then pebbles around the boarders. There were some pine trees and elms within the planters around the outside on the south and each side of the cemetery. Dalen's plot was closer to the south end. Everyone walked around and just took it all in. They seemed comfortable. It was peaceful too.

"It's pretty quiet here," Alyssa commented.

"Yeah, I like the trees," Kailee added.

They tried to make some jokes like: "Well, everyone's just dying to get in here", so we could all laugh. That was also a different way to express our experience as enjoyable. We were comfortable and laughing just a bit, but enough that we didn't sense any stress or heartache for anyone. They all liked the places we picked. They all felt like we made a good choice.

"I think Dalen will like it here." Again Kailee was trying to contribute to the event.

We didn't stay long—maybe ten minutes, and then they didn't really know what to do except walk around and look at tombstones. Very interesting that on Dalen's isle and about three spaces to the right of his plot, was a tombstone with the last name of Graham on it. We found that a bit funny too.

"Hey look we will be in the Graham section," Mariah stated.

We all went over to look. Sure enough, there was a tombstone that had Graham as the last name on it. It was about 3 spaces away from Dalen. That was kind of another little experience that made the situation a bit lighter.

"Sounds good to me," stated Scott.

Alyssa actually liked walking around and looking at names. There were several graves where spouses were going to be buried so they would have both names on the headstone and of course the date of the one that passed and blank death date for the one still alive. We saw sights of babies that only lived a day or two. There were even some with names and no dates as they had chosen the spot they liked with the tombstone they wanted, but were still alive.

I had been in cemetaries many times in my life. When I was growing up, we used to ride our bikes over to the cemetary that was about a mile from my house, and my friends and I would play tag or have a lunch. There were many times I would go by myself and just read a book. I never liked to think of all the scary things that people had associated with graveyards. Mind you, I would never be there in the dark.

I had been to funerals before, and burials, so I was okay to walk around and my family seemed comfortable too.

I hadn't really studied any headstones though. I might have seen a name or date but never thought a whole lot about the process. This time I would question: 'I wondered what their story was.' Each person that was buried there would have a story.

As the girls were walking around, we speculated as to what some of the stories might have been based on the graphics on the headstones or the decorations around them. Some had scenery or wildlife pictures. Some had a scripture quoted. Some were super plain with only a name and date. It was now very interesting as thoughts began for all of us as to what we would have put on Dalen's headstone.

Altogether, we might have spent about twenty minutes there. Everyone was happy with our choices and content with the time we stayed there.

"Okay, we all good? Then let's go," Mariah was done. She was never one to hold back her emotions and she was done and ready to go. I could see that she was getting uncomfortable. We had all made sure that she was okay and that it was okay that we spent what time we needed to be there. She was good, but now it was time to leave.

"Okay, so let's go."

The Tombstone

From the cemetery, we were going to go to the place to get the headstone made.

Scott had remembered seeing a place once when he drove around so we started out to find it. We drove down a street and actually came to a headstone place that Scott didn't know about. He did get us in the right direction though. We stopped to check it out. We all got out of the car and walked up and there saw a note on the door saying: "Closed for lunch, will be back at 1:00 p.m."

"Well, that's no good," Alyssa said.

"Nope," Scott replied. "I think I know where this other place is."

I asked how he would know where there was a masonary.

"Well it's over by the muffler place. I remember seeing it when I drove to the shop a few times. Sure enough, we drove to the muffler place—one of Scott's favorite places in St. George as they had helped him once, and he always seemed to stop and visit with them each time he drove through town. They were good to Scott. We turned right at the intersection and past the muffler shop and saw the sign for St. George Monuments. Scott was right again, and there it was.

12:18 p.m. Again we unloaded the car and started to walk around the courtyard where they had all these different samples of colors and sizes and designs of headstones. Some were black, gray, salmon and various shades.

About one minute later I heard: "I like this one. What do you think?" Alyssa asked.

It was a salmon colored stone.

"Oh I like it!" Mariah announced with actually excitement in her voice.

"Hey, that's not bad," Scott added.

"It looks like Dalen's blanket," Kailee said and that was it. That was it. It was even the shape we liked. It was one that stood up so it would have a base. We even liked the size of the sample. It was perfect.

"Well if everything is that easy—then we should be able to get through this quickly," Brandon commented.

Just as we decided what we liked; the owner came out to greet us. We introduced ourselves and explained our situation. He started to explain what some of the possibilities were and pointed out certain sections as of some were sandstone, and some were of marble.

"Well, I think we just decided on this one," Scott stated. He pointed to the headstone we all liked.

"Really—you already decided?" The owner seemed soo very puzzled as to how quickly our decision was made.

"Yup, we like this one," Scott reiterated.

"Well that was the fastest decision making I've ever seen," he said.

"That's what I said," Brandon added.

"Well, I guess then we can go in and we will go through what you want on it and we will get things going." The man continued to give us a few instructions.

In the shop straight ahead of us was a computer on a desk. There was another desk and computer to the left. That was where the man sat.

"Well, since you decided on the color and shape already, then we just need to figure out what you want on the headstone." He pulled up a website that had all types of lettering, sayings, fonts and sizes. Alyssa sat down and manipulated her way through the samples as we all looked from behind her to get some ideas.

"We need to have this on it," Alyssa pointed to the sport section and a volleyball player.

"And this," Mariah pointed out the style of a font.

"I don't know his favorite scripture. Maybe we could have a set of scriptures on it."

"Yeah that sounds good," Alyssa and Scott agreed.

The man reminded us that we could do the back and front of the stone. Of course that made sense. It also made it easier because of all the desires of everyone It was a given that we would have his name with his birth and death dates on it.

"I would really like "Buddy Boy' on it if I could," I suggested.

Everyone agreed that was important to have on it. So far, we came up with:

"Our Buddy-boy"
Dalen Scott Graham
November 28, 1995–February 10, 2018

Scriptures would be in one corner. Mariah suggested a flag since Dalen was very patriotic and would want one, and that could go in the other corner.

"Yup, he would want that Mariah. Good idea," Scott stated.

A flag would be perfect and could balance the space across from the scriptures. It really was that easy again. The decisions were made, and all agreed. The man was starting to draw up what we were suggesting and we all liked it.

"Our Buddy Boy" Dalen Scott Graham

November 28, 1995
February 10, 2018

Flag	Scriptures

"Anything else that you want on it?" The man petitioned. "This just never happens."

"What doesn't happen?" Scott asked.

"People don't just come in and make their decisions so quickly. So many times I'm needed to walk them through on every step. It takes a while for them to decide even the color of the headstone. Many people are just so distraught that they have a very hard time making any decisions. I don't ever push them, but I'm usually guiding the conversations. Seldom are we done under an hour. You guys walked in, saw what you liked and that was it. You've decided on what you want and where. This is just amazing," stated the man.

It was very apparent to us that none of our experiences with our son's passing were what you might call *'normal'*. We were very much in control of our emotions. We had so much peace and comfort with us that we just kept going. We didn't stop or wonder what we had to do. We weren't sitting in a room crying and overcome with emotions. We just moved forward. A decision needed to be made and it was done. There was little pondering or questioning of our choices. It was just what had to be done, we were there, so why not take care of it all. From the hospital and the donor process; to the coffin and funeral issues; then the burial, and now the headstone and it all just fell into place. Most people take a bit longer to have to make all these decisions.

I didn't want to have to come back and take care of things. I didn't want to worry about anything after the burial (which also was an option), and it just seemed to be exactly what it should have been. It was very overwhelming to all of us. And everywhere we went, we heard of how abnormal our situation was including our decision making. 'I've just never seen that!"

"I've just never heard of that!"

"'I've just never had this done so quickly!"

"Your family had just made this so easy for us."

"I've never seen anything like this!"

"We don't know that we aren't normal, but we just know what we want I guess, and it seems to make sense and is what we all want. Believe me, we really don't know that we aren't normal in this process. We just keep getting told that we aren't. We have been so grateful and humbled by all this though," was my statement.

"Like my wife said, I guess we just know what we want," Scott added.

"That's kind of how we do things," Mariah added.

Alyssa was looking at the fonts while we were talking.

"So, I like this one," she said.

"Could we make it bolder?" I asked. I wanted to make sure the font would be readable.

We experimented for a few minutes to decide which font and size we wanted and then it was selected.

Now we needed to design the back of the tombstone. From the beginning, Mariah wanted a volleyball player on it and I just couldn't see that on the front. But it would work perfectly on the back. Alyssa was looking again through the graphics. We found a volleyball player spiking the ball.

"What about this one?" Alyssa asked.

"I like it," Mariah said.

"I like it too," Kailee added.

"Well, I think that works. That's perfect. Maybe we could get it flipped so it would look like a left-handed player.' I suggested.

"That would be perfect. Yea that's perfect," Mariah added.

"Yup, that's it," Scott said.

"So can we put Dalen's favorite saying on it too?" Kailee asked.

We hadn't thought of that, but as soon as she said it, Mariah was looking it up on her phone. She read it to us and we all liked it. So, it was a matter of where we wanted it to be.

"If we put the volleyball player at the top, we could put the saying below it," Alyssa suggested.

We laid it out on the computer and again, we all liked it. It took a minute to design it and then it was done. We all liked it and all agreed, so I guess we were done.

The man asked us: "You designed the back already too?"

"Yup, I think we are done," replied Scott.

"That's amazing. I really can't believe it. You guys just know what you want. I've spent hours with people trying to help them with everything. This is amazing. I can tell you I've never seen this before, and that you all are so positive and just seemed to make this so easy for me and you," said the man. Then he drew out our wishes for the back with the font, color and size. He let us check it over with the design and it looked good.

"I'm sure there might be some questions that will come up so we will just keep in touch and I'll send you pictures with the progress," stated the man.

"That will be perfect. Thank you."

He started to fill out the bill of sale. He again checked over everything. I again asked if he could flip the volleyball player, and he made a star by the diagram and noted it on the side of his paper stating such. We paid for the work to be done and then stood there for a minute like there was something more we needed to do, but there wasn't.

"Thank you so much for your help." Scott said as he extended his hand out for a handshake. "Well, this was definitely the easiest plan and design I've ever done. Again I'm sorry for your loss, but we will do our best to make this headstone what you want. We should have it done by Memorial Day.

"Wow, that sounds good. We will keep in touch."

And we were done. That fast and that simple. Again it almost seemed easy. There was no stress or worry that we weren't doing it right. There were no thoughts of Dalen not liking it either. We were on a mission today and we completed it. It was just that simple.[60]

We surprised ourselves and made comments that we couldn't believe how fast we did all that we needed to do. There wasn't anything else we could think of that we needed to take care of. Mortuary stuff—all done. Coffin situation—resolved.

Burial and plot—check. Tombstone—completed. Funeral—planned and now it was just a matter of time to see things come to fruition. Whatever we paid for, we would get reimbursed for, and then it was all taken care of. Don't tell me my God isn't good.

We drove back to Scott's mom's house and were in a sort of happy state of mind. Everyone was very pleased how things turned out and we were all surprised also, by how quickly we were able to accomplish our desires. We got to the house and were laughing with each other. It was easy to talk about our experiences with Scott's mom, and she seemed surprised too that all was so easy.

Everyone had to gather up their things as we were getting ready to head home. It had been a very good morning, but we still had a good seven hours ahead of us, so we needed to get going. I also had been informed that people wanting to help us back home, would have a dinner waiting for us around 7:00 p.m. even though I wasn't sure of the time we would get home. It was time to go.

---

[60] We walked on the premises and saw what we liked for a memorial, and it was done. The writing and graphics were selected and there was nothing but agreement from everyone on the specific details. Wow.

Heading to California—Finally

1:00 p.m. The drive home started. This time we would leave Kailee's car again as she would drive with me to California. Scott and Mariah again were in Dalen's truck, and Alyssa and Brandon were driving in his dad's suburban. Kailee would be able to drive back with any of the family that would be coming back through for the burial. We had driven this road many times. Nothing was new. The miles just went by. We all stayed together and were communicating the whole way.

2:45 p.m. (back on California Time) The normal stops occurred where we ate and went to the bathroom. We had to stop in Vegas for an 'In & Out' burger. They were Dalen's favorites and besides that, everyone liked them. It was an easy choice with easy access off the highway too. Both Scott and Brandon wanted to remember Dalen, so they got the quad—four patties, no lettuce or tomato. Mariah got the animal fries which looked like Thousand Island dressing on fries. I didn't like it too much, but Dalen did. Mind you being from Canada, we would put vinegar or gravy on our fries so I guess salad dressing wasn't that bad. Five more hours to drive and I was getting a bit anxious. It wasn't an exciting anxious feeling; it was more like I just wanted this to be over.

We told everyone that they didn't have to drive together, but it just happened. Usually, Baker was a good bathroom break, and then Yermo and that usually got us home. Scott might have an extra stop in there somewhere for just one more Diet Coke.

Victorville was where we turned off the #15 and headed home. There was a mountain range we followed, and the tops of the mountains still had snow of them. It was really very 'deserty' the whole drive home. Not my favorite view but definitely the normal one.

6:21 p.m. We drove through part of Victorville and then we headed west. It used to be known as the roller-coaster road as there were lots of dips. It was actually pretty fun back in the day. There was nothing but the odd house. It was a fun ride. But now, there had been so much development. There were lights about every two or three miles with an intersection at each. There were shops and stores all along the way. The development almost went out to Pear Blossom almost twenty miles away.

Kailee and I kept talking about wanting to be home. It had been a very good day and again we were all in good spirits. This time, my anxiousness facing what would occur once we would arrive at home, was minimal. The unknown again was pretty powerful compared to what we did know and had experienced.

6:45 p.m. Little Rock and the new McDonald's landmark was coming into view. It was interesting how something would be built and it would immediately be packed and you wonder how they ever survived without that place. That was this McDonald's.

"Well, we are almost home. Do you need to stop or just go home?" I asked Kailee.

"Nope, I'm good. Looks like dad isn't stopping either." She looked behind us, which wasn't always normal because Scott would need just one more large Diet Coke easy ice, to get him home. No one stopped so we were homeward bound. Once we passed through Little Rock, you could see Palmdale lights which meant we were almost home.

6:56 p.m. We turned off Highway 38 onto the Pear Blossom Road. We were only fifteen miles from home. Of course we hit every red light. It almost became like a joke for Kailee and me.

"Let's see if you can make this one Mom," One I did, and one I didn't.

It was pretty dark outside. There wasn't a moon out yet and there weren't many lights off the main streets.

7:07 p.m. We all drove into the housing track and followed the mile and a half road up to our street. We could see our house. The porch lights were on which was a surprise because when we left for somewhere, we don't leave them on. It was like a welcoming beacon though. We drove up the driveway into the far-right spot. Scott was right behind me, and Alyssa and Brandon pulled up onto the gravel which was left of the house.

"Hey Mom, look we got heart-attacked." Kailee pointed out.

"What the heck. On my gosh, that is so cool."

To get heart-attacked meant that cut out hearts are placed all over your outside yard. It's like toilet papering someone. It meant you had been thought of. The first time this happened to us was when Alyssa got asked to Prom and our lawn was filled with a whole bunch of hearts staked into our grass. It was so cute.

We were all exiting our vehicles and standing near the porch looking at the scene and taking it all in. We walked across the grass and were reading the messages.

"You are so loved."

"We love you."

"You're the best."

"Love, love love you."

"Prayers for you all."

The hearts were all over the lawn, taped to the door and strung on the railings.

I knew immediately that the Sister Missionaries were a part of this as they had our house key and were helping take care of the animals. We were so touched. It was so amazing.[61]

---

[61] The heart is always the symbol of love and our lives were filled with them tonight.

We opened the door to the house.

"Well here we go—reality is here."

"Yup, it's real—that's for sure." Scott added his thought to mine.

When you first walk into our house, you saw our living room and dining room and there were already plants and flower arrangements on the table.

"What the heck," Alyssa stated.

From the dining room you could walk into the kitchen and there was more than a surprise. Our entire island was filled, and I mean filled with personal notes. They were all different colors, and some were addressed to individuals and others were to the whole family. It was beautiful. There were a few more floral arrangements on the kitchen table. If you continued around the kitchen you entered the family room. It was kind of like a circle but in more of a square shape I guess.

My first thought was how did they know when we would be home? But then I realized that several of my friends who were in constant contact with me while we were gone, had asked when we would be home. The Relief Society also had asked as they tried to arrange meals to be brought in and for how many persons.

We had all carried in our luggage, so I then set mine down in the family room. I just paused and admired the scene. I remembered telling the Relief Society Sisters not to worry about Tuesday night as we didn't know when we would be home. With that information, I was told they would have meals from Wednesday—Saturday for us. We knew that we would be heading back up to St. George Sunday afternoon for Dalen's burial on Monday. That was so awesome. I knew it's what we did as church members and I have helped many times with similar situations; but this was for us.

Scott and I also talked that we reminded each other that we needed to let others serve us as that would be their way of grieving. I went back to the island. Everyone was looking through the names on the cards. We started to separate them and again just looked through everything. I started to count them. Kailee assisted as we put them into groups of ten. Then everyone caught on and helped with the pattern.

"Really Mom, there has to be 100 cards here," Alyssa said.

"I know, this is crazy. I can't believe this. I wonder who did this for us." I knew that someone had to lead this and how they would get so many letters so quickly.

I learned later who the master mind was and that at church after Dalen passed, that we were the conversation of all the meetings and one sweet lady; Michelle Cooke had all these cards that were distributed in every class during the second hour of our services. Instead of their prepared lessons, they wrote us letters and discussed our situation and their heartaches. We were so humbled by all of this. Then Michelle came over with the Sister Missionaries and set everything up, literally just a few hours before we got home.

"I think I just counted 153 cards—could that be real?" I asked.

"I think so Mom, I got up to 150 so yeah," Kailee added.

"Wow, that is amazing," Scott was impressed too.[62]

I had brought the flowers in that we had received from Dalen's apartment and set them on the table with the others. There were three plants and two flower arrangements. I then took time to read the cards and who they were sent from. A couple of them were from people out of State and I also learned that once the accident occurred, the sisters came over daily just to see if there were any deliveries. This was just so amazing. We felt so loved. There was actually a gift card on the table from Subway with a note; "Not sure when you'll get home but maybe this could help." It had a $50.00 amount written on it.

Alyssa and Mariah again announced they were hungry, so we sent them on a run to subway. What a huge blessing for sure. We had no idea how people would take care of us but to immediately get some food with no concern for where it would come from was a godsend.

No one had posted anything yet that we were home and yet we all were getting "Welcome home" messages and of course concerns for our wellbeing.

I had to go feed the animals as I told the sisters previously that I would be home to take care of them. When I walked into the shed to get the hay—I was surprised again as there were several more hearts taped all around the shed. It was so cute.

I learned that all the hearts were from the Young Women of the ward. It was just so touching. Again, I took a moment and just tried to soak up all this outpour of love. Often when I fed the horses; I stood for a minute and just caressed them while they began to eat. I loved the feel of their coats. Tonight, I gave them a few more minutes

---

[62] The cards were on the island and the table. They were covered with words of love. We couldn't believe that there were more than 100 cards.

of my time. Their coats were so plush because of the winter coats, and it just felt so good. It really did feel like velvet.

I made my way back into the house and started to read some of the notes. I gave some to Scott and Kailee, so they were reading a few too. Once they were opened and read, we would set them into a pile so someone else would then be able to read a different pile. There were notes from everyone in the ward. The little kids that couldn't write would draw a picture of a smile or one was a stick figure of two people, one small and one tall. The caption (written by the leaders); "Dalen and me." Dalen had helped in primary a few times so the kids knew him and loved him. Every single one of them expressed their love for us—it was overwhelming. Alyssa, Brandon and Mariah returned with the sandwiches. They set them on the table as we made some room with the flower arrangements. Mariah immediately went to the fridge to get some milk. I knew there wasn't any. There was only a very little left before I left to go and visit Kailee. I knew that it would either be bad, or Scott would have used it. When she opened the door, there were two full gallons, and a load of bread. Seriously, someone even had the intuition to look in our fridge and make sure we had a few things needed when we would get home. So many people were blessing our lives and we didn't even know who or how to thank them. We were just so overwhelmed. We sat at the table and ate our sandwiches with of course our prayer of gratitude first. Our phones were still ringing with messages and concerns throughout the next few hours.

> **—I want you to know that I'm coming for Dalen's funeral. I have to come and say goodbye and give you and Scott a hug. I love you dearly.**
>
> **—We are part of a prayer group. I reached out to them and asked to say a prayer for your family. I know this loss is unbearable, but our faith reminds us that our loved ones are in a better place.**

>—You are in our prayers. We put your family names in the temple.
>
>—We are not close by, but we are only a phone call away. We haven't stopped thinking of you and your family.
>
>—We would like to offer a light lunch after the burial in Washington on Monday. We hope that helps in some way.
>
>—We love, love, love, love you so much. Words cannot express my deep feelings for you and your family. Gary and I love you.
>
>—My heart hurts for you.
>
>—Thinking of you. Not going to lie, you and your family have all been on my mind and in our prayers constantly. I'm over here bawling my eyes out and seeing your strength and the peace you have in your heart. Dalen was a gem!!!!!! One of my favorite.
>
>—Our minds and prayers are with you. Such a great young man with his whole life ahead…this is one of life's hardest challenges and so difficult to understand. We love you.

Okay ladies—you were the only ones with a key. Please thank and thank again everyone for the incredible display of love. So overwhelmed. (I sent the Sisters a text. I knew that the ladies in our ward were having an activity at the church tonight).

>—We love you!!!!!!
>
>—Hey Sis (from Rory) I know things must be a little crazy right now so I wanted you to know that I won't be able to be with you in person, but I will be there in spirit. Much love. Can you take a picture of me with you to the funeral so I can be there too.

"Of course, I'll take one of mom to."

While we were eating, there was a knock at the door. I went to go and open it and Brother Harris was there—a dear friend of ours. As soon as I opened the door he started to cry. I invited him in and he just hugged me.

"I'm just so sorry. I'm just so sorry," he repeated.

"Oh Robert, thank you so much for coming over. We are doing great. We really are doing okay. Come on in."

He followed me down the hall to the family room and kitchen where everyone was. Scott got up and came over to greet him. Robert and his family have kids our kids ages. We have hung out together for years. Our kids were friends and his friendship to Scott was treasured. He really was just a good guy.

Again, you could hear of his condolences as he was embracing Scott.

"Sorry to interrupt your meal. I don't need to bother you, I just wanted to see you." Robert said.

"You aren't bothering us man. You can stay." Scott responded.

"Are you sure? I don't want to interfere with your family. I just wanted you to know how sorry I am for you," and he wiped more tears away.

"Robert, we really are good. We would love to have you stay. I can't eat a whole sandwich, so you're welcome to my half," as I was still standing by him.

Mariah walked over to get her hug. There was another long embrace.

"I'm so sorry Mariah. You know how much we love you and are just very worried about you." Robert and Mariah were really close. She thought of him as a second dad and would go to him often for advice or consoling if Scott wasn't around.

"I'm okay," Mariah commented. That was her response again to most expressions of concern, but I really had to believe her. It wasn't like she said it and walked away or pulled from the situation. Upon hearing her words, she would remain with no alterations in her body language. Robert made his way around the table as he acknowledged the girls and Brandon.

I turned his attention to the cards all over the island and it was then I heard of the happenings at church. Robert proceeded to tell us what occurred.

"Well, the Bishop got up and 1st thing he announced was that Dalen had passed away. You could hear all the shocked responses. He asked that your family be in their prayers and announced when the funeral was. There was silence after the initial shock. Everyone was just so stunned. Some were crying," he said.

"Wow that's amazing!"

"Yeah, it really was. The spirit was so strong though. Everything that was said, was then focused on Dalen. Then Michelle had all these baskets for everyone and everyone in the rooms wrote letters. It was so amazing to see. Everyone loved Dalen that's for sure," Robert said.

Robert was only known as Robert to us. Not Bobby or Rob, just Robert. I remember one of the first times we met him; he introduced himself as Robert and that's all it's ever been.

Even though everyone was eating—they responded to what they just heard.

"Wow," Kailee said.

"That's amazing," was Alyssa's response.

"Cool," Mariah added.

There were more communications about some of our amazing experiences over the last few days. "I had come to learn of the differences between the mercies of God and the miracles. I think tender mercies are when we petition the Lord for something we need. 'Help me find the keys.' 'Where should I go to school?' 'Please bless me to remember what I studied.' We ask for help and because the Lord loves us, he answers our prayers."

"But miracles are when we let Him lead. Our lives are forever changed and the peace that we have felt has been amazing. They have become mighty miracles and they just keep coming".

I reflected on how I had now described mercies and miracles and the difference between them to everyone I spoke with. This would be my motto, my understanding, my knowledge of what had transpired, and I wanted to tell everyone about what I had experienced.

Robert concurred with my definition.

We all talked about a bit of our experiences and Robert listened. The review from the family members was all positive and again expressed our amazing miracles. It was just so nice to have Robert visit us, but he didn't want to intrude on our time anymore and felt it was time to leave. He just kept mentioning that he didn't want to bother us even though we enjoyed his company. He hugged everyone again and Scott offered to walk him out.

Scott was gone for about five minutes. As soon as I heard the door open for him to come back in, he called me over.

"Hey Sharon, come here," he insisted. We were in the entry way and away from the rest of the family in the kitchen. Scott started crying. "Look—look! "He started crying harder. He held out his hand with a stack of money. I took the money in my hand and began to count it.

"No way! We can't take this. What is he doing? You need to give this back to him." It was $400.00.

"I tried. He wouldn't take it. I tried; I really did. I told him we didn't need it. That we were doing okay, and he said that it would help to make him feel better if he could help."

My mind had an immediate flashback to the profound words of our Bishop: *'Everyone will need to mourn in their own way, so let them.'*[63]

"Oh my gosh Scott," and we hugged each other very tightly. "What do we do?"

"I don't know," replied Scott as we both cried. "I really couldn't grasp all this."

Gratitude, humility, sincerity, and overwhelming love were our immediate emotions. We kept hugging each other. Scott excused himself as he went to the bathroom to blow his nose and wipe his eyes. I went back into the kitchen.

"So you guys need to know how blessed we are. Brother Harris just gave dad a lot of money because he wanted to help us all."

"Really—that is so amazing," Alyssa said.

---

[63] To be given money in any situation was humbling—but this amount was shocking. And we couldn't do anything but accept it.

"We told him we don't need it, but he needed to give it to us. We are so blessed."

"It's kind of a bit overwhelming with all this," Kailee said. Again, I was so proud that she was able to analyze the situation and answer correctly how everything was connected together.

"Wow!" Mariah repeated about four times.

Scott rejoined us and we all finished our supper almost in reverence at what had just occurred.

I went back to the cards. Right from the start I had a list of the many miracles we had received so I went and got my book out of the bedroom. I brought it out to the island. I had written everything on the back of the packet that Jared had given us. I wanted to add all that had happened to us since we arrived at home. I wish I could find new words to truly express our thoughts, but I just didn't know any different ones. 'Amazing' 'Awesome' 'Miracles' 'Gratitude' 'Humbling'—there really weren't other words to say or express our love to God through all these amazing people touching our lives.

Everyone started settling in. The kids all knew that coming home they may not get the room they grew up in because they all had been converted to guest rooms. The couple (Alyssa and Brandon) would get Mariah's room because it had the queen-sized bed. Mariah and Kailee would be in the other room where there were two twin beds. It had also been discussed that when my family started coming, we would have to move people around. For now, they all took their stuff upstairs.

It was decided during dinner that we wanted to watch a movie and just vedge for a bit and not think about anything. It had been a very good day. We drove safely and in good time. We were shown an abundance of love. A movie would be the perfect end to our day.

Kailee's turn for family prayers. Kailee was very factual so in her prayer it was: "Thank you for the six cards I got, and the three Alyssa got and the ten Mariah got." It was touching. Heavenly Father just hadn't stopped blessing us, it just hadn't stopped!! Time for bed.

"Good night honey," Scott commented.

"Good night. Isn't this all just amazing?"

"It sure is," and he rolled over into his sleeping position after kissing me goodnight.

Day of Love

Wednesday, February 14, 2018 Happy Valentine's Day! I don't think it would be the normal, romantic day where Scott and I would have cards on the dresser for each other. We would plan a dinner date and I would usually get flowers. Scott liked to get me flowers. They didn't have to be these huge arrangements. More than likely, he would go to a Vons and pick up a bouquet. Scott even tried to get me flowers almost on a monthly basis. Yup, I was spoiled in that way. He liked to get them for me and I like to have them.

Since I was gone and then Dalen passing, there would be no flowers today from Scott. There were however, other arrangements and they were beautiful. I loved the smell always. Some people think flowers were just a waste of money because they just died. I disagreed. If something brought you joy and pleasure in this life and smelt good and created from God, it was not a waste. Flowers were meant for man, to bring us joy.

Throughout the morning, everyone was slowly getting up. I didn't like to have hours of a meal, so after I took care of breakfast and if they weren't there; then they were on their own to find what they wanted for breakfast.

10:45 a.m. There were already a few knocks on the door with a couple more of arrangements. Again, feeling so blessed. They were so pretty.

11:18 a.m. I received a very unique phone call.

"Hello, Sister Graham—My name is Sherry Nichols and I believe you know my daughter.

'I don't think I do, I'm sorry."

"She's Dalen's girlfriend," she reported.

"His what? We never really knew Dalen had a new girlfriend for sure."

"My daughter is Chloe, and she had been dating Dalen for about two weeks before he passed away," She continued to inform me of their relationship.

"Well, that's new news to us. We heard mention of a girlfriend from the paper but thought they were misinformed. Anyways, how can I help you?"

"Chloe feels she needs to be there and would so like to come and meet you. She is flying out tomorrow and was just hoping you would be okay with her coming over." Sherry continued.

I was quite surprised. 'Well honestly I recalled a message and I hadn't responded yet. I just didn't know if it would be a good time. Actually, we have family coming in tomorrow and I'm not sure if we would have time to visit with a young lady that we don't know." It's kind of a unique request don't you think?' I asked the mother.

"Oh please, just let her visit for a minute. She is staying with her Uncle in San Dimas. She will be there tomorrow and would just like to meet you for a minute. She has been so devastated and has truly felt like she needs to be with your family to meet you and know who you are."

"I can't say that we will get to visit much but if she wants to come—it would have to be tomorrow between one to three. I'm not sure where else we will be, but my family is expected then. We have family plans for Friday and Saturday of course, is the funeral. I think we are going to be busy. I'm really not sure about this. I just don't think we are in a position to entertain someone yet. That's the best I can do." I wasn't feeling very comfortable about this. I just didn't want to have to be polite to a stranger that liked my son and to worry about how things would be. I really knew that I was being just a bit selfish and that I needed to get over it. It would be fine, and it wasn't going to be forever. I could do this.

"I will let her know. Thank you so much for letting her come to meet you. She just felt it was more important to meet you before the funeral. She will be very excited. Thank you." You could hear the almost pleading from the mother's voice. This was very important to her and her daughter as the mother expressed that she loved Dalen too. They knew him from his mission. He served close to their area, and they had a family restaurant that Dalen ate at a lot. I was told that Dalen made them laugh all the time and they just loved the time he spent with them. That I believed.

After his mission, he got in contact with Chloe, who knew of the breakup with Delany. She believed in her heart that they were dating, and I couldn't put it past Dalen. Again, he was fast with his emotions and latched on quickly to a young lady, but would also be the most dedicated to the relationship.

I was a bit nervous about this whole thing. In some way, I didn't want to cater to this girl. I didn't want to have to worry about her too. I didn't know of her except for an article written by one of the papers that wrote a quote from 'Dalen's girlfriend.' I really didn't want to entertain or divide my time with family for this young lady. That really wasn't who I was though, and my son knew that. He knew I would accept whoever came to my door and welcome them. Usually if I found someone with a need, I tried to help them as I could. If someone asked for my time—I would normally give it to them. Why should this young girl be any different? Of course she could come. She liked our son and wanted to be here. I couldn't deny her impressions either. I told her mom that she could come. We had it arranged that she would come tomorrow around 1:00 p.m. Her train wouldn't leave till 5:00 p.m. so we would have to see how the afternoon went. If at any time she felt she didn't need to be there, or it might be awkward we could then make that decision for her to stay or not and she was good with that.

11:30 a.m. A knock at the door. This time it was our friend Tracy Packer. Tracy was a unique guy. Very short in stature but had a huge heart and was married to the Saint of all Saints. He had a few daughters—one Alyssa's age and another Kailee's age and even had the same name (spelled differently though). Tracy usually said what he felt and usually didn't sugar coat anything.

"Hello there, can I come in?" he asked.

"Of course, come on in."

He acknowledged the flowers and the cards.

"Looks like people are thinking of you," he commented.

"Actually, it's been very overwhelming," I replied. I escorted Tracy to the family room and had him sit on the couch. Scott came out from the bedroom and the girls were all there too. We were all looking through our photo albums to find pictures that we could put together as a slide show for the funeral.

I have always taken pictures and lots of them. I thought I was pretty good too. I even had done some weddings and taken some photography classes. I learned early after listening to many people how they would have pictures but that the family would have to fight over who got them. I would also hear that they have tons of pictures, but they were all on their phones. Sometimes they would transfer them to their computers but mostly I heard how they would eventually have to delete pictures. When I first was married, we used cameras. We would get the rolls of film developed. I knew then that I would: 1)—print off all my pictures and 2) that there would be one set for Scott and I of our lives, but as our children came along—that every picture they were in, would also get a copy for them. So, each one of my children have their lives in picture books. Sometimes I would spend quite a bit to get them developed but I felt it was very much worth it.

It wasn't hard at all to find pictures of Dalen. I just went to his photo bin and the albums were all numbered. Since he left for his mission and college and all his things were packed up, I just went and found the bin of his photo books and there they were. Everyone picked a few books and each of us chose twenty to twenty-five pictures. Then Kailee wanted to put them into a slide show after the other girls scanned them into the computer. That was our activity for the morning knowing it might take some time. We put the number of the photo album on the back of the picture, so I could return them to their proper place.

"So how are you all really doing? I just can't imagine what you're going through, I really can't," Tracy commented.

"Well thanks for coming." Scott sat in the chair by the computer. "We really are doing good. It's been humbling and we have been very blessed."

Mariah, who had been in the kitchen, came out to see Tracy. He got up to hug her.

"We all just have been so very worried about you and what you're going through and how you're handling what happened." Tracy's voice showed great concern.

"I'm doing okay. I really am," Mariah stated.

"Well that's amazing because you're who everyone is worried about," Tracy responded.

"I wish they wouldn't. I'm fine," Mariah said and retreated to the couch. She really wanted to be left alone and not have everyone talk about her.

We all visited for a few minutes. Of course again, we were reminded how we all were going through this traumatic event, but that Mariah's experience would always be worse. She would have to deal with the fact that she was driving the truck that caused the death (by accident) of Dalen.

Tracy talked about church and how everyone was affected and how sad it was for everyone. He asked how our travels were and how we made all the arrangements.

Scott mostly responded to Tracy's questions unless there was a direct question to one of us. It wasn't as hard as some of us thought, to talk about our experiences. We were just so at peace and comforted.

Tracy stayed for about half an hour and then decided it was time to go. We appreciated so much of him taking the time to visit.

The girls went back to looking through photo albums. All the pictures they picked just went into a pile in the middle of the floor. I let them pick theirs and then I would go through all the albums and add my choices.

Instead, I decided to take all the notes and cards and string them up throughout the house. I was hole punching a corner on all the cards and then took some string to tie them together. I would put about ten on a string as I didn't want them to get too heavy for the stick pins. There were so many of them. As I strung them up, I reread each one again. I started hanging them all around. At the top of the stairs, before the loft; there was a spot where we would often hang posters or happy birthday anniversary signs, so I had a few of the strings hung from there. I put them in the entries to the kitchen. I hung them from the fan in the family room. I hung them from the kitchen lights. It was awesome to look at and again be reminded of the outpouring of love we received.

The girls concluded with getting the pictures done. Kailee immediately started to work on the slideshow. I didn't care if they were chronological or not. We just mixed them all up. Mariah actually helped with some scanning of the pictures into the computer.

We were still receiving many messages on our phones. I knew my family was making arrangements of coming down. I was in communications with our Relief Society President on how many beds we would need to house everyone. There were also discussions about our family dinner that would be at our building in Acton after the funeral. It was explained to me that the ward would provide everything, but that we would have to get all the meat. We were very okay with that. We had planned on pulled pork on buns with salads and desserts. I knew our ward would help. Then we started guessing who might be there. Initially we planned for one hundred people, but by Wednesday afternoon, we thought it would better to think of 150 people. We just kept hearing about people who wanted to be there. Our position was anyone that needed to travel most definitely deserved a luncheon.

Through various phone calls, it was decided that Sister Bennett (my Relief Society President) would come and pick up the check for the meat and because there were soo many that wanted to help, I wouldn't have to do any of the cooking. That part I was grateful for. It was so overwhelming to hear of the numbers that wanted to help. Phone calls were received from members of our stake. It got to a point where she didn't know how to let them all help, one ward to set up, one to do salads, one to do desserts, one to help with take down. It really was amazing. I had heard of fifteen families outside of our ward that wanted to help so badly. That wasn't including my own ward that also wanted to help however they could. All of this was to assist those that would attend our family luncheon. I was told that they would set up all the round tables that our building had, with nine to ten persons per table. I think there were sixteen tables in all.[64]

We made sure that every person we heard from either with a text, phone call, or IM, also knew that they were invited to the family luncheon and that they would come so we could get some kind of a headcount.

We made sandwiches for lunch.

1:30p.m. It was decided that we would go shopping for dresses for everyone for the funeral. We had talked about getting a pedicure and then go shopping. So that was the plan. We got the pedicure first at my little shop that I went to in Palmdale next to one of the gyms in the city. It's a little place. They knew my name, and all were Vietnamese. They did a good job though. There was usually plenty of parking so no issues with that. Kailee wasn't sure if she wanted a pedicure, but she went ahead anyways and got one. There wasn't much traffic on an early Wednesday so we just walked in and none of us had to wait. I love the chairs that give you the massage. I hated

---

[64] We were told that there were so many people that wanted to help and from other ward too. To let them all help, they split up all the food lists and added servers and table decorations. It was amazing to hear of.

the filing on the toes though. It really makes me cringe. I loved the heat rocks and the massages on the legs most of all. We enjoyed our conversations and had a pleasant time. It was a nice little change from the events we were enduring.

The mall wasn't very far away from the nail place. The girls didn't want to walk the whole mall, but they had the stores they wanted to go to in mind.

We started walking in. Mariah was complaining a bit. She has never liked shopping. Alyssa was more on the picky side. She would go to twenty stores because she had to find just the right item and she had to look good in it. Kailee would follow. If we suggested to look at something, she would. If she had to try it on, it really would determine what someone said about what she was wearing.

We started at the end of the mall where Sears was. I have always liked Sears, probably because that's where my mom shopped. I didn't buy lots there, but they usually had good sales. The girls didn't really find anything they liked. Mind you, they didn't take too long to look either. It wasn't a store they liked. So on to the mall.

They had their favorite stores that we looked at. The question always was: "Well, what's appropriate for a funeral? What should we wear?" Within the church, black really isn't a choice of color for a funeral. Death is a passing and even though it's hard, the mourning time is different. We generally wear any color but black. Kailee was looking at dresses with flowers. Mariah just wanted pockets and Alyssa wasn't sure.

Four stores down and not a lot of success. I said I wanted to go to JCPenney. I always seemed to find something there. All the girls were actually picking out things for each other once we got there. After about fifteen minutes, we all had some dresses that we were going to try on.

"So everyone will be looking at me—I have to find something that really makes me look thin—at least I could wish it did and that I felt good in it." We all had to come out of the dressing rooms and show off what we had chosen.

I had success. It was a dress with a jacket. The top was white with black embroidered appliqués on it and the bottom was black. I thought it looked pretty good on me. The girls liked it, so I thought it would work.

"So girls, why aren't you going to get your dresses?" I asked them.

"I'm not sure if I like this," Alyssa said.

"I really don't need any more dresses," Kailee commented.

"But that one really looks good on you," Mariah said. "Mom, I kind of like this one."

"Look girls. This is a unique experience. We want to buy you something new for the funeral. Seriously, find something, anything you like and let's get it for you."

The girls continued to look. All of them went into the dressing rooms together after they helped look for something. One would suggest: "You would look good in this", "I like this color on you", or "I need help deciding". It was actually kind of fun to watch. I stayed out while they tried on their dresses. While I was there, I saw another one of the exact dress I had, but it was more the size I preferred. The one I had was good and I fit in it, but I didn't like things too tight across my chest. So, I took the other dress and tried it on. I felt much better. The girls all came out at the same time. It was like a mini runway. We all looked pretty good, and they said they felt good. Kailee's was black but very flowered with red and blue hues. It looked nice on her. Mariah had a maroon-colored dress that of course had pockets, and she looked good. Alyssa actually had a blue-striped dress that looked really good on her, but she decided at the last minute that she really didn't want the dress.

"Alyssa, then pick something else. It's okay. We aren't in a hurry."

"Yeah, but I don't want to. I'm okay. Let's just go home," she insisted.

"Okay, you're sure though?"

"Yup," and she walked over to get in line to pay for the dresses for everyone else.

We had our bag of new dresses and started to walk back down the mall. We had had a good time together. We were relaxed due to our pedicures, and we looked good. It made me think that I needed to get my hair done too. That would be a miracle if I could get in. I called my lady while we were walking through the mall. She was shocked that I was on the phone and devastated about our news. Her husband worked with Scott, so she knew all about what we were going through. I mentioned that I was just wondering if she would have any openings within the next few days.

"We are going to the beach at 10:00 a.m. on Friday but other than that, I'm pretty open.

She looked at her booking book.

"No matter what, I will get you in. How about tomorrow morning? Would 9:30 a.m. be okay?" Debbie (my hairdresser) asked.

"Really, that would be perfect. I would love to come in tomorrow. Thank you so much."

"Of course," she said. "How are you doing—we are just so sad. Rob (her husband) wants to do something for Scott. He is just beside himself." Of course again, you could hear the concern in Debbie's voice.

"Well, we are doing pretty good. I will see you tomorrow and thank you again."

3:52 p.m. We started to drive home. I was told that dinner would be delivered between 5:00 and 5:30 p.m. I didn't know who would bring the food or what was coming. It didn't matter—we were just grateful. I asked the girls if they needed a milkshake or ice cream or anything, and they all said they were good. We drove home.

The guys said they just messed around. Scott was on his phone constantly reading emails or messages. He was in his office. Brandon was watching TV and relaxing. Of course, when we all walked in, the house again was noisy. We showed our new treasures off. Then all the girls went to the computer to finish scanning photos so Kailee could put them into a power point slide show. That was most of our evening. There had been two more flower arrangement delivered while we were gone. We were just so in awe of all these thoughts and concerns.

4:30 p.m. The sound of the doorbell rang, so I went to answer the door. Kim Bennett (my Relief Society President) wanted to come over and go over a few things with me. When I opened the door, she just hugged me.

"I'm just so sorry. I don't know what to think," she stated.

"We are doing pretty good actually. Really, we are doing good. I bet you need my check, don't you?" The check was to pay for the meat for the family luncheon. We had discussed that it would just be easier to give her the money and she could get all the meat that we would need. Initially Kim had asked me to get the meat and I was willing to do that, but then she just said she would do it and then we wouldn't have to transfer the meat over to her. I had the check waiting on the corner of the table for her.

She commented on the flowers and how amazing it was to have Michelle Cooke have everyone write a card. They were hung from the ceiling fan, from the door archways, from the ceiling in the kitchen so they could all be seen. You couldn't have really missed them.

Then we sat at the table and went over not only the menu, but the housing issues that we might need. She stated that she had never seen so many people want to help. We added ushers and whatever she could to try and include everyone that wanted to help.

"I've had to turn people away. Seriously!" she stated. "I've just never seen anything like it. You are so blessed."

"Believe me, this is very humbling."

Kim and I had spent some time together over the past few months. You see, Dalen was told he had to come home early from his mission. We didn't know why and neither did Dalen. Kim could relate. Her son couldn't finish his mission. He had made a mistake and was sent home. We had talked about the feelings of failure, how to help our sons and what to expect. The judgmental looks from those at church knowing that a mission was for two years. There were only two reasons someone came home early from a mission: (1) sin and (2) couldn't handle it. Dalen received a phone call from his mission president and our Stake President. They both told us that they would treat Dalen as though he had served a full-term mission. That phone call was devastating to Scott and I and our family. We only had two days' notice that Dalen would be at the airport. We had called the girls home and wanted them there to welcome their brother home. We had heard that there was an issue that occurred about six months prior. Dalen had repented and both his local and

Stake leaders felt his repentance was complete. However, the issue was still being wrestled with in Salt Lake where the church headquarters resided. We had spoken to Dalen on the phone.

"Mom, I really don't know why I have to come home early. I have repented of whatever was wrong. There really isn't any reason I need to come home Mom, except Heavenly Father wants me to so I will obey. Six weeks Mom. I only have six more weeks," Dalen said.

I cried. My son was worthy. We couldn't explain all of this, but we would face it together. Kim could understand our feelings. Looking back, I've come to realize that my son came home to be with me. Heavenly Father knew, and my son came home to be with me even if it wasn't for very long. We didn't know that at the time, but came to that understanding after speaking with Dalen's mission President and our Stake President. We all didn't want him to be home and be idle. We made the decision to have him go to BYUIdaho for the block semester. He also, after a while, thought it would also be a good idea. There was no way we were going to have him just sit around. He needed to be around others that were his age, home from missions, and moving on with their lives. He needed to be busy. In making that decision though, it meant he would only be home for five days before we would need to drive him up to Idaho and get him settled in for the block to begin. He would get home on a Friday and school would start the following Thursday. There was a bit of arranging that had to be done to get him there, but we got it all worked out.

At that moment, Kim and I were talking about our son's worthiness. Dalen's Facebook mentioned that he was heading to the temple to get his answers. He had such a strong testimony. He knew who he was and where he was going. He knew he had been cleared of any wrongdoing and he had continued to live his life as he should have. He really was so very worthy of the spirit in his life. I was so grateful.

Kim and I shared our feelings as only mothers could of the worries few had for our children and the choices they made that could wrench your heart or fill it up. We hugged and cried for a moment.

Our conversation continued and then turned our thoughts to the food, décor for the tables, and all who wanted to help.

There had been four homes offered to help house my family coming in. Our former Bishop offered the loft over their garage which could house ten people if needed. That would be a great place for Cody's family, as I was surprised that all of his family was coming. Etchells offered two rooms for two couples and lots of couches. We weren't sure who would be where yet. Alyssa had some friends coming too, but they begged to just sleep on our couches because they wanted to be there to help with anything. There was another house offered, the Becks, where she again had two extra beds and three couches. Then the VanOrnums mentioned we could have their whole house. They were heading up to Idaho for a family funeral. That was more than amazing. They had seven bedrooms. I could put Gord's whole family up, and they could all be together. There were about fourteen of them. The offers were just so big for us. Kim and I arranged what I knew could be arranged. The rest would have to be tentatively arranged for now. She needed to get things going and sensed it was time that she left. She was such a blessing to me and was huge comfort that she came by.

5:23 p.m. The doorbell rang and it was Kelly Jensen and her husband Tony. She lived just up the street from us. She had her arms full of food, so I offered to help carry something into the kitchen for her and set them on the island. She didn't know what to say.

"Oh, this is so amazing. Thank you so much. It's looks so good."

"Oh of course. Wendy was a few minutes late because she had to finish cooking the dinner rolls." Kelly announced. Wendy was the culinary arts teacher at the High School. We also were each other's visiting teachers. Sometimes I would go check on her and sometimes she would check on me. Either way, her food was amazing. She made everything taste so incredibly good.

Kelly was setting things up that she had brought us.

The doorbell rang again. I went to the door and it was Wendy with of course, her arms full. All the girls came into the kitchen to greet them and called them for dinner. I pointed out the flowers and all the cards hanging. They enlightened us more about church and what happened.

"We were all just so mortified. It was amazing how the bishop led us all. The spirit was so strong. It was so strong," Kelly said.

"Some were crying and some were gasping when they announced that Dalen had passed. Everyone was in shock. For those of us that knew—it was another realization of what had happened," Wendy added.

"It was just awesome. Michelle had her baskets out everywhere and everyone wanted to write on them. It was so neat how it all came together. None of the ladies wanted to do anything but talk about Dalen during Relief Society. We all just talked about Dalen and your family and what you were going through," Kelly added.

"We just cried and hugged each other, and then we cried some more." Wendy herself was crying as she was telling us of the events.

"We have just been blown away by your strength and how you have handled this." Kelly paused for a minute as she tried to gain her composure. "How are you really holding it together so well?"

"Honestly, we don't know how else to hold up or what we think needs to be done. It all has just fallen into place. It's actually been amazing, and we have been so blessed. There had just been so many miracles."

"I know. I've seen all your posts and you have had a lot of blessings," Wendy added.

"Well, I've learned what mighty miracles are and how they are different from tender mercies. Mercies are when we ask Heavenly Father for something. And because he loves us, he answers us and blesses us. With the mighty miracles, we are just following His lead and we are seeing all these amazing things happen that we have to call miracles. I call them our mighty miracles-like getting us all up to Idaho. It was just so amazing how everything happened. There had to be divine intervention. It just wasn't a normal thing. It was hard to watch Dalen die, but it was amazing too."

"I just got chills," Wendy informed us of her raw emotions.

"See, I just don't know how you do this. You are amazing," and Kelly got emotional again. I've never really sensed Kelly as a touchy-feely kind of woman. She was very much a matter-of-fact kind of person. She was an administrator for one of the school districts near us and could handle almost anything that came her way. But I walked over to her and rubbed her back to console her a bit.

"I know it's very different to describe, but everything has been absolutely perfect Kelly. It has been just amazing," I responded.

"Wow—I'm just blown away by how you are able to respond," Kelly iterated.

"So, what actually happened?" Wendy inquired.

I told them of the accident and how things happened. I rehearsed with them the hospital visits and the profound process with the donor center. I told them of when Dalen was taken off life support and all the care he was given. I quickly spoke about our stay in Rexburg and then coming home. My heart rejoiced again as I rehearsed all that had transpired and how blessed we had been. The ladies mentioned Dalen's last Facebook post. They said how profound it was that he was that in tune. He was ready.

"It really hit me that we can't take every day for granted. That we need to live worthy and be obedient," Kelly added her thoughts to our conversation.

The ladies didn't want to interfere with our family time (which they weren't), I reassured them they weren't and that we loved their visit. But they had set up the food and didn't want it to get cold. They both hugged me tightly and cried as we embraced. They were so sweet. We all thanked them again as the family gathered around the table to have our dinner. You knew that if Wendy was involved in food, that it would be very delicious. She had made homemade buns and a salad with craisins, walnuts, spinach and her homemade dressing. Kelly made chicken quesadillas. It smelt incredible and looked good too. We called everyone up to the table after the ladies had left. We sat down and after the prayer—all dug in. It was good. Our conversations at dinner were about how good the food was and how we loved to eat Wendy's food. The girls mentioned her cinnamon rolls that we got each year as our Christmas gifts. The dough would be made Christmas Eve, and then she would deliver her goodies sometime during Christmas morning. For years, as her friends, we all tried to get her to deliver her goodies Christmas Eve so she could spend the morning with her family although they all would be at the door with the delivery. They were just so good though and she always wanted them delivered when they were still hot. No matter when you would receive them, they wouldn't last long.

Our evening was spent finalizing the arrivals of when people would be coming. We continued to receive messages and shared them with one another. The family members were relaxed and able to sleep when they chose to. In fact, that had been another blessing for all of us, even from day one, we could all sleep. I hadn't thought of that as a miracle. In fact, I didn't even think anything of it, but so many people that I had talked to after there had been a death in their family, didn't sleep or they didn't sleep very much. This could go on for months. Even in our sleep we were blessed so abundantly.[65]

The time came for us all to go to bed.

"Good night family." We all expressed our love for each other.

---

[65] We could sleep and be refreshed. We all were given enough peace that we could sleep and sleep we did.

The Arrivals Commenced

Thursday, February 15th I was up early of course. I don't think I've slept past 5:30 a.m. since we had moved to our house in Acton sixteen years ago. Even before that, I hadn't woken up to an alarm clock our whole married life. If Scott had to get up early, he would set his alarm and I would always wake up before his alarm went off to make sure he was awake. He worked nights for eighteen years, so he was always coming home in the middle of the night, or he was getting up for a shift change in the middle of the night.

As our kids got older, our church had an early morning scripture study class which started at 6:30 a.m. Of course I was up to get the kids up and make sure they had breakfast and lunches made for them. We would do our own family scripture study and prayers before I would need to drive them to seminary. For some reason all our kids didn't want to get their driver's license at age sixteen, which annoyed Scott and I. That meant I got to drive them to seminary and did so for twelve years. Once I was up, I was up, so there never was even a thought to go back to bed. And if they weren't old enough yet to go to seminary, once I returned from dropping the kids off, I would need to make sure the others were ready for the other schools. Seminary was only for ninth to twelfth grades.

Any early activity was very normal for me. I got up and started to compile the messages we had received and put them together. I didn't want to forget who had supported us and sent their blessing, so I began to type out first, my text messages. There were so many, but I copied every single one.

I had to take care of the bills too. That usually took me about an hour or so. It always surprised me that we made good money, but would never have extra. We paid our mortgage on the first and almost all our other bills on the fifteenth. I spent my morning doing that. There were a few more expenses too this month, as we had two vehicles that we paid gas for driving up to Idaho and back, and then helping the kids with their expenses too. And yet, we always had enough. We were blessed so many times that we wouldn't have extra, but we would always have enough. I also strongly believed that those blessings also came because we always paid our tithing. In our church, we are asked to give 10% of our gross worth to the church. It's called tithing. We think of it as spiritual insurance. The Lord truly has given us everything and only asks for 10%. We all have very strong testimonies of paying tithing and acknowledge the blessings that have come from it. These sacred funds pay for our buildings, which exist throughout the world. They pay for needs of people in our area. They pay for our church schools, all the materials and supplies needed for schools to function. It pays for our lesson manuals. Tithing pays for the running of a building such as the electrical and maintenance or water bills. Because the members pay an honest tithe, blessings are promised and given. There have been some tight situations throughout our lives, but because we obeyed God first and paid our tithing, we had the right to call down blessings from heaven.[66]

Once I recalled that I literally had to count pennies from our coin jar to pay for milk for our family. There was enough though. We prayed that our money would last till the next pay period. The very next day, there was a knock at our door. When I opened it, no one was there, but there were four grocery bags full of food. It overwhelmed us and we instantly knew our prayers were answered because we paid our tithing. which meant we were entitled to ask for blessings, and then they came abundantly. I would never not pay my tithing. It was just way to important to me to be obedient and follow Heavenly Father's plan and we definitely had testimonies of its importance.

The family started waking up. They didn't have to get up as we didn't really have any plans that had to be done during the day. I didn't want them just sleeping all day though. People would start to

---

[66] Blessings of financial help were always available to us because of our obedience to paying our tithing.

arrive, and the arrangements had to be completed. The house didn't really need cleaning because we arrived home Tuesday night, and when we looked around, we realized that the house had already been cleaned. The bathrooms were shiny, and the floors had been swept and the vacuum had been used in the family room. Again, "*Who does this?*" It was just such a nice gesture. The kitchen needed a touch up, but other than that, the house was pretty clean. Mind you, we never left the house that it wasn't cleaned, but everything was fresh.

Breakfast was simple today, cereal and toast. Everyone could pretty much fend for themselves.

Again, I finished the bills. I remained at the computer and started the process of either copying or typing out some more of the messages we had received.

9:15 a.m. Sheila called. "I just called the boarder and they aren't letting anyone cross because of the severe snowstorm, or unless it's an emergency.

"I'm so sorry. Just breathe. We will all just do what we can. You aren't less important to me if you can't make it down for the funeral, and it won't be for lack of trying."

"Yes, but that doesn't help me get there either. We aren't giving up. We will try again and again. Second attempt in about two hours," Sheila added. To get to the boarder was about an hour away. They wouldn't say if the boarder was open through the phone system, so unless you were there in person, you wouldn't know if the boarder was allowing anyone through, but if you did make it through then you would be driving in a storm. I was worried for her.

10:30 a.m. Paul and Heather were getting close to the house. It was arranged that they would also be bringing Mariah's boyfriend Rick down with them. That was kind of a funny thought-here my nephew would pick this kid up that he never met and have an eighteen-hour ride with him. Paul would drill this kid for sure. But Rick was a good sport and was up for the challenge. He would then go back with Mariah as she thought she would be okay to return to school within the week. We told her to take more time, but we were going to try this. We didn't want another vehicle at the house if we could get help from someone else. Even if Mariah didn't go back to Idaho, Paul would have to drive back up to get to Canada, so it wasn't a big deal, but Mariah wanted him here so the arrangements were made. Our friends offered to have Rick stay with them for the few days, so it was all working out. He and Kailee's boyfriend would be at the same place when Chris would come down tomorrow. Until then, Mariah would drive Rick back and forth between homes.

Paul wanted to be at our house as soon as he could get there, so he drove all night long. Paul was Susan's only son and the middle of her children. Susan was my older sister. Paul brought his family down. They had rented a van and were the first to arrive from Canada. Paul was special to our family. When he was fourteen, he was a bit of a rebel and Susan struggled with him. She didn't know what to do with him, so we offered for him to come live with us for the summer. Scott was of course, working nights, so most of the time, Paul was with me and the kids and trying to find some things to do for fun. With that experience, Paul had always been special to our family and loved everything about Scott's race car and career. He was even able to go on a ride along with Scott one night at work, which was a highlight for Paul. He thought it was very cool which made Scott even more cool. Most of our nieces and nephews thought Scott had a pretty exciting job.

Over the years, Paul was one of those family members that actually kept in contact with us. He would call or communicate with Scott on a pretty regular basis. We were excited to see Paul. He has the cutest wife. She was very quick at being sarcastic with Scott which he loved. They had two cute kids too.

We would go home to Canada every year. I knew all my nieces and nephews; I just didn't get to spend too much time with them though. Again, Gord's family were the closest physically. I made many attempts to be with them at least once every two months. But Paul was just a bit closer to us emotionally.

The Crapos (Paul's family) arrived at the door and of course we were just hugging once the door was opened. He cried as he hugged me and again expressed his condolences. I said we were doing good and that we all were okay. We had previously decided that Paul's family could stay out in our camping trailer. It slept eight. For now, it would house their family and then if we needed it, we would add a few more people to it. Scott would pull it up from the back field where we parked it to be beside the house. That way we could also plug in the motor home to the house so inside they could have power and air/heat if needed. It also meant the septic could be hooked up. Scott was actually taking care of that when Paul's family arrived.

The kids were shy and didn't say much, but with our kids trying to play with them, they warmed up quickly. Mariah had a new best friend in Naomi and they didn't go too far without the other.

Kailee was pretty much on the computer making sure the Power Point, with all Dalen's pictures, were ready. That also meant we had to make sure the church would have two TV sets—one on each side of the building by the main entrances to be seen before people went into the chapel area for the funeral.

Our morning seemed to pass quickly. Paul and his family had settled in and everyone was just hanging around in the family room.

There were a few more flower deliveries made and they again, were so beautiful.

We thought the messages and texts might have slowed down and maybe just a bit, but they still came on strong.

Scott was glad he was home and could do what he wanted. He was gone for most of the morning doing car stuff. I think it entailed picking up parts and getting sponsor checks for the month. It was what he did, but I also think it was an out for just a few minutes of what we had been experiencing.

Lunch time came and we decided that sandwiches would work out fine. The girls helped to make them. Our table seated six but it was a taller table that was easy to stand around and so we did. There was laughing and jokes and stories told. Again, we enjoyed our time together.

1:15 p.m. There was a knock at the door. When I opened it, there was a very young girl standing in front of me. She had brown shoulder length hair. She was wearing jeans and heeled shoes, with a jean jacket and nice dress shirt on.

"Hi, I'm Chloe," she announced.

"Chloe, as in the girlfriend of two weeks Chloe?" There was a question in my voice.

"Yes, it's me," she replied.

"Well, come on in," and I then greeted her with a hug. "We are just eating lunch, so come in and join us. Would you like something to eat? We won't force you, but there won't be any problem to make another sandwich."

She consented. I walked her into the family room and to the kitchen where everyone was introduced. Everyone came up to meet her.

"I know this is awkward and I'm so very sorry for that, but I just had to be here," Chloe stated.

"You're fine, come on in," Alyssa invited her in with a hug for her greeting.

"Thank you," and Chloe joined our circle.

"What kind of sandwich would you like? Nothing fancy but what would you like?' I asked.

Chloe expressed her desires and I proceeded to make her sandwich.' The family immediately started to ask her questions about how she and Dalen had a relationship.

We all wanted to know the story especially since we only knew of her because of a newspaper quote.

Chloe proceeded to explain her story. She had met Dalen while he was serving his mission in Dallas. Chloe's family owned a restaurant and would often invite the missionaries to eat there. It was always free to them.

"Of course Dalen would eat there if it was free to him. He's so cheap," Mariah stated to which we all agreed and laughed.

Chloe explained that every year her family would have a booth at the fair and her dad always asked the missionaries to help them set up. Gong out in public, missionaries were always to dress in their white shirts and ties, but this time, Dalen was wearing shorts and a T-shirt. If he was going to be working really hard, then he was going to be comfortable. They also got permission from their mission president too, so it was okay. Chloe's dad was impressed with that. In fact, he said that Dalen worked the hardest of the young men. He was very grateful for all the hard work Dalen had done, and so they were always invited to come eat at the restaurant. They would be welcomed any time.

Dalen would never refuse food, so he went to the restaurant every once in a while. Chloe met him there and even though he was there as a missionary, they both honored the rules. Elders were to remain clear of all relations during their mission. As a missionary, they were to stay with their companions always and be reserved as to communications with others. Their sole purpose was to bring souls unto Christ. She did mention that she did like Elder Graham though and had hoped he would look her up after his mission.

"There was innocent flirting I guess. Dalen promised me always that he was just being friendly and that he was following the mission rules," Chloe stated.

I was always asking Dalen about exact obedience because he was my son, and he usually found a way around a rule at home to fit him. He was really good at it too. So, I was checking on his understanding of the rules and he did honor all of them.

Once Dalen was grounded from his Nintendo for something he had done. Sure enough, I would hear things upstairs, and the next day when I approached Dalen, I would inquire about him playing his game. "What are you doing Dalen, you're grounded for the week. What the heck is going on?"

"You said I couldn't play my Nintendo and I'm not Mom. This is my friend's. He said I could use it." Dalen replied.

"Dalen, you knew what we meant. You were to be confined from Nintendo no matter whose it was."

That's the way Dalen would get around things. He would always find a way to make things work out for him. Funny guy.

Scott joined us as we knew the curiosity of Chloe was something he needed and wanted to resolve.

Chloe was charming. It really only took a few minutes before we all liked her. She had a sweet voice and we all seemed to enjoy her conversations. Chloe talked a bit about her family. She was the second oldest and first daughter of eight kids. She mentioned about the restaurant and how their whole family worked there except for the little ones that would generally be home with their grandma. Chloe talked about her family with tenderness, but it also was evident that they didn't really have normal lives as their parents were never home and they were pretty much raised in the restaurant. I'm sure that wasn't the first family that lived in the family's business. We could sense that Chloe loved her family very much; she just knew her up-bringing was a bit different that's all.

Everyone just kept asking questions. We all wanted to know about her, and it was okay. The awkwardness that I was previously nervous about, wasn't there.

We learned about the last two weeks of Dalen's life. He had contacted Chloe knowing that things weren't going to work out with Delanie. Then once they broke up—Dalen immediately began to pursue Chloe. They talked and messaged and video chatted daily. Chloe wanted to serve a mission and she was scared. She informed us how Dalen would help her learn how to teach and that he would then ask her to role play with him. She said he was amazing and that he really helped to give her clarity and confidence. Chloe felt so honored and humbled. We knew that his last Facebook post was that of mentioning going to the temple with a question and that he got his answer. His question was if he should marry Chloe or let her go on the mission first. What freaked me out though, was that he came to that conclusion only after two weeks of dating. This kid was crazy for sure. But his answer was to let her serve a mission first and all would work out after.

Chloe would cry for a minute when she talked of Dalen.

It even came up that there was mention of love between them. I found that hard to believe, but then again, it was my son, and he gave his heart away quickly. He was very loyal, but he did move fast, with his emotions. Chloe was different though. Normally Dalen liked pretty girls but usually they didn't have much self-esteem. Dalen would let them see their worth. But Chloe had a confidence with her. It was weird, but as we all sat and talked together, we also fell in love with Chloe. We were grateful that she came and that we were getting to know her.

We hung around the house for most of the afternoon. Mariah wanted to go see some of her friends, so she took Chloe with her. It was like they were instant friends. It was also decided that she would drop Chloe off at the train station on her way back. That seemed to be a good plan. Her train was to leave at 5:06 p.m. We said our goodbyes and that we enjoyed getting to know her. Chloe was an exceptional young lady. Our son had made a very good choice in Chloe. We liked her a lot and instantly.

Alyssa and Brandon were just 'veggin' and Kailee again was going through the power point to make sure it would be perfect. Scott went to the garage and I again worked on gathering all our messages and typing them out.

5:12 p.m. "Mom, what do we do? Chloe missed the train. We were here and trying to get a ticket and then the train just went by us. It didn't stop. What do we do?" Mariah asked.

I had actually been in that situation as well. At our depot, you have to know to stand on the other side of the tracks if you are heading a certain direction. I had to learn that the hard way too. There wasn't another train for today. We were kind of in a pickle.

"Well, I guess you have to bring her back home and we will figure things out." It really wasn't what I wanted, but it wasn't a big problem either. Scott and I had conversed that he could drive her down to her uncle's, but then I really wanted him to be with the family. I didn't want him to leave. We could ask her uncle to come get her. We also had the option of asking one of Scott's team members to come and pick her up or get an Uber driver. We had options and would figure them out when she got back home.

"Okay, we will be home in a minute," Mariah stated.

"Okay, see you then. Drive carefully." I was still hesitant to have Mariah drive. '*What if……*' became very strong with me. If she was driving and had a flashback, or couldn't process things in a certain way, or if she just would freeze; the thoughts were still so very real to me as a mother. I was very worried for her to be behind the wheel. She promised that she was good and would be fine. Again, I had to trust her.

Mariah and Chloe arrived back at the house. They were all giggly and happy when they walked back in as they had missed the train. They were a bit perplexed as to what to do next and we would have to figure something out quickly. However, it was supper time so we would discuss the situation after.

5:30 p.m. There was a knock at the door again and this time it was Sister Carrillo. She was pretty upset when she greeted me. Her son and Dalen were pretty good friends growing up and Dalen had many meals at their house. He loved her Hispanic cooking. She had brought us dinner. I knew this lady well and she would spend all day in the kitchen to prepare a meal. She also knew that Scott's favorite dish was carni-assada and that I loved her home-made chips and salsa. So that was what she had made for us, with rice and a salad too. I was so grateful to her. Her chips were so good. She also made me my own salsa as I couldn't eat the one she normally made; it was too spicy. She and her family had come to our house on several national holidays, and we enjoyed our barbecues together. I thanked her again and she set things up and wanted to leave. I told her she could stay and visit for a minute, but I knew more that she didn't know what to say or do, so it was easier for her to set up and leave.

I began to set things up with plates and cups so that when Alyssa and Brandon returned (from running an errand) we could eat. They were sent a message to come home.

The family was amazed at the spread of food and how very good it was.

We spoke with Chloe in private and asked her wishes and what were the options available to us. We decided that it wouldn't be too bad if she wanted to stay the night and have to go with us to the beach tomorrow. She hadn't been to the beach but maybe twice in her life, when she was a very little girl and they would visit her grandfather. So, we thought that we wanted to give that to her. We also came to the conclusion that we could have one of Scott's team members drive to her uncle's house and get her things. That way she wouldn't feel quite out of place. And again, the officers were more than willing to help us out with this request. We were growing fonder of Chloe too. She was good to have around and Mariah seemed to lean on her.

8:00 p.m.   The evening was pretty quiet. There was another knock at the door. This time it was my cousin Kelli (Cody's sister). She had just been dropped off from her Uber driver. She had a later flight then she wanted, but it didn't matter to her as long as she got to our house. We had been in communication since the accident, and I knew she was coming. She could have the room upstairs and the girls would move to the couches. Kelli said she would rather have the couch, so it still worked out just fine.

I probably heard ten or fifteen times from Kelli that: "I'm here just for you—so whatever you need just let me know." Kelli's twin had passed away a year ago and it was very devastating to her. She had epilepsy and had an attack and died. So Kelli and I could relate now on many levels. I appreciated her being willing to be there for me. We sat around and again rehearsed some of our experiences.

Everyone sat in the family room. We watched TV and relaxed. I sat at the computer and typed some more messages out. There were just so many, and I didn't want to miss any. One more day down and one more day closer to the funeral.

Beach Day

Friday, February 16th The plan all along was to take the family to the beach. The girls and Dalen really loved going to the beach and smelling the ocean. They loved to all play in the water. We would go camping to this one place where there was a campground on the left of a highway. We would walk under the highway bridge and be at the beach. It was a natural thing that I would suggest we go and just have a good time. Paul and his family had never been to the ocean and Kelli hadn't been there for many years so we all actually were excited to go.

I figured we would get up and eat breakfast. I would prepare the food to take and that we would try to leave about 10:00 a.m. That meant we would be at the beach by 11:30 a.m.(ish) and we could have the whole afternoon together.

I made sure everyone was up by 9:00 a.m., so we could get things ready.

My favorite beach was in Ventura, California. It was called Silverstrand, off the Channel Island Harbor and a great cove where the waves weren't very big. Not really a surfing spot, but great for boogie boarding. You could go way out and it was only waste high. It was just a shallow area and great for just playing in the water and not worry about undertows or high currents. I loved it.

We had to take two vehicles to fit everyone, so we loaded up. Made sure we took our beach equipment and of course the cooler with our food. I also had lunchmeat, cheese, lettuce (all in separate baggies), chips and then all the munchies such as cucumbers sliced, carrots, grapes, snack packs and whatever else the kids grabbed.

The drive to the beach was one of my favorite ones in California. Once we got passed the main city, it was all farming. The crops were beautiful. Palm tree farms, strawberries (best ever), all veggies, oranges and lemons, and some lime trees too. It was always a beautiful drive. There was always a crop in the fields throughout the year.

The sun was shining. There was a bit of a wind but not much. Paul said that is was a long ways away, but for us, not too far. As soon as we got there, Paul was so very excited. We found 'our spot' and set up our chairs and blankets. The cooler always went to the shady side of the chairs, and then we headed to the beach. Paul's family was all a bit hesitant to put their feet in the water, but the rest of us just walked in. It was amazing. There was a bit of a bite to the coldness of the water. It took a minute to stand there and not feel like it was freezing. Kelli was so excited too. She loved the smell of the beach. We all tried to walk in, but you could tell the novice beach goers from the first timers. We all laughed. Chloe was speechless and just kept saying how beautiful it was. It was a very good decision for sure. We were all in wonder of the scene. It really was beautiful.

We always made everyone eat lunch first before they really went into the water. That way, they weren't wet when they tried to eat. So, I went back and began making the sandwiches for everyone. Heather and Kelli helped me. It didn't take long, but each person got the sandwich of their choice.

Then the clothes came off and the bathing suits were exposed and we all ran into the water. Kailee once she was in the water would be almost the last one out. It was a bit too cold for Paul's kids, so they went to the rocks and looked at the tide pools. Rick, Mariah, Kailee, Chloe and Brandon all went in. The boogie boards were well used. Alyssa stayed with Paul's family and Kelli and I walked down the beach. I forgot to mention that Mariah brought our dog Titan, so he was with me. It was a gorgeous day. It was about 74 degrees at the beach. The water was probably about 63 degrees. That's pretty normal for the Pacific coast in February. There weren't very many people there either, probably too chilly for the natives.

We all had our own time and then we would come together. We were never very far from each other.

(Kailee and Brandon were in the water.)

The sky was clear blue. You could see a few boats out on the ocean. We saw a dolphin which was always such a favorite thing especially for Kailee and me. Everyone else were screaming with excitement. It was too far out to get a picture. We also saw a seal and Naomi was over ecstatic. She was pretty cute. It really was a perfect day. There were seagulls, pelicans and sandpipers. Naomi and Landon were given the seashells that someone would find as later in the afternoon we all walked the cove. It was literally a perfect day.

3:00 p.m. We started to pack up our things. It was time to go home. We always had a rule that they had to get out of the water and dry off before we loaded up into the car. It helped to keep the sand out. We also didn't wash our feet off like many did because when the sand was dry, it brushed off way faster than wet sand.

The drive home again was about one and a half hours away. It really was beautiful and clear. Coming home, my kids always brought the cooler into the front of the car so they could eat all the way home.

We have three bathrooms and I knew they would all be going at the same time when we got home. I let them all shower first and I would take my turn after. I received a call that my cousin Cody was almost to our house. He would be there in about half an hour. That gave me time to shower. It's funny how no matter how careful you are at the beach, sand finds a way in. I was grateful for the penetrating water to wash it all away even though I love the ocean so much.

4:30 p.m. There was another knock at the door. This time it was my cousin Cody and his family. He had his five kids with their six grandkids, and they were all in the family room. They noticed all the hanging notes as they walked in.

"Wow, that's a lot of cards," Cody announced.

"Yes, they were from our ward and were all over the island when we got home. It was pretty amazing," I replied.

"So how are you really doing?" JoEllen asked (Cody's wife).

I would explain again that we were good. We have just had so many miracles that we couldn't deny them. I explained some of the miracles and mercies and the peace that we had received. They too, seemed surprised by our actions, but we really didn't know how to be any different.

Cody's family was going to be staying with our former Bishop. He had a big loft over the garage which could sleep eight adults. We figured those kids would sleep on the floor. Again, it was amazing that such a place was opened up to us and that it could house all of Cody's family. They didn't want to stay long. Again, they didn't want to interfere with our family time, but we reassured them they weren't in the way. They still chose to leave so Alyssa and Brandon would have them follow her in her car and they in theirs, over to the Higley's (house offered). I asked if they wanted to stay for dinner, but they said they would take care of themselves.

I had learned that every house that was hosting persons, also said they would make sure they had breakfast for the time they would be staying with them. Most people were going to be leaving Saturday after the funeral except for the family that would be going to the burial as well. Again, I was just so grateful for all the kindness of soo many people.[67]

---

[67] We weren't just offered housing for our family coming down, but we were offered enough housing. Each home had several spots for family to stay with. Such a huge blessing.

There was another call that came to the house that was mentioning our dinner was on the way. Michelle Cooke was bringing it over. Bless this woman's heart. She had already done so much for us. She arranged all the cards. She was constantly in contact with me. She was already such a devoted friend whom I loved dearly. Now a beautiful home cooked meal for fourteen people. That was a lot of food and of course she made it all herself. She didn't want any other help. There was a beautiful salad and enchiladas and brownies for dessert. Again, I was just so blown away with the size of this woman's heart. I loved her so very much. Dinner was so good. Somehow, it just always seemed better when you didn't have to fix it. We were so grateful for sure.

5:45 p.m. More people were coming. Dad and Susan were almost there. Sheila and her family had some major trials for sure, but they weren't giving up and would be there before 9:30 p.m. Sylvia and her husband were going to arrive at about 8:30 p.m. and Kailee's boyfriend was pulling into the housing track. He was coming down from Salt Lake City near where Sylvia lived. The house was getting full, but also full of love. Gord and his family arrived first. I had called the one family that were allowing us to use their whole house to ask for the key. She said that her husband said after talking to the Bishop, that we wouldn't need their house. They didn't leave the key. I was floored. I was very upset. Why would they do that? Now what do we do? A little panic came over me because there were thirteen people now that had no place to stay. My mind raced with possible options, but there really weren't many. I was concerned about the cost too, because now we would have to get hotel rooms for them. I was more upset that our Bishop relayed the message that we were all good and that we didn't need this house.

"Scott, we are going to have to get them hotel rooms. What else can we do?" I asked.

"I know, we don't really have much of a choice," he replied.

"They just said they are at Victorville, which meant they would be at our home within the hour. What do you think of the Cotton Tree or something like that? That hotel is pretty close."

"Why don't you call them and see if you can get them reservations."

"Okay, so let's figure out how many rooms. Gord and Maria could be with Kyle and Bryce (their sons). Dallin (son) will be by himself so maybe he could go with Blake (son) and Melissa (Blake's wife), and their two little kids could sleep on the floor. Then Stacey (daughter) and Brent (her Husband) could have the third room with their two kids. What do you think, we need three rooms?"

"Yeah probably," Scott commented.

"Wow that's going to be expensive. But for how long, just two nights right, because we're driving up to St George Sunday?"

"That should work, so call and check it out," Scott was as confused as I was about what had happened to the house we thought we would have use of. But it was what it was and this now had to be done. It took a little bit of time to handle all the details. In fact, I barely ate before I was looking online at hotels and getting a good price. When I found one that included breakfast, because if they were staying at someone house, I knew that breakfast would be included. We needed three rooms with two queen beds in each. I explained the emergency and asked if they could help in any way. I had AAA, Scott was a government official—whatever I could think of to lighten this load. Even with a discount, it was over $1200 for the three rooms and two nights. That was a lot for me. Scott didn't want certain hotels because of their locations in town and they were pretty scummy. We had to also realize that we hadn't had to pay for hardly anything through this whole ordeal except our travel and food expenses, so we would make this work. We also only had an hour to book everything. Looking back, it was a trial but also solvable. So here was the outcome. Dad / Sue and Glade (her husband) /and Kelli —my house. Gord's family— at the hotel. Cody's family at the Higleys. Paul's family in the trailer. Courtney and Taylor/ Sylvia and Chris (her husband) were now going to be at the Etchells. Initially the missionaries that were coming down, were going to stay there, but they were going to be so late that we made some changes. They would now be upstairs in the loft. Kailee's boyfriend and Rick were also at the Etchells. They said they had three rooms and three couches, so we were needing to use them. Sheila's family and Colette Williamson (from Dallas) were going to the Beck's home. Wow, that was a lot of detailing and figuring out.

6:25 p.m and on. It seemed the front door kept revolving as people were coming. It was very busy. The tone was jovial as all were greeted. Everyone was always very sensitive with Mariah. People were starting to fill up every room. Dad and Susan and Glade (Susan's husband) would be upstairs. I put a cot in the room and Dad said he was good with that. Kelli was on the couch upstairs, but I would soon need that space, so she chose to sleep on the floor in Susan and Dad's room. The missionaries weren't able to leave when they had planned, so it made sense that they could come to our house because I wouldn't want' anyone else to have to stay up and wait for them. I was so excited that they were willing to come. I knew of five that would be coming to our house. My thoughts were also that I didn't want the boyfriends here as there were enough emotions. I didn't want to have any other issues. I just thought it was the safest thing to do. Gord and his family all arrived at the same time. Scott and I decided to take them over to their hotel and let them get settled in. Alyssa took Courtney and Taylor over to the Etchells just to show them where they needed to be and then they could come back to our house if they wanted to. At the house, I had spent some time in gathering up items that we would want to have on display at the church. I knew I wanted displays on both sides of the chapel. We had over the past few days, pulled out things we wanted shown, and had chosen pictures that we also had enlarged and framed. We had some of his sport equipment. I wanted the guilt I had must made him after his mission. Each square of the quilt was a white shirt and a name tag of one of his companions on it with a tie from that particular companion. So, I was making sure we had all this stuff. We were supposed to be at the church by 8:00 p.m. to set up. We took two volleyballs that we had received at the house through the week. One was of all the kids Dalen played with every night while up at Rexburg. There were seventy-five names on the ball plus a shirt also with signatures. Another ball was from the BYU team where a few of Dalen's friends played on the team and also had the whole team's signature on it. We also received letters from the coaches expressing their condolences because Dalen had made himself known to the team. It was so amazing. We received pictures of Christ and poems and letters that I also wanted on display. We had some of Dalen's trophies and his mission scrapbook I had made. I also had his high school scrapbooks. We also had the life-sized figure of Dalen that we had made while he was on his mission, to use at Alyssa's wedding to show a representation of him. I went to look for my tablecloths and realized it would be easier to take this huge roll of orange material I had from Alyssa's wedding which I had about 50 yards of. That way we could take as much as we needed and just cut it off. I had asked the man setting up the church if we could have two long tables at each entrance. If we needed more we could get all that we needed.

7:30 p.m. It was time to leave to set up the church. The girls and Brandon, Maria and Kelli all wanted to come help. Courtney and Taylor came with Alyssa and Brandon too. Driving to the church took about thirty-five to forty minutes and then we arrived. Of course, it was dark outside. I backed into a parking stall closest to the door and the prayer was that the church door would be opened, and it was. Everyone started grabbing boxes and whatever else was in the car to bring the items into the church. I had taken two loads into the church and when I walked out the second time, there were these two pretty big guys with big bushy beards coming toward me. As they got closer, I could see their faces, but still wasn't sure I knew who they were. "Elder, what are you doing here?" I asked. The one Elder had served in our ward during the time between Ecuador and Dallas missions for Dalen. He was a good Elder and went out with Dalen a lot. He spent quite a bit of time at our house. He was from Missouri, and he was here. I for the life of me though, couldn't remember his name. He was just Elder. He came up to me and gave me a huge hug. "Oh my gosh. How are you Elder? What are you doing here?" He heard about Dalen and just had to be here.

"We called the house and they said you were here, so we came to help. This is my cousin. He also served his mission in Bakersfield," the Elder commented.

Okay, so there was a memory now coming back into my mind of this Elder and the story of not only serving in the same mission with his best friend and cousin, but that they even got to be companions for a time. They took the items out of my hands and carried them into the church with me.

"Elder Allan?" Mariah shouted with a questioned voice. "What the heck!"

That's his name. It's all good now. He then introduced himself and his cousin to the rest of the family standing in the lobby.

It took a minute to compose and then it was time to arrange the tables.

"So how about if we divide the pictures up. We can lay the material over first and then see where we want to place things."

Maria was right on it. She and Stacy started rolling the material out and covered the tables. While she went to the other side, the rest of us started laying things out. I asked the boys to find four of the classroom tables that I wanted by each door with the sign in books on them. I would also need the little tables covered with material too.

I started organizing what items I wanted in the main entrance. We had a few picture stands, but I would need more. Then I saw the gentleman that had made the arrangements for all the chairs to be set up and opened the door for us. He had a key to the library, so I followed him to get stands for some of the pictures. When I walked back, Maria had already laid out the pictures and was putting books under the material to alter the height of some of the pictures. Everyone found something to do, or they were visiting in the lobby, but we were productive and quickly completed the task at hand. We were done in about fifteen, twenty minutes. I looked over both displays. The table on the other side of the chapel was a little bearer, so I got a few more things from the main side and put them on the other side. It looked good and no one would see both sides at the same time anyway so they wouldn't know the difference.

I had Dalen's Eagle Scout uniform, his scriptures, missionary tags, awards and scrapbooks, and I thought it looked pretty good. I was happy with it all. Everyone was very gentle in asking where I wanted things. Each door had a sign-in book and a picture on them with space for the programs.

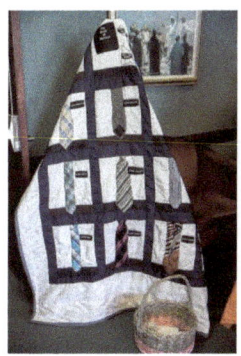

Back at the house it was full of family that just sat around and visited. We had dropped Maria and Stacy off at their hotel on our way home. I wanted to start herding people off to their host houses so it wouldn't be too inconvient for the hosts to keep waiting for them. Courtney and Taylor then led the boyfriends to where they were going.

9:30 p.m. Sheila finally arrived. Just to hug my twin meant everything. You could tell by looking at her that she had a rough trip. She had the worst time in coming down. With three attempts to cross the boarder; daughter drove while Sheila took a nap and the daughter drove in the wrong direction, and that took them four hours out of the way; storms and road issues, and yet she persevered and made it. We hugged each other for a while. Of course they were invited in and said their hellos to everyone. They were tired though, so Mariah had them follow her to where they were going and then came back home.

There were fifty-four people in my house during the evening. It was such a good feeling to have all this love and support. So now we just had to wait for the missionaries to arrive, Elder Bunker and Elder Shelton. They at least were on the road. It was about a twelve hour drive from the Salt Lake area, and they were about to Vegas which meant about five more hours to go. They kept texting me and expressed how bad they felt for with how late they would be arriving. It didn't matter to me, I just wanted them there and safe.

It was about **11:30 p. m.** before I made it to bed. Everyone was in their place and things were settling down.

2:10 a.m. (the following morning) I heard the door open and got out of bed to meet and see the missionaries that Dalen not only loved, but had altered his life along the way. There were two sister missionaries and Elder Fifi (the big Elder we met in Rexburg that was afraid of Dalen), that came with the other Elders. We all hugged.

"I'm so glad you are here and safe," as I hugged them all again.

"We can't believe that you stayed up to meet us. You are so amazing. I'm just so glad we can be here for you. Is there anything we can do for you?" Elder Bunker asked.

Of course I told them I was fine. I asked if they needed anything and they all just said they were good. I started to walk upstairs and showed them the loft where I had put blankets on the couches and the other cot. I had a blow-up mattress where I had bedding arranged on the floor. They all found their places and said thank you again. I showed them where the bathroom was and that all the towels on the edge of the couch were clean and for them. I again thanked them for coming.

"We need to be at the church by 9:00 a.m. which meant you would have to leave around 8:30 a.m. at the latest."

"What time are you leaving?" Elder Bunker asked.

"I will be leaving by 8:00–8:15 a.m. I need to be there to make sure things are set."

"Then we will plan on leaving with you." Elder Shelton said. They all agreed. I told them they didn't have to and that they could rest a bit longer if they wanted to, but they wanted to be with us at the church. They all thanked me again for letting them stay there. I said goodnight and went back to my bed for maybe a few more hours of sleep. Tomorrow would be a big day.[68]

---

[68] Everyone arrived and arrived safely. I was glad and felt very humbled. It was just so amazing to have all this support.

The Arrival of the Funeral Day

I was up by **5:30 a.m**. which was very normal for me. There were so many thoughts running through my head. We were expecting a lot of people and weren't really sure who would be at the funeral. We had been so supported. Today was a way to thank everyone and for them to have their closure. This would be a day where many eyes would be on me. My hair was just cut, but I wanted it straightened. I wanted to look good and feel that I looked good. Kelli was up about 6:00 a.m., and wanted to make sure she was available for me. The tables were set in the church, the powerpoint was done, the clipboard was ready, the dress was laying on the bed to put on, the house was ready and cleaned. Kelli wanted to do my hair, so I went and got dressed first. I woke everyone up by **7:00 a.m**. I didn't want anything to be rushed this morning, and I wanted everyone to have enough time for themselves to get ready. Some of the family were going to be there by 9:00 a.m., but I needed my immediate family with me and no questions were offered.

7:30 a.m. There was a knock at the door. The gentleman with the hearse had arrived. Brandon was up and dressed and Elder Fifi (our big Elder) and myself went outside to help. We had to pull out the box from the back of Brandon's suburban. We opened the box and took all the packing off.

"Well this is a unique experience."

"Who would have thought we would unpack a coffin for a funeral?" Brandon said.

"I've never seen anything like this," replied the man from the mortuary.

"Me neither," said Elder FiFi.

Good thing was that it was the coffin we had ordered. It was a beautiful pearl smokey blue. The man had brought the rolling cart up the driveway. The coffin was then loaded onto the cart.

Elder Fifi was so anxious to help and do whatever he could. He was so cool.

Then from our driveway, the visable picture of the hearse at our house now had a coffin inside of it. There was a moment to reflect on what that represented today. Again a flood of gratitude surrounded me. The gentleman said he had some time to spare, so he was going to get some breakfast. I offered to give him something, but he said he would rather do his thing.

"That would be a funny picture of you in a drive-through," Brandon commented.

"That would be something different especially with an empty coffin inside!" Again, we told him to be at the church by 9:00 a.m., which he concurred he knew and understood.

Brandon and Alyssa were going to head out because they had offered to go and get the flowers that we had ordered for pick up at 8:15 a.m. from the flower shop in Palmdale. It was the place where we got Alyssa's wedding flowers from, so she knew it well. I was glad they wanted to take care of that, but I also wanted to go to make sure

I was getting what I had ordered. I would let it go and it would all work out.

Check—one more item off my 'to do list' which I carried with me. I had a clipboard which allowed me to jot down all my thoughts of what to do and when. Since Rory's phone call, I also had a picture of Rory and his family and one of my mom that I also carried on the clipboard. Today I would have the talks and thoughts of the program as well in case someone lost their copy also on my clipboard. I would have my page of thank yous from Scott and I that we wanted to express. I also had a picture of Gary and the two stories of others' that described their dreams. Brandon and I looked at some of the flower arrangements and asked each other if we should take some to decorate the church as we didn't know if there would be any others.

"Well, if you want them, I will put them in my truck," Brandon offered.

"I just don't know if we need them. Let's take the big arrangement. We will have at least two there, and I have one that your picking up for the viewing. I think we will be good."

Brandon picked up the arrangement and put it into his suburban. We had to have his vehicle at the church because after the funeral, the coffin again would be put into his vehicle for us to take up to Utah for the trade at the burial. I then walked back into the house. Everyone was up and eating. I had cereal and muffins for them.

7:50 a.m. I was getting a bit anxious. It was almost an excitement. I reminded everyone of the time and that we were needing to leave in about fifteen minutes. I walked upstairs to check on the missionaries. It was pretty funny as all five of them were in the bathroom trying to get ready. I told them we had other bathrooms, but they said they were fine. They were just so cute. Most followed me down.

Everyone was now in the kitchen and introductions were made. We got to spend a few minutes with those amazing missionaries that served in Texas with our son. I instantly loved them and they loved us because of our son. There were also a few phone calls making sure everything was taken care of and that people knew where they needed to go.

8:07 a.m. It was time to start loading everyone up in the various cars. We had a family prayer. It was quite the circle as dad, Susan and Glade, Kelli, Paul's family, us and the five missioinaries knelt together. Talk about feeling loved. Again there was a lot of peace and comfort with us. I had asked for my immediate family to be with me and that everyone else could follow us. If they wanted to come a bit later they could as they really didn't have to be there for the receiving line if they didn't want to. Once loaded up, we had a train of four cars behind us as they all decided to just come now.

"Are you ready dear?" I asked Scott.

"I think so. I don't know what to expect but can't do anything about it anyways," he said. "I'm good. I'm good.

"Me too. I'm actually kind of excited to see who will be there. I just want to see everyone."

"Yeah, me too," Scott replied.

8:15 a.m. We arrived at the church. It was opened. We walked in. I reviewed the look of the tables in the entry way and was pleased. Harris's were there with the Romanos. Of course we hugged each other. Sabrina had been put in charge of writing out the hymns for the meeting and she was inserting them into the programs. The Romanos were helping.

"Would't it be easier to just place them along the benches and chairs?" I asked. That was really what I wanted because I knew if we just left them at the doors, that not everyone would take one and I didn't want a lot left over.

"I think this way will be better," Sabrina commented, and so I let it go.

We walked to the back of the buiding into what is known as The Relief Society Room. I was asked where I wanted our receiving line to be. I showed the brethern who were there to help arrange all the chairs, and it was arranged.

Frankie (Dalen's friend and palbearer) came in. He was very beside himself. I commented on how handsome he looked. Then I went over to my bag of supplies that I might have needed something and pulled out a blue silk tie that I had for him to wear. Dalen had seven silk ties, so I had it planned that the palbearers would each get and wear one of Dalen's ties. Elder Bunder and Shelton picked theirs out at the house as did Paul who got the first pick.

About that time, Jordan Castro walked in. Jordan and Dalen had played sports together for years and became very good friends. He came from such a good family. His dad was a fireman that got along very well with Scott. They both harassed each other about their jobs. I worked with his mother at the school as she was a clerk in the office. Just a good family for sure. So Jordan walked over to see me and I embraced him.

He held me really tight and cried for a minute. Jordan's suit looked so good.

"Does this look okay?" he asked. He had purposely gone out and bought a suit for us. Previously he had asked what he should wear. When we told him generally they wore suits, he said okay—but I didn't know that he didn't have one. Because he respected us so much, his dad made sure he had a suit. I purposely had saved Dalen's favorite neon green tie for Jordan. He cried some more when I gave it to him. Since he was the last pallbear to arrive. I then gathered all the young men together and we went out into the hall to go over what was expected of them.

Other people were showing up too. Brother Hill had been asked to be the official photographer, and I had asked Cody if he would be a backup and mostly do family shots. Dad and Susan, who had been out in the lobby, and Sheila all walked in about the same time.

I had the pallbearers together in the hallway.

"First off, I want to thank you so very much for being here and a part of this special day. Please know how much you meant to my son. He loved you all very much. Also I love you too." I paused for a second to gain my composure. "The hearse should be here any moment and basically we will have to go out to meet them and then carry in the coffin. When we go into the church, you will walk right behind the immedite family. There is a place at the front of the chapel on the right side for you to sit at. After the service you will be directed when to come up. Brandon will help you line up and answer any questions. Are you all okay with this?" I asked.

Responses were unanamous to yes. I returned to the room and Brandon lined up the young men so they would know where to go.

8:45 a.m. "Hey Mom, this man is looking for you," Mariah stated.

I went back out to the hall and saw the man with the hearse. Mariah wouldn't have known who he was because no one but Brandon and Elder Fifi saw the gentleman when he was at the house. I told him that I would get the palbearers and meet him outside. He was parked at the side door and would then move to the front of the building once the coffin was removed. I called the young men. You could see almost a fear come over Frankie and Jordan's faces.

"Don't worry guys, you will be fine. You look great. Just breathe and you will be able to do this."

I think my reasurrance in them calmed them down. I walked out with them. Again, the conductor told the boys where to grab onto the coffin and that they would just place the coffin on the wheels, and then it would be pushed into the room where the family was waiting. Elder Bunker made the comment that it was lighter than he thought it would be. Everyone stood up in reverance as the coffin was brought into the area. That was again another numbing moment. The coffin was now in front of us all.

We went back into the room and sure enough Alyssa and Brandon had walked in with the flowers. Perfect timing. I was told that I would have to place the orchids on the netting that would be hung over the coffin. There were two arrangements for the coffin and one standing that we placed near where the people would first be greeting us. I immediately started to put the flowers on the coffin. I layed the arrangements on and then the net over the coffin. I had a box of orchids that I had to individually put into the net. I was very pleased with the way it looked. I really thought it was simple and yet reflected Dalen a bit with the net especially. Again, he loved the ocean and it gave it an added feel.

Once I was done, I pulled Elder Bunker to the side for a quick second.

"Dalen's body isn't in the coffin. It was going to be very expensive to cross four state lines so we are just borrowing the coffin for today. We will get the coffin with his body at the burial," I explained.

"Well, that makes sense," Elder Bunker stated.

There was a picture of Christ right over where we placed the coffin. It was perfect. I had also asked for a single rose for each of the girls to hold with my order. More were gathering in the room.

8:55 a.m. We had a few minutes, so I walked up and looked at the back of the culture hall which had been opened up into the chapel. I was surprised that there were already people there. I met with the man who had the chairs set up. He said that he didn't have all the chairs set up, but that there were about eight hundred. I wondered if it really would fill up. I had a moment, so I went to the bathroom and just had a little prayer that all would go well which I knew it would.

Trisha and George came in. The kids were excited to see their grandparents. Sylvia and her husband came in. I knew that if I introduced each other they would find plenty to talk about. It was just amazing to have Sylvia there. Everyone fell in love with her immediately.

Sylvia, red hair / Susan—to the right /
George and Trisha—on the left

9:05 a.m. Robert Harris thought that we should have a prayer to start and we all agreed. Robert offered the prayer. We had kind of asked Robert to lead our events of the day. He was grateful to help however he could. We positionied ourselves and then asked those gathered in the room if they would start the line and come through the reception line to meet us. Robert would then go to the chapel and announce that anyone who would like to come see the family would be invited to the Relief Society Room in the back of the building and the family would greatly appreciate it.

Immediately a line was formed and family and friends began to come through. Kailee was first. Then Scott and I were next with Alyssa and Brandon with Mariah at the tail. We wanted Brandon to be with us. He was our family, and he belonged. Mariah would change positions once in a while and stand between Kailee and Scott. During the processions, there were some times when we were quite busy and others when we weren't. I was so surprized at who came. They all were so sad for us. There were also times when no one was even in the room and we almost felt awkward. We would break the line and just visit with those family in the room. We would even ask Robert to go again and make another invitation. There were a few jokes and laughter heard. We had to remind ourselves that we probably should be a bit quieter. Every person was very important to us. I was so grateful for the pictures that were taken because I wanted to remember them all.

We had many members of the Sheriff's department want to be with us and help us however they could. I think I mentioned before that we decided to have them help with driving people from the airport to the church. They brought Sister Williamson who came out from Texas. She had a house that Dalen liked to hang out a lot at. She was actually from my hometown of Lethbridge, Alberta, Canada, and found out that I went to school with her younger brother. That was way cool to find out. She arrived wearing a very beautiful red dress. When she came through the line—I just held her and told her how much our son loved her and how much it meant to us that she was there.

One other pickup from one of the deputies was for my best friend Carol Parker that was coming from Colorado, and could only stay for part of the day and then would have to return. Her flight wouldn't land till almost 9:45 a.m., and we were a good one and a half hours away from the airport on a good day. So we knew she would be late, but she would be there. I told her there would be a space for her next to Sylvia and Colette on the second row. I had earlier put her reserved name on the bench in the chapel. I had told Carol that she would be picked up in a black and white police car and that they would have a sign looking for her. Also I described to the officer what Carol would be wearing.

Everyone that got picked up by on officer, said it was pretty neat to be in a police car, in the front seat of course. We all thought that was pretty cool.

Throughout the morning, I kept wondering how Carol was doing and when she would actually make it.

The attendance for the reception was just so amazing. There was one young man that I didn't even know, but he was beside himself. He was so emotional and just couldn't seem to control himself. The line was pretty slow, so I went over to him and invited him up to the coffin to say goodbye. As I was standing beside him, I had my arm around him.

"Are you ok?" I asked.

"No, I don't know how to handle this," the young man stated. "How did you know Dalen?"

"We played video games together. I've known him for years. He almost had me talked into going to school with him up in Idaho." (Again, I had a flashback of Dalen telling me about this young man and how he wanted to provide a spiritual guidance in his life). "I just can't believe that he's gone. I don't know how to do this," and he continued to cry.

"I want you to know that there can be great peace. That there will be a spirit that you will feel today. I want you to know that Dalen is in a good spot. He is happy and will be with us today."

He then placed his hand on the coffin.

"I want you to know that Dalen had a very strong testimony of who his Savior was. He loved him and it's because of that knowledge, he is really in a good place. When you hear the funeral today, I want you to sit with the family. I want you to hear our words and you will have an experience like you have never felt before. I need to know that you will be okay. You can stay here as long as you need to."

I hugged this young man and he just kept thanking me. It was a touching moment, but a joy to testify of what we believed and to know that our funeral would affect lives and without a doubt, that the spirit of God that testifies of truth would be present. I knew it.[69]

Scott's Lieutenant Stefanie and her husband flew in from Arizona. That was awesome to see them. She was the means for Scott getting a flight up to Idaho. We really wouldn't ever be able to repay her for that. There were so many officers that came through. Teachers' of Dalen or even the girl's teachers were there. We had distant relatives and friends from Virgina, Utah, Nevada, Colorado, Arizona, Missouri, Texas, Wyoming, and of course from various places in California too. We couldn't forget the family from Canada that sacrificed so much to be with us. Scott's whole family came, which also was a very big deal. They hadn't been together for over seventeen years. Scott's sister was moving from Hawaii, but not for two more

---

[69] To comfort someone so in need was a blessing. I totally felt inspired to assist this young men. That was a blessing for sure.

weeks. When Dalen died, she altered her plans so she could be with us, which was so amazing.

At one point I scanned the line of persons coming through, and I noticed a young man in the back of the room first talking with other people he knew. I then released myself from the line and went over to him. He flew in from Hawaii also. He was in school over there and flew home for the funeral. Tyler Morris was his name. He, Dalen and Brad Harolson were the three musketeers. These were Dalen's church friends. They were in a different ward, but they hung out all the time and these young men were at out house a lot. They always came over to go swimming. I was in shock to see Tyler. He hugged me so tight. I shed a few tears. He also had brought a lei and asked if we would mind if he put it on the coffin. Of course I thought that would be so perfect. We walked up together to the coffin and Tyler took the lei off his neck and placed it over the coffiin. That picture will never be erased from my memory. It was like the room went silent for a second as everyone watched him present his gesture of love. Tyler then went through the line and joined his family that had just gone through.

The girls were holding up. We all did so extremely well. Generally there were smiles on our faces and they were genuine. But there were a few times when they had their moments too.

The hour and a half seemed to go well. Sheila played the piano for us the whole time. In the chapel, I had an organist play for twenty minutes, and then she switched out with a family (Tori Odom that took Titan for us) and the Odom kids that sang and played guitar also. They were so excited to help out and to be involved that this was the perfect solution. I heard from others that their singing and playing was just beautiful. I wish I would have been able to hear a bit, but I also needed to see people on an individual basis.

Scott's friends from thirty years ago came by. They helped Scott build his very first engine in our garage for his race car. They spent many a day at our house fixing something or other on the car. They too were family.

Our entire family had people there for them, it wasn't just for Dalen or it wasn't just for Scott. We were all blessed to have people express their concerns for each of our individual state of minds and well-being.

10:38 a.m. I looked at the clock and hoped that Carol was making good time.

There were several times when we hoped more people would come see us. I took a minute and walked up the hall way and just peeked in the back of the cultural hall. It looked like there were a lot of empty chairs still.

"I hope this fills up," was my thought. I went back into the room and there were a few more people that came through.

10:43 a.m. Carol walked into the room and I immediately ran over to her. We embraced and cried. She and I have always been there for each other even when one had moved away. I so needed her and just could't believe she was there and how quickly she made it to the chapel. She was shocked too how fast they got there. She said she mentioned that Sylvia (her officer driver), even put the lights on a few times to get through traffic. Sylvia was on Scott's team and just wanted so badly to stay and be a part of this all. She was designated as Carol's driver for the day which also meant she would get to be with us, and we were very glad that she could. She now too, was adopted into our family group. Carol was in the room and made it on time. She really was here. Driving through LA traffic and having time to spare, not by chance.[70]

10:45 a.m. It was time to have the family prayer. The doors were closed to the public and it was then mentioned that we would have our family prayer before we went into the chapel. Everyone took their seats. Scott would offer the prayer. After that, the casket would then lead the procession with the immediate family behind and then the rest of the family group would file into the chapel row by row.

---

[70] Carol made it through LA and was there for me and in time. Such an amazing reunion.

Scott's prayer was mostly of gratitude and for all the people that had come to honor us. He prayed that we would feel the spirit and be enlightened through this experience. He did a nice job.

A few of us went to the bathroom before the procession began. Then we walked down the hallway which was lined with people. Chloe was standing there, so I grabbed her and said that she needed to be with Carol on the second row with Sylvia and her husband too.

Scott and I found ourselves waving to a few people and thanking them all for coming. We walked past the back door of the cultural hall, and this time when I peeked in, it was full which surprized me. We continued up the hall and came to the lobby area that again was full of people standing waiting for us. Again we were noticing people and thanking them for coming. We got to the chapel doors and it became silent.

The Funeral Service

We walked in and looked over the audience and were so suprised at faces we knew. There were so many people there. We walked past the aisles and took our places on the front row as the casket was locked into place. It was kind of funny because the family didn't fill in the two rows behind us so they were blank except for our out of town friends. The family kept coming in and filled up the remaining rows. We had eight rows saved, but I think Sister Harris might have extended it to ten rows. I just wanted to stand and look at all the people, but we took our spots and just waited for everyone else to find their places. I had my clipboard with me. I wanted Rory and Mom to know I wanted them with me. Scott and I then looked at the amazing flower arrangements.

"Look at that one—it's from Jack-In-The-Box."

"Wow that's so cool," Scott replied. Dalen and Mariah had both worked there and Scott went there every day to get his Diet Coke, easy ice. They were very good to him too. He never had to pay. The flowers were a very nice gesture.

There was an arrangement from Scott's department as well as his union. There was also one from his team family that could't be with us, but sent flowers. We were in awe as there were fourteen arrangements there spaced all over the front of the chapel. It was so beautiful.

As the family settled in, I turned and looked at a few of them and checked to see that they were okay.

"There's a whole lot of people here," Mariah stated.

On the bench were Scott and me in the center. Kailee and Chris were on Scott's left. Mariah, Rick, Alyssa and Brandon were to my right. And then all of a sudden we are shuffled over as George and

Trisha came up to our row and sat down. We weren't expecting that, but it was fine.

I had all the girls look at the flowers. I really wanted to walk up to each arrangement and read who they were from, but I didn't. It was just so beautiful and over whelming to see.

"Are you girls ready for this?" Scott asked them.

"Yup, I'm ready," Alyssa announced.

"Me too," was Mariah's comment.

"I don't know," said Kailee. "I don't know what Im supposed to be ready for," said as only Kailee would say. That just meant she had never been in that situation before, so she didn't really know how to feel or what to expect. She had been to a funeral before (my mom's) though, so that helped her a bit.

And then it began.

President Knowles was conducting. He thanked those who had played the prelude and all those who attended. He made a comment that it looked like Stake Conference with so many people there and how loved our family was, and we felt it.

The opening song was changed. Sabrina thought I said one when I said another, so it was: "I Know that my Redeemer Lives." The words were typed out and in the programs. After which George Graham (grandpa) would offer the opening prayer. The program was announced and all of a sudden I was getting upset because President Knowles had changed the lineup. Usually a Stake President was the last speaker when we had regular meetings, but this wasn't regular. This was my son's funeral. I wanted the euology done, Pres Knowles to speak on the Plan of Happiness. A musical number, and then the girls' remarks. Blake was to read his post then Scott and I were going to say a few words with Pres. Knowles giving closing remarks. That was the program that as a family we decided on. So now to hear that he changed things around, I wasn't very happy with that. I felt like it would ruin our program. I felt like I wanted to correct it, but I didn't.

The program was the euology, Blake's talk, musical, the girls and then Scott and me, which I really didn't want us next to each other on the program. I wanted there to be a space betwen our family comments, for the reason that I wanted people not to be overwhelmed with their emotions relating to ours. After Scott and I would comment, President Knowles would speak. If Dalen's mission President would have been there to speak, there wouldn't have been an issue. So it was what it was.

Eric was very nervous and worried about reading the eulogy. I had given it to him a few days earlier and I had him read it to me a few times to get rid of his nerves. I was so proud of him. He did a good job. There were only a few times when he had to regain his composure. In fact, we had it arranged that if he could't do it, he would look at me and I would come join him and together we would read it. But Eric did it.

<u>Dalen's Story (read by Eric Lewis)</u>

Dalen Scott Graham was born November 28th 1995, in Thousand Oaks California at 3:14 in the afternoon. He was born to Scott and Sharon Graham and he was their third child of four, and the first and only son.

Dalen was a fun child. He loved to be the center of attention.

As a child, he had this thing for sneaking into the back yard and jumping on the trampoline naked.

Dalen moved to Acton California when he was 6 years old.

He went to the local schools there. He played with the Sierra Youth Sports and was noticed as a very versatile baseball player. Every Coach said he had so much potential. Truth be said, he could have been an awesome pitcher, but Dalen wanted to play instead of practice.

In Junior High he even tried the trumpet. Mom and dad actually discouraged that one quickly and made him practice outside.

Dalen's father ordained him to the priesthood when he was twelve, which Dalen was always very aware of and knew that if he made a mistake, he really tried to clear it up quickly. He understood that being a priesthood holder meant you represented the Savior on the earth. Repentance became a blessing to Dalen. He truly loved his Savior.

In High School he played on the football and volleyball teams.

He was one of the fastest runners. One play, Dalen punted the ball and then ran past everyone down the field 40 + yards and tackled the guy hard.

Volleyball was his favorite thing and he had played it ever since. He had learned how to hit, place the ball, and had an awesome vertical. No one was ever prouder than his mom who was his loudest and biggest cheerleader. He knew his mom's whistle very well.

Dalen loved guns and was either having a nerf gun war or an air soft gun war. For 5 years in a row on his birthday, there would be 10-16 kids come and battle it out on the hill behind the house.

Dalen was a tinker kind of guy. He loved to take things apart. The problem was that he wasn't very good at putting them back together.

The outdoors was his thing. He and Dino Lauricella could survive scout camp on nothing but top ramen soup and a tarp for a canopy. That was because he didn't pack any food and thought he wouldn't need any more clothes. His claim to fame was calling his family from the top of Mt. Whitney. "Hi Mommy, guess where I am?." His mom was way nervous because he *was supposed to not have any reception on this hike, so she thought something was wrong. "I just peed off the top of Mt. Whitney". He was way proud too.*

Dalen loved being with his family. He loved the ocean and the way it smelt. He wanted to learn to fish. We were at June Lake and fishing was definitely not his dad's thing. So, his mom took him out on the boat, and he caught his first fish. But then to clean it, he backed way out, and mom had to do it. However, fishing on the ocean with Uncle Gordon in Mexico, was another story. Dalen puked for 4 hours. Poor guy. I guess that's why he liked the beach, but not so much being on the ocean.

He's had a few semesters at Brigham Young University Idaho in Rexburg, where he had great influences with awesome friends and roommates.

He had served a mission for the Church of Jesus Christ of Latter-Day Saints in the Dallas Texas Spanish speaking mission where he returned four months after a two-year period. He influenced not only those seeking for the true word of God but helped many to remember those same principles.

Dalen loved people. He loved life. If you knew Dalen you knew he was ALWAYS happy. Dalen wasn't the best in an emergency because it was usually him that was the emergency. He broke his color bone, sprained ankles six times and he dislocated fingers from volleyball all the time.

Dalen had a way of searching out that one person that might be alone. They would always leave as buddies. Dalen didn't have just friends because everyone was his best friend.

He was the joker of the family. He would run in at any time and stick his butt out and wiggled it literally in your face. You couldn't see anything, and he wouldn't stop till he heard you laugh.

He was best friends with his sisters. They would talk about everything, and he had a way of letting them know that they were very important and were treated individually. Dalen was very protective of his sisters even if he was years younger than the person. If you would hurt his sister, he would hunt you down. He wasn't big enough to do anything or even appear threatening, but they knew where he stood.

You definitely knew where you stood with Dalen. Whether good or bad he would express his feelings for you and in return, most people knew of his sincerity.

Dalen can't be replaced and won't be, but the relief is that we believe our families are eternal and will be together again after this life. So now it's up to us. We have to keep going. If Dalen's life can be an example of how we truly should live, then remember him and do as he did. Dalen truly has touched 1000s with his life. The 'one' mattered. Judgments were few. Everyone was important and Dalen would remind you of that. Dalen knew he was a child of God. "And if it so be that ye shall labor all the days of your life and bring save one soul unto me, how great shall be your joy." Not only did Dalen find the one (meaning himself) but he is also taking many with him. Dalen Graham- our son, brother, friend, leader, councilor, comforter, insightful, funny, energetic, loyal, child of God. We love you "Buddy Boy".

His death occurred February 10th, 2018, at 5:16 a.m. in the Pocatello Portneuf Medical Center in Pocatello Idaho, after a tragic car accident.

He will be buried at the Washington Cemetery on Monday, February 19 @ 2:00pm.
His Father will dedicate the grave.

It was good to hear the crowd laugh and seemed as if they were enjoying themselves. It released some stress felt from everyone. It went over well.

Blake then read his Facebook post. He added a bit for the funeral, but again it was touching and a nice tribute to how Dalen influenced him to be a better person.

Sister Pam Castagna was a Sunday school teacher of Dalen's and had a great love for him. She decided to sing one of Dalen's favorite songs a cappella. She sang "How Great Thou Art". It brought tears to all of us.

The girls then went up. We had previously talked about some of their memories and as they talked, I wrote them down. Then they decided which ones wanted to say which memory. They all stood at the pulpit together. Alyssa introduced their memories. It was pretty cute. They did a great job and handled themselves with great composure. Alyssa at the end thanked everyone for being there and said how much she would miss her brother and best friend but knew that we would all see and be with him again.

Memories of Dalen

Mariah's Memories

- *Road trip home from grandmas at like 1:30 am.*
- *We were forever road trip buddies and we always had so much fun.*
- *Monsters.*
- *Hot Cheetos.*
- *His testimony.*
- *He was the most supportive big brother ever.*
- *One time I sprained my ankle in a soccer game really bad and he carried me off the field because I couldn't walk, I went back out and won the game after a few minutes.*
- *So, when Dalen came home for the first time from Ecuador he and my mom surprised me at school, and he picked me up and spun me around and was so happy to see me.*
- *Sometimes we would drive around the neighborhood just to listen to some great songs in the car together.*
- *He always posted literally the ugliest pictures of me on his Instagram.*
- *When on road trips or anything and it was raining we would both stick our heads out the window and get pelted with the drops.*
- *We both slept on grandma's couches and would stay up all the time and just talk or watch movies.*
- *Whenever he told me to play a video game with him he would always kill me so I would just stand and turn in circles and shoot until he found me.*
- *Dalen was very spiritual, very in tune with the Lord.*
- *He was a social butterfly.*
- *Dalen was a hard-core Republican.*

Kailee's Memories

- *Dalen would talk in his sleep all the time. Sometimes he would just yell out and other times he would scare you like "Kailee, give me that*
- *Dalen was the fastest runner on the team. He had proven this several times. But one other good play, he was punting the ball and after about a 40-yard punt, Dalen took off and ran like crazy and passed his entire team to reach the kid returning the ball, and Dalen just plowed into him. That was a good tackle.*
- *His practice of shooting would be at the rabbits on the hill. He shot 3 in one day.*
- *Sisters taking him through the girl's sections of the stores, and he loved the bra section specially.*
- *He was always hyper. He couldn't sit very long. After we would do air soft, he would want to go some more and the rest of us would be tired.*
- *Whenever we had family prayers, many times Dalen would fart, and we would all start to laugh. We couldn't finish the prayer.*
- *He really liked to build things like Legos everywhere. We would have competitions on who could build them higher.*
- *At the dinner table if he had to fart he would stick his butt out the door.*
- *When Dalen was about 2, he loved to escape the house and go and jump on the trampoline and would be naked. He and I were buddies at this. He would just run and run and run around and laugh because we couldn't catch him.*
- *Dalen loved to take things apart. He could dissemble almost anything electrical. He loved to figure out how it went together. The problem was that he couldn't put it back together. We went through a lot of remotes for some reason.*

- One time in Vegas dad challenged Dalen to eat 3 double doubles. which he did. He was sick for the rest of the day.
- Whenever he would take down trash out of the kitchen, he would always leave the back door open so eventually we start locking the back and the front door so he couldn't get in.
- Dalen and his friends would do the cha-cha slide backwards. Legendary.
- Dalen's stupid pink blanket-went everywhere with him.
- He loved video games. When he played, we would hear him talking and thought it was to us, but it was always with someone in his game.

<u>Alyssa's Memories</u>

- Really loved techno music.
- Driving up in the desert we passed a sign and Dalen read it what's Mojave (mo-jay-ve).
- He was always available to talk to you and could make any conversation interesting.
- Had a dorky smile that lit up a room.
- Dalen got in trouble a lot, but he really loved his family.
- Everyone was his friend.
- He gave all of us Wet Willys but especially Alyssa.
- When we were younger we would go on road trips and have to share drinks because we usually didn't drink one by ourselves. So, we bought a large drink with four straws in it; but then Dalen would spit in it so no one else would want any more of the drink.
- Dalen was really good with kids, especially Ashley's son Michael.
- Triple decker pb&j.
- Dalen would pee in the back yard.
- The Dalen special at In N Out was a four by four with spread and onion only, and animal fries. We have no idea how he ate it all because he was so small.

- *He ate soooo much ketchup.*
- *He slept in the most awkward positions all the time.*
- *His cool socks.*
- *He wore shorts and neon socks every day until he went on his mission. Then after, he wore his maroon jacket, and his tan pants every day!!!*
- *When at the beach in the water his pants would fall down a little because he was so tiny.*

The girls took turns reading one of their bullet points. It worked out perfectly. We told them that they might not get to read them all and to kind of look at me if the time was going on too long. So that was what they did. Again it wasn't easy, but it was so perfect. Everyone commented after on the good job the girls did and how their memeories touched them.

Then Scott and I got up. We wanted to thank everyone for all they had done for us. We first figured out where we wanted to stand and then I spoke.

> *"We knew that we couldn't let this opportunity go by without thanking everyone personally. Scott agreed, but he also said that I would be the one to do the talking.'"* Everyone laughed.
>
> *"To say thank you truly isn't enough. There aren't words big enough to describe our emotions."*
>
> *"We have been so amazingly taken care of. Thank you especially for all the messages, texts, facebook, IM. We are just so extremely grateful, just so grateful. For four days we did nothing but read your messages and felt uplifted and carried."*
>
> *"Thank you to Bobby and Gina for ochestrating so many events, so many."*
>
> *"Special thank you to all the members of the Sheriff's Department, and again for their*

huge contributions in all aspects. From checking in on Scott to being our personal drivers and again, all the phone calls."

"Colonial Funeral Home in Pocatello has made this process so calming and peaceful. Just so very blessed."

"We accept this tragedy as now a blessing to us and so many. Of course it's sad, but when we allow God to really lead our lives, it can only be described as perfection."

"We have learned the difference between 'tender mercies and mighty miracles. Mercies are God answering our prayers. We have lost our keys or we have need of direction in our lives, but we petition Him. He answers us because He can and He loves us. Miracles are when we let Him lead. We have done that and the miracles have been mighty. The death part wasn't easy, but the aftermath has truly been perfect. We think we understand some of this, so to clarify let me share a few stories of the 'WHY.'"

(I reread my cousin Kathy Hudson's dream)

"I know you're probably overwhelmed but I had a dream last night that I wanted to share with you. Dalen and Mariah were in heaven standing with Heavenly Father. Heavenly Father was explaining to them what their life would be like when they came to earth. He talked to them about the famliy they would come to and the work they would do here. Heavenly Father turned to Dalen and told him that a time would come when he would be called home to do a work critical in the building of the kingdom of the Lord and that only

Dalen could do. Then Heavenly Father turned to Mariah and explained to her that she would have a huge roll in helping her brother get back to Heaven. He knew that it would not be easy but He chose her because of her faithfulness and strength. They both told Heavenly Father that they were willing to do whatever He asked of them. Heavenly Father then expressed the deep love He had for them and promised that their family would be blessed far beyond what they could imagine for their obedience and faithfulness."

You could hear the emotions of the people in the audience.

"This story touched us very deeply, but we knew it was true too. The second story was from Sylvia Richins."

Sylvia stated—"I saw your son's story on the news. I am so sorry and heartbroken for your great loss at this time. Right now I am sitting in the hospital room at IMC in Murray, Utah and my son, who has been on dialysis for five and a half years, is about to receive a kidney transplant that will give him a new life. May you find comfort in knowing that your selfless decision to donate is bringing life, hope and joy to many others. One of those could be my son. I pray you all will be blessed for your great selfless gift of life to others and find that peace that passes all understanding in your time of deep grief."

Me—"Oh my gosh, thank you so very much. We will be praying for your son as well.

I know my son's organs went into the valley. Would't that be something if your son received my son's kidney?'"

Sylvia—"That would be more than amazing. My son's last name is Graham also."

(There was a huge gasp from the audience.)

Sylvia—"I will message you later. We were asking who the donor was and they told us we could go through the donor center and that they couldn't tell us who the donor was other wise."

The next morning I messaged Sylvia back.

Me—"We just heard that both of Dalen's kidneys were not just received but accepted. Did your son have his surgery? Please oh please!! The director said after I told her about you that; "If we were to put 2 + 2 together, I couldn't tell you if it was right, but I'm sure you could figure it out. We knew it was a match."

Sylvia—"Yes!! My son had his transplant last night at 10:00 p.m. There was another recipient in surgery just before my son. I am sure they both received Dalen's kidneys. It's Dalen's. I just know it."

I showed the congregation a picture of Gary in the hospital and introduced him to everyone along with his family. I then pointed out Sylvia who was in the audience, and how grateful I was that she was there with us. It was really amazing.

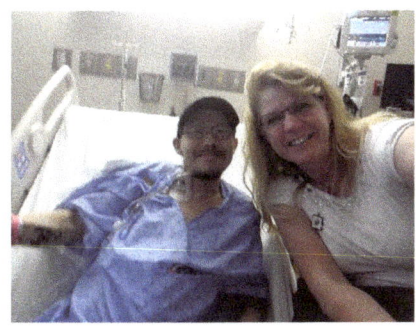 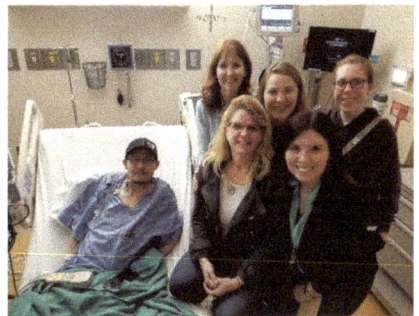

> *"We just want to say how much we love you all and are so grateful that you are here. We have been so blessed. We have so much peace with us and we know God has taken our boy home. We miss you Buddy boy. We miss you so much. But I love my Savior more. We know where our son is. We know what he is doing. We are so grateful for our knowledge of the after life because of our Savior. Thank you all again for coming. Our lives will never be the same. And I say these things in the name of Jesus Christ, Amen."*

I thought we were then going to walk down but Scott walked up to the mic. He also expressed how grateful he was for the out pour of love and how the department had comforted him so much.

> *"This is in no way easy to do. We have been humbled and blessed in so many ways. We wish our son didn't die, but he did and in knowing what we know, we have great peace. Thank you all for coming. This really does mean the world to us. We love you. I love my Savior. I know he lives. I say these things, in the name of Jesus Christ, amen."*

We then walked down from the pulpit to our pew.

It was now turn for President Knowles to give his talk. It was good. He talked about our Savior and his gifts to all of us through the resurrection. He expressed his love for Dalen and how he could make everyone smile. That Dalen was friends with the Lord. Dalen knew his master and served him well. He spoke of the necessity of death. He talked about how this gift of living again, is now given to every person that ever lived on the earth. There was mention of three main gifts that we all have received: 1)—peace 2)—comfort and 3)-the resurrection. There was a bit of explanation of each point.

> *"The knowledge of the resurrection gives us hope. It increases our desire to do good, it helps us as we prepare to see our loved ones again... It is a comfort to know that Dalen will live again, that he will be resurrected. What a comfort it is to know that after we die, we will also be resurrected! We will meet Dalen again, and enjoy the presence of his company!"*

President Knowles than gave his closing remarks of how uplifted we all have been and how our lives will be altered through the life of Dalen Graham.

There was a closing song: "I Believe in Christ" and the final closing prayer was offered by my dad (Grandpa Hudson).

The pallbeares then approached the coffin and walked behind the conductor as he moved the coffin outside. The family followed and then the congregation was excused to come out and see us. What an absolutely perfect morning. It may not have been easy, but it was perfect.

Pallbearers-Elder Shelton, Brandon, Paul, Jordan, Frankie, Elder Bunker, Eric and Matt Lewis

The sun was shining when we walked out. It was warm and there was no wind. The sky was clear. We walked out and immediately were hugging all around us. So many people came and expressed their condolences again, but also mentioned how amazing our program was and that we should be proud of our family. So many people mentioned that they were so sad when they arrived but that they were leaving uplifted. We felt blessed again that our desires had been met. It was a very uplifting mood. It was really good and fun to see everyone.[71]

---

[71] Miracles of who came and from how far away they came. Just in Awe of it al.

Some of Dalen's school friends: Matt, Devin, Jordyn and Alec (who also died of a car accident eight months after Dalen), came from three states and it meant a lot to Scott and I.

These were missionaries that had served with Dalen. There were ten of them that drove down from Provo Utah, to be with us. What an honor. They were so fun and cute. We instantly loved them.

Surprised as a high school friend of mine who now lived in Lancaster and had come to see me. "No way, I can't believe it's you."

We were at the church for about forty-five minutes after the services as we spoke with people and gave them individual time as they came out of the church. We really enjoyed seeing who was there and appreciate so much the huge amount of support.

During the visiting outside, Brandon all of a sudden said he needed to go.

"Where are you going?" I asked.

"I have to go down the street and meet the hearse so he can put the coffin back in the suburban. I'll be right back," he mentioned.

"Yeah, that is a good idea. We don't want the driver to have to wait any longer."

"Yeah, he was the one that told me his time was up. I'll be back when all the people are gone so they don't see the coffin inside. Then we can put flowers in there if you want, there will be room." Brandon stated.

"Sounds good. The people will probably be gone in about ten minutes I think." Most of the people had already left. Many were invited to our family luncheon so we would see them there too.

Brandon was then gone. When I walked back into the church, Maria and Sheila had already taken down the display tables and put our supplies into boxes. The chairs were almost put away from the gym and the flowers had all been gathered, and we were figuring out how to transport them all to the house. I saw the Castro family all together and went over to thank Jordan again for his help and the family for coming. Jordan's dad was very specific in how he felt of the funeral. He cried as he expressed how uplifting it was and how amazing it was to see the family in the state of mind that we were in. He loved the girls comments and hearing about Gary. His wife also commented on how sad of an event she thought this would be and she didn't know what to expect, but that our funeral was amazing. She related that she felt uplifted and at peace. They felt of the Holy Spirit, and they actually were leaving happier than they thought they would from attending a funeral. I encouraged them to continue with all these good feelings and to relate them to others. The same response happened to almost all that we spoke with after. They all said that it wasn't just a good funeral, but that they were leaving uplifted and enlightened. What a blessing. It was a good service.[72]

---

[72] Our goal for the service was to have people uplifted and enlightened, to feel at peace. Goal achieved.

Is It Time to Eat Yet?

1:52 p.m. We all found our way to Agua Dulce and as we drove into our ward building, the parking lot was full. We had to unload a few flower arrangements so Scott and I carried one in and set them up around the gym. The girls had driven over with their boyfriends, so Scott and I were alone. The gym was full. We had asked for 150 people to feed and they were all there. It was like a wedding reception with family and friends everywhere. It was so neat to see everyone now on a more casual level. I saw people from the 5th Ward and 3rd Ward that came to help. They were serving food, or there to clear tables or just fill water glasses, but they were there. Every table had a beautiful tablecloth on it, a 4 x 6 photo of Dalen's last Facebook post that Kelly Jenson and Wendy Barnes were instrumental in planning. That was so cool. Each table had a centerpiece that was just perfect and a little plant with matching colors of the tablecloths. It looked so nice. There were desserts on the side tables. The menu was pulled pork, with hoagie buns, salads, and fresh fruit were available. There were three long tables with helpers behind the tables ready to serve all that came through. We got so say hi to just a few people, but then they wanted to have a blessing and begin eating as everyone was hungry. It was overwhelming how much food there was. This was what Sister Jenson was talking about earlier when she said they had so many people that had offered to help. I paid for the meat, but all the rest was donated, and it was a lot.

We had the video again playing of the life of Dalen for all who wanted to see it. There was just such a good vibe in the room. Everyone was laughing and having a good time. Scott and I just kept walking around thanking everyone for coming. I purposely went to every table and took a picture, so I could remember who was there. It was so good to spend some time with people and again thank them for coming. There were a lot of people. It was just fun to have them around us. It was also funny that by the time I got to sit down to eat, they had already started cleaning up the tables. That made me laugh.

Sitting with Carol and Darrin Neilson—(a missionary
I served with in Bolivia). Such a fun time.

People just stayed. They all wanted to visit and it was good. All that were from out of town or family, were of course invited over to the house to hang out and just visit some more. It's not often that we get to be together and I wanted them in my house.

Sylvia (Gary's mom) Chloe (Dalen's girlfriend)
Kathy Rosito (friend) Sylvia & Husband /Bobby & Gina

And…Colette Williamson (From Texas) and Carol

Elder Bunker & Shelton Scott's Family

Best friend Carol with Scott photo bombing us.

Facebook (Kailee) Funeral service was amazing for my brother. The love and support is unbelievable. Calculated around 800 people there with love and support for our family with friends, friends of Dalen, and friends of my parents. Couldn't have been anything without you guys there. From all and any kind of help to support, it wouldn't have been possible without you all.

3:30 (ish) p.m. The church was now empty and all was cleaned up. We were told that we didn't have to help, but we wanted to, and we were still visiting too.

It was time to go home. We turned down the street arriving at the house. There again were cars everywhere. It was a nice sight. When I walked in, everyone was now in their casual clothes, and they seemed relaxed. There were people everywhere. There really wasn't a room that didn't have people in it.

4:00 p. m. It had been determined that Carol and Chloe could go to the airport together. Their flights were only an hour apart so that would make it easier for the person transporting them. It was sad that they were the first to go. Chloe had become a part of us now for three days. We just loved her and all the time we were able to spend together. We were so sad that we wouldn't get to have her as part of our family, but we still adopted her quickly. It had been a very good time together. And to have Carol here, if only for a few hours, was so worth it all too. How I love this lady. She had always been there for me, and this was no exception. They were just family to me today, and I didn't want them to leave.

Our evening was amazing. We sat and talked. There were lots of comments about Dalen and the funeral. Lots of laughter heard and for food, they got whatever was left over from the luncheon. It pretty much was a help yourself and no one seemed to mind. It really couldn't have been any better of a day, afternoon, or evening, nope not in any way. Rick decided to drive up to Utah with Chris, who was heading home, to visit with his grandma, and we would meet up with him again on Monday for the burial. That way Chris wouldn't have to drive alone either, as he had to leave to get back to Salt Lake City. It seemed like a good plan.

We were so grateful and blessed for words spoken, messages received, flowers, cards, attendance for the funeral, and the abundance of love we felt in all directions.

WOW—WHAT A DAY!!!! 68 people passed through our doors this evening—SPECTACULAR

Michelle Lyche—our very first and forever babysitter

My siblings and dad

The Hudson Clan

Cousin Kelly

Facebook (Sharon) From all the support, pictures, prayers, thoughts, the morning couldn't have been better. We are so truly blessed and grateful. We have born witness today of God and have testified of the truth of His words. Thank you everyone. Thank you. Friday night we had 56 people over to the house and today there had been 68 counted. WooHoo—so amazing!!!

9:30 p.m. The house was almost quiet as so many people had already left. Dad, Susan and Glade, and our kids were the only ones remaining. Colette Williamson had joined us, but had an early Uber ride at 5:30 a.m., so she just wanted to stay on the couch. Everyone reflected on our day and how well we all thought it went. No TV, just visiting. All the flowers had been taken into the garage and I was finally at a place where I could go look at them all. Alyssa and Kailee followed me. I took a picture of each arrangement and who they were sent from. They smelled so good and we were just overwhelmed by them all. The kitchen table, dining table, blanket chest and garage floor were covered with flowers. I love flowers and these were beautiful for sure. The family stayed up for a bit while we visited together before we decided to go to bed. The beds were inviting to us all as we were waiting for our day of extreme love to almost to be over.

Sunday—Church and More Driving

I wasn't sure who would be going to church with us, but I got up early and made breakfast for everyone. The missionaries had left after the luncheon yesterday so they could get to one of their family members in St. George before it got too late. Cody's family said they would also head home. Gord's family was still around, as was dad, Susan and Kelly were also here.

The house started stirring with people deciding when they might need the use of the bathrooms, for those that might have wanted to shower. The time seemed to go quickly. We let everyone know that they needed to be ready by 8:40 a.m., as that's when we would leave for church. I was excited to be there. I loved going to church. I loved the spirit I felt, seeing the people, and feeling like I belonged. I didn't always feel that way, but I had for a while, and it was just a good thing.

The kitchen got cleaned up. I also knew we wouldn't need a lunch as one more angel would be bringing lunch to us. I had contacted them to say that we would be driving to Utah later in the afternoon, so that meant we wouldn't be home for dinner. They were thrilled to bring lunch for us instead. They had planned for fourteen persons.

The cars were filled and we headed to church. As we started to walk in, everyone came up to greet us. Some were surprised that we were even there. Why wouldn't we be there? It was Sunday, and on Sundays we go to church. The family members that wanted to be with us, would also go to church knowing that we would stay the full two hours, and not come home after the first hour, which many people did when they had family visiting. So many commented on how wonderful they thought the funeral was and that they were uplifted by being there. We thanked them and appreciated their comments. There were lots of hugs.

We took our seats. The meeting began. The Bishop conducted. He too, mentioned that he was surprised that we were there, but that he wasn't really surprised because he expected our family to be there. He also mentioned how wonderful the funeral was and how many people were there. He was impressed by the numbers that attended and how many non-members were there. There was a sensitiveness throughout the meeting. The tears weren't far away from the eyes, but mostly because of gratitude and just overwhelming feelings from everything that had transpired. The sacrament portion was so sweet. The spirit was really strong. We knew that the bread and water which represented the body and blood of our Savior, were tender reminders to us, because of His sacrifice, that our family would be together again. His resurrection meant our son would also be resurrected. It was such a bitter-sweet experience with way sweeter than the bitter.

During Sunday School, there were a few more family members that needed to leave. I went outside to say goodbye to them and thank them for coming. Kelli was the first to leave. She had been so awesome to attend to my needs and I so appreciated her being there. Gord and Maria were at Sacrament along with Blake and his family. Blake stayed for all the meetings. Gord left after sacrament as some of his family were also leaving and he wanted to say goodbye to them. I was so proud of Blake for staying. He was doing what he felt was right and wanting to show that he was changing his thoughts and actions. Sheila felt she needed to leave too, because she had to get her kids home for work. It was good to have her with me. I just love her so much. To me, having a twin meant she was always a part of my life. She was half of me and was always there for me. I had expressed my love to her and prayers for a safe return. Then I returned to the Sunday School class.

The third hour we were in Relief Society. As a region, we hadn't completely switched over to the new church programming with only two hours of service. Our area was going to make the adjustments starting in March. So, Relief Society was about conversations dealing with Dalen. The topic was on gratitude and so how could I not express mine with all those there. It was a very good day of meetings.

The love just kept flowing. We were again hugged by everyone, and condolences were expressed.

12:30 p.m. We headed home and our lunch was only about ten minutes behind us. This too, was a very special moment. The sister that wanted to bring us lunch, was inactive. She had only been a member for a short while and just missed her old Baptist church. She felt that our church was true, but just wanted to be where she could express herself differently. For her to bring us a meal meant so much to me. I was so grateful. She arrived and just mentioned how much she loved our family and that she was strengthened by how we had handled ourselves. She hugged and cried on my shoulder. I hugged her back and expressed my love for her. She had brought sandwiches, fruit, salad and drinks. It was so good. Again, we were very grateful for the day and all our continued support.[73]

It came time for the family to get things together so we could start the drive back up towards St. George. Dad and Susan were going to stay in a hotel once they got to St. George. We were going to stay at Alyssa's for the night in Vegas, and just be us together. She wanted us to stay at her house. We would then get up early and head to St George in the morning as Grandma Graham said she would have pancakes ready for everyone. We really didn't know who might go to the burial. So it was just our family that drove up. We again took two cars. Brandon was hauling the empty coffin again and all the flowers that we wanted to put on the grave. I took a few arrangements and of course the coffin flowers. We had left Dalen's truck in St George because we thought Mariah would want to take it back up to school. She didn't think she would want to just sit at home even though we told her to take more time and the school said she could. Mariah wanted to get back to her normal life. We would be careful with her and watch closely for how she was dealing with things.

We followed each other up, and the time seemed to go pretty quickly. It wasn't a bad drive at all. We stopped for gas at the usual

---

[73] To have an inactive member want to serve us, meant so much and graciously we accepted her efforts.

spots and would get a drink. We arrived at Alyssa's house about **7:00 p.m**. We were all kind of quiet. We found our spots and moved our suitcases in. We all visited in the kitchen for a bit and of course since it was Sunday night, we suggested a movie and popcorn. That was our tradition and maybe a nice diversion for the evening. It was a good day. The visits continued till about **10:00 p.m.** where again, I suggested that we all go to bed, which we did after our family prayers. There was a crispness to the air that you could feel with the temperature changing. Only the morning would tell. Goodnight to our Sabbath day.

Burial day—With All We Had Experienced, It Now Became Final

6:00 a.m. It was a very crisp morning. In fact, when I got up there was a heavy frost on the windshields of the cars as I looked out the upstairs bedroom window. When I walked outside for a bit, I could see snow on the mountains surrounding us. That wasn't a normal sight. Dalen loved fresh snow. It was a sight he would have loved. There wasn't a need to rush anything since the burial wasn't till 2:00 p.m. So, the family that was there could relax and the others that needed to drive could do so. I had at least an hour to myself with my thoughts of what today would be. Again and again and again, it was just so amazing to reflect on all our blessings and what had transpired over the past week. Nine days and how our lives had changed. My prayer that morning, was again of gratitude for how we had been taken care of. There was an abundance of peace.

6:15 a.m. We had to leave pretty early because going into Utah, we would lose an hour of time so the family started to get up.

My Dad, Susan and Glade along with Gord and Maria, were at a hotel somewhere in St. George. I didn't even know which one they stayed at. Gord and Maria called to inform me that they decided to head home when they heard of the incoming blizzard. I agreed with them and thanked them for coming. I again thanked Gord for going to the hospital with Mariah and wished them a safe ride home. I suggested the same for Dad and Sue, but they wanted to stay which really meant a lot to me. We would meet up with them at the burial.

Scott's sister Debbie was staying with her daughter Sarah, who also lived in St. George, and they would be there. Family support was amazing. Scott's other sister was staying with Scott's mom, and we would see all of them for breakfast.

Mariah and Kailee were on the couches in Alyssa's front room, and Mariah was actually up first which wasn't normal.

"It might have snowed last night," I mentioned to her.

"Of course it did. Thanks Dalen. I know it's his joke, so we all freeze today standing outside," she replied.

"It might be chilly, but it will warm up by then. There isn't snow on the ground just a heavy frost. We will be fine. And it might be very different in St. George too."

We got up and dressed and again loaded up in the cars to get to grandma's house because breakfast would be waiting for us all. Grandma's special breakfast was her pancakes and the heated syrup. Mariah had asked grandma last night if she could have pancakes for breakfast. Sandy didn't ever sleep well, so for her to be up by 8:30 a.m. was a big deal, but she was up and preparing breakfast for all of us. I gotta say—her pancakes were always really thin, but they were so good. We got there about **9:00 a.m.**, Utah time, just in time for breakfast. It was as good as I always remembered.

Denise and her family also started getting up. They were everywhere: two rooms downstairs, couches in front room and family rooms. They just kept coming. How perfect though, that they could stay at grandma's house for the burial today, so appreciated. With them all getting up, we could eat together.

I had previously told my family that I would like them to be ready by 12:30 p.m.(ish) We were supposed to be at the cemetery a bit earlier than others so we could meet up with Jared, switch the coffins and set up the flowers we had brought to be put around the burial plot. I wasn't going to be stressed about hurrying to get there either. My concern was also that the hearse wouldn't make it on time. Jared had contacted me and mentioned that there was a storm that he was trying to stay ahead of, but he could only go so fast. I prayed for his safety. The blizzard was going through the Salt Lake area, exactly where all our family had to go through that had come down. He mentioned that there were even some roads closed. That caused some more anxiety for sure. He had at least a six-hour drive and would just keep trying to get there, but with the snow, he might need more time. We were just again baffled by his generosity and now determination to make our event of high priority even over bad roads.

"Please protect him Heavenly Father." That prayer didn't leave my mind or heart as well, for all those who had decided to drive and were heading into the same storm. "Let them all be safe. Let them all just be safe."

While Jared was on the phone with me, I just had him reassure me again that he did have Dalen's body with him and that things were ready that way.

Jared assured me that he had Dalen's coffin and his remains were inside. I appreciated his ability to calm my nerves, especially with him facing such bad weather.

Jared would keep us informed of the weather and his progress. He actually had left at about 5:30 a.m. to be there on time. He wanted to give himself plenty of time especially knowing that the storm was getting worse. Again, I just couldn't believe this blessing he was giving to our family. I did pray again that God would really protect and guide him during his travels.

8:50 a.m. We arrived at Grandma's house. Everyone was now up as breakfast had been announced. I think they might have been up already because we could hear communications in all the various rooms, and they were all filled. My family were all on their phones. Normally that would have been an issue, but not now. Our phones were our support. They were lifelines to all who wanted to help and be there for us and we weren't going to deny that opportunity for any of our family.

The bathroom doors seemed like one of those revolving saloon doors. There were three bathrooms, but since we all were downstairs—it seemed logical to use the downstairs bathroom, and it remained busy.

9:00 a.m. Grandma's kitchen had a pretty big island that we all gathered around, and the plate of pancakes lay in front of us all. A blessing was offered and the feast began. I ran through the time frame of today. Again, I reminded my family that we needed to leave about 12:45 p.m. to meet Jared with Dalen. We also had heard that Grandma's ward had offered a luncheon for all in attendance. That too, was amazing. After the luncheon, we knew that Dad and Sue would also head home. So we wanted them and anyone else that needed to travel, to get ahead of the storm coming in.

9:56 a.m. I was getting a bit antsy because it wasn't time to go yet and the morning seemed to just drag on. I needed to go out and do something. I actually went into town and drove around a bit. We needed something at the house, so it was a good excuse for me to get out. As I was driving, I could see the tops of the mountains and they were covered with snow. It was beautiful. Kailee was with me and we both kept trying to take pictures. It was peaceful. Dalen would have loved the view.

11:15 a.m. Still had a couple of hours to go. We were receiving messages and support from people that wanted to be there and couldn't. The family was still sitting around together and reading our messages.

> **—This is Brad your neighbor. We have known you guys for 18 years. We have been praying for your family for the last week. We are so sorry for the loss of your son; we were at the service on Saturday, and it was amazing. It was strange, I ran into Dalen maybe two years**

ago. He was working at Jack-in-the-Box and he was like; "Hey Brad. What are you doing?" He was going on and on and on about normal life. When I left, his face just stuck in my heart and his smile stayed with me. When I heard what happened, I cried my eyes out. Just meeting him those 2 days made me crack up and smile when I thought about him. What a great young man.

—Thinking about you. Hoping all your travels go well. Thinking about you all day.

—I was remembering a day when Dalen was at my house, and we were going out to eat with a group of friends. I wanted to pray on my food, but I felt ashamed cause other people were there and might look at me. I wasn't brave enough I guess. Then I started eating. Dalen was sitting in front of me, and he opened his food and put them on his legs then, closed his eyes and prayed. I felt speechless and admired him for his strength to pray without caring what others might think of him. Since that day, I pray every time before eating no matter where I'm at. Dalen would come to my mind, and he would motivate me.

—Snowing and rain in St. George, it's Dalen pranking us one more time.

—My heart is with you right now. Sending my love.

—Can't be an easy day. Thoughts and prayers are with you and your family.

—I love you. Remember your mighty miracles. Write them down while they are fresh in your mind. They will comfort you especially with the day you will have ahead of you.

—Just wanted you to know I was thinking of you and your family. Our prayers are with you.

12:45 p.m. Our family started loading up into the various cars. The Graham family members would join us later especially for Sandy who wouldn't be able to be outside for that long. It would be hard for her. Again, our family got into one car. Alyssa and Brandon took the suburban. Dad and Susan and the rest of my family knew to meet us at the cemetery around 1:30 p.m.

We started to drive into St. George, and everyone commented how cool the temperature was and how much snow was on the mountains. It really was beautiful outside. It was perfect. It was cold, but I prayed that it wouldn't get worse or at least wait till our service was completed.

To get to Dalen's plot, you had to drive through the old end of the cemetery. It just surprised us how people decorated the grave sites.

"Why do they do that?" Mariah asked.

"I think that's a little extreme," Alyssa replied.

We again were commenting on all the decorations we saw as we drove to the burial place. Again, it was agreed that that wouldn't happen to Dalen's space. Still, it was very interesting for sure. But the cemetery area where Dalen would be, was newer and less decorated, so it was good. The area was just very peaceful.

"You aren't going to do any of that are you Mom?" Mariah asked.

"I don't think that's something I would do. I reassured Mariah.

"I hope Jared was able to make it okay. I still can't believe all that he has done for us. He really has blessed us so much." Scott said.

"I know. He is just a good guy. How can we really thank him?" I asked.

"I'll offer to pay for his gas, even though he said he already included that into the funds for coming down," Scott mentioned.

"That's a good idea Dad. You should do that," Kailee commented.

We passed the one side of the ballpark and made a left turn into the area. There were two other cars there and Jared with the hearse literally had just parked. We reached the cemetery and Jared was there. It was such a huge blessing to see him. He was amazing and we just couldn't thank him enough for all he had done for us. We parked, got out of the car and walked towards Jared.

"Well, I made it. I didn't know if I would actually. There were some tough times for sure," Jared said.[74]

"We are so grateful to you and glad you made it. So, for sure you have my son?" I asked again as we offered hugs to each other.

"Yes, he is here." We went over and he opened the door to show us all Dalen's coffin. That motion took me back for a second. Up to now we weren't really worried about Dalen. We were greeting people and attending to what the situation was, but this was now my son in a coffin and not just an empty one. My son would be buried soon and this now, was very real and very final to me. I regained my composure.

"I'm kind of excited to get rid of this thing. It hasn't been bad, but just a bit different." Brandon commented.

I could understand that too. He had been so good to take care of everything related to the borrowed coffin and exchanging it for the real one. Bless his heart. I love that man.

"Do you have pallbearers to move the coffin with you?" asked Jared.

I hadn't thought of that at all and really it was just Scott and Brandon there. Jared said we would work it out. Then I looked over to the area set up for the funeral. There was a tent, chairs set out and a cement box propped up, along with some flowers that had been delivered there. That surprised me, but what a very nice surprise. Then I saw some young men. I walked over towards them and as I got closer, I realized that they were Dalen's roommates from Rexburg. That stunned me. I was in shock that they would drive so far to be with us. Talk about another blessing. That was amazing. I hugged them all and thanked them for coming. There wasn't much time, so I quickly asked if they could help us.

"We knew we couldn't make the funeral, but we all wanted to be here for his.

"Even the weather wasn't going to keep us away," replied another of the young men. "Dalen changed my life and I owe him this," he responded. "Of course, I would be here."

---

[74] Jared had made the drive from Pocatello, Idaho while driving through a storm and made it safely. What a miracle.

I was just so grateful. And here they were, the exact number of young men we needed to help with the coffin.

"Well, we actually could use your help if you're willing," I stated.

"Of course, anything you need," Will replied.

"Well, we need some pallbearers to move the casket from the hearse and then take it to the stand. Would you be willing to help with that?"

"You bet," seemed to be the response from all the young men.

"Of course!"

"It would be a great honor for us all."

What a miracle. First that they came, but then that they were there early enough (and literally no one else) to help us move Dalen's casket into place.[75]

We started walking toward the hearse. Scott came to greet the boys and Will's now fiancé. I told Jared and Brandon that they were willing to help.

"That's great. So then if you come over here, I can show you what to do." Jared said as he led the young men over to the back of the hearse with the opened door there.

Brandon gave them the rundown of how to lift the coffin. "Once it's up we readjust the weight so we can carry it."

The past few days really were about the life of Dalen. All of a sudden, it was about the body of Dalen. His body was inside the coffin being lifted to the plot. His body was here. This was his final resting place. This would be where my son would rise from the dead when Christ comes again. My son was here. I again so wanted to see inside the coffin to make sure Dalen was there, but I trusted Jared and he had been so generous to us with everything, there was no way I would doubt his words now.

It was a bit of a carry for the young men. Jared asked if they thought they would be able to carry the coffin to the block because

---

[75] All of Dalen's roommates made it down to St. George which was an eight-hour drive. They were a beautiful sight and definitely an answer to a prayer that I didn't know I would need.

if it was an issue, then they would put the coffin on the cart with wheels. It was just really hard to maneuver on grass.

The boys didn't question it at all. They just said they would carry him. It was that fast and Dalen's coffin was being pulled out of the hearse and the boys each grabbed a corner. Just then, Eric and Matt pulled up and literally jumped out of the car and offered to help. That balanced the sides a bit more, so there were now seven young men that were helping. No sooner had I thought that, when Paul arrived, and he too wanted to assist since he was one of the original pallbearers. Jared could now direct the boys and aid with the placing of the coffin.

"Now that makes things easier. This is perfect," Jared said.

That word '*perfect*', just kept being expressed when mentioning events that occurred during the passing of Dalen and all that was involved with the situation **'*perfect*'**.

The four young men, Brandon, Erik, Matt and Paul, with the help of Jared, made the task at hand easier. As the girls, Scott and I stood in reverence, the coffin was then lifted and they began the walk through the gate of the cemetery and headed to the stand. We followed. We watched as Jared made sure Dalen's head would be facing the correct way. I wondered how he knew where Dalen's head was.

"When we put them into the coffin, we know how we lay them, so they go in headfirst into the hearse and come out feet first. We always have them face east so they come up facing the direction Christ will call those from the graves. Scriptures teach us that when the graves are opened, Christ will come in from the east to receive them. To us as members, we believe it's important that they face the right way," Jared explained. That really was important to him and made again the experience so much more sacred. When my son would be called up from the grave, he would be facing his Savior. I loved that.

"Wow, I had never thought of that. That's awesome." Alyssa stated.

"Yeah, that's pretty cool. Thank you." Scott replied.

There was a brief moment that I then got to say hello to Matt, Eric and his wife Janna, and thank them for coming. Hugs were given all around to all that helped.

I asked the girls if they could then help me get the flowers out of the vehicles and place them on the gravesite. I really was amazed that people had flowers delivered to the cemetery though. That was very special. It really made the area look nice and it was again, full of flowers. The coolness from the night actually helped the flowers to not wilt. We had brought what we thought would look like it could go on the burial place. I think there were seven or eight arrangements that we brought from California and then we added them to the other five that had been delivered out there. I also had the casket flowers to drape over. They didn't look fresh or new but were fine. I was grateful for them all. There was one beautiful huge pot that had all kinds of greenery in it that was gorgeous. That would be going home with me.

People started arriving. Dad and Susan and some friends came first. I was placing the flowers out and trying to acknowledge those that were coming in. I had the sign-in books and asked Eric to make sure that they got signed by everyone. I started to seat my family and any others arriving. There was a briskness to the air and it looked like it could have rained or snowed but the prayer was that it wouldn't. For a moment, there were even a few snow flurries. So grateful they didn't continue.

Rick walked in and Mariah seemed relieved that he was there. I saw Holly and Jim Guard. He had been struggling with health issues and to see him there was so amazing. Holly was a special angel and would always hold a very special place in my heart. I saw the Cottoms. She too, had just gone through cancer so for her to make the effort to be there was inspiring to me. I loved that family. I saw the Andersons (use to live in our ward), John and Lisa Petsco (friends of Scotts) from Vegas. Of course, Trish and George were there. Sandy and David came in. Debbie and her girls were there. Denise and her family were there. The crowd just kept getting bigger. We were all blown away. My cousin Kathy and her husband came. The Goodsells (friends met from racing in Mesquite) and so many others. Great Uncle Doyle and Aunt Kam and their daughter came. Boltons, (old ward friends), McNabbs (from Vegas), Ericksons (Scott went to high school with), Maynards (also from Thousand Oaks, Ca) and the crowd kept coming. Phil Painter and his wife, who were also at the funeral, were there from Vegas. Stirlings came too. It's just so awesome that Brandon's family had become part of our family too. I really just wanted to go around and hug everyone, but I only was able to hug a few. Todd Lisenbee (an elder that served in our ward a few years back) came from northern Utah. Sylvia and her husband were there and of course Dad, Susan and Glade who were heading home immediately after, but they stayed for the burial. Paul and his family of course joined us too.

I was just surprised that: 1) that with the weather conditions, these people came to honor our son; 2) that Dalen and our family meant so much, to again, so many people. My silent prayer of gratitude again consumed my thoughts. I was just so overwhelmed to see all these people and feel of their love and support. We found out later that there were over seventy-five persons in attendance. I just couldn't comprehend that, so many people came to honor us and Dalen, and we were very humbled by the sight.

Jared had mentioned previously that he would lead the program. We mentioned that we would repeat just a bit of the funeral program. The girls would repeat some of their memories, and Scott and I would give our thanks. Susan said she would lead the music.

We quickly had to think of a song that people would know and easy enough to sing. We chose "I Know that My Redeemer Lives".

2:00 p.m. Jared welcomed everyone and invited them to all move in a bit closer to make the situation a bit more intimate, and so everyone could hear. Scott and I again took a minute to look through the crowd. We were overwhelmed with all the support. Jared announced that we would have an opening song that Aunt Suzie would lead and an opening prayer by Brandon, Dalen's brother-in-law.

Jared spoke for just a moment on how sad the passing of a loved one was, but also how amazing it was to feel how close the other side was. Jared acknowledged our family and how easy we had made the process for him. He spoke of our visible strength and the power of the testimonies as a family that he felt. He spoke of the restoration for just a moment and how that made this ordeal more comforting. Jared then invited Scott up to give the dedicatory prayer for the burial plot of Dalen.

In our church, we dedicate a burial plot. It is a special blessing offered by a man holding the priesthood power. In the blessing, Scott asked that the ground protect Dalen's body and that no harm would come to his plot. He thanked our Heavenly Father for the life of our son and for his testimony. He blessed the spot that no animals would alter any of the components and that Dalen would rest in peace. He petitioned the angels to watch over our boy's grave and expressed joy for the reunion we would one day have when we would see him again. Scott was very composed. The prayer literally asked for protection upon the person residing there and that on the morning of the resurrection, he would come forth with honor and blessings. "I now dedicate this gravesite unto thee." It was pretty short but important to us, and he finished the prayer.

Scott did a nice job and I complimented him on it when he sat down again. Jared then continued with the brief little program. He invited the girls up to share some of their memories.

The girls came over to me because I had my clipboard with all the notes on it from the funeral program. They asked to see the pages to help remind them of what they had said.

"If you were at the funeral this might be repetitive, but for the rest of you, we just have a few memories of our brother that we would like to share with you," Alyssa led the memoirs.

The girls each mentioned about five memories of their brother and the fun or craziness they shared. They all spoke of the love they had for Dalen and that even though this was hard and sad, it wasn't empty. They were covered with peace, and they all could testify of where Dalen was. They didn't take a lot of time, but it was good.

Scott and I then again stood up and thanked everyone for coming. I rehearsed a bit of Gary's story and then repeated the dream of my cousin about the hardships Mariah and Dalen would face, but that she would help him with his progression. We again bore witness of how much God loves us and so wants us to invite him into our lives.

"We have learned the difference between tender mercies and miracles which we now refer to as 'the mighty miracles'. A mercy is when we petition our Heavenly Father for help and guidance and because he loves us so much, he answers us. A miracle is when we let Him lead, and when you are willing to submit ourselves to God, he will guide us perfectly." I stated.

Scott added a few thoughts. "It's not easy to have your son die. It's not easy watching your family struggle for understanding, but like Sharon mentioned, we have been very blessed. We have seen God's love through all of you. Dalen was in a good place. His last Facebook post was of him going to the temple. He knew who he was and he loved his Savior. I love him. He will always be our '*Buddy Boy*'."

After Scott spoke and sat down, Jared did something we didn't know about and that was he gave everyone the opportunity to say a few words if they desired, about Dalen and how he touched their lives.

A few moments of silence went by, which made me a bit uncomfortable. It was like being in church when we have a testimony meeting (monthly) and no one gets up to express their feelings and testimony. I had always been taught that we should never fear in bearing witness of our Heavenly Father and His son. The awkward silence was kind of loud for me.

Debbie, Scott's sister, got up first. She mentioned how funny Dalen was and that he always made her laugh. She watched his growth through his mission and how much he loved the people. Debbie was one of Scott's siblings that was inactive with the church. She chose to not follow it's teaching when she was about sixteen. She mentioned how much she knew Dalen loved his Lord. "I know that I haven't been active in the church for years, but Dalen always invited me to come back and to remember that the Lord loves me. I've been a basket case through this and haven't understood how my brother has handled this so well, but he has and it has inspired me for sure. I'm really glad I knew Dalen like I did."

She said a few more things that were very touching. She was crying during most of her tribute. Then what surprised me most was her daughter Sarah got up and spoke next.

"Our families really hadn't spent a lot of time together, but Dalen's family were our closest cousins. I remember playing together as kids at grandma's house. I was really surprised when I heard Dalen died. It was actually pretty hard on me. I haven't stopped crying, but I needed to say how Dalen always made me laugh. He was just funny all the time and I really liked that." Sarah also mentioned a few more details.

The contact Dalen had with all our family members that weren't active in the church was very strong and apparent today, and he let all of them know that he loved them. It was just so overwhelming to me. Dalen wrote to every inactive or nonmember cousin or family member during his whole mission, and said how much he loved them as he would bear his testimony to them of the truthfulness of the church and always invited them to come back. He affected their lives and did it sincerely.[76]

Eric Lewis then got up. He talked about how Dalen helped him with the church even at his young age. Eric spent lots of time at our house and was converted and served a mission for the church with the help of Dalen and our family. "Dalen always told me I was like a big brother he never had. We would talk about everything. I see now why he might not have contacted me as much after his mis-

---

[76] I heard from six of Dalen's cousins that weren't active in our church and all mentioned that Dalen would write them monthly while he was on his mission and that he always told them he loved them.

sion because he was too busy being a brother to everyone else. I love Dalen so much. This has been so very hard for me. I can't believe he's gone. I really love you Dalen."

What a sweet moment Eric shared with us.

I looked over at the coffin and thought: *'This was our boy. This was our boy's burial. Our boy—who touched so many lives that we never would have known. Our boy was loved by so many and our boy, my boy, had a testimony of the truthfulness of The Church of Jesus Christ of Ladder-Day Saints. They were all talking about 'my boy.'* I was in awe.

Jordan (Denise's son, Dalen's cousin) also spoke and mentioned how Dalen was a very good example for him and that he now wanted to be more like him, even if he was younger. He loved Dalen's ability to always make you laugh.

Tommy Cottom was an old boyfriend of Alyssa during her senior year of high school. We loved Tommy dearly. He mentioned how hard this was for him and such a big shock. He was really struggling with Dalen's accident. He was the youngest in his family, but Dalen was his little brother, and he loved to play with him whenever they could be together.

A couple more people spoke of how sad this was and how much they would miss Dalen. Then my dad got up. He actually didn't talk much about Dalen, but spoke about how important it was to believe in the atonement of our Savior.

"I know firsthand how hard it is to lose a loved one, and I wouldn't be able to go on without the knowledge of the next life. Our Savior gave His all for all of us. His atonement applies to all of us. There's more to life and death; it isn't the end. The atonement is real, and I love my Savior and I'm grateful for the gift He gave me." My dad then returned to his seat.

It was peaceful and uplifting. Hearts were touched. We felt that Dalen was there. I hoped he was, but Alyssa and Mariah knew it for sure. I've just not been blessed to feel of his spirit yet even though I have prayed that I would. I was okay though, that my daughters were given that special gift to feel of Dalen and witness of his spirit.

Jared again stated how amazing Dalen was. This was a sad occasion, but also an amazing one. We all had felt the spirit there that day, and we would go on and remember Dalen. He called for the closing prayer and then the Bishop of Sandy's ward stood up and invited everyone to their building for a luncheon, and they were planning for everyone, so he made sure all knew of the invite. "*Who does that?*" We didn't know this Bishop. We have seen him at church the odd time that we would come and visit Sandy, but he didn't know us and yet his ward was offering us this blessing.[77]

For about the next half hour, hugs were given and pictures were taken. We made sure our family pictures were taken. It was still a bit cool out, but it didn't snow and we all survived. News also came of the storm and that it was coming quickly. So, everyone that needed to travel or head north, decided they needed to get out on the road. We said our goodbyes so they could head out. That meant less people to attend the luncheon, but the invite was still there. I tried to talk everyone there into coming by the church. Jared said his goodbyes. This

---

[77] The generosity of the people of the Bloomington Ward, to feed our family, was just the sweetest gesture. They said they would have enough for all that were there. How awesome was that.

man had done so much for us. He had carried all our concerns and solved so many of our issues. He leant us a coffin, traded one, and then delivered our son after six hours of driving. How could we honestly reveal our depth of gratitude we had for this man? We hugged and again tried to express our thanks for everything. He pulled away with the borrowed coffin now in its proper place and Brandon finally could drive his vehicle without a coffin in it. I hadn't mentioned that all the roommates had carried Dalen's borrowed coffin to the stand and then had put in into the hearse as soon as they had placed Dalen's real coffin on the cement block for the burial. Jared had pulled all the curtains shut so no one would look inside and wonder why Dalen wasn't over by the burial. We hugged Jared again and said our goodbyes.

Susan and Dad also needed to get going. I was just so grateful for their efforts to be there. Susan didn't like to travel much. It really meant a lot to me that she was there. This wasn't an easy trip in such a short time, but it was so appreciated. Paul and his family had decided to take a few days and make a vacation out of the trip. We too, had to get one more family picture.

I tried to convince everyone to go to the church especially the locals. They kept saying they didn't want to interfere with family and I reassured them it would be okay, especially since most of our family was getting on the road.

(Dad, Paul's family, Susan & Glade, Sylvia and her husband)

The cars dwindled out. I told the girls and anyone else that was still there that they could take some flowers from the gravesite. Everyone had left. Several that were going to the church followed the Bishop over. Scott struggled for a bit while hugging his daughters' before they all headed over to the church The girls all went together since the coffin and flowers were no longer in the suburban. Scott and I were left alone. We were just standing and thinking of all that had transpired. We tried to say our goodbyes. It was getting dark because of the clouds coming in. I went over to the casket for my FINAL goodbye.

"Goodbye my 'Buddy-boy'. I so love you. I love you so much."

It wasn't very long before we saw a big truck back into the burial spot. They were going to lower the casket right then. Scott and I had moved to the car, but sat there and watched. Our son was going to be buried and very shortly. They dropped the coffin down and closed the cement stand and covered it up. I wanted to stay and watch, but Scott said he didn't. I wanted to put the flowers on the plot, but Scott said the guy in the truck would do it. That was it. It was over. There was a moment of silence between us. Then Scott started the car and put it in gear and we backed out. I wanted to stay. I just wanted to stay but again, the thought of another person's feelings was more important. I didn't want Scott to be uncomfortable.

"Let's go now—it's over," Scott said.

I agreed and we pulled out of the cemetery parking lot. While we were driving I looked through the sign-in book. It was verified again that there were over 75 persons there. REALLY??!!!! UNBELIEVABLE!!!!!!! Again, we just couldn't believe how much support we had received. I actually wiped a tear that rolled down my cheek in gratitude once again[78].

We drove to the church and went inside. We weren't sure where things were set up, so we started walking down the hallway. I looked in the gym and nothing was there. Mariah then found us.

"Finally, we've been waiting for you and I'm starving," Mariah said.

"I didn't think they would wait for us." I felt bad that they had because we were about forty-five minutes later than the rest of the crowd. We barely walked into the Relief Society room when the Bishop announced they were ready to start and that a blessing would be offered on the food. There were six tables set up with a beautiful arrangement in the center of each. The food smelt so good. I think we were all hungry as the burial was over and we could now move on. For some, it was a relief which I understood so they could let other feelings come in. Hunger was it. I found a table and had our kids sit with us. There were cheese potatoes, salads, veggies and pulled pork with homemade dinner rolls. Our plates were filled as were our hearts. This was amazing again because our family didn't even know anyone that was serving us. They just wanted to serve, and they did so well.

You heard laughter and good times during the meal. People sat at a table, but also visited with others that sat at different tables. Our little family had increased immensely through this experience. Everyone was just now our family. Scott and I made sure we went to all the tables and spent some time with everyone. I think we counted forty-six people at the church for our luncheon.

---

[78] A count of 75 persons attended Dalen's burial. That was huge to me and all but 20 drove from another area. We were so blown away by the support of everyone.

4:30 p.m. We were all finishing up. Again, from the church people were saying goodbye and heading to their own homes. Scott had invited some of his high school friends that were there, to come over to his mom's house. Sylvia and her husband came too. Maynards, McNabbs and Erickson's came. They just visited and seemed to have a good time. There were lots of stories about their high school days, but also thoughts about Dalen and the experiences they all had. The kids all went downstairs to change their clothes. Teri (McNabb) had brought in this gift. It was a prayer quilt. She worked with a Christian foundation that made quilts for those who had lost someone. There it was again, that word '*lost*'. I hated that word, but I knew it was used respectively. The quilt had scriptures all over it. It was so very thoughtful of her.

It was about another hour or so before everyone left. We appreciated the visits. There were talks about our experiences and how amazing this whole thing had been.

5:30 p.m. Scott wanted to go back to the gravesite: I was glad to go with him. He just wanted to see that everything was okay. I'm not sure what Scott was expecting, but he wanted to see that everything was good. As we drove over, we were talking about the day and how well it went. We were so blown away by all the support and his mom's ward feeding us. It was pretty dark by now and I wasn't sure that we would see things clearly, but it was important to Scott that he be there. We got to the cemetery, and it was very quiet. We were the only ones there. We walked up to the area. All the flower arrangements were laid over the grave. I was actually hoping that the casket flowers would remain on the casket, but they got moved. I wanted them buried with Dalen, but it really didn't matter at this point. It was fine. The ground around the plot was covered with dirt, and the flowers covered the gravesite spot. I loved the smell and the sight. There wasn't any empty space.

9:45 p.m. It was really nice that evening to just have quiet. We sat downstairs in Sandy's house and watched some TV. We were all there and spoke somewhat of our day and the blessings that were poured over us. The only thing left to do was to go home and learn what a new normal life would be like. We all went to bed around 10:00 p.m. (ish). We had the house now to ourselves. Alyssa and Brandon got the other room downstairs and Mariah, and Kailee were on the couches and that was normal for us at Grandma's house.

"Goodnight everyone. Again, another day of miracles and blessings that I hoped you all saw," I stated as we walked to our various bedrooms for the night.

"Yup, it was a good one," Alyssa replied.

"I'm glad it's over," Mariah commented.

"Me too," Scott said.

"Good night Mom. I love you." Alyssa said.

"Love you too," Mariah said.

"Love you girls," Scott replied.

Driving Home

10:30 a.m. It was time to go home. We got up and took our time getting things together. There came a point when it was time to start out on this new normal life. We loaded our things into the various vehicles. Alyssa & Brandon were going to Alamo to swap the suburban back for their vehicle and then head home to Vegas. Mariah and Rick were going to drive back up to Idaho in Dalen's truck. I was super nervous about that. Mariah assured me that Dalen's truck would be way better to drive in the snow up in Idaho than the truck she just totaled. Still didn't help me. I was just nervous for her to be behind the wheel. Rick reassured me that he would drive if Mariah had problems. That helped.

Scott and I were heading home, and Kailee would get ready to go back to work tomorrow. She could take more time if she needed, but she also didn't want to just sit around. That would make it harder on her, so she wanted to be busy. All of us spoke of us returning to our 'normal life':

"Whatever that means now," Kailee commented.

"Yeah, I don't know what that means either," Alyssa commented.

"It means we take one day at a time. It means if we need help, we ask. It means we stay in touch for a while and constantly make sure the other is good. It means we call often, and it means we continue to be close to our Heavenly Father and not drop our relationship with him. It means we are there for each other no matter what. We are here for you all. If you need us, we will be there," I replied.

"Yup, we'll be there at any time. Don't forget that. Don't forget we love you and stay in touch with us, okay." Scott said.

We gave hugs to grandma and started to exit out the door. We got to the parking lot and said our goodbyes. It was a very different feeling, one that we never thought we would experience. Our goodbyes forever now would be one less person. There would always be an empty spot. One day at a time. One day at a time. Scott and I watched as Alyssa drove away. Mariah and Rick were also ready to go. Rick could take as much time as he needed from his work to be with Mariah. That was a comfort. I just prayed that Mariah would be okay back up there, back where it all happened and so quickly after the incident. Driving past the spot and rehearsing in her mind over and over and over again what transpired. I was just so worried for this girl. She promised that if she felt overwhelmed that she would contact her Bishop and seek counseling. Kailee watched as Scott and I started to back out. I hated leaving her there. I wanted us to be together for a little bit more. It was hard to drive away.

Scott of course, had to stop in town so he could get his Diet Coke, but when he did, he also said he wanted to visit the gravesite. That surprised me, but again I wasn't going to say no. So, one more time we drove over to the cemetery and spent just a few minutes where Dalen's body was now laid to rest; one last visit.

There was a frost last night so the flowers didn't handle that too well, but we could still see the expressions of love from everyone.

The drive home was full of phone calls making sure all were okay and safe. Friends still were keeping tabs on us. I don't remember much of the drive, as we were numbed by the event. I stayed busy trying to compile some of the paperwork we had and went through the sign-in books again and was overwhelmed by all the support we didn't just feel, but saw.

3:00 p.m. There wasn't anything that stood out on the drive home except for when we came into our housing track. We were alone. We wouldn't have anyone around us. The kids were gone. We would have to also deal with this new normal on our own. It already seemed so empty and we weren't even in the house yet. When we opened the door this time, there weren't any notes or flowers, but the smell of the flowers still in the garage was amazing. We put our things down and just hugged each other for a minute. During this time, Scott had been a lot more physical than he had been in the past. He needed me, and I him. It was peaceful though. I looked at the cards hanging and the few flower arrangements that were on the table. We would have the whole afternoon and evening to figure out what we wanted to do next.

Alyssa and Brandon had made it to Alamo and decided to head home to Vegas that afternoon, so they were almost home too. Mariah was just coming into the Salt Lake Area. I was nervous for her. About two more hours before the crash site would come into view. She said she was okay.

Scott found his way out to the garage and asked what we could do with the flowers. I brought what was left into the house and again had them all over the place. Some flowers had died. I would rearrange a bit the ones that were still good. That was one part that I just loved seeing all the flowers. It was very nice.

The evening was again super quiet. We sat and Scott watched TV and I wrote out more messages on the computer that we had received on our phones. I had everyone send me all their messages. I typed them all out, every single message sent to any one of the family members. What a treasure for sure. It was about this time that I toyed with the idea that I should write a book because of all the miracles. This couldn't have been normal. This was amazing. This was so peaceful. This was more than just right. I was feeling very prompted. I challenged that idea, that it would be a good idea. The thought process literally began. I was feeling inspired that I needed to tell our story.

7:45 p.m. Mariah made it to Idaho and she said she was okay. She said it was weird with her roommates because they didn't know what to say or do. I told her that if she talked about what happened and her feelings, that that would help her roommates in knowing what to say back. She agreed. Rick was home now, but I know that he was close enough if Mariah needed him and his family would be right there too.

Mariah would face a lot of that—awkward silence as people wouldn't know what to say. The campus knew of Dalen's death and knew that she was his sister driving the truck. She would have to face it alone. I felt so bad for her, but she was the strong enough one to handle it. She thought she would be okay. I reminded her to tell us what was going on with her and that we would be there if she needed us. She said she would be fine. She just wanted to get back to a normal life. It would never be like the normal life we knew, but still a normal life, the routine of work and school and all that was involved with going to college. That part could be normal.

A Week—A Month

There were lots of phone calls to everyone over the next few days and weeks making sure we were all okay. It was interesting how someone would be having a hard time, whether a family member or a friend. They just wanted someone to talk to. I was glad I could be that person for so many. I stayed home that week and again spent most of my time writing out messages and starting to gather my thoughts and vision for a possibility of writing my book. It really was an awesome thought. I wasn't a writer and I wasn't experienced in writing, but I had a good story and I felt like it might be worth reading to someone else. Time would tell. I would continue to just think about the whole thing. For now, I would finish typing all the messages. That would come to be one of the biggest helpers in deciding to write my story because everything was typed out chronologically and the time frame would be right in front of me. I continued. Scott kept saying that it was just something I had to do. It wasn't a healing for me, but an acknowledgement of all the good that came into our lives. It was in recognizing how many times God sent angels to touch our lives. It was the essence of peace all around us. It was to testify of God taking the lead in our lives and the peace that came with that. It was in knowing where my son was and how amazing it all had been. That would be the purpose for me in writing out the messages and thinking of writing this book.

I decided to write the book. I began writing my notes out and was amazed at how the thoughts were coming. Every time we drove somewhere, it seemed to be the best time to write. I had very little distractions and the pages seemed to just keep flowing.

Stacy (my niece) had made an enlarged poster of Dalen's last Facebook post that we had used for the funeral. I had gotten a shadow box and had the idea to put the poster board in it with a flower from all the arrangements. It was what I thought, a pretty neat idea. I spent a day and designed Dalen's memorial post. I thought that the end result was pretty nice looking. I didn't want a shrine or anything like I had seen in other peoples' homes, but I wanted something that would not only remind us of Dalen, but help us feel blessed.[79]

The girls all struggled a bit getting back to the job routine and somewhat of their normal lives. I understood some of their struggles. Several times a day, Alyssa would call.

"Mom, this is just so hard. I just miss him so much. I just don't want to do this," Alyssa would comment.

I would then remind her of all our blessings and miracles. I would remind her of the peace and comfort we had been given and that she could have that peace again, but she would have to ask for it.

One day, Kailee and Alyssa both called and said they were struggling. Kailee couldn't work, she just couldn't focus. She had her Aunt Debbie go to Grandma's house and find her necklace of Dalen's fingerprint. All the girls wore them regularly. Once Kailee had her necklace, she felt better.

---

[79] One flower from each arrangement. The roses held up the best but still a major show of love from our friends and family.

Alyssa's print one time fell out of the capsule. She was lost emotionally. I did everything I could to calm her. I told her I had other prints and I did. When LaNae was making them in the hospital, I had asked for extra copies of Dalen's fingerprint. I didn't know why I might need them, but I had them and now they would be a blessing. I assured Alyssa that I could fix it. I even called LaNae again after I spoke with Alyssa, to see if I could get some more of the charms and explained what had happened. She had mentioned that she had heard of the prints falling out. So our solution was to super glue the cover over the print to keep them more secure. LaNae said she would send me some more charms that very day. I then reported to Alyssa that it would take a few days, but I would get her another charm. She didn't know if she could handle things till then. I offered to mail her my print and would next day air it to her. She said that wasn't necessary. Alyssa was calmer knowing that she could get another print, but was still upset that it wouldn't be her original one, even though all the prints were made at the same time. It made me fix mine though, as soon as I hung up from talking with Alyssa and I passed on to the other girls to do the same. They said they would.

Daily I was checking in with the girls or they were calling me. Mariah was surprisingly doing pretty good. She said it was hard to focus on studying, but she was starting to get back into it. She really liked work. It wasn't a hard job. She worked at a sandwich shop, so no major thinking to it just make a sandwich.

Scott was taking care of the yard and things. I spent a little more time with the dogs and horses. The dogs definitely knew there was a difference. They were another lifeline for me, always there and always ready for me to love them. What a blessing they were to me. I never felt lonely, just alone sometimes. The house was still pretty quiet.

Another Desperate Call

Wednesday March 7, 2018, Scott and I were up in Vegas for the Mint 400 Off Road Race with our LASDMOTORSPORTS team. We were there to help the team unload things and they were planning out who would be where during the event. It was in the evening that we got there, and Scott wanted to stop off at Alyssa's first and take our things in. I actually decided to stay with Alyssa as Scott continued on into the city to meet up with the guys. It was my first time there, but I wasn't really needed there tonight as they were having a parade of all the vehicles in town. All the streets were closed off, and it was supposedly a really big thing. Scott mentioned that he didn't know the time period, so I was happy that I stayed and visited with Alyssa. This was supposed to be a three-day event and a really big deal. It was such a cool thing to have our daughter live there so we could visit her every time we went to Vegas. It was very convenient.

I was getting ready for bed knowing that Scott could be there all night. I never slept well in another bed, so I was glad to try and get what rest I could. Alyssa and Brandon spent the evening with me and they too had to get to bed. Brandon had to work in the morning and had the early shift. Alyssa also had work at 9:00 a.m., so she was tired too. I went upstairs and went to bed.

During this event, we had it planned that we would stay with Alyssa and had decided to spend a few extra days with her after the event to just make sure she was good too.

Scott got home about 1:00 a.m. He said he had a good time and that they really were excited we were there to help them tomorrow and that we would have fun with the team. I was excited. I didn't know what to expect, but we were there to help and it was all a good thing.

1:38 a.m. My phone rang and that startled me. I sensed something was wrong, so I knew I had to answer it and then I heard the desperate voice of Mariah. She wasn't hysterical, but was very upset.

"Mom, I can't do this anymore. I don't want to be here. I want to come home. I can't handle the way everyone looks at me or avoids me. I don't like having to not look at people that seem to stare at me all the time. I just want to come home. I thought I could do this, but I can't. I can't focus any more. School sucks. Please come get me. I just want to come home," Mariah expressed.

I was very shocked. Scott was able to hear some of the conversation and so we both were worried and very concerned for Mariah. I tried as a mother does, to calm her down.

"Mariah we will come get you. We actually are in Vegas at Alyssa's right now. Let me talk to dad and see what he says. We can either fly you home or if you can wait, we will drive up and get you. We can be there tomorrow. What would you like us to do?" I asked.

"Come get me Mom!" she insisted.

Scott could hear that Mariah was struggling. He gave me the look that he knew that we would be going to Idaho. There wouldn't be a question about that either. We talked for a bit with Mariah to calm her down and assured her that we would be heading up to Idaho first thing in the morning, but that we at least needed to talk with Alyssa in the morning to explain to her what we were doing. We also didn't' think it would be good to get up at that moment (1:30 a.m.) and drive up, we would just be too tired. Mariah wasn't asking us to come up that very moment, but did want us to come and get her. Again—a huge blessing. One more time, we were already five hours closer to Mariah than we should have been. We had planned to stay with Alyssa for a few days, so we had our suitcases with us and they were packed for a week. Mariah said she would be okay for now and that we reassured her enough to where she could go to sleep. Our hearts were broken for what this girl had to experience. Scott and I stayed up for a while and expressed our concerns for her. We had to try to sleep though, as we decided that we needed to get up to Idaho as soon as possible so we would be leaving very early.

Alyssa would be getting up early as Brandon had to leave for work about 6:30 a.m. I was already up and had taken Oakley out for her walk. It was just what I did when I was at her house. That way, Alyssa usually could sleep in for a bit except for saying goodbye to Brandon when he left for work. When I got back to the house after walking the dog, Alyssa and Brandon were there, and so I explained what had happened last night and that we would be leaving as soon as Scott got up which would be around 7:00a.m. They were both very concerned for Mariah and what she was struggling with. We didn't know what would happen once we got up to Idaho, but we had clothes to last us for about a week. Another phone call to our neighbor to attend the animals and all was set. I was so overwhelmed again that our blessings and miracles just kept coming. We were closer and had enough clothes.[80]

Thursday March 8, 7:18 a.m. We were about ten hours away from Mariah. I got Scott up and we both showered so we could get going. We gathered our things and headed out the door after saying goodbye to Alyssa. We of course had to stop and get Scott's drink which also meant we would grab our McDonald's breakfast and eat in the car. Scott wanted to get up there. Mariah needed us and he felt there was an urgency.

8:04 a.m. And on the road again. The road seemed pretty clear. It was another time that I could dedicate to my writing. The long trips seemed to be productive for me. It also helped direct my thoughts especially with our concerns for Mariah. We contacted Kailee to let her know what was happening. We told her we wouldn't have a lot of time, but we could stop if she needed us to. She said she was okay. I reassured her then that we would stop on our way home. She was happy with that and told us to drive carefully. We said we would.

We passed through St George, Beaver, Nephi and then went through the valley of Salt Lake. The time was going by pretty quickly.

---

[80] We were needed in Idaho which meant we would be gone for a few more days. We had packed the proper clothes and were ready to be a few days with Mariah.

We still had about five more hours, but we were making good time. The road was still very long but it didn't seem to be as long as the last time we drove up to Idaho. There was a need to get up there, but at least there was no accident that ended with a family member in a hospital. Still, it was an emergency for Mariah.

5:10 p.m. We were coming into Pocatello and I wasn't sure how I would feel. We passed the sign of Colonial Funeral Home, and I had a flood of memories flash across my mind. We then were coming to the hospital exit and I was reminded of the time that I was coming into the hospital parking lot one month earlier. This time Scott was driving. I could see the hill where the hospital was. All of a sudden, I took a few deep breaths. I could feel a tightness come into my muscles. I grabbed the door handle.

"Are you okay honey?" Scott asked.

"I think so, but I wasn't expecting to act this way." I actually shed a few tears as we came to the off ramp. "Wow, what an experience that I don't want to have again. Just think of everything that happened up there and how many blessings we received. I'm just a bit overwhelmed right now," I stated.

Scott grabbed my hand. It wasn't really very often that I had a 'Dalen moment'. Through most of our driving, I was focusing on writing the book. It was very exciting for me to see how things came together; but coming into Pocatello, left me with a big pause. This one hit me a bit harder than I was expecting. I was still good. It was a moment, and it was sad, but also we just kept driving so we could move on with the reality of the scene too. That was a very good overview. I just quickly thanked again all those persons that were there helping Dalen and all they did for him and us. That tenth floor was an amazing place.

We continued on. We got off in Blackfoot to get something to eat. It was an exit that Scott knew what was there, so it made it easy for us. We decided to stay at the same hotel in Rexburg that we stayed at before, so I called and made a reservation. The room was booked and we were set. Now we just needed to finish the drive.

7:30 p.m. We were arriving in Rexburg. We had made great time and the roads were clear. There wasn't much snow till about Blackfoot and even then, it was just on the sides of the road. We drove to the hotel. The snow seemed to pile up a bit more on the road, but that was Rexburg. The snow never left once the first snow came. It would be cold for another month or so. Mariah wanted us to call her when we got there, and she sounded relieved hearing that we made it in town.

We walked into the hotel and checked in. As I was standing at the counter, I noticed a manila envelope that caught my eye. Dalen's name was on the envelope. That really surprised me.

"What are you doing with this envelope that has my son's name on it? Why would you have that? My son passed away last month so why would this be here?" I inquired.

"Well, actually we just found these the other day and needed to look up your information because we were supposed to mail this to you after you left from your last visit," the lady behind the counter said.

"Wait a minute, seriously you had these from our last visit a month ago and you didn't think to mail them to us, or make sure that we got this? What's inside?" Again, I asked, but wasn't too thrilled that this envelope had been sitting there for a month and they chose to do nothing about it. I thought that was pretty poor PR. Scott didn't look very thrilled either.

"The last time you were here, the Bishop brought these over Sunday night after they had their memorial and we forgot to give them to you. When you called in for your reservation today, we recalled hearing that name and remembered the folder sitting in on the desk, so we brought it out," she reported.

Now I was a bit more irritated. I gestured for them to hand me the envelope and I proceeded to look inside while Scott finished signing for the room.

"You didn't give us this packet of what looks like a bunch of letters to our family on the day our son died. You couldn't have mailed this to us? You forgot about them and then just re-found them and still chose not to mail them. Can I ask you how would you have felt being the parent of a son that died and we didn't receive all these words of love and support? I don't count this as a miracle that we are signing in again to this hotel. It's lucky for you and I hope you would feel bad on the lack of attention you gave to our situation. May I take this envelope now?" That was the strongest negative emotion I had felt through this whole ordeal. I didn't feel so good about me lashing out at them, but I was irritated on their lack of integrity.

We both wondered how much longer that envelope would have sat on the desk. You could even see a Post-it Note with our address on the envelope so they really only had to put postage on it and mail it. AGGGGGGGG.

I know I wasn't very happy. The envelope was full, so who ever took all this time to get all these letters probably wouldn't have been very happy either, to know that we didn't receive them. The Bishop that had been in the hospital with Dalen; had also arranged the memorial for Dalen and collected all these written letters. All this happened because of this Bishop, and I couldn't thank him for all his efforts because we never received them.

"Or would you like to mail them to our house?" Scott showed that he was irritated too. "Actually, this wasn't very cool."

The staff apologized and said they were sorry they didn't do anything with them. They felt bad and apologized again. We thanked them and were given our room key. We then found our way to our room and immediately after setting down my suitcase, I looked inside the envelope and sure enough, the ward had written letters about Dalen the day after he passed away. It was amazing. They again had only known of Dalen for about five weeks and yet so many messages were of how they knew Dalen and how happy he always was and how he made them smile. He made them all smile.

There were over one hundred notes. The impact my kid had again on so many people just astonished me. He wasn't just a name. He was known and loved by many. He made a difference in the lives of this ward. The Bishop had delivered the envelope actually before the fireside at the apartment. That was frustrating to hear. That would have meant so much for the other kids to have seen as well. Well now, it was again an incident where we reflected on how our goofy boy touched lives. Our hearts were warmed. I was grateful again.[81]

I felt bad about how I communicated with the front desk, so I called down to apologize to them. They were very sorry and apologized again to me. It was late and time to go to bed.

8:00 p.m. Mariah just got off work and came over to see us. Mariah just hugged me when she came in the door. She just didn't want to let go. "Thanks for coming Mom. Thanks," she said.

"Of course, honey. We told you if you needed us, that we would be there. I'm glad we were able to come," I replied. "That's all I needed Mom, was your hug. I'm good now. I'll be fine." Mariah again, sounded of her ability to handle all this and that she would be fine.

"Good to see you sweetie," Scott said while hugging Mariah.

"Hi Dad, love you," Mariah also was hugging Scott for a few minutes.

We all just sat down and visited. It was good to just be together. We could see that Mariah was struggling emotionally, and this was a big deal for her to ask for help. We were so grateful that we could be together. Mariah stayed for about two hours and then we decided it was time for her to go and us to go to bed. Mariah had mentioned that after she had talked to us last night, that she spent what free time she had in packing up her things. That impressed me, but I was also there to help however I could. I had planned on packing for her which now meant, that I would be there for whatever else she needed. It was late and now time to go to bed. Tomorrow would be another day.

Friday March 9, 2018 I always woke up early, but in a hotel, sometimes it was hard to find a place where I could do something and not wake up anyone. But this hotel had the couch area and so

---

[81] We received an envelope filled with letters from the young adults of Dalen's ward. Their words were amazing and they all spoke of how Dalen affected their lives, even the ones that didn't know him very well. This bishop was truly a servant of God.

that was my spot. There was a half wall that separated the areas. I said my morning prayers and read some scriptures, and then read again all the letters that were in the envelope. I wrote the Bishop a letter back and would ask the front desk if they could mail that for us especially after the mistake that had occurred.

A couple of hours later, Scott decided to get up. We were going to meet up with Mariah at McDonald's for breakfast and then decide what we would do during the day.

"Well, I'm hungry so let's go eat," Scott said. And then sure enough, Rick also arrived. We weren't surprised to see him, so we asked him to join us and we all had our McDonald's breakfast.

The plans were to hang around till Mariah was finished with work. She had to work from ten to two, but then we would have the rest of the day to do what needed to be done. We really didn't do much. It gave me time to work some more on my writing. If nothing else, Mariah knew we were there for her. We talked several times during the day while she was at work. You could hear some relief in her voice.

It was decided that we would have some fun while we were in town. Mariah had tomorrow off from work and could take a day off from her studies. It was decided that we would go skiing at Kelly Canyon. Boy would that bring back memories for Scott. I felt that I shouldn't go as it was meant as a daddy-daughter date and that Mariah needed that time with her dad. I also had a unique sense that I shouldn't go. I didn't know why, but there was something that told me that if I went, I would somehow hurt myself. I would hurt my knee. I didn't know what that meant, but I felt something would go wrong. Then Rick said he could get the day off. And then Mariah's friend Aubree said she would love to go and then it was a party. I didn't want to be left out, so I decided I would go.

Throughout the day, Scott and I drove around town a bit. We needed to go up to the campus and let the school know we were taking Mariah home and wondered what they could do. They were so helpful and told us that it wouldn't be hard to contact the instructors and have them put their classes online for her. That was a great solution.

There was only five or six weeks left and to just throw away all her work wasn't good. That was a huge blessing for sure.[82]

While we were on campus, Scott wanted to look up the man he knew that worked there. We looked him up and found him. His name was Glen. Scott knew him from way back when Scott attended what was then 'Ricks College'. This guy was in Scott's dorm and now was working there. We went to his office, and it didn't take long to discuss the reason we were there. Glen's sister had died several years ago, and so he could relate to what Mariah was going through. We had an amazing visit. It was just not normal to talk about our son's passing as such a positive experience. It was just a comfort. We could only talk about all the miracles and the support that we received. Our visit was enriched.

Mariah was now off work, and I thought it would be good if we could exert some physical activity, so I talked her into playing racquetball with me. It had been years for me, but I used to love it. I knew I wasn't the greatest athlete, but we could have some fun. We went up to the campus and got the things we needed. Mariah was not into it.

"What the heck Mom, why are you hitting it so hard?" Mariah asked.

"You're supposed to. That's the game. Try to hit it so the other person can't return it." I had to give her the basics on racquetball. I had a blast and Mariah put up with me. She was figuring it out and things were just fun. Scott was watching from above for a bit and then he ran to get his Diet Coke. It felt so good to sweat, and we just laughed. We both made some pretty good shots too. When our hour was up, we both felt good. We had played hard and laughed more. From there, we went over to Kevin's house. He was the fireman that helped Mariah in the hospital with Dalen. His daughter was Aubree (Mariah's good friend that also was at the hospital).

We just sat and visited in their front room. They talked about their family happenings and somehow the conversation always ended

---

[82] The school was very helpful with Mariah's classes. They arranged with all her teachers that her classes could be put online and she could finish out her semester at home. What a blessing for sure.

up on Dalen and how things were going for us to which we said, "All was well".

It was getting close to dinner time, so we decided to all go eat out at Applebees, one of the only restaurants in Rexburg, again. Mariah had Rick come and meet us there too. Kevin's son worked there, and Aubree would join us after her shift at work. Party on. It was a good time. There were moments that we had to take and reflect on our past month, but they were only moments. We did however, explain to those following us on social media why we were there, and that was because Mariah was struggling. Everyone was super surprised when Mariah said she wanted to go back to school so quickly. We agreed that the atmosphere with students her age and schoolwork and work would all help her adjust better than sitting at home and having nothing to do. They weren't really surprised when she felt it was too much. We were okay with that too.

Mariah and Rick came back to the hotel with us. I think she wanted to be with us and we were good with that. Mariah wanted some more discussion on our 'fun' day tomorrow that we all wanted.

I still felt that I didn't need to go skiing, but then Rick and Mariah were trying to convince me again, that it would be fun and they kept inviting me. It did sound fun, but in my mind, I just kept hearing that if I went, I would hurt my knee. I said again that I didn't need to go, but they pleaded some more and I consented. We had brought up our winter things (jackets and gloves) because there was still snow in Vegas when we were at Alyssa's, and we knew it would be cold helping with the race. How amazing that we were prepared to be in Idaho where it was very cold. It was going to be fun. It had been quite a few years since Scott and I had skied. No worries, we would pick it up, or I hoped we would.[83]

9:30 p.m. It was still pretty early for Mariah, even though it was late for us. So she suggested that we go up on campus and watch

---

[83] We had the proper attire to head up to Idaho and be with Mariah. Not really in our plans, but again a major blessing. We were prepared for snow and that led to the opportunity for fun in the snow later.

the guys play volleyball. It would be fun and I was already to go. We got to the field house, and I saw the ten or more courts all being used in one area. We went into another room and there were about eight more courts. We walked into the room and someone immediately recognized Mariah and yelled out: "Hey Mariah is here, Dalen's sister", and the room stopped. Everyone looked at us.

One young man came over and as he approached us he asked: "Aren't you Dalen's parents?" and he shook our hands.

"Yes we are," Scott replied.

The entire room started to gather around us. They were amazing. They all were so solemn and yet they wanted to be by us.

"So you all knew our son Dalen?" I asked.

"Yes" were the answers along with some comments on how they knew him.

Everything stopped and we all just grouped together and spoke of Dalen. We heard how fun he was and how he saved one team and helped another. I heard of the 'underdogs' that he helped make into a team. It was just so much fun to hear all their stories. I thanked them all so much for the volleyball and shirt with all their names on it that they sent us after Dalen died, that we used for the funeral. It was just so fulfilling and rewarding to be with this group. I wanted to talk with each one and hug them. They just couldn't stop talking about Dalen and how he changed their playing of volleyball. It was awesome. I reflected on all the conversations I had with Dalen as he was running off to play volleyball instead of studying. I didn't get mad at him, but strongly encouraged him to spend a bit more time with his studies. But now I understood. This was where he felt at home. This was where he could play, and he did with all his heart. This was where he lived. This was where he could shine. I loved it. We didn't want to take all of their time, but we asked for a picture first and it was just a lot of fun. Another amazing experience where we saw where our son had touched so many lives.[84]

---

[84] We physically saw the number of people that not only played with Dalen, but like him and commented on how he made them better. So very humbling to experience for sure.

This was just some of the students that played with Dalen but what a treasure to meet them.

Such a highlight for us. We couldn't stop talking about what an amazing experience that was. They were all just good kids and in those few minutes, they all became family and were just fun to hang with them. I will personally never forget what they all did for Dalen. Just so amazing.

We got back to the hotel and it was about **10:30 p.m**. Since we were going skiing tomorrow around nine, we thought it was time to get some sleep. We had asked Mariah if she just wanted to stay with us or go to her apartment. She actually wanted to stay with us, and I was okay again with that, so we drove by her apartment on our way home from the gym and she got some of her things. I loved having her with us and knowing that she needed us meant a lot to me too.

Another day down. Another day down.

Lesson Learned the Hard Way

March 10, 2018 We all got up and were excited to start our day of fun. We ate our McDonald's breakfast and then headed up to Kelly Canyon so we could get the ski rentals. It was bringing back a lot of memories and good times for both Scott and me. It was a very pretty drive and although the snow wasn't very thick at first, there was a good base when we started through the mountains and were getting closer to the resort. Scott knew it well as he had a ski class there when he was going to Ricks College. I skied quite a bit in high school but only one other time since then. Mariah and Aubree were actually the beginners and Rick was the daredevil with no fear.

We got our skies and started on our way to the top of the mountain. It was pretty funny to watch Mariah try and figure out how to use the ski board. We had taken all our kids one year, but she only had one day, and she was probably only ten years old. Today, Mariah learned that in order for her to stop, she had to fall on her butt. It took a minute for all of us to get situated and ready to go down the hill. Rick was pretty good. He would go just a short way and then wait for all of us. There were some obstacles all the way down for boarders to play with and Rick was all over them.

Scott and I were skiing, and the others were snowboarding. It took a minute, but then it was starting to feel good. I was cutting and heading down the hill. We took our time as Mariah was still figuring things out. We were doing better and moving down the hill when I was cutting over to a place closer to the left of the mountain, and I cut wrong and felt my knee pop out. I couldn't stand. It hurt, and it hurt a lot. We were only about one hundred feet from the bottom of the mountain. No one saw me or was with me, so I literally started scooting myself down the hill. Finally, Mariah looked up and saw me and yelled up to me:

"What happened Mom? Are you okay? Do you need help?" and they were also kind of laughing because I was so close to the bottom and just missed it.

They called for the ski patrol. I was so embarrassed and told them not to worry about me and that I could make it down. I started scooting down. I was told not to move. So, I stayed up on the hill until someone could ski down to me and help out. This was such a bummer. I was just so upset with myself, but I was also so very humbled as I remembered my impression.

After being put into the cage and taken to be looked at by a paramedic in the back room, I was hurting and it was intense pain. They examined me a bit and said I needed to go to the hospital. One run, not even one run. It was just not fair. One run. They suspected that I might have broken my knee. Scott was making a joke that he didn't want to take me to the hospital.

"I'm just getting started and only had one run." Scott proclaimed.

We were all laughing but reality was, I had to go to the hospital. Rick offered to take me in, but I wasn't too excited for that, so I made Scott agree to take me in.

"You owe me a ski trip. You owe me big time. Seriously, one run. You owe me," Scott exclaimed.

He was right. I had to agree. We were still laughing when I wasn't hurting. We encouraged the kids to stay and have some fun. Scott would run me into town (only about twenty-two miles away), and then come back and join the kids for hopefully half the day. I was good with that.

"Really Mom! One month. Only one month since Dalen passed and on the one-month anniversary, there was another incident involving a hospital. Seriously Mom, you had to pick today," Mariah stated jokingly.

Scott drove the car up to the lodge and backed in. I slid myself into the back. It wasn't the worst I've been in, but I was still in pain and my leg was swollen pretty badly. The bumps were a little hard to take, but Scott did his best to hit every one of them I'm sure. We laughed again.

I just kept thinking of the prompting I had had. I was told that if I went, I would hurt my knee and badly. I wasn't going to go, but then I gave in to the invitation of my daughter and her friends. I had dismissed a prompting that was very real. I was mad at myself for not listening, but again thanking my Heavenly Father that my accident wasn't worse. I believe my lesson was learned. I would try really hard to head the promptings I from now on would feel.

We drove up to the ER and no one was there. Literally, Scott couldn't find anyone for a minute when he walked in. That was different—small town thing I guess. A nurse then came in and two other nurses with her. They immediately came to my attention and brought the gurney to the car for me to slide onto. The doctor came into the room probably about three minutes later. In fact, they were still doing my vitals when he appeared. That was quick. He knew I would need x-rays and ordered them immediately. I was only in the ER for about twenty minutes, and I had blood drawn and x-rays taken and results. That was pretty cool. I liked having the full attention. I heard the radio though, that a possible heart attack was coming in. With that, they asked me to move to the next bed because the one I was on, had all the emergency things connected to it. They moved me to the next bed. I also had to go to the bathroom but didn't know how much I was supposed to move. My leg was in a brace, and they gave me crutches. I was told that I had broken my knee and would need to keep it elevated and take some medication. They told me to see my primary doctor when I got home and until then, I really only could take it easy. I got that.

I had to go the bathroom, so I picked up the crutches and had Scott help me as I tried to make my way down the hall. I again couldn't see the nurses because they were prepping for the next patient coming in. When I was coming out of the bathroom, I saw one of the nurses.

"What are you doing?" she asked.

"I really had to go to the bathroom and I couldn't find anyone," I replied.

"Are you okay? Did you need any help? I'm so sorry that we weren't here to help you. But it looks like you figured things out for yourself," replied the nurse. I think she was impressed with my gumption.

"Yeah, I think I got it. Do I need to do anything else or are we okay to leave? I know you have an emergency coming in," I commented.

Literally as soon as I said that, the doors opened and a man was being wheeled into the exam room.

The nurse gave her consent for us to leave if we wanted to. There was a form on the nurses' counter that she needed me to sign, but they had already explained what I needed to do when I got home. We were good to go. She ran into the other room to assist the other medical staff.

I told Scott we could go and since I was already on the crutches, why not. We picked up my prescription on the way back to the hotel. I was okay now that I had my knee wrapped and some pain medication.

"This changed our plans," I stated as again, Scott and I were laughing. One run. Not even one run—kept running through my mind. I urged Scott to go back to the hill and have some fun. It was only **11:30 a.m.**, so there was still a lot of time for playing. Scott called Mariah and she actually said that they were probably ready to come home too. She was tired of skiing on her butt. Scott said he would go get them. I encouraged them to stay and play. I asked her to just have fun. They all said they would figure it out when Scott got back up to the mountain. I would be fine with the remote and a drink and some munchies till everyone got back. I couldn't do a whole lot anyway, but it was all okay.

I only reflected on not listening to my prompting. The impression really was strong. I had never felt anything like that before. That in itself was a miracle—even with the wrong choice, I had felt the impression and heard the warning. I heard the Lord trying to guide me and I put it aside. I prayed that I would have learned my lesson and try hard to follow what I had felt. It would forever be one of my prayers from now on.[85]

---

[85] I had felt and heard an impression from the spirit and I didn't follow. The miracle was though, that I heard it. The lesson learned was that I would try harder to follow promptings and not question them.

The gang arrived in a few hours. They were all laughing and having a good time, but they cut their day short probably because of me. I felt bad for that, but I couldn't change it either.

There wasn't much I could do now so when they got to the hotel, we were figuring out a way to get all of Mariah's things over to Rick's. Mariah's semester would end in April, but then the Spring semester would start almost right away. Since she could finish her semester online, we knew that she would want to be back for the spring semester to continue on. Well, it made sense to just leave her things there in Rexburg instead of hauling it to California and then back again. Mariah had boxed almost everything up the day we drove up, but we decided to go to her apartment and see what else we could help her with. Rick said there wouldn't be an issue for her to leave her things at his house. We were going to leave Dalen's truck there too because as a family, we had planned to go on a cruise between semesters in April. Rick was now going with us and would be driving down and then would bring Mariah back up for school after the cruise. Again, the plan seemed perfect.

We decided to have Scott and Rick go with Mariah to her place and load up everything. I wanted to go too, so I did. There were only a few things that weren't boxed up yet, so Mariah did that while Scott and Rick started loading everything up into Dalen's truck. I was surprised how full it was. Mariah had a lot of stuff. The truck was pretty full. I thought that this was still the best idea though, so we then drove over to Rick's house. We got to see his parents for a minute. They were good people, and it was nice to see them. Once we got there, we noticed that it might be getting cold again. Quickly we made the decision to get a tarp and cover the truck as it would be outside with all of Mariah's stuff in it. Everything were in bins, so it all was protected. We put as much as we could in the cab to help out, but there was still a lot in the back. Rick remembered there was a tarp in the garage. We had offered to go get one, but he thought it might be big enough. Sure enough, it was. We tied it down. I guess I should say, the men tied it down. I was sitting in the Durango watching. We felt that we had accomplished what we needed to. The decision was also made, that we would leave in the morning and start our drive home. When it got close to church time, we would find a building and attend at least Sacrament. Then we could continue on. We also thought that we would stop at Grandma's and spend Monday with Kailee. Well, let's see where this goes. And the night now was back in the hotel room and relaxing with Mariah with us.

Good night my family wherever you are.

Fast Forward in Time

Jordan Castro's Dream

I had a dream that I was hosting at a really nice restaurant. In walks Dalen Graham, smile big as ever. We catch up. He tells me that he's doing awesome and that he is happy. I go to seat him in a special room where there was a reservation for Dalen. God sat at a table with all of these amazing guardian angels who were all wearing white. They were all very peaceful and inviting. They all looked like normal people, but just had this aura about them. I believe there were twelve seats, ten angels and God, with God reserving the last seat for Dalen. Dalen was wearing white too. There was a chair right beside God for Dalen, as God invited him to take the seat which was to his immediate right, and join him. It was a super long table, and they had all been waiting to have dinner with Dalen. All I can say is that I can't tell you what God looked like, but I can say that he was there, and it was the most peaceful and uplifting dream I had ever had. It was the most humbling thing I had ever experienced, and I felt truly blessed to have been able to have, and remember, a dream like that. Dalen was so at peace and at the side of God; we can sleep comfortably knowing he was happy and was where he should be. If our faith had ever been shaken, don't worry.

My Facebook Post March 18, 2018 Some very good news. We just got the list of organs and tissues that Dalen contributed.
*__Kidneys__ went to two male recipients, one we had just met.

*<u>His liver</u> 3 minutes late for transplant but used for 3d bio studying. They had never seen such a good sample.
*<u>Heart valves</u> which could be used for up to a year for transplants.
*<u>Tendons</u> because he was so tall, they would help several patients.
*<u>Lg veins in his legs</u> used for heart bypass surgeries.
*<u>Corneas</u> Dalen helped someone see—his favorite sense.
*<u>Skin off his back</u> for burned victims.
*<u>Bones from legs/arms</u> whoever needed a bone fragment or the bone.

Felt so overwhelmed and blessed. What an amazing thing. Everyone involved with transplants were given such special gifts. I'm grateful for the skills and dedications of all the team members and for what they do. Thank you to all.

March 20, 2018

All the stories we received over the next little while were just so powerful to me. I'm so grateful for their insight. Thank You Heavenly Father for again sending so many angels. Another story about Dalen came from my sister Susan.

I had an experience happen to me as I was driving down to your place for the funeral. I only drove the car once on the whole trip. It was quiet and I don't really remember what I was thinking about when all of a sudden this story played out in my mind. It was very real to me and I hope I can convey the reverent feeling it left me with……

<u>Heavenly Father:</u> Dalen it's time.
<u>Dalen:</u> I know.

<u>Heavenly Father</u>: It's time to make your decision. You can choose to come home now, with your testimony intact, or you can choose to stay and risk your demons coming back to haunt you and possibly destroy your testimony.

<u>Dalen</u>: I don't ever want to lose how I am feeling right now…so, I choose to come home.

<u>Heavenly Father</u>: All right, but now you get to decide HOW.

<u>Dalen</u>: I've been thinking about it, and I think I know what I would like to have happen. I want to go when I am feeling totally happy. And if I have to go now, I don't want to just have some boring heart attack. I wanna go in memorable style! It's gotta include a car, cause my family is all about cars. I want to be doing something that I really like, and I want to have my sister with me because she always makes me laugh.

<u>Heavenly Father</u>: Are you sure you want to put your sister in this situation?

<u>Dalen</u>: Yes. I think it will be okay. You see, Father, I have had a lifetime of seeing my sisters forgive me for so many stupid things that I have done. I know Mariah will forgive me for requesting this very difficult thing of her. Oh, don't get me wrong, she will deck me when she sees me again, but I really believe she will understand that it is because I love being with her, that I am asking her to take part. I know it is selfish of me, but I want to go laughing and joking, and being excited about WHERE I AM HEADED! My only request is that Mariah be kept safe.

Heavenly Father: If this is what you want, then it shall be done as you have requested.

As quickly as my impression started, it ended. It was very real to me, and I kept reflecting upon it over and over for the next several hours. I don't know if this is how it works. But what I think it has taught me, is that there is NO reason for the "What if's" or the "If Only" thoughts. That would supersede God's will and none of us have the right or power to do that. The only reality is that hard as it is to accept, you were asked to be a part of God's plan and not the cause.

With all my love, your sister Susan.

March 23, 2018 A document came in the mail today that I never would have thought in my lifetime that I would receive. Scott and I just stood and stared at the piece of paper when we opened it. This made everything very final.

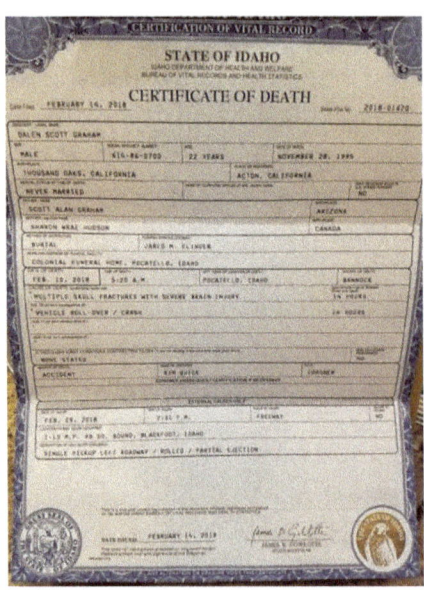

We all tried to regulate our lives. We were doing pretty good. There was constant communications with each other, and the days seemed to go by. Then there would be a moment or a day, when someone just couldn't handle what they were going through. We just reflected on our blessings and the calmness and peace returned.

I was surprised how many times Scott for example, would just start to cry and really couldn't figure out why except he missed his son.

For the girls, we made quite a few trips up to either Idaho, Utah or Nevada to check on them and make sure they were okay. Each of the girls needed us at one time or another. Through the next several months, we made eleven trips to check on someone at some time.

> **Jordan Jepperson (Dalen's cousin) Driving down the highway one of the overhead signs read: "Eleven lives lost on Utah roads in February." My cousin Dalen lost his life a few weeks ago not on Utah roads but up in Idaho. I had a chance while driving to just think about him and his passing. There are going to be triggers in life that remind us of him and of his tragic accident. This was a trigger for me, but I choose to accept those triggers and enjoy the moments where his memory comes to mind. I'm grateful for these triggers, it's how his memory will live on, through little things we see and hear. Thanks to that one sign, I was able to reminisce a little. I was taken away from reality and saw in my mind Dalen's smiling face. What a blessing these little triggers of the mind can be. I'm thankful for that one today. I miss Dalen but know his memory will live on. He left a mighty impression on the world.**

April 10, 2018 There was just something about this date, two months since Dalen passed away. Today we also had to make a decision that would affect most of our family. Our one dog Sierra was seventeen years old. She had been struggling lately in climbing up our hill from the horse corral to the house. She simply couldn't move. I pushed her many times. She looked like she was in pain. Her one eye was getting a cataract too. She didn't eat as much. I was very worried for her. A decision had to be made. Our family's cruise was coming up and we would be gone for a week. Our neighbor was going to watch our animals which she had done many times, but with Sierra getting worse, I asked the girls what they thought we should do.

"Mom, you just can't put her down because you want to. She is fine," Alyssa stated.

"She hasn't been fine for a while Alyssa. She has been struggling and it's hard to watch sometimes," I stated.

"I think you should put her down Mom. We aren't going to be here and to have someone else worry about her wouldn't be right," Mariah stated.

"I agree with Mariah." Kailee also thought we should put her down. "It wouldn't be fair for her to suffer and not be there to watch over her and help her."

I called my neighbor and asked her for her vet's number. I would get his opinion and go from there. "Well, you are in luck. He just happened to stop by a few minutes ago because he was in the area and wanted to see that my horse was good. He had given her some medicine a few days ago and wanted to know that it was working. I'll just have him come over. I'm sure he would love to help you out," my neighbor responded.

I was in shock. It literally took away my decision and my fear of putting Sierra down. This way, I had no choice. It was already made which made things so much easier for me. I couldn't believe another miracle from our Heavenly Father so quickly. It was amazing.[86]

I told the girls what was happening. They too, said it was a good thing and a blessing. I asked Mariah if she wanted to be with me when the vet put Sierra down. She said no.

---

[86] The Vet just happened to be at my neighbor's house. Not only that, but he had time to put Sierra down right then which meant I wouldn't have to try and decide when to put our loved dog down.

The vet drove up into our driveway. He had been to our house before when he helped one of my horses who was colicky, so he knew me.

"So I was in the neighborhood, so why not help you out. I literally was just right here. I understand you want to put your dog down. It's the black one right?" he asked. Again, since he had been here, he knew my animals.

"Well, I actually wasn't sure, but then I called Christine and here you are." I commented.

We talked for just a bit, and I explained our situation. I paid him first because I wanted to spend that time with Sierra once it was done. He agreed that it was a hard decision, but he would do the same thing if it was his dog. He explained how it would happen. He would give her a needle with medicine. Some dogs have some convulsions and others just twitch a bit and then it's over. Then they would just be still and it would be finished. They would have passed.

"It happens very quickly though." He asked again if this was what I wanted to do, and I said 'yes'.

Within two minutes I was holding Sierra's head and stroking her as I had her lying beside me on a blanket I had brought out. I loved this dog. She was amazing. She had been with me on so many adventures. She was our coyote chaser. She was the horse chaser. She would go on all my rides with me. She was my comfort when Scott was gone for a few days and we would bring her into the house. Dalen would try to claim her as his dog and take tried to take her up to his room, but she would usually come down to mine. She was my comfort so many times when I would just go outside and hug her. I knew Dalen would be greeting her. He claimed her as his dog, but he knew she really was mine. I really loved this dog. We all loved her so very much, even though Scott would never admit that he even liked her. The injection was given. And then there was no more movement. She was gone. My beloved dog of seventeen years was gone. It was so peaceful. I thanked the vet. He said I was welcomed and sat with us for a minute and then decided he needed to go. He listened for a heartbeat and there was none. I just sat on the lawn for a while with Sierra. This amazing dog had outlived Dalen in this house. We got her only after being in the house for a few weeks. She was the main Christmas present that year—2001. She was Dalen's dog (so he claimed) and my best friend. I loved this dog.

Titan would be very lonely. He would miss Sierra terribly as they did everything together.

Scott came home and I told him we needed to bury Sierra in the back. He and Mariah dug the hole. I had a blanket under Sierra for the purpose of moving her when it came time. We just picked her up carefully and put her in the wheelbarrow so we could transfer her to the back yard. We laid her down gently in her resting place and then covered her up with the blanket. Then they slowly started covering her with dirt and we placed rocks over her after so no animal would harm her. I just loved this dog so very much. There again was another whole in my heart that would never be filled.

Another type of—'just moving on'.

April 14–21, 2018 Scott and I had purchased a cruise for the family a year ago. Then Dalen passed away, and we couldn't get our money back. The family thought it would be good to go and enjoy ourselves for a bit. We couldn't get Dalen's refund, but they mentioned that it would be only $6.00 to change the name to someone else so we chose Rick to come with us. We were all so excited to go.

We left from Long Beach and were sailing down the Mexican Riviera. We had three stops along the way. I had been there before, once with Mom and once with Sheila, and I loved it. Scott didn't want to go because he said he would never support anything Mexico did. But he went. We went on an ATV ride along the coast. We went snorkeling for the most of us, and scuba diving for Brandon. We went fishing and Mariah caught one. We saw whales and followed them for a bit. We went zip-lining and had a blast. The food of course was amazing. It couldn't have been better. How do we describe things?—Oh yeah—PERFECT!!! It was perfect. Such a blessing for all.

As soon as we got into port, our phones were on again, and I got a huge message from Sylvia saying that Gary's kidney was awake and functioning perfectly. There couldn't have been a better message. How exciting for him.[87] Gary still had some issues, but he was feeling better than he had in years. What a blessing for him. Everyone was so excited to hear the news about Gary as we exited the ship and our trip that would forever remind us of good times, fun adventures, and family time, had come to an end.

April 27–30, 2018 Every year, Scott is in charge of a race that we put on in Vegas. There are police officers from across the country and Canada that come together and race each other. They all had become a second family; they were good people. April was our month. Scott worked so hard getting the track personal to include our group in their race. We would get two or three runs each day. We got sponsors to donate prizes and handouts. Everyone left with something which wasn't a normal thing when racing. It was a lot of work, but it always ended up being a really good experience.

There were fourteen teams there this year. We had Frank from Louisiana, Gary and Reggie from Nevada, Mike, Blair, Terry, Kien from Canada, to name a few.

---

[87] Gary, who had suffered so much in his life, was getting better and his kidney was functioning. It was working. Dalen's kidney had been accepted and was now awake and working well.

We were all staged together and just become an extended family as we mingled with each other and got caught up on our lives. This year was different with Dalen absent.

The first day, after all the cars had done a test run, everyone was invited to join together. We weren't sure what was going on, but Gary Davis came forth. Gary was a member of the church that had been so fun to get to know over the years. His family always came to support him, and it was fun watching them grow each year too. Dalen would always play with their grandkids. Gary was choked up as he looked at our family and related that he couldn't understand the pain that we were going through. The track and all the racers there, were then going to dedicate this race to Dalen whom they all loved. There were stickers that were handed out to each team that would be on each car for the weekend. That was so humbling. As a family, we just were blown away.

Everyone was emotional. Our family were the rocks. Scott thanked them again and expressed that this was just amazing. There really weren't words to describe how full our hearts were and how overwhelming the love between all these members of our race family was. Then they presented us with a banner about Dalen and again were just so grateful. We hung it up in our pit for the weekend. It was visible to all that came around.

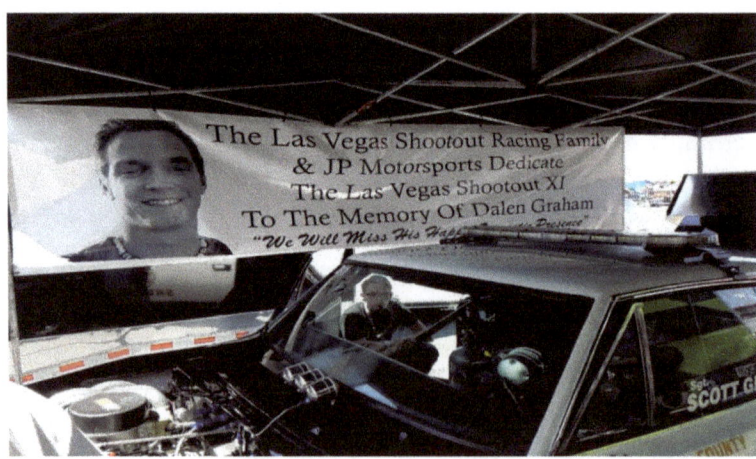

The weekend went pretty much as planned. Scott would stay at the track with BJ (engine builder) and Chris (friend and racer). Sometimes the group would go out for dinner Thursday night so I would try to get there for that, but usually I would be there Friday, Saturday and Sunday with the kids, and we would stay at the hotel. We learned quickly that we would pay for an extra day at the hotel rather than to fight the traffic going back to California on the weekend. It was usually pretty quiet by then too. The Hilton Towers were pretty close to the track, and we knew the place well. The girls always had fun even though we would arrive quite late at night and leave very early in the morning. That was just the usual racing weekend. Even though Alyssa now lived in Vegas, we didn't all fit well in her home with only one extra bed, so we still stayed at the Hilton. It was just easier.

Thursday we had a few runs with the car and Friday, we had a few more. That's usually called 'Test and Tune' at the track. The personnel from the track were so kind to us. One of the managers kept asking about Dalen and how we were doing. He had mentioned that they would do a memorial for our son. I didn't really know what that meant, but was very appreciated. He asked me Dalen's favorite hymn. I thought that too was an interesting question. I had to think for a minute of the answer. I'm not sure that I mentioned his exact favorite, but I did mention one that he liked.

Friday, after a day at the track, we had a meal sponsored for us all for dinner. What a treat to sit with each other and eat such a great meal. What a highlight of the weekend.

Saturday we got to the track early. Scott had made a trial run and things were going well. At the track, it was always funny that we hurried, hurried, and then would wait and wait and wait to make a pass. Scott's runs were about 9.3 seconds, so it was also over very quickly. It was definitely a thrill though when he ran. It was just over so quickly.

The track personnel came over to our pit area and said that they would do the memorial around 11:00 a.m. We said we would be there. The whole group with all the race cars were up for our runs. Each car came up and ran their race, but something was different at the end. Usually after each race they would reach the end and just come back, pick up their time slot and go back to their pit area. This run, all the cars stayed up at the top.

The announcer in the tower then did something I had never seen before.

"Ladies and gentlemen. We have a very unique moment that we would like your attention for. There is a member of our racing family that have had a tragic loss and we are here today to honor them and their son Dalen who passed away just a few months ago. If you would all rise please, we will have a procession from our police officers as they come back down the track. We ask you for a moment of silence when they pass."

Just then, the cars came rolling down. All the lights were on. They were amazing. Our family had now gathered behind the banner that was placed on the track. Each car backed into position and were lined up. The drivers all then met us on the track. What I heard next just blew me away. Over the loudspeaker, they were reading Dalen's obituary that was in the paper and we were all crying a bit. Alyssa was next to me. I grabbed her hand.

"This is more than overwhelming," I said.

"Mom, this is amazing. It's kind of hard to take in." Alyssa replied.

The tower then played Dalen's favorite hymn, and I lost it. I couldn't stop the tears from flowing. Why were we so honored by these people? What had our son done with any of them and how was his passing so influential to so many? I just couldn't understand. It was just so powerful.

There was nothing more we could say. The track had honored our family and son in such a way that reverence was encircling us. We all lined up and took pictures and hung around for a minute just because we were there.[88]

---

[88] We had been so blown away as the racers and track honored us and our son. They had a moment of silence, read his eulogy and played his hymn. The spirit bore witness again of the love that surrounded us. Talk about miracle—this again was a biggie.

The racing then continued.

Miracles and More Miracles

April 30, 2018 I received a picture of Dalen's tombstone and that it was completed. That was quick. Initially the man said that we might have to wait for four or five months. It was good to hear.[89]

May 3, 2018 I received a letter from the donor center mentioning that they had heard from Dalen's other kidney recipient and that he wanted to get in touch with me. I was ecstatic. It was just amazing. I knew in my heart that he was the man in the next room at the hospital when I met Gary, and I had since kicked myself so many times that I didn't go in his room and say who I was. I was just so excited that he finally wanted to get in touch with me. I called him immediately.[90]

May 5, 2018 One of my emails touched me deeply today. It was from Dalen's mission president, and he had something special for us.

---

[89] Dalen's tombstone was finished 2 ½ months earlier than expected. Told doesn't normally happen.
[90] I was going to meet the second kidney recipient. Amazing for sure.

We understood that his whole mission had a special fast for our family and that the president also asked any missionary that knew Dalen, to write a note or letter that he would compile and get to us. The email was of those letters. It was amazing. Here the missionaries spoke of how they knew Dalen and more importantly, how he touched their lives. What a treasure. There were fifteen letters included.[91]

May 23, 2018 Before Dalen's winter semester, his friend James Lewis got married in Bountiful on January 6th. We were there as we brought up some things for the Lewis's and had planned on visiting with our family along the way. Today I was sent a video from the wedding photographer of Dalen and me dancing. It was so fun. He always thought he knew more than me and I was trying to teach him again correctly, how to dance the waltz. I loved it. Dalen and I dancing for the last time. Another treasure for sure.[92]

May 27, 2018 Mariah submitted her mission papers. What an enormous event for her at this time in her life.[93]

June 16, 2018 Mariah opened her call to serve in the Nashville, Tennessee Mission and would report October 3rd, 2018.

June 29, 2018 Mariah wanted to go through the temple and chose the Salt Lake City Temple. It was an issue to get all the family up there, but we did, and it was such an amazing experience. She was given a special blessing because of her testimony of the atonement and how she would use that to teach all around her. This was a very sacred event for our family.[94]

---

[91] The letters from co-missionaries of Dalen all sent pictures with stories of how they loved Dalen.
[92] To have a video of the last dance between Dalen and I was priceless. Such a treasure.
[93] Mariah being willing to serve a mission was a huge miracle. That she could go and testify and move on, can only be because of the Savior's healing power.
[94] Mariah was promised that her testimony would change lives and many would be touched.

August 22, 2018 It was our anniversary date. We had been invited to participate in the yearly Celebration of Life Memorial. This was where the city of Salt Lake, put the names of all the donors for that year, on a wall in one of the city parks. It was a pretty big ordeal for these families. These names would forever then be on the wall. Each year they would just add another panel to the wall. I wanted to be there. We made it our anniversary trip. We would stay with Gordon and try to make the most of our weekend. Somehow we filled our time up touring and running around. We visited a nephew and his family. We went to dinner with a mission companion and her husband. Somehow our time got filled.

The ceremony was Saturday morning and was actually pretty casual. There were people everywhere looking for their loved one's name on the wall. They gave you a guide to find your family member's name and it wasn't hard to find after that. There were balloons released and music playing. Tables of snacks were around and it was a beautiful day. We found Dalen's name. It was a bit surreal. It almost immobilized Dalen. His name was etched on the glass wall.

We walked around with a name tag of our loved one on our chest. I was over by Dalen's name and I thought I would like to etch it onto a piece of paper. So, I had some paper, but I needed to find a pencil. There were lots of people there, but I looked at this one girl that had a shoulder bag.

"'Excuse me, would you happen to have a pencil I could borrow?" I asked…

Immediately I heard: "Dalen Graham, is Dalen your son?" from a voice behind me.

"Um, yes he was." I answered with a question in my voice.

"We are the Peterson family. We are the ones that sent you the book when Dalen died. Our daughter died three weeks before Dalen," replied Julie (the mom).

"Oh my gosh. I can't believe it's you and that you knew who my son was," was my shocked reply, as we hugged each other.

I borrowed the pencil and scratched over Dalen's name on the paper, but not until after we had visited with this amazing family and were again stunned that out of the hundreds of people that were there, we found the one family that had known of our son's story and had blessed us with the gift of a book about the afterlife. Coincidence? No, we call that a miracle.[95]

Scott even said that meeting this family was worth going. That made it purposeful for him.

That evening I also knew of a wedding reception for the son of Dalen's former mission president, the man that we wanted to speak at Dalen's funeral. They had invited us to this reception as they heard we were in town. I told Scott we were heading over there. He wasn't sure about that, but it was my year for planning our anniversary so he couldn't argue.

The house was in a really nice area in Bountiful. It was beautiful and the homes were huge. We pulled up. The reception was in the backyard. I knew who the Taylors were immediately. They were conversing with a couple and then they were free. I approached them.

"Sister Taylor, I'm Elder Graham's mom," I announced.

She just hugged me. She cried on my shoulder for a minute and just hugged me.

"We loved our Elder Graham. Oh how that boy won my heart. We just loved your boy," she stated while grabbing the arm of her husband and announcing to him who we were. He in turn also hugged me tightly and just reinforced his love for our son.

President did what a president does and immediately took us over to meet missionaries that Dalen served with. I recognized two of them as the missionaries that came to our house for Dalen's funeral. It was awesome to see them. What a blessing. We were honored to be given that moment. Again our son mattered and we were humbled by the love these people had for him. We didn't stay long but so worth all our effort to be there.

We needed to get up early the next day and drive the rental car back near the airport and then just the waiting for our flight and the return home. Pretty much our plan for the day—to just get home again. We had a very worthwhile weekend with those mighty miracles all around us.

---

[95] We had met a family that were touched so much by Dalen's story that they contacted us and shared their similar story of their daughter, and we were right beside them. God led us again.

Mariah's Account of the Accident
August 22, 2018

February 9, 2018 I picked Dalen up around 1:00 p.m. or 2:00 p.m. and then we left. He was all excited about his new IPod he just got for his upcoming summer job. We were jamming to music like always, and he was taking funny snap chats of me. He told me about Chloe. We talked about how lucky we got with our parents and family. I made sure we were both wearing seat belts. I had him send me a cool playlist Collin made, and we were having a blast like usual. Then the road started to lean. I wasn't paying attention because he was taking a funny snap chat of me. We started going left and then I over corrected right as he was yelling at me to slow down. I was awake the whole time. We rolled multiple times. His head was crushed, but I didn't know that until he was in the ambulance. When the truck stopped rolling on the hill, I looked at Dalen and tried to wake him up. I kept screaming and screaming his name. He wouldn't wake up. I unbuckled my seatbelt and fell to the ground.

    I had to climb out of my window which was shattered. I couldn't feel my left side or open my left eye. I scrambled around looking for anything useful like a phone or even a pair of shoes. People began showing up and trying to help. They already called 911. I checked four times. I scrambled around looking for a phone to call Mom. I found his phone. It was still playing music. Some of the song that started with M and the snap chat video he was taking when we crashed. It kept repeating him screaming: "slow down, slow down," I turned off the video and the music and called my mom. I told her what happened and apologized for crashing and not being safe. Then I called Rick and told him what happened and where we were going. He said he was coming, and I can't remember much after that. I called my dad. Mom posted it on Facebook, which was annoying because I didn't have time to answer stupid questions from people I could care less about. Mom said we needed the prayers.

I kept telling everyone to help my brother, and they kept telling me I was in shock. I wasn't in shock. I was fine and my brother needed help, not me. I tried to help as much as I could. I got in the ambulance and had a quick exam and then handled more phone calls. Everything sucked. All the calls and texts. I asked the paramedics if Dalen was breathing. They didn't answer, so I started yelling trying to get them to answer me.

They said yes, but I knew it was a lie.

They landed a helicopter, but didn't even use it. They wasted time waiting for the helicopter and then sending it back while we just sat there blocking traffic and waiting for what seemed like hours. It felt like years. I just sat there crying and hating myself. We finally started moving to the hospital and I talked with the driver while making jokes because that's who I am. I got angry because cars wouldn't move out of the way for the ambulance.

We get to the hospital. Everyone starts fussing. I told twelve people how old he was, his birthday and everything about him. And they kept getting it wrong, so I yelled at them because they were idiots. I talked to a paramedic. He was nice. Then the cop came for the first time, which pissed me off because I had other things to do. Talked with him—don't remember what he asked or what I said.

I get back to Dalen and Rick got there—thank goodness. They move Dalen into some surgery to do something and started checking me out. Got an x-ray on my shoulder. I was fine. It hurt so bad I could barely get my shirt off to change. Someone called Elders which I could not care about. They gave me a blessing and told me Dalen would be fine. They lied. They were nice, but they couldn't take a hint to leave.

I did not appreciate everyone telling everyone what had happened. It made me feel worse.

Someone else came, I don't remember who, and they sat and talked in my exam room for a while. I talked to the cop again while waiting for my x-ray results. They came and gave me a card to get into the ICU where Dalen was. Went up and saw Aubree and her parents there I think. Talked to the cop again. He told me I could have been charged with murder. Checked my phone to make sure I wasn't on it. It wasn't on before the accident happened. I wasn't speeding or doing anything wrong.

I went in and saw Dalen. His face was so swollen and so was the rest of his body. He was already dead. There was no way he was alive. I sat and held his hand for a while and just pleaded with God to wake him up, or give me some kind of miracle. Sat around waiting forever. The worst part was when I had to hold the phone up to Dalen's ear for every single member of my family to say their goodbye over the phone because of the accident I caused.

I sat next to his bed for a while, held his hand again and waited for him to die. Mom and dad and Kailee showed up and Rick's family and then Alyssa and Brandon.

Our phones were constantly blowing up with messages of love and support, but they could do nothing about the pain being felt. It was my nature to try and make crappy situations better but for this one, I was out of luck. I have never been so stressed out, sad and destroyed all in one day. It felt like minutes that I was in the hospital, but in reality it was the next day. 5:16 in the morning they finally pronounced him dead. The whole family was there. Since then, everything sucks. I feel nothing.

Time Can Heal Pain-and Blessings Still Come

Wednesday, October 3, 2018 Mariah was starting her mission. We had driven up to Utah again, knowing that we were going to go to Conference for our church up in Salt Lake City that weekend. It was again perfect timing.

Chloe had arranged to come for Mariah's farewell, and then we would take her to conference as she had never been. She would then visit with her brother and fly home from there. It was just awesome to have her with us.

Dropping Mariah off was just so exciting. We were so proud of her for going. It wasn't going to be easy, but she had her conviction. The spirit was so strong on the Missionary Training Center grounds. It was just awesome. We literally drove into a parking lot, she opened the door and was greeted by other missionaries, we got a hug and she was gone. It was that quick, and then she was gone.[96]

So now we filled our time by showing Chloe around Salt Lake. We of course went to the memorial wall where Dalen's name was placed and thought she might like to see that. We did a bunch of church history sites and had a great time.

Thursday, October 4, 2018 One highlight we had was related to Dalen's mission. During conference week, there are always mission reunions all over the valley. I knew the Texas, Dallas Mission was

---

[96] Dropping Mariah off at the MTC wasn't just a drop off—it was sensing the protection of all the angels guarding Mariah to be on guard. There was such a strong power there.

having one and I had planned it out, and that we would be there. There was a very nice restaurant upstairs in a building that overlooks the Salt Lake Temple, and it was in that building that Dalen's mission reunion was taking place. We so went to eat. While we were waiting to be seated, I dismissed myself and ran downstairs. I found Sister Taylor and expressed how happy I was to just be in the building. She begged me to come back after our dinner and visit with everyone. I couldn't promise because I knew Scott wouldn't want to go, but I would try and pray so hard that it would come to be.

Dinner was great. My anxiety was bigger though. Dinner was coming to a close, and I gathered up my courage and mentioned to Scott that I happened to know that the Texas Mission Reunion was going on downstairs and that we had been invited to stop in by the Taylors. Scott said he didn't want to go, but with Chloe there, and her excitement to see some missionaries that served in her area, it sounded fun for her too.

"Scott, please. I know we need to be there. I have felt strongly that we need to be there. This was a thought from a while ago that I've had. Come on. Let's go. We won't stay long, but I want to thank the Taylors for all they did for Dalen," I pleaded.

Scott consented.

We walked into one of the conference rooms downstairs, and it was packed. There were missionaries from wall to wall. There wasn't much room, but we made our way in and went kind of in the upper corner. The Taylors were addressing all the missionaries.

Sister Taylor was speaking of how much she loved her missionaries and that they would always be their missionaries. Then she saw us and stopped for a minute.

"In expressing our love to our missionaries, it's in that thought that we can see them again. There is one missionary that we won't have that option in this life to see. We only lost one missionary during our time and that was our dear Elder Graham. His parents just walked in. This elder had the biggest heart I've ever seen. He was happy all the time. He loved everyone. He just made me laugh. I'm sure that the Grahams," and she motioned for us to come out of the corner which we did; "would love to visit with any of you that knew of their son." she continued.

We stood in awe. We weren't expecting anything like this. It again was so humbling. We kind of snuck back near the wall for a bit while President Taylor spoke.

Immediately when they finished the meeting, there was this line that formed in front of us of missionaries that wanted to shake our hand and talk of Dalen. This was just so awesome! It was like a reception line. Most expressed that they were sorry for what we had to experience. Some had stories of how they met or how they played together. Dalen was comp to two that were there. He was in a zone of a few others. There were a few that had some amazing stories. It was so uplifting. There weren't any tears of sadness, but definitely ones of gratitude.[97]

One young man came up quickly and shook our hands. The line was increasing, but he said he had to tell us a story and would wait to do so. We stood there for about forty-five minutes conversing with these amazing young returned missionaries. They just kept coming. The room was becoming cleared. And we again met up with this one young man.

"I have to tell you this story of your son. He changed my life. I just have to tell you how important he was to me and how my life was better because of him." This young man was so adamant that we hear this story, and he was emotional in telling it to us.

"Please we would love to hear it," I stated.

"Your son and I weren't companions, but we were on exchanges one day," the young man stated. We found out his name was Todd.

On a mission a young person is assigned to a companion that they serve with twenty-four hours a day for weeks or months until a change is directed from the mission president. During that time however, the missionaries would go on what they call 'splits'. It just meant that for a day, they would switch companions and serve with someone else. It was to help leaders see how missionaries taught and

---

[97] The abundance of love from the Taylors and missionaries was so strong. We felt as if the heavens had been opened and Dalen was standing beside us.

to get a change for the missionaries, so they in turn, could learn from a new experience.

"We weren't sure where we were going to go, but your son said; 'Well, let's pray and we will get the answer,' without any hesitation. I had prayed several times in asking for guidance, but his no hesitation nor questioning which was impressive to me. So, he stopped right there, and bowed his head and started to pray. He didn't care if anyone was watching or not. He wanted his answer now," Todd explained.

"Dalen usually didn't care what others thought, but we hadn't seen that on a spiritual side," Scott replied.

"Then we rode down this street and he jumps off his bike and said, 'Let's go Elder. We have work to do.' He just was so eager. We got to this door and this lady asked us in. Elder Graham looked at me and said, 'This is it'. The lady said she was struggling with God and wanting to know if she mattered to him. Elder Graham immediately started addressing this lady in a story form. He presented to her a play. If God was in charge of the characters on the stage, each one had a place, what would happen if one person wasn't where they were supposed to be. He continued and asked me to help. He then came to the atonement of Christ to help this lady know that she was of great worth. She was expected to play a role in this play and God would direct her and lead her and help her along the way. She wouldn't be alone. There was always a prompter in the wings. Dalen was amazing. He was crying, and so was I and this lady. I had never seen or heard anything like that in my life. I had been a member my whole life. I had some rough teenage years. I repented and went on a mission. I thought I knew the gospel pretty good. I questioned the atonement for me. I was told that I mattered, but it was nothing like what I experienced with your son. Hearing your son explain how important one person is to God, it hit me like a ton of bricks. I was converted that day and can't go a day that I don't think of your son and how he altered my life," Todd said.[98]

---

[98] Dalen knew his Savior and the power of the atonement. He knew it.

We were all crying together. I had to hug him again. My son did that. Again, I was dumfounded at his spiritual insight. It was an amazing story. Todd thanked us again for our son's life and again he wanted us to know that our son changed his life. What a depth of gratitude we felt from this young man. We wanted to stay and hear more stories, but it really was time to go. The witnesses were profound from these missionaries and of our son's association with them. I will never forget this event, never.

Conference weekend was such a spiritual highlight of our lives. We heard from church leaders that spiritually uplifted us. We heard from a Prophet of God who guided us with his words as he expressed his love for us. We sent our daughter on her mission, and we met and were loved by the missionaries from the Dallas, Texas Mission,. WOW!

October 20, 2018 Mariah's boyfriend got his mission call to Zimbabwe and had to wait for his visa. He had been at the training center for about two months and was being assigned to a States side mission until his visa came. He was assigned to the Dallas, Texas Mission. I was floored. I immediately contacted Rick through email.

"That is so cool. I want you do to me a favor when you meet President Dalton (Dalen's second Mission President), I want you to ask him if he remembers Elder Graham. You will have the best reunion. He will treat you so special because of that. I know you will do good there. You have a lot to live up to for sure," I stated.

Rick's email conquered that he agreed.

October 22, 2018 "Dear Sister Graham: Your son is amazing! Getting off the airplane at the airport, I met mission President Dalton. I took your advice and said, 'Do you remember Elder Graham?' He stopped what he was doing, looked at me and asked: "You know our Dear Elder Graham?!"

I explained how I knew him, and he told me he misses him very much. And he hugged me.

Yesterday at church I was asked to give a brief testimony in sacrament. I got up and talked about how much I've seen Christ's hand in my life. I explained that I had a dear friend that served his mission here in Dallas, and that I hoped to live up to his example. I gave no name or any specifics about my relationship with him or that he had even passed away. As I was walking back to sit down, a teenager grabbed my arm and said: "You knew Elder Graham?"

And I looked at him and said; "Yes, but how did you know who I was talking about?"

He said Elder Graham taught and baptized him. It brought tears to my eyes. I just wanted you to know that your son continues to bless lives and today he blessed mine. I know God put me here so I could see this. It has been the coolest experience. Thank you for raising someone I can look up to for the rest of my life.

The next day was our preparation day and I had asked Jesus if he could come to the church and get a picture together. Get this other miracle, I got my visa today and will be leaving for Africa tomorrow.[99]

Rick Hamilton and Jesus Lopez.

November 28, 2018. Today was Dalen's birthday. I had wanted to do something special. Dalen loved to party. He was happy most of

---

[99] Jesus and Rick met. Jesus meant the world to Dalen and now a testimony for Rick and how God leads us. Rick was only in the Dallas mission for 5 days. Talk about miracle.

the time. So I wanted to have some fun. I had posted on Facebook and Instagram previously and had all the girls forward my post onto theirs. We invited everyone we knew to celebrate with us.

> **November 28, 2018**
> **The Party:** All Day Long
> **Where:** In & Out Burger place (or any burger joint close to you)
> **Request:** For all who wish to join us in celebrating Dalen's life, get a burger, and take a picture of you eating it. We hope a few can join us. Again, take and send a picture of you eating a burger in memory of Dalen. Come join the party.

The day went on and a few people actually sent in their pictures. I thought: *'Awe, that was nice of them'*. The day continued on and a few more pictures. By **3:00 p.m.**, they just kept coming. I was blown away. Picture after picture came in. Everyone had huge smiles on their faces, and it was just so exciting and fun to see.

265 people sent in pictures-265 persons !!!!!!!.[100]

December 25, 2018 Christmas was always a fun loving day. Today was the same. Alyssa, Kailee, Scott and I were all together and we got to talk to Mariah who was on her mission, all day long, so it was great. Everyone was happy. We always miss Dalen, but it was never with bitterness or regrets or frustration. It was from love and happiness. Another great day at the home front. Merry Christmas Buddy! I wondered what he got to do to celebrate it and who he would be with. I would one day learn the answer to those questions. For now, a day of treasured memories.

---

[100] Some of the most amazing support. We couldn't post all the pictures but thank you everyone. Thank you. And that the 100th miracle was on Dalen's b-day. AMAZING!

Anniversary Fun—February, 2019

February 7, 2019 I had arranged for months to finally meet Paul Slaughter, Dalen's other kidney recipient and I thought that the year mark would be a good time. Paul, after a few conversations finally agreed. I had arranged to go up to Salt Lake City. I would be by myself, but that was okay because this probably meant the most to me.

I flew into Salt Lake City Thursday morning. Got the rental car and kind of wondered what I wanted to do. I went to Gord's house and settled in. I had previously arranged to meet with friends that I usually didn't have time to enjoy. Kelli (my cousin) and I wanted to spend some girl time together. We had the late afternoon and evening planned. We got our nails done, went out for dinner and hit the movies. Great girl time and so needed.

It was late when I got back, but I visited for a bit with Gord and Maria and just enjoyed the conversation. When I went to bed, I was pretty tired. The prayer was just that I was able to sleep. I should have some good dreams from the fun evening I just experienced.

February 8, 7:15 a.m. The next day. Of course I woke up early, but I really didn't have any plans for the morning. The only plan I had made was dinner with a couple that used to live by us when we were first married in California. We have stayed in touch for all these years, so I was excited to see them. I didn't need to get up or really do anything. I finally went upstairs and saw Gord getting ready for work. We said our hellos and he left. Maria was already at work. I lingered around and thought that I could, should get my day started.

I had tried to make contact with Dalen's mission president. When I reached his office, I mentioned to his secretary that I was just announcing that I was in town and that if they had any time, I would love to see them. His secretary was trying to see how she could make the connection when all of a sudden she asked; "How long are you in town?"

"Just till tomorrow. I know he's busy. I was just hoping to say hello."

"Well actually, he's having a lunch today with some of his missionaries and why don't you just meet them at the City Creek Eatery. I know he would love to see you," she reported.

"Wow, I actually could do that. That would be incredible. Thank you so much. That is so nice of you," I stated.

"No, I'm sure President would love to see you. I'll let him know you'll be coming, so he can look for you." The secretary seemed excited that the plan might work out.

"Thank you—I'll be there."

Well now I had a purpose for the day. I showered and headed in. I knew I would be early, but I was pretty excited, so I didn't care if I had some time to waste. I walked through the mall to the end where the eatery was and just kind of walked around wondering if I would be able to find them and recognize them and feel accepted with these missionaries. A Mission President is forever a hero. They have helped you through a process of becoming a disciple of Jesus Christ and when you have heeded their council, you are accomplished as a returned missionary. I loved Pres. and Sister Taylor; I think almost as much as Dalen did. I was in line getting a sandwich when I saw President and Sister Taylor walking around. I was at the register paying for my lunch and literally jumped out of line after excusing myself for just a second, to catch the Taylors and say hello. They hugged me and had the biggest smiles on their faces. I quickly realized that I needed to finish my business at the register and thanked everyone in line for waiting for that moment.

Once I finished, I again returned to the Taylors and Sister Taylor commented: "Oh we are so excited to see you. How awesome is this." She is such a beautiful lady in and out. I almost felt like they were my Mission Presidents with that desire to be with them, and just hold that hug for a few seconds longer.

The Taylors still needed to get their lunch so they asked me to find a spot and see if I could notice any missionaries coming. I didn't think I would know what any of the missionaries looked like, but I found a spot to eat. I watched as the Taylors walked around and a missionary would run up to them and give them a big hug. It happened over and over again. What an amazing experience. They finally were able to get their lunch and we sat at the table. The missionaries kept coming. Every time another missionary arrived, the Taylors got up and hugged that person and let them know how much they loved them. I was in awe that on a Friday lunch time, so many returned missionaries were able to come and have lunch with their president. President Taylor was very careful to announce me to every missionary as Dalen's mom and that Elder Graham had passed away. Most of them had served before Dalen had, but they were cordial to me anyways.

One Elder did know Dalen, and he expressed how much he loved him and how much fun he was. They weren't ever companions, but they were in the same district. There were fourteen missionaries that came: two with their spouses, and one with their new baby. Life really does move on as the missionaries now were all talking about dating, marriage and starting families. There was reminiscing too and talk of different companions and their experiences. I felt a bit out of place because I really didn't have any information to contribute, but I enjoyed seeing the Taylors for sure.

"Sister Taylor—how often do you have lunch with your missionaries?"

President Taylor replied: "We have never done this before. This was the first time."

"Seriously, this is your first and again I'm here for a monumental mission event (reflecting on the experience we had with General Conference and the mission reunion). This was so amazing!"

"It's another show of God's love for you." Sister Taylor always seemed to have the perfect answer.[101]

---

[101] I had the prompting to make contact with President Taylor. Not only would I get to see him, but a luncheon with other missionaries and this was their first time to get together. It was such a blessing. God gave me such another amazing gift.

I was in awe again. Here I was in Salt Lake City and on a whim—eating lunch with missionaries and their first luncheon with their president, President Taylor and his beautiful wife. I was amazed that these missionaries would come for a lunch and many from as far away as Provo (forty-five-mile drive) and that I was there with them.

Then I had a Dalen moment. That usually meant that a thought brought a tear or two to my eyes. It was usually just a memory or a wish, never a big deal and literally only about a minute or so. This was Dalen's hero, so my moment was a lot more intense. Dalen had spoken about President Taylor on almost every occasion that he wrote home. He loved this man. So, the impression that I received was the most profound Dalen moment I had had. I was overwhelmed for a minute and actually had to leave the table. I made it look like I needed to go to the bathroom which I did, but I actually just sat and cried for a minute. I had a thought: "*Hey mom, get him to give you a blessing.*"

What the heck? I had waited for a year to feel or hear my son. So many other people had experiences with regards to Dalen, and I was actually jealous. I felt that I, as the mother, was entitled to some feeling, thought, dream, impression, or hearing of his voice, and it never came. Today it was strong. I heard it several times in my head. Now I had to process what I was feeling and what the reality was of where I was at. How would I ask his president for a blessing? I had never felt of Dalen near me before. We were in a food court and all these missionaries were with us. That was an amazing thought though, and I also knew that I couldn't let it go. I regained some composure and went back to the table. It was hard to focus especially since I knew what I should be doing. I haven't always been good at understanding a prompting or following it, but this, I just couldn't ignore something like this.

I just kept hearing Dalen's voice in my head; "*He gives really good blessing Mom—really good ones.*" Usually when someone was given a blessing it occurred for two reasons: 1) the person is sick and needs that power of healing or, 2) they want a blessing of comfort for some struggles they might be going through. I had neither reason to ask for a blessing except my son had prompted me to, and it definitely couldn't hurt.[102]

I returned to the Taylors. Sister Taylor was afraid that I was going to leave. It was a thought of mine since I didn't really fit in with the discussions, but then I conceded and went back. Within a few minutes, there was a moment, where I heard again: *"Ask him Mom."* And I took control of the moment. I grabbed Sister Taylor's hand.

"I have a very unusual request from you and in asking I'm going to cry." I was overwhelmed for just a minute. "I'm just really feeling prompted from Dalen to ask your husband for a blessing. I don't know why, but I just feel that Dalen wants me to receive a blessing from his President."

"That would be such a good thing. I know he is supper busy today, but I would love to ask him, and we can go from there," Sister Taylor stated.

"I've never done anything like this before and it feels weird, but I just keep feeling that Dalen would like me to get a blessing." I was crying and felt a bit awkward because I didn't want the missionaries to see me. But it was kind of at a moment where there was the understanding that people were starting to say goodbyes. So the attention wasn't directed to me in any way and yet I still was visible, which caused the awareness of others that might be viewing my emotions.

"Well, let's see what we can do. I have your phone number right?"

"Yes, I believe you do. I can send you a message to make sure though." And I opened my phone and sent a text message to Sister Taylor. She smiled and I got a thumbs up, meaning she received my message. Of course we took pictures together and the day was now perfect.

---

[102] I had actually felt an impression from Dalen. I heard his voice and felt of his spirit so strongly. I knew that he was with me. That was so exciting for me. I have wanted to have a 'Dalen Moment' throughout this year, and here is was, on his year mark. I felt so very loved. My boy was there.

"I'll call you later after I talk to President and see if he has any time."

"Thank you so much. I really think I should go though. Thank you so much for letting me be with you and your missionaries. What an amazing thing and that I was here to share a part of it with you. Just so very cool."

"Well, you don't have to go. I would love to have you stay, but I understand. Thank you for coming. We love you and our Elder Graham," stated Sister Taylor.

She guided me next to her husband and the circle of missionaries, and we said our goodbyes with another hug.

"I love my Elder Graham. I just love that kid," President. Taylor commented.

That hug felt like an eternal bond of forever. I was in awe again of another amazing experience that God was guiding me through. If I did nothing else that whole weekend, I would have been uplifted, inspired and humbled. I heard words in my head that were from my son. Dalen was actually speaking to my mind, and I heard his voice. I was with my son's mortal Savior. I ate with him and felt profoundly of his love for my son and myself. I wouldn't receive the blessing, but I was more than uplifted and touched by the spirit.

In Salt Lake City, I had a dinner date in the Joseph Smith Building in the Garden Restaurant, which happened to be across the street from where I was at. I had about four hours to fill. So shopping would be the resolution.

Dinner was also such a great experience. The restaurant on was the tenth floor overlooking the Salt Lake Temple square. The lights were coming on, so I sat in the lobby pondering on it all. The word eternal now was a daily thought. I knew I wouldn't see Dalen again in this life, but I would live with him and our family forever. Eternity seemed exciting of course. The hard part would just be this earthly separation. The temple—where eternity takes place, was a beacon with the lights illuminating The House of the Lord.

My friends then came, and we greeted each other with big hugs. I loved when you saw someone after years, and it seemed like you hadn't really missed any time. It was that kind of feeling. We had kept in touch with each other with our Christmas letters and posts and that helped as we knew a bit of what the other family had been doing.

We sat down in the restaurant and were by the windows so we could keep looking at the temple. It took a bit for the food to come, but our conversation filled the time. As parents there really wasn't much else to life that was more important than the family and how they had chosen to live their lives. The food was really good, but the conversation was way better. We talked more about what had happened since we had been together. We talked about our children and how most of our trials were family centered. Of course, our discussion led to Dalen and again I got to testify of all the amazing miracles that had happened to our family and that tomorrow would be another amazing experience as both kidney recipients would be together.

Sean (the male side of the couple) talked about his mother's passing. Ironically, she was a co-worker of mine from years ago when we were waitresses' together back in California. The couple of hours went by unnoticeably—we simply enjoyed our time. We sat and visited literally for over two hours and just felt so uplifted and enlightened by the others. They thanked me so much for talking about Dalen and giving my perspective. They said they felt humbled and uplifted which surprised me. I guess I should have learned that my talking of Dalen became a strength for me. I was able to bear witness of God's hand in our lives and how it seemed so normal to talk about. Another day of blessings and amazing experiences because I was in a place that I felt Heavenly Father had prompted me to be at.

The Awaited Meeting

February 9, 2019 Meeting Paul The awaited morning finally arrived. I was anxious. I knew Gary would be there, but Paul had left some concern in my mind. Sometimes on the phone I couldn't read him very well. It just seemed that his life and issues were always greater than my desire to meet. But I knew I needed to meet him and today was the day. I just wished that more of my family felt the need for these experiences. These persons just enhance all that Dalen was. I didn't think of them as 'Oh my gosh, you have a part of my son in you and that means I have meaning. I need to be a part of your life' NOT AT ALL! I merely just wanted to see that their lives were better and that they were happier from where they were at, especially physically. That really was my full intent. I have never liked being alone or doing things by myself, but for this instance, I was ready.

We were to meet at the memorial wall in Salt Lake City. I got there a bit early. The decided time was **11:00 a.m.** I didn't want to make it hard on anyone there especially since there was a lot of snow that had been plowed up. The streets were pretty cleared, but the ground was covered by a very nice blanket of snow, maybe even six to eight inches deep. To get to the memorial, I had to trudge through the snow. No one had walked around the park as there were no footprints near the donor's wall. I again found Dalen's name and enjoyed a moment of solace with my thoughts of Dalen and how this year had been so amazingly inspirational. I had an 8 x 10 picture of Dalen with me that was one he took while on his mission. I took a picture of his picture by his name on the wall. And then Paul called me.

"Hi, this is Paul. So where are you?"

"I'm standing by the wall," I mentioned.

"I'm at the library, so where is the wall," Paul asked.

"You need to go to the back side of the library. I would drive down to 300 E and then turn onto 500 S. The memorial wall was on that corner. I'm wearing a purple coat. You can't miss me—I'm the only one here," I instructed.

"Okay. I'll drive around," he said.

"Very exciting—I'll see you in a minute."

I knew he was driving a PT Cruiser as he had mentioned that before on one of our phone calls. After just a few minutes I saw Paul approaching. I watched him park just a ways down from me. He got out of his car and walked back toward the library. I thought: '*Okay, maybe that wasn't him.*' Then he walked back almost to me near the entrance of the underground parking lot and again turned away. I thought it might be him, but I never said anything because I just wasn't sure. He was about six feet tall with white hair. He was a pretty big guy physically. He walked away from me again, which I didn't understand.

Within a few seconds literally, I saw Sylvia and her daughter coming to greet me. Oh I was excited to see her. We ran into each other and just hugged tightly. "Oh, how are you? How I love you," she said.

"I'm so glad you are here. How are you and where is Gary?" It was explained to me that Gary was called into work and was quite upset that he couldn't be with us. I was way sad. My mind had pictured this moment so many times with both recipients standing next to me holding Dalen's picture. I just really thought of the magic of that moment. I was sad, but also grateful that Sylvia was there as I loved her dearly.

"We are doing good. I'm feeling better now." Sylvia and I were in contact with each other on a very regular basis and I knew that she was trying to recover from bronchitis. We hugged again. Then at the corner of my eye, I saw that man approaching again and so I called out to him this time.

"Paul." He paused and looked over toward me. "Paul, we are over here."

"Oh, there you are. I came over but didn't see you." In front of me was a man that had received my son's kidney. He looked good.

We hugged and he held me tightly. Just for a moment, time stopped. I was a bit surprised at his size. I knew he was sixty-five years old. I knew he was a musician and that he loved to ski and was very athletic. He was pretty large in stature though. That surprised me but was also easy to accept. I knew he was a grandfather. On our first conversation, I asked him if he was a member of our church and he said he was, but that he wasn't and wouldn't be active. That was sad to hear because Dalen had gone through a lot to finally have his conviction and testimony. Paul really just kept telling me about himself and his life on our previous phone calls. At one point, I actually stopped him and asked him if he wouldn't like to know anything about Dalen at all. So I knew he cared about Dalen, but it just seemed that he wanted me to know more about all his accomplishments in life rather than what Dalen was like. I had to accept that. To meet him was a relief. He seemed gracious and grateful. I was very happy.

"How are you?" he asked.

"I'm good. How are you?" I responded.

"I'm really good," and he looked happy.

"I'm so happy to meet you. This is Sylvia. She is the mother of Gary who is the other kidney recipient," I replied.

"Oh, so nice to meet you", and they hugged.

"You too." replied Sylvia.

We stood there for a few minutes and just looked at each other.

"You look so good Paul. You look healthy and so very happy," I commented.

"I am very healthy. I feel good and I am happy," Paul ensured us again.

We took pictures of course, and we talked just a bit. It was cold though, so we decided to go to a little restaurant that was across the street and share more time together. It was a tiny little Mexican restaurant, but it was the only thing around that was opened and I was grateful to sit down and be out of the cold.

We talked about the lives of Gary and Paul and all their medical issues. They both had suffered so much and had constant struggles and pain. I felt so bad for them and what they had to endure. I couldn't image a life with that much pain, constantly wondering if you would ever feel better or live through it. I was just in awe of their lives. They both had suffered so much. Gary's was very intense as he had issues from birth; but Paul had suffered for over twenty years and in his words: "I've been to Hell and back." I know they felt bad about Dalen, but he didn't suffer. He wasn't in pain. He was healthy and enjoyed his life. Paul was pretty active. He was a musician that played all over the place and enjoyed most sports. He was an avid skier and his goal of today with his healthy body was to teach his granddaughter how to ski. I was grateful to know that their lives were blessed. I wanted them to enjoy life.

During our luncheon, we talked about their past, our present situations, and our hopes for the future. I just asked that they serve others. Of course I wasn't expecting them to be 'Oh Dalen' every minute but that they would take care of their bodies and do all they could to be healthy, that maybe every once in a while they would think of Dalen and be happy. We talked for about two hours. I loved being there. What a joy.

"So, what would you say to Dalen if you could?" I asked.

"I would say thank you. He saved my life. Literally I've been to Hell and back and your son has given me a new life. Thank you." Paul seemed to pause for just a second and looked down. He was grateful and he showed it. For that, I was very relieved. Dalen did mean something to him, and he had thought about my son a bit.

"Our lives have forever been changed. You are always in our thoughts. We are so grateful for you and your family. We will never be able to repay you." Sylvia cried a bit which led me to shed a few tears too. I just loved this woman and all her strength. She was an amazing woman whose personal story would be worth a book series. She truly had an amazing faith and had led her family in that way.

"We don't want to be repaid. But to know that your lives are better was worth it." We had talked about their ages and how I wasn't expecting them to be so old. They also were so surprised to get the call that a kidney was available to them. Protocol was usually kids first and then emergencies and then older cliental. They were both just so grateful and I was humbled. Such a blessing to be with them, and I still missed Gary. This donor process is such an amazing world, and I was just (there has to be another word for grateful), to be a part of it. My God was so good. He was just so good. My heart was so full of love.[103]

Sylvia and I then spent a few hours together as we didn't really have plans but didn't want to let go of each other either. We went shopping again. I loved being with her. We wanted to make a special memory of our day, so we bought matching shirts.

We were silly and playing and just enjoyed each other. Of course, I took pictures. We were brought together by a tragedy but choosing to stay together because of our sisterhood. I only had an hour till my flight, so we decided to say our goodbyes so I could head to the airport and drop off my rental car. We hugged each other so tightly.

"I just will never be able to repay you for all you've done for my family. I love you so very much. You are an amazing woman and have so much faith. You are an example for me, and I want to be as strong as you are one day." Sylvia stated.

"That wasn't exactly right—you have been way stronger than I have been and have shown so much courage. I love you Sylvia. I'm so grateful you are in my life. I love you," was my reply.

I headed to my car after I helped Sylvia find her car. We hugged again very tightly and said goodbye. Once I returned the rental car, I walked to the ticket booth and made the arrangement necessary to

---

[103] I had met Dalen's second kidney recipient. So very worthwhile. Just amazed again.

board my flight. I got to my gate and could only reflect again on my past few days and how amazing they were. When you let God lead-you will always see miracles.

I love flying when I can recognize parts of the scenic topography. I got to see some of the Salt Lake area, but the sun was setting while we were taking off so there wasn't much light. I had learned that as soon as you get on a plane, if you make contact with the person next to you, there is never awkwardness. So, I spoke to the man next to me. He looked Indian and said hello, but didn't take long to put his earplugs in and listen to his phone. That was okay. I was so happy for the few hours I got to spend with everyone throughout my weekend. It was just an overwhelming feeling with everything. Such a good trip that I was again, very grateful I made the arrangements to go.

  Sheila Robinson—So glad you could meet.
  —How exciting.
  —Amazing.
  Kelly Jensen—Awesome! That's incredible—!!!!!!!—One miracle after another!!!!!!!!
  Sylvia KcKee—So grateful to you and your sweet spirit. Twin spirits forever.

  February 9, 2018-8:10 a.m. Heather Crapo—Thinking about the Grahams today. #lovedonesinheaven "In Memory of all those you left us too soon… We remember you in the morning, in the night, when we look at the stars, a song, a place, a smell. You are always with us.

  February 9, 2018 12:14 p.m. LASD Motorsports (Scott—picture with him and the girls in front of the car)**—Today I'm at the track with two of my girls. We are together this weekend as a family. One year ago today**

I received the dreadful phone call that two of our kids had been in an accident. Tomorrow. February 10th is the one year anniversary of my son's death. Not a lot to say, but we are together as a family doing what we love at the racetrack.

> **Sharon Graham**—I love it. I'm coming.
> **Debbie Coulombe**—Love you guys.

—Great Photo.

—What a testimonial of faith through you and your family Scott. Love you brother.

—You're doing good work! It's great that the girls can still be with you at the track. Prayers for you all!!!

—Good to see you Friday Scott. My thoughts are with your family on this sad anniversary.

—You and the family are GREAT EXAMPLES of FAITH…

—Hugs to you and your family Scott. I have prayed many times for your hearts to heal. I will say another as well. God bless you and to the family! So glad you guys are hanging out at the track together!

—Sending prayers.

—I'm here for you and your family always…

—Prayers, thumbs up, and hearts.

—My son turns 21 in two weeks. I can't imagine what you're going thru. It was great seeing you at Fontana couple weeks ago, thanks for stopping by out pit.

—My hero!!!!

—You are in my thoughts and heart.

—**Much love and prayers for the Graham family as Dalen's anniversary approaches.**
—**God bless you brother.**
—**You're #1**

It was the start of the NHRA racing season. Scott usually had his car on display at one of our sponsor's trailers in Pomona. Scott had asked Alyssa and Kailee to come home, so he could have his girls with him. He wanted his family together for Dalen's anniversary except I wouldn't be there till later. We could all be together on Sunday, the actual anniversary of Dalen's death.

I flew into L.A. about **9:30 p.m**. I loved seeing the lights. I was always amazed at how big LA county was. It just didn't stop and on a clear night, you can see lights for as far as you can see with no open spaces. It was a good flight. We made good time and I was now excited to be home. Scott said he would take everyone out for dinner after the track and then they would just drop by the airport and pick me up. So that actually worked out really well. I literally got off the plane and walked down what seemed like the forever tunnel to the baggage claim, I got my bag and went outside and they drove in. I only waited for a few minutes.

Brandon was the first to get out of the car. I loved his hugs. I could never get enough of family hugs. Then the rest came out to greet me. Scott gave me a hug and then took my bag to put it into the back of the car, so we could keep moving. I sat in the back with the girls because Brandon really did need as much leg room as he could get being 6'6, and I was fine in the back with the girls. We talked about their day and how it was cold, but they had a good time. They asked how my adventure went too, and I was excited to report all the details to them. They were glad they were home and that we were all together.

The drive home seemed pretty quick. We all mentioned some anxiousness about how we might feel tomorrow. It was pretty late when we arrived at home, but our home once again was filled with family, the best thing ever.

One Year Mark

Sunday February 10, 2018 I didn't sleep much as I was rehearsing the events of the previous year—where we needed to go and what had occurred. At **5:16 am**-Dalen's body finally stopped breathing. He was gone. The event of our today now, was again back at the track. It was to start out early. We had to leave by 6:30 a.m. to get to the track in time, and get the car prepped. We all got up and ready to go. Kailee was the first to be ready of course. Mention a car thing, and she would be right there and ready to go. Brandon was excited because he hadn't done too much with the car, but was learning and really enjoyed it. It was just a fun thing to do now, but mostly because we got to do this with the family. About ten miles from Pomona, Scott got a call saying that their event was planned for 10 a.m. and all was ready. He would get to drive his car down the track and represent all those first responders that save, change and alter lives. Cool!

> **February 10, Facebook 7:27 a.m. I have a friend and his family dealing with the first-year anniversary of the loss of their son today. This amazing family gets their strength to move forward with a great amount of faith each day.**

Normally I would not attend the track with Scott on Sundays, but this time they had asked Scott to participate in the first responders' run. What was supposed to happen was, after the national anthem, they would have a few vehicles go down the track as first responders and a moment of silence for those who had lost their lives in trying to help others. We thought it was pretty coincidental that on Dalen's anniversary, we could honor those first responders that helped him too.

9:25 a.m. Facebook 5:16a.m. A year ago today we said our final goodbye to Dalen. How we miss him. How our lives have been blessed. Never to be forgotten. Love my son.

96 likes-29 pictures (Including meeting Paul and Gary's family, the kidney recipients) 3 shares.

We got to the track, and it started to rain. We went to where the car was and said hello to our friends. Then we waited and waited for the rain to stop. It was crazy how many people were still there. We uncovered the car and cleaned it and hung around. Usually, we answered questions people had or took pictures for people or just cleaned the car. Today was different. We just tried to stay dry. There were a few people that stopped, but when it kept raining, people were just taking cover. The midway was pretty empty.

10:29 a.m. Kailee's Facebook Post 5:16 am a year ago today we said our final goodbye to my one and only brother Dalen. How we miss him. How our lives have been blessed, changed, but never forgotten. As much as I want him around since I had the same interests he did from video games, airsoft, Lego building etc. I know he was called home for a reason and that's what's important to me.—145 likes — 9 Picture.

11:25 a.m. Gary Graham (Kidney Recipient)

(Picture of meeting Gary and his family in the hospital the day after he got Dalen's kidney).

> One year ago, a wonderful family lost a son and a brother Dalen Scott Graham, but in that tragedy he gave life to several other people. That's because he chose to be a Donor. On that tragic day when that family faced the worst day any family could face he gave life back to me. I received one of his kidneys one year ago today. I have met his wonderful and awesome parents and they are so like family to me. I want them to know I feel their pain of losing their son and wish I could take their pain away; I also feel guilty that they lost their son so I could live on. I love you Scott & Sharon and I am so sorry for your loss.
>
> **Sylvia** (Gary's mom responded)—**What a precious moment for all of us. I still marvel how quickly we found you and knew my Gary got your Dalen's kidney. Hearts and prayers.**

Sharon—We love you Gary. Thank you, but don't feel guilty. The blessing is that your life is better. My son would have died either way, but to give part of him to you, has been so amazing and worth it all.

We decided to go see our friend in the tower, Pat Weir. He was just the nicest man. When you went to the tower, you were right behind the starting line in a suite with food and drinks being offered to us. There wasn't a better view of the track and there was quite a bit of excitement when you got to watch the cars speed down. It was amazing. Mariah and Dalen loved to just stay there and felt comfortable enough to do so for good portions of the day. They did become too comfortable sometimes. Those in the suite were always very cordial to our family and we really appreciated it. Today was no different except they too, honored Dalen and remembered him. Pat and his son gave their condolences as they hugged us tightly. It was so thoughtful.

—Hugs and prayers from us to you.

—May you find peace and comfort with each other today.

—We are so sorry for your loss. My husband Brett Woodland served his mission in California eighteen years ago and was very fond of your family! He remembers your son and was so sad to hear of his passing. It looks like your daughter is serving a mission. Sister Lenhart was in my ward growing up and we are friends with the family! What a small world! Lots of love and prayers for your family.

—He is still in our hearts.

—Sending love your way. Glad you could make it home to be with your family.

—We are thinking of y'all today!

—My heart hurts with your heart and rejoices with your heart. Love you guys.

—Love and prayers for you, Scott and all your family today. May that peace that passes all understanding abide with you all today.

They cancelled the 'first responders' thing because of the fact that the rain was coming and expected all day. They felt there was a shortness of time. The races of course were the main event. We were bummed just a bit, but understood. So, they had The National Anthem sung, and the races began. We watched as the big guys came out. The top fuel cars approached the track. They were the crowd attractions. It was so amazing how many people are involved with one car. Six cars ran. The stands were still pretty full even with the rain forecast. These race car fans were crazy. But only six cars ran and then the rain came again. That was it. We stayed for maybe another half hour in the tower and then decided we needed to go back to the car and see how things were. The downpour came.

Everyone was taking cover or leaving. All the vehicles in the midway were trying to keep their displays dry with not much success.

There were no more runs made. At **2:00 p.m.**, we started to pack up the car and get things ready to close everything up. We towed the car out to where our trailer was parked and packed it all up. Not quite the day we had planned, but kind of a quiet day spent with the family.

>—Love, thoughts, and prayers are with you all today.
>
>—So glad you are all together today, he's right there with you too. Sending love and comfort! Glad you came for a visit!
>
>—Sharon, thanks for the amazing visit the other night. Thanks for testifying of God's amazing miracles in your life through this journey. You've changed the lives of many, including mine! Much love to you all today.
>
>—May you all remember the great times with your goofy brother and son. Thinking of you all.
>
>—Your understanding of His plan and faith has been a strength to me. We miss your handsome vivacious boy. With you and your family today in love and comfort. Hugs...
>
>—We miss him terribly. Michael still sleeps with the stuffed dog that Dalen gave him. He calls it Dalen Dog.
>
>—I am so grateful to have served my mission in the TDM office because I had the opportunity to serve with amazing missionaries, of which elder Graham was one of the best!
>
>—I've had thoughts of you and your sweet family. Love you.

Throughout the day, we kept getting messages of all these people thinking of Dalen and our anniversary. It was amazing how many people remembered and that they made a point to think of us. Our dear friend Michelle had once again gone above and beyond the call of a friend, when she had made little heart pins that she gave to our ward family, and they wrote messages again. We kept getting pictures sent to us with the members of our ward wearing the heart pins in remembrance of Dalen throughout the day. They were so sweet and heartfelt. It was the best. One of our neighbors even brought over a fruit basket. Once again, we were shown how our son had touched so many lives and felt very loved.[104]

Michelle made little pins with hearts on them and handed them out to everyone in the ward even though we weren't there. So amazing and grateful. Then they all sent us their pictures wearing the pins, and also received more heart letters.

—Sending my love to you guys! Thanks for all you taught me.

—Dalen was in my district and a great missionary to work with. I wish I could tell you some of his great moments at district meeting! His hand language of being guided by the Spirit go here, turn left, stop! (something like that), with his finger against his forehead motioning and he and Elder Brown going to teach some

---

[104] I had worn the heart pin on my jean jacket ever since this day. I love the reminder it gives me of the love that we had been shown. Again an incredible out pour of love from our ward family and friends. We were not forgotten.

of my investigators. He said he loved the King Follet Discourse. NOTHING like seeing the power of God in these young Elders and being with them and experiencing it.
—Sending hearts.
—Thinking about the Graham family. Love you guys.

The drive home seemed quick. We got home and had a very relaxed afternoon.

There were some that took their naps and others just read all the notes and again were in awe of all the love and support we had received. The love demonstrated to us just never seemed to stop.

I finally had time to read the Facebook posts.

11:50 a.m. Karen DeHemmer (FBPost—picture with heart pins) Karen, Robert Harris and Michelle Cooke. **Sharing our hearts with yours.**

12:09 p.m. Talicia Larson (FBPost—picture with heart pins) **Sending our love to your family!**

12:29 p.m. Mari McLaws (FBPost—picture with heart pins) **Sending you our love.**

12:40 p.m. Barbara Harwick (FBPost—picture with heart pins) **Today we are sharing our hearts with your hearts.**

12:42 p.m. Shel Cooke (FBPost—picture with heart pins) **Dalen Graham, we love you buddy! You have our hearts forever. Sharon Graham & Scott Graham.**

1:15 p.m. Alyssa's FBPost—Contemplating what to say and this is probably the best I got.

A year ago, I said goodbye to my one and only brother. Today on the year anniversary of that time I can't help but reflect and think about how much I have grown from then till now, and the wonderful blessings that have been placed in my life to help me when I have hard times. I'm so grateful for my family and that I get to be with them today. (Huge blessings) I'm grateful for God's plan of love and life also known as the Plan of Salvation. I am grateful for the love and support constantly given to me and my family. I'm grateful I get to see my brother again. I miss you lots buddy! Of course, there are times that hit me harder, but I hope I can honor and live up to your example every day. I want to focus on the life you lived and the good rather than the fact that you are no longer here. I will miss you forever but my love for you is much stronger. Till we meet again. #dalenscott #familiesareforever #lds #199502918 #gratituderatherthanloss #loveyoumissyou #yearanniversary #oneyearagotoday.

Mom—He misses us just as much.

    Your best is an amazing testimony of the plan of salvation, forever families, and your love for your brother. Couldn't get any better, Squirt. Sure love you.
    Your faith in God strengthens mine.

    4:56 p.m.   Eric Lewis (FBPost) One year later and you are still missed by many every day Dalen. (Picture of Eric and Dalen together).

6:00 p.m. Mariah was also given special permission because of the circumstances of the day; that she could Facetime her family and so we waited for the call. When we got home, we gathered around the computer and were able to talk with Mariah. She looked happy and excited to talk to us. Her and her companion started out with a song that they had prepared. It was so cute. We talked about our past few days. We laughed and enjoyed one another. Mariah was always such a character. She made us laugh all the time. She talked about her mission and the people that she was teaching. She was so very excited. She talked about the area and the amazing blessings she had seen and how she had been able to help so many people come to know of the Savior and in return, they all seemed to love her. It was time to say goodbye. There were a few tears, but definitely a treasured time. We were very grateful to Mariah's Mission President for allowing us this opportunity. They had planned to drive the 2 hours to be with Mariah so they could give her a hug or whatever she needed from them. What a huge blessing and that this anniversary was thought of again by so many people. So good—just so blessed.[105]

Our evening was again with family and our normal routine. We popped our popcorn and watched a DVD which we have done since Scott and I have been married, every Sunday night. We settled in to watch the movie and enjoyed one another, and then we all spent some time and reflected on Dalen before our night ended. Some family had reservations about the day and how they might have felt or would make it through. I kept reassuring them that it would all be good though. It was a very happy day with laughter and smiles. Where it may have been dreaded before, it was now another blessing, and I don't think any of us were even sad. Of course, when we thought of Dalen's anniversary of his passing, it was a very sad thought but not devastation in any way. No regrets. Miracles in abundance and God leading the way.

---

[105] Mariah's mission president allowed our family to be together. He was willing to take his time and drive 2 hours to be with our daughter.

Scott—I came home and was feasting upon a Jimmy john's triple chocolate chip cookie that was given to us. My thoughts are drawn to thinking about my three daughters. I've been thinking about how grateful I am for each of you and how much I love each of you. I'm proud of each of you and all of your accomplishments so far. You all have so much potential to achieve greatness, but you don't realize it. You guys have been able to do hard things all of your lives. Success doesn't come easy for most, but success is only achieved after failures. I went and watched mom's production she had a while back of the Women's Conference our Stake had the week Dalen died. Your mom promised to help them and did even though we had only been home for a few days. She promised and it was done. She directed it and decorated it. I was in awe of her strength. But then, this play had to do with many women of the scriptures and Latter-Day pioneers. I was in awe of their strength, courage and determination each of these women had. I was most impressed with the mothers of the stripling warriors. One of the things about you girls is that you have the ability to demonstrate and do so much good in your lives and for the lives of others. The world is in need of righteous women who will influence not only the men but children to make good decisions. Each of you girls has what it takes to accomplish this Each of you may need to push yourself a little harder at times in order to find the better job or be the better person or be more spiritual, but it will all be worth it! I love you all, Dad.

—Mariah—Thank you dad. I love you so much.

—Allyssa—Thank you daddy. I love you too. And I love you all very much.

—Kailee—That's cool. Thanks dad for sharing. Love ya.

So the year mark came. Dalen Scott Graham had passed away one year ago today. Our lives have forever changed. Blessings and miracles hadn't stopped. We had been led through this experience by our loving Heavenly Father. It was hard sometimes to think we wouldn't ever see Dalen again physically. Many times, I waited to get a phone call that I knew would never be coming. I yearned to hear his voice and laughter. But I couldn't deny what had transpired through this year. We had literally seen 100's of lives that had been influenced and touched by Dalen. My son knew who he was and his purpose and lived the latter part of his life with the desire to make someone else's life better along the way. There was no way to ever replace a son, a loved one, a child; but knowing how mine lived, had guided and comforted and blessed others, would lead us into eternity.[106]

DALEN'S Final Facebook Post: (one more time)
Feb 7, @2:15 p.m.
My brothers and sisters in the work of the Lord. He truly is there. He answers our prayers. He wants to guide us. Yesterday I prepared to go to the temple. I had questions I wanted answers to. I was praying beforehand, listening to hymns while I walked there. I got my answers, I got my direction.

---

[106] The family was together and on a day that brought us enlightenment and peace. A good day for all.

Intermountain Donor Services

April 24, 2019

Dear Sharon and Scott and Family,

    I am providing you with information in regard to the outcome of how many people Dalen was able to help through his <u>tissue donation</u>.

    In highlighting the outcome of Dalen's gifts, his **bone grafts and soft tissue (tendon and Fascia) were transplanted into 120 people, ranging in ages 17—84 years of age, from 19 states including: Utah, Colorado, Arizona, Nevada, California, Oregon, Washington, Hawaii, Missouri, Michigan, Indiana, Ohio, Minnesota, Iowa, Texas, Oklahoma, Tennessee, Florida and New Jersey.** Most of the grafts were used in spinal fusion surgeries, helping to relieve back, neck and ankle pain, or for general orthopedic surgeries to repair injuries from trauma and other defects.

    There were also a number of **soft tissue (tendon and Fascia)** grafts that were used to **reconstruct damaged joints**, either from sport's injuries or trauma.

    The tissue processing company would like you to know, "On behalf of these recipients, please accept our heartfelt thanks to you, for Dalen's generous gift. It is through his generosity that these current and future recipients have an opportunity for a healthier future."

Karan Elizabeth Hannahs, LCSW
Director Donor Family Services

<u>AND SO THEY, AND WE, LIVE ON.</u>

About the Author

Sharon Graham was born and raised in Alberta, Canada, where most of her family still resides. She has been married for over thirty-four years to her husband Scott, and they have four children-three girls, and one boy. Her family resided in California for most of her married life until a recent retirement from Scott's employment led them to southern Utah where they currently live.

Sharon has always been active in her church. The entire family have all served missions for The Church of Jesus Christ of Latter-Day Saints and have remained faithful.

Sharon speaks Spanish (because of her mission) and had used it almost every day in her educational career where she taught English as a Second Language for more than twenty-six years. Sharon loves everything about nature and is constantly in awe of all God's creations. She loves family time, nothing more precious to her. And has found a new love in writing. She enjoys working with her hands and loves helping all around her with whatever she can.

Sharon wants her story told of her son's passing, so that others may be uplifted and touched and see how God is involved in our lives and DOES bless us.

CPSIA information can be obtained
at www.ICGtesting.com
Printed in the USA
BVHW061103060423
661868BV00017B/844